HOPES AND FEARS

HOPES AND FEARS

The Future of the Internet
Volume 2

LEE RAINIE
AND
JANNA QUITNEY ANDERSON

CAMBRIA
PRESS

AMHERST, NEW YORK

Requests for permission should be directed to:
permissions@cambriapress.com, or mailed to:
Cambria Press
20 Northpointe Parkway, Suite 188
Amherst, NY 14228

Library of Congress Cataloging-in-Publication Data

Anderson, Janna Quitney, 1955-
    Hopes and fears : the future of the Internet II / Janna Quitney Anderson, Lee Rainie.
        p. cm.
    Includes bibliographical references and index.
    ISBN 978-1-60497-571-0 (alk. paper)
    1. Internet—Social aspects. 2. Internet—Forecasting. 3. Internet—History. I. Rainie, Harrison. II. Title.

    HM851.A628 2008
    303.48'330112—dc22

2008040348

FOR VINT CERF AND BOB KAHN

These co-innovators of the transmission control protocol and Internet protocol (TCP/IP)—the method by which packets are switched on networks, allowing information exchange—will forever be remembered as the "fathers of the Internet." Their work started in the 1970s, and it has grown exponentially more demanding with each passing year, yet they remain fully dedicated to their cause. They have given themselves over completely to support the "end-to-end" model of the open Internet that allows people at all levels of the network to innovate free of any central control. Their work is representative of the work of many hundreds of dedicated technology leaders of the 21st century. Cerf and Kahn have worked together and individually in inspiring the thousands of global contributors who are continually engineering the positive evolution of the Internet. For this, we are truly thankful.

A SURVEY OF TECHNOLOGY THINKERS
AND STAKEHOLDERS SHOWS THEY BELIEVE
THE INTERNET WILL CONTINUE TO SPREAD
IN A "FLATTENING" AND IMPROVING WORLD.
THERE ARE MANY, THOUGH, WHO THINK
MAJOR PROBLEMS WILL ACCOMPANY
TECHNOLOGY ADVANCES BY 2020.

TABLE OF CONTENTS

FOREWORD

We learned so much and had such a good time asking experts to predict the future of the Internet in 2002 that we did it again in a survey in late 2005 and 2006. In the intervening period, the business of looking into the future of technology had boomed. There were many more sources of insight—and wackiness—to draw upon. So, the results reported in this volume are somewhat sharper and more pointed than in our first volume. Truth to tell, we learned from our research into the burgeoning field of futurology about how to ask questions more directly.

We also took inspiration to continue this work from the thoughtful and widely quoted epigram of Alan Kay (1989), a brilliant digital innovator: "The best way to predict the future is to invent it" (p. 1). That gave us reason enough to consult as many of the creators, builders, and shapers of the Internet as we could in this next round of work.

We went back to survey those we could find who were in the extensive Imagining the Internet database of expert commentators on the Internet in the early to mid-1990s and those who were added to the list as we conducted the first *Future of the Internet* survey in 2002.[1] We also built the list of respondents by inviting commentary from the membership of several prominent Internet-related organizations: Internet Society, Association for Computing Machinery, the World Wide Web Consortium, the UN Working Group on Internet Governance, Internet2, Institute of Electrical and Electronics Engineers, Internet Corporation for Assigned Names and Numbers, International Telecommunication Union, Computer Professionals for Social Responsibility, Association of Internet Researchers, and the American Sociological Association's Information Technology Research section.

The results yield a fascinating mix of consensus about the future development of technology and argument about the likely social, political, and economic impact of that development. The nature of this amalgam is captured in several forms.

First, there is considerable expectation that a global, low-cost network will be thriving in 2020 and will be available to most people around the world at low cost and with great potential to improve the lives of many who are now distant from the grid. At the same time, there is notable argument about whether businesses and governments will work and play well with each other and with their citizens/consumers.

Second, despite the growing capacity of technology to assume more and more of the work done by humans, most respondents said they think people will remain in charge of machines. Some fear, though, that technological progress will eventually lead to machines and processes that move beyond human control, in part because human oversight of some technology functions is waning. Others said they worried that the leaders who exercise control of the technology might use this power inappropriately.

Third, many respondents agreed with the notion that those who are connected online will spend more time immersing themselves in more sophisticated, compelling, networked, and synthetic worlds by 2020. This was my favorite revelation in this piece of research, not because it seemed counterconventional, but because it made perfect sense and I had not given it any thought before my coauthor Janna Anderson convinced me to ask the question. After we ventured into this area of inquiry, we also began to pay attention to the growing amount of research devoted to serious gaming and the increasing real-world applications of gaming "magic" in classrooms and training endeavors. Our respondents agreed with the prediction language that the emergence of virtual worlds will foster productivity and connectedness and be an advantage to many, but there was significant dispute among them about whether some level of tech "addictions" would also show up in the general population.

A fourth major finding in this survey was widely noted in press coverage and somewhat overemphasized. Most respondents agreed with a prediction that resistance to the effects of technological change may inspire some acts of violence. Yet, the more significant argument of these respondents about violence was largely ignored in the first wave of coverage, which left an impression, I fear, that our survey found that a notable class of Unabomber types would become an important part of the cultural landscape. The more salient assertion of this group was that most violent struggle in the future will emerge from classic sources: religious ideologies, politics, and economics. The consensus here was that a cohort of technology refuseniks will emerge between now and 2020 and choose not to participate in the digital communications network, but that this group would not necessarily be linked to any major level of violence.

For me, the "money" question in this survey involved this prediction:

> As sensing, storage, and communication technologies get cheaper and better, individuals' public and private lives will become increasingly "transparent" globally. Everything will be more visible to everyone, with good and bad results. Looking at the big picture—at all of the lives affected on the planet in every way possible—this will make the world a better place by the year 2020. The benefits will outweigh the costs.

A fifth major theme of this survey was that there was such sharp and even dispute in the responses to this scenario. Some 46% of survey takers agreed with the prediction, 49% disagreed, and 5% did not respond. There was nearly unanimous feeling that some level of privacy must be retained, but no firm sense of how that would happen. Some argued that new privacy protections would be built into the law.

Others believed that recalibrated social contracts would be a more likely avenue of privacy protection. There is an expectation in this group that governments and corporations will continue to escalate surveillance and "own" access to information; while they do that, the powerful and privileged will find growing transparency more to their advantage than others in society. In short, there is a cynical sense in this group that the flow of information will trend more heavily in the direction of average people becoming more "transparent" (and less private), while those who have power will find ways to protect their privacy at the same time that they exploit their new insights into others who are less powerful. Some believed technology could help re-right that imbalance and allow individual citizens to become watchdogs in a kind of system of distributed vigilance of the powerful. Still, the pushback against this benign vision of greater transparency was heated and heartfelt.

In the most fundamental sense, these respondents made clear that key elements of the future are up in the air. One way to read into this mixture of hopes and fears is to highlight the critical uncertainties these respondents addressed that hover over the development of digital technologies. The way these uncertainties are handled will determine how technology affects people in the future.

The first uncertainty involves the nature of the Internet itself. The current architecture is seen as inadequate and dangerously vulnerable. When MIT's David Clark, a giant among those who created the first version of the Internet and a leading proponent of building a do-over version, worries about the security and interoperability of the network as he does here, it is important to take note. A related issue involves the struggle for control over the flow of information on the current Internet. Many of the respondents here said they were unsure that the policy climate will be favorable for the kind of improvements Clark is seeking or even for maintenance of the current mechanisms of how material passes its way through the existing Internet. These respondents were anxious about those who build the pipes and control the information spigots and whether they will hurt the way the Internet is, *in principle*, supposed to work as an equitable end-to-end system.

A second critical uncertainty that gets a great deal of attention here is the way businesses and Internet users will treat intellectual property. The majority of respondents believed that the clash over free file sharing by Internet users and copyright holders is unresolved and will play out indefinitely in courts, legislatures, and even on technology platforms. Their bias is against companies that are too stringent in their restrictions and toward users wanting to sample, share, and remix material. And they dread the prospect that businesses will marshal resources to preserve their current advantages. At the same time, the responses of this group indicate there is nothing approaching a consensus position on where a new equilibrium might be struck that would satisfy both camps. They expect conflict, but cannot collectively see how it will end.

A third critical uncertainty rests at the social and cultural level: How will people behave toward each other in an environment where so much more can be known about others and where people have less control over their privacy? These respondents have a clear expectation that people will wittingly or unwittingly disclose more about themselves, gaining some benefits in the process of losing their privacy to varying degrees, as governments and corporations escalate the collection and analysis of personal data. In the process of addressing our specific query about the social benefits and harms of transparency, these experts showed that they expect behavior and interpersonal relations to change. Yet, they are not as clear about the new social norms and elements of etiquette that will emerge.

A final uncertainty relates to how information markets will perform. How will important truths be upheld or discovered when the process of publishing and broadcasting becomes open to all? This group hopes the ever-greater flow of information and communication will bring the world closer to essential truths. Yet, they wonder if an "information market" corollary of Gresham's law will prevail: that bad information will drive out good. As some framed the question, will gossip, spin, disinformation, degraded commercial speech, and the bleating of the ignorant overwhelm serious news and consequential views in the marketplace of ideas?

If we had asked that question directly, my guess is that we would have had a split verdict. In the end, this group has a mixed view of humans themselves. On the one hand, respondents see people as capable of retaining control of the technology they have created. On the other hand, they fret that the human race *in toto* perhaps is not up to the job of living masterfully in the techo-world to come.

That uncertainty is reason enough to continue asking these kinds of questions and eliciting reaction to possible scenarios. By the same token, this book is also meant to provoke your reaction and inspire your own contribution. We invite you to add your own insights to the collective intelligence amassed at http://www.imaginingtheinternet. org. Why bother? Because, eventually, we will be feeling the results.

Lee Rainie, Director
Pew Internet & American Life Project

ENDNOTE

1. The experts and their predictions can be found at Elon's *Imagining the Internet* Web site, available at http://www.elon.edu/predictions/.

ACKNOWLEDGMENTS

PEW INTERNET & AMERICAN LIFE PROJECT

The Pew Internet Project is a nonprofit, nonpartisan "fact tank" that explores the impact of the Internet on children, families, communities, the workplace, schools, health care, and civic/political life. The Project takes no positions on policy questions. Support for the Project is provided by The Pew Charitable Trusts and is an initiative of the Pew Research Center. The Project's Web site is http://www.pewinternet.org.

At the Pew Charitable Trusts, the support of two people in particular has sustained the Project: President and CEO Rebecca Rimel and the Managing Director for Information and Civic Initiatives Donald Kimelman. Inside the Pew Research Center, the Project profits handsomely from the expertise of President Andrew Kohut and Executive Vice President Paul Taylor.

Lee Rainie is especially thankful for the help and support of his colleagues at the Pew Internet Project: Susannah Fox, John Horrigan, Deborah Fallows, Amanda Lenhart, Mary Madden, Jessica Vitak, and Cornelia Carter. He also appreciates the help on the *Future of the*

Internet surveys from Prof. Steve Jones of the University of Illinois–Chicago, a longtime advisor to the Project.

PRINCETON SURVEY RESEARCH ASSOCIATES

PSRA conducted the survey that is covered in this report. It is an independent research company specializing in social and policy work. The firm designs, conducts, and analyzes surveys worldwide. Its expertise also includes qualitative research and content analysis. The firm can be reached at 911 Commons Way, Princeton, NJ, 08540, by telephone at 609-924-9204, by fax at 609-924-7499, or by e-mail at ResearchNJ@PSRA.com.

ELON UNIVERSITY SCHOOL OF COMMUNICATIONS

Elon University has teamed with the Pew Internet Project to complete a number of research studies, including the building of the Early '90s Predictions Database and the Predictions Surveys on the site, Imagining the Internet (http://www.imaginingtheinternet.org), and a 2001 ethnographic study of families' use of the Internet in a small town, "One Neighborhood, One Week on the Internet" (http://org.elon.edu/pew/oneweek/), both under the direction of Janna Quitney Anderson. For contact regarding the Predictions Database send e-mail to predictions@elon.edu. The university's Web site is http://www.elon.edu/.

Many people at the university made this work possible. We owe special thanks to Elon's President Leo Lambert and Provost Gerry Francis, School of Communications leaders Paul Parsons and Constance Book, University Relations Director Dan Anderson, designer Christopher Eyl, and copy editor Colin Donohue.

ITHIEL DE SOLA POOL

Pool, a leading communications researcher of the 20th century, died in the mid-1980s, but he was a significant influence when vital decisions were being made regarding freedom on the Internet in the decades to follow. He inspired many Internet stakeholders with his book *Technologies of Freedom*. In it, he projected that interconnected computing devices would be joined to form an open-ended, all-encompassing structure. He described it as "the largest machine that man has ever constructed—the global telecommunications network; the full map of it no one knows; it changes every day" (1983, p. 56), and he projected that it would be questioned by regulators fearing the challenge to the economic and political status quo. He warned that a positive future would be delayed if regulators chose to interfere. His research was an inspiration for the initiation of the Imagining the Internet project and surveys.

SURVEY RESPONDENTS

We are thankful for the thoughtful and revealing contributions of the thousands of international participants in the *Future of the Internet* surveys. Their insights are helping to create significant knowledge about the past, present, and future of information technologies.

Respondents Reflect on the Future

Predictions Inspire Lively Discussion About the Future and Allow Stakeholders to Prepare Everyone for Expected Adjustments Associated With Technological Change

Those who think about the future are best poised to influence it. The visionary 20th-century engineer, mathematician, and architect R. Buckminster Fuller said, "We are called to be architects of the future, not its victims."

Those sentiments guide this effort. Many futurists, scientists, and long-term thinkers today argue that the acceleration of technological change over the past decade has greatly increased the importance of strategic vision. Technology innovations will continue to impact us. The question is whether this process will reflect thoughtful planning or wash over us like an unstoppable wave. If the developmental record of 20th-century computing continues for only another 30 years, we will rapidly and permanently move to a different world.

Are we prepared to act and react in ways that will make that world a good one?

HOW THE SURVEY ORIGINATED AND WAS CONDUCTED

This research project got its start in mid-2001 when Lee Rainie, the director of the Pew Internet & American Life Project, approached officials at Elon University with an idea that the Project and the university might replicate the work of Ithiel de Sola Pool in his 1983 book, *Forecasting the Telephone: A Retrospective Technology Assessment*. Pool and his students had looked at primary official documents, technology community publications, speeches given by government and business leaders, and marketing literature at the turn of the 20th century to examine the kind of impacts experts thought the telephone would have on Americans' social and economic lives.

Rainie's idea was to apply Pool's research method to the Internet, particularly focused on the period between 1990 and 1995 when the World Wide Web and Web browsers emerged. In the spring semester of 2003, Janna Quitney Anderson, a professor of journalism and communications at Elon, led a research initiative that set out to accomplish this goal. More than 4,200 amazingly prescient predictive statements made in the early 1990s by 1,000 people were logged and categorized. The fruits of that work are available at the online site Imagining the Internet (http://wwwimaginingtheinternet.org).

Next, Rainie and Anderson reasoned that if experts and technologists had been so thoughtful in the early 1990s about what was going to happen, they might be equally as insightful in looking ahead from this moment. Thus began an effort to track down most of those whose predictions were in the 1990–1995 database. In 2004 they and other experts since identified by the Pew Internet Project were asked to assess a number of predictions about the coming decade. Their answers were codified in the first report of this effort, *The Future of the Internet I* (http://www.pewinternet.org/pdfs/PIP_Future_of_Internet.pdf).

In late 2005 and the first quarter of 2006, the Pew Internet Project issued an e-mail invitation to a select group of technology thinkers, stakeholders, and social analysts, asking them to complete a second, scenario-based quantitative and qualitative survey about the future of the Internet—*The Future of the Internet II*. Rainie and Anderson also asked the initial group of respondents to forward the invitation to colleagues and friends who might provide interesting perspectives.

Some 742 people responded to the *Future II* survey between November 30, 2005, and April 4, 2006. More than half are Internet pioneers who were online before 1993. Roughly one-quarter of the respondents said they live and work in a nation outside of North America.

The respondents' answers represent their personal views and in no way reflect the perspectives of their employers. Many survey participants were hand picked due to their positions as stakeholders in the development of the Internet or they were reached through the leadership listservs of top technology organizations, including the Internet Society, Association for Computing Machinery, the World Wide Web Consortium, the UN Working Group on Internet Governance, Internet2, Institute of Electrical and Electronics Engineers, Internet Corporation for Assigned Names and Numbers, International Telecommunication Union, Computer Professionals for Social Responsibility, Association of Internet Researchers, and the American Sociological Association's Information Technology Research section.

ABOUT THE SURVEY PARTICIPANTS

Many top Internet leaders, activists, and commentators participated in the survey, including David Clark, Gordon Bell, Esther Dyson, Fred Baker, Scott Hollenbeck, Robert Shaw, Ted Hardie, Pekka Nikander, Alejandro Pisanty, Bob Metcalfe, Peng Hwa Ang, Hal Varian, Geert Lovink, Cory Doctorow, Anthony Rutkowski, Robert Anderson, Ellen Hume, Howard Rheingold, Douglas Rushkoff, Steve Cisler, Marilyn Cade, Marc Rotenberg, Alan Levin, Eugene Spafford, Veni

Markovski, Franck Martin, Greg Cole, Paul Saffo, Thomas Narten, Alan Inouye, Seth Finkelstein, Teddy Purwadi, Luc Faubert, John Browning, and David Weinberger, to name a few.

A sampling of the workplaces of respondents includes the Internet Society, VeriSign, BBN Technologies, Fing, Yahoo Japan, France Telecom, the International Telecommunication Union, Nanyang Technological University, the Electronic Frontier Foundation, TDCLA Chile, AfriNIC, Qualcomm, Wairua Consulting, Electronic Privacy Information Center, Universiteit Maastricht, RAND, IBM, the Austrian Academy of Sciences, Sony, Google, Telematica Instituut, Habitat for Humanity, Cisco, Greenpeace, the University of Haifa, AT&T, Unisinos, Goteborg University, Jupiter Research, Sheffield University, CNET, Microsoft, the University of Sao Paulo, Intel, ISTOE Online, NASSCOM, Amazon.com, Walmart.com, Universidad Nacional Autonoma de México, Sprint, Intuit, HP Laboratories, the Centre for Policy Modelling, ICT Strategies, Bipolar Dream, the Benton Foundation, Semacode, Widgetwonder, Curtin University of Technology, the Hearst Corporation, Imaginova, CNN, Adobe Systems, Forrester Research, the Community Broadband Coalition, Universidad de Navarra, The Center on Media and Society, the Association for the Advancement of Information Technology, Massachusetts Institute of Technology, the Institute of Network Cultures, The Institute for the Future, O'Reilly, Yomux Media, Nortel, Radboud University Nijmegen, Disney, Harvard University, the London School of Economics, Geekcorps, Polaris Venture Partners, InternetPerils, Consumer's Union, the University of Copenhagen, the University of California–Berkeley, the Singapore Internet Research Center, Princeton University, the federal government of Canada, the U.S. Congress, several technology policy divisions of the U.S. government, and many dozens of others.

Participants described their primary area of Internet interest as "research scientist" (19%), "entrepreneur/business leader" (12%), "technology developer or administrator" (11%), "author/editor/journalist" (10%), "futurist/consultant" (9%), "advocate/voice of the people/activist user" (8%), "legislator/politician" (2%), or "pioneer/

originator" (1%); the remainder of participants (29%) chose "other" for this survey question or did not respond.

The Scenarios Were Built to Elicit Deeply Felt Opinions

The Pew Internet & American Life Project and Elon University do not advocate policy outcomes related to the Internet. The predictive scenarios included in the survey were structured to inspire the illumination of issues, not because we think any of them will necessarily come to fruition.

The scenarios themselves were drawn from some of the responses about the future that were made in our 2004 survey. The scenarios were also crafted from predictions made in reports by the U.S. National Intelligence Council, the UN Working Group on Internet Governance, The Institute for the Future, Global Business Network, and other foresight organizations and individual foresight leaders.[1]

The 2020 scenarios were constructed to elicit responses to many-layered issues, so it was sometimes the case that survey participants would agree with most of a scenario, but not all of it. In addition to trying to pack several ideas into each scenario, we tried to balance them with "good," "bad," and "neutral" outcomes. History is full of evidence that technology adoption brings *both* positive and negative results.

After each portion of the survey—each of seven proposed scenarios and the question that was really a request to rank priorities for the future of the Internet—we invited participants to write narrative responses providing an explanation for their answers. Not surprisingly, the most interesting product of the survey is the ensuing collection of open-ended predictions and analyses written by the participants in response to our material. We have included many of those responses in this report.

Since participants' answers evolved in both tone and content as they went through the questionnaire, the findings in this report are presented in the same order as the original survey. The respondents were asked to "sign" each written response they were willing to have credited to them in the Elon-Pew database and in this report. The quotations in the report are attributed to those who agreed to have their words quoted. When a quote is not attributed to someone, it is because that person chose not to sign his or her written answer. To make this report more readable and to include many voices, some of the lengthier written elaborations have been edited.

ENDNOTE

1. Among the reports consulted as background for scenario construction were various documents from the UN/ITU World Summits on the Information Society and from their Working Group on Internet Governance (2005); U.S. National Science Foundation (2005); Kapur (2005); Neild and Pearson (2005); U.S. National Intelligence Council (2004); Institute for the Future (2005); Glenn and Gordon (2005); Dutton, di Gennaro, and Millwood Hargrave (2005); Hoare and Milner (2004); Frey (2004); and Internet Society (2005).

SUMMARY OF FINDINGS

TECHNOLOGY THINKERS AND STAKEHOLDERS ASSESS THE
FUTURE SOCIAL, POLITICAL, AND ECONOMIC IMPACT
OF THE INTERNET

Hundreds of Internet leaders, activists, builders, and commentators were asked about the effect of the Internet on social, political, and economic life by the year 2020. The views of the 742 respondents who completed this survey were varied; while there is notable agreement about how technology might evolve, there is not consensus among these respondents about the overall results of this evolution. Among the topics discussed were the pros and cons of pervasive, autonomous technology; the loss of privacy; the impact of virtual reality; the "flat world" revolution; the possibility that some people living "off the grid" may protest violently against accelerating technology; and the ordering of world priorities in regard to developing information and communication technologies.

Reacting to several scenarios constructed by the Pew Internet & American Life Project about the possible future impact of the Internet, the respondents struck on several themes and challenges in their answers:

- **The deployment of a global network:** A majority of respondents agreed with a scenario that argued that a global network will be thriving in 2020 and will be available to most people around the world at low cost. They argued, though, that this will only be accomplished through a great deal of innovation, investment, and collaboration among technologists, policy makers, and businesses. A majority of respondents have optimistic views about the continued spread and adoption of the network. They agreed that a "flattening" of the world will open up opportunities for success for many people who will compete globally. Still, the members of a vocal and sizeable minority of respondents said they are unsure that the policy climate will be favorable for such Internet expansion. The center of the resistance, they said, will be in the businesses anxious to preserve their current advantages and in policy circles where control over information and communication is a central value. In addition, a contingent of respondents predicted significant barriers to the development of a "flattening" world, most noting that social inequities will persist.
- **Human control over technology:** Most respondents said they think humans will remain in charge of technology between now and 2020 even as advances continue. Some do fear, however, that technological progress will eventually lead to machines and processes that move beyond human control, in part because human oversight of some technology functions is waning. Others said they fear that the leaders who exercise control of the technology might use this power inappropriately.
- **Transparency versus privacy:** There is a widespread expectation that people will wittingly or unwittingly disclose more about themselves, gaining some benefits in the process of losing their privacy to varying degrees, as governments and corporations escalate the collection and analysis of personal data.

Many respondents said they expect some level of privacy to be retained. There was disagreement over whether this privacy protection is best accomplished by law or by social contract. Respondents split evenly on a central question of whether the world will be a better place in 2020 due to the greater transparency of people and institutions afforded by the Internet. Our scenario asked respondents to weigh the benefits of transparency against the costs in privacy, and they responded this way: 46% agreed that the benefits of greater transparency would outweigh the privacy costs, and 49% disagreed that the benefits would outweigh the costs.

- **Violence, Luddites, and technological "refuseniks":** Most respondents agreed that resistance to the effects of technological change may inspire some acts of violence, but most violent struggle in the future will emerge from classic sources: religious ideologies, politics, and economics. Many people will remain unconnected to the network because of their economic circumstances. Still, some respondents believe that a class of technology refuseniks will emerge between now and 2020 and choose not to participate in the digital communications network. They will form their own cultural group that lives apart from "modern" society.

- **Compelling or "addictive" virtual worlds:** Many respondents agreed with the notion that those who are connected online will spend more time immersing themselves in more sophisticated, compelling, networked, synthetic worlds by 2020. While this will foster productivity and connectedness and be an advantage to many, it will lead to addiction problems for some. The word "addiction" struck some respondents as an inappropriate term for the problems they foresaw, while others thought it appropriate.

- **The fate of language online:** Many respondents said they accept the idea that English will be the world's lingua franca for cross-cultural communications in the next few decades. But notable numbers maintained that English will not overwhelm other languages and crowd them into obscurity. Instead, these respondents believe that as the Internet continues to improve,

Mandarin and other languages will expand their influence. Most respondents stressed that linguistic diversity is good and that the Internet will allow the preservation of languages and associated cultures. Some respondents noted that all languages evolve over time and that the Internet will abet that evolution.

- **Investment priorities:** Asked what their priority would be for future investments of time and money in networking, 78% of the *Future of the Internet II* survey respondents identified two goals for the world's policy makers and the technology industry to pursue: building network capacity and spreading knowledge about technology to help people of all nations.

Some Cautions About Methodology and Interpreting the Findings

This is the second specific canvassing of Internet specialists and analysts by the Pew Internet & American Life Project. While a wide range of opinion from experts and the representatives of key organizations and interested institutions was sought, this survey should not be taken as a representative sample of all Internet experts, nor as a comprehensive overview of all the best thinking about the future of information and communication technologies and methods. By design, this survey was an "opt in," self-selecting effort. Only the views of those who chose to respond to our invitation are represented. That process does not yield a random, representative sample.

This survey is our best effort to prompt some of the leaders in the field to share their thoughts and predictions. The limitations of the sample should inform any discussion of these findings. More than half of the respondents are Internet pioneers who were online before 1993. Roughly one-quarter of the respondents said they live and work in a nation outside of North America. While many respondents are at the pinnacle of Internet leadership, some of the survey respondents are "working in the trenches" of building the Web. Most of the people in this latter segment of responders came to the survey by invitation because they are on the e-mail list of the Pew Internet & American Life Project. They are not necessarily opinion leaders for their industries or well-known futurists, but it is striking how much their responses were distributed in ways that paralleled those who are celebrated in the technology field or are affiliated with premier academic or industry organizations. More detail regarding the respondents is included in the introduction and "Biographies" section of the full report.

This report presents the views of respondents in two ways. First, we cite the aggregate views of those who responded to our survey. These answers strike us as most interesting for the fact that there is such wide variance in their views about whether the general direction of technological change will be helpful or harmful to people. Second, we have quoted many of their opinions and predictions in the body of this report.

RESPONDENTS REACT TO SEVEN SCENARIOS ABOUT THE FUTURE

Respondents were asked if they agreed or disagreed with seven scenarios about the future. They were given the opportunity to elaborate on their answers. The scenarios—woven from material collected in recent industry and research reports and predictive statements by leaders in science, technology, business, and politics—were layered with overlapping elements to spur discussion and elicit nuanced views of the future. They were constructed in a way to provoke responses and conversation. They were not written to reflect the views of the Pew Internet Project or Elon University about the most likely or desirable future. Neither Pew Internet nor Elon takes positions on the policy matters or forecasts the likely impact of technological change.

In many cases, respondents' written answers indicate that they agreed with one part of the scenario and disagreed with another, so their final answer was often a qualified "agree" or "disagree"—with elaboration that sometimes reflected the respondents' challenges to the nature of the scenario we drafted.

RESPONDENTS SAY BUILDING NETWORK CAPACITY AND TECHNOLOGICAL KNOWLEDGE SHOULD BE THE TOP PRIORITY

We asked a separate question about setting priorities for future investments in communications technology. Most respondents identified building network capacity and technological literacy as the first or second priority for policy makers and technology leaders to pursue.

Following closely as a priority was "creating a legal and operating environment that allows people to use the Internet the way they want, using the software they want."

Internet sociologist **Howard Rheingold** expressed the consensus of the respondents reflecting on the setting of priorities. "Without affordable access, knowledge of how to use the technology, and the legal and operating environment that permits innovation," he wrote, "we won't see the creative explosion we saw with personal computers and the Internet. Digital rights management, 'trusted computing' that bakes restrictions into hardware, and extensions of copyright law such as the Digital Millennium Copyright Act are roadblocks that could strangle a global creative renaissance before it can take root worldwide." Internet Society board chairman and Internet Engineering Task Force member **Fred Baker** wrote, "Education is key to Internet deployment and use...I therefore placed it first."

Thinking Ahead to 2020: A Sampling of Revealing Predictions Selected From the Thousands of Answers That Were Submitted to Open-Ended Questions in the Survey

> "In 2020 it may no longer be 'screens' with which we interact. What I mean by 'screen time' in 2020 is time spent thinking about and interacting with artificially generated stimuli. Human-to-human nonmediated interaction counts as 'face time' even if you do it with a telephone or video wall." —**Glenn Ricart**, executive director, PricewaterhouseCoopers Advanced Research; member of the board of trustees of the Internet Society

"Privacy is a thing of the past. Technologically, it is obsolete. However, there will be social norms and legal barriers that will dampen out the worst excesses." —**Hal Varian**, University of California–Berkeley and Google

"Fear of enslavement by our creations is an old fear and a literary tritism. But I fear something worse and much more likely—that sometime after 2020 our machines will become intelligent, evolve rapidly, and end up treating us as pets. We can at least take comfort that there is one worse fate—becoming food—that, mercifully, is highly unlikely." —**Paul Saffo**, director, The Institute for the Future

"English will be a prominent language on the Internet because it is a complete trollop willing to be remade by any of its speakers (after all, English is just a bunch of mispronounced German, French, and Latin words)…That said—so what? Chinese is every bit as plausible a winner. Spanish, too. Russian! Korean!" —**Cory Doctorow**, blogger and cofounder of Boing Boing; EFF Fellow

"Profit motives will impede data flow…Networks will conform to the public utility model, with stakeholders in generation, transmission, and distribution. Companies playing in each piece of the game will enact roadblocks to collect what they see as their fair share of tariff revenue." —**Peter Kim**, senior analyst, marketing strategy and technology team, Forrester Research

"There will be a bigger push for both 'national walled gardens' and international cooperation." —**Robert Shaw**, Internet strategy and policy advisor, International Telecommunication Union

"The more autonomous agents, the better. The steeper the 'J-curve,' the better. Automation, including through autonomous agents, will help boost standards of living, freeing us from drudgery." —**Rob Atkinson**, director, Technology and New Economy Project, Progressive Policy Institute

"We are constructing architectures of surveillance over which we will lose control. It's time to think carefully about *Frankenstein*, the Three Laws of Robotics, *Animatrix*, and *Gattaca*." —**Marc Rotenberg**, executive director, Electronic Privacy Information Center

"Until testing, bug fixing, user interfaces, usefulness, and basic application by subject-matter experts is given a higher priority than pure programmer skill, we are totally in danger of evolving into an out-of-control situation with autonomous technology." —**Elle Tracy**, president and e-strategies consultant, The Results Group

"Before 2020 every newborn child in industrialized countries will be implanted with an RFID or similar chip. Ostensibly providing important personal and medical data, these may also be used for tracking and surveillance." —**Michael Dahan**, professor, Sapir Academic College, Israel; Digital Jerusalem

"There is a strong likelihood that virtual reality will become less virtual and more reality for many. However, I see this as an addiction phenomenon that will likely inspire us to understand unexplored dimensions of being human." —**Barry Chudakov**, principal, the Chudakov Company

"While area codes might still define geographic locations in 2020, reality codes may define virtual locations. Multiple personalities will become commonplace, and cyber-psychiatry will proliferate." —**Daniel Wang**, principal, Roadmap Associates

"These technologies allow us to find cohorts that eventually will serve to decrease mass shared values and experiences. More than cultural fragmentation, it will aid a fragmentation of deeper levels of shared reality." —**Denzil Meyers**, founder and president, Widgetwonder, Applied Improvisation Network

"A human's desire to reinvent himself, live out his fantasies, overindulge, addiction will definitely increase. Whole communities/subcultures, which even today are a growing faction, will materialise. We may see a vast blurring of virtual/real reality with many participants living an in-effect secluded lifestyle. Only in the online world will they participate in any form of human interaction." —**Robert Eller**, Concept Omega, Media & Verteiler, Celler Blitz

"Behavior is the function of learning, and the networks shall be the common source of learning, a common platform where all netizens stand equal." —**Alik Khanna**, Smart Analyst Inc., a business employing financial analysts in India

"Corporation-based cultural groupings may actually be one of the most destructive forces if not enough cultural, relational, and bottom-up social forces are built up. This does not detract from the prediction that a lot more people than today will have a good life through extensive networked collaboration."
—**Alejandro Pisanty**, CIO for UNAM (National University of Mexico); vice chairman of the board for ICANN; member of UN Working Group for Internet Governance; active in ISOC

"The information age needs the flow of ideas—the political form always follows the economic need. We will see a flattening of the nation-state in Western society. In Third World countries and networks of ethnic grouping such as the Arab world, we will see a desperate attempt to hold onto the framework as is." —**Amos Davidowitz**, director of education, training, and special programs for Institute of World Affairs; Association for Progressive Education

"By becoming a valuable infrastructure, the Internet itself will become a target. For some, the motivation will be the Internet's power (and impact); for others, it will just be a target to disrupt because of potential impact of such a disruption."
—**Thomas Narten**, IBM open-Internet standards development

"Random acts of senseless violence and destruction will continue and expand due to a feeling of 21st-century anomie, and an increasing sense of lack of individual control." —**Martin Kwapinski**, senior content manager for FirstGov, the U.S. government's official Web portal

"We really need a series of well-supported, lower-level watchdog organizations to ensure that ICTs [information and communications technologies] are not utilized by those in power to serve the interests of profit at the expense of human rights." —**Lynn Schofield Clark**, director of Teens and the New Media @ Home Project, University of Colorado

How Respondents Assessed Scenarios for 2020

Exact prediction language, presented in the order in which the scenarios were posed in the survey	*Agree*	*Disagree*	*Did Not Respond*
A global, low-cost network thrives: By 2020, worldwide network interoperability will be perfected, allowing smooth data flow, authentication, and billing; mobile wireless communications will be available to anyone anywhere on the globe at an extremely low cost.	56%	43%	1%
English displaces other languages: In 2020 networked communications have leveled the world into one big political, social, and economic space in which people everywhere can meet and have verbal and visual exchanges regularly, face-to-face, over the Internet. English will be so indispensable in communicating that it displaces some languages.	42%	57%	1%
Autonomous technology is a problem: By 2020, intelligent agents and distributed control will cut direct human input so completely out of some key activities such as surveillance, security, and tracking systems that technology beyond our control will generate dangers and dependencies that will not be recognized until it is impossible to reverse them. We will be on a "J-curve" of continued acceleration of change.	42%	54%	4%
Transparency builds a better world, even at the expense of privacy: As sensing, storage, and communication technologies get cheaper and better, individuals' public and private lives will become increasingly "transparent" globally. Everything will be more visible to everyone, with good and bad results. Looking at the big picture—at all of the lives affected on the planet in every way possible—this will make the world a better place by the year 2020. The benefits will outweigh the costs.	46%	49%	5%

Virtual reality is a drain for some: By the year 2020, virtual reality on the Internet will come to allow more productivity from most people in technologically savvy communities than working in the "real world." But the attractive nature of virtual-reality worlds will also lead to serious addiction problems for many, as we lose people to alternate realities.	56%	39%	5%
The Internet opens worldwide access to success: In the current best-seller *The World Is Flat*, Thomas Friedman writes that the latest world revolution is found in the fact that the power of the Internet makes it possible for *individuals* to collaborate and compete *globally*. By 2020, this free flow of information will completely blur current national boundaries as they are replaced by city-states, corporation-based cultural groupings, and/or other geographically diverse and reconfigured human organizations tied together by global networks.	52%	44%	5%
Some Luddites/refuseniks will commit terror acts: By 2020, the people left behind (many by their own choice) by accelerating information and communications technologies will form a new cultural group of technology refuseniks who self-segregate from "modern" society. Some will live mostly "off the grid" simply to seek peace and a cure for information overload, while others will commit acts of terror or violence in protest against technology.	58%	35%	7%

Source. Pew Internet & American Life Project Survey, November 30, 2005–April 4, 2006. Results are based on a nonrandom Web-based survey sample of 742 Internet users recruited via e-mail. Since the data are based on a nonrandom sample, a margin of error cannot be computed.

Setting Priorities for Development of Global Information and Communication Technologies

Respondents were asked the following: If you were in charge of setting priorities about where to spend the available funds for developing information and communications technologies (predominantly the Internet) to improve the world, how would you rank order the following international concerns? Please number these from 1 to 4, with 1 being the highest priority.

	First Priority	Second Priority	Third Priority	Fourth Priority	Did Not Respond	Mean Rank
Building the capacity of the network and passing along technological knowledge to those not currently online	51	27	11	4	7	1.67
Creating a legal and operating environment that allows people to use the Internet the way they want, using the software they want	32	32	21	8	7	2.05
Establishing an easy-to-use, secure international monetary microcredit system	8	21	36	28	7	2.90
Developing and "arming" an effective international security watchdog organization	8	12	23	50	7	3.25

Source. Pew Internet & American Life Project, Internet Issues 2020, November 30–April 4, 2006. Results are based on a nonrandom sample of 742 Internet users recruited via e-mail. Since the data are based on a nonrandom sample, a margin of error cannot be computed.

HOPES AND FEARS

A GLOBAL, LOW-COST NETWORK THRIVES

PREDICTION: *By 2020, worldwide network interoperability will be perfected, allowing smooth data flow, authentication, and billing; mobile wireless communications will be available to anyone anywhere on the globe at an extremely low cost.*

Respondents' Reactions to This Scenario	
Agree	56%
Disagree	43%
Did not respond	1%

Note. Because results are based on a nonrandom sample, a margin of error cannot be computed.

CONSENSUS OF OPINION: A great deal of innovation, investment of resources, and successful collaboration will have to be accomplished at the global level during the next 15 years for the elements of this proposed scenario to unfold in a positive manner.

A majority of respondents reflect optimism, while a significant minority expresses pessimism.

This future scenario really won only qualified agreement. A majority of those who chose to "agree" did so while expressing some reservations about parts of the scenario. Some pointed out the probability of government and/or corporate control that limits some types of access in certain parts of the world, and others noted a likely lack of "perfected" interoperability in a world of changing technology. Those who supported all or most of this scenario noted the rapid acceleration of technology innovation in their answers.

"The advances in wireless technologies are pretty much a natural consequence of Moore's law," wrote **Christian Huitema**, a longtime Internet Society leader and a pioneering Internet engineer. "Better computers mean more advanced signal processing, and the possibility to harness higher frequencies. More frequencies mean an abundant 'primary resource,' thus natural competition increasing service availability and driving down prices."

Bob Metcalfe—Internet pioneer, founder of 3Com, and inventor of Ethernet, now of Polaris Venture Partners—chose to reflect on the arrival of "IP on everything," the idea that networked sensors and other devices using an Internet protocol (IP) will proliferate. "The Internet will have gone beyond personal communications" by 2020, he wrote. "Many more of today's 10 billion new embedded micros per year will be on the Internet."

Louis Nauges, president of Microcost, a French information technology firm, sees mobile devices at the forefront. "Mobile Internet will be dominant," he explained. "By 2020, most mobile networks will provide 1-gigabit-per-second-minimum speed, anywhere, anytime. Dominant access tools will be mobile, with powerful infrastructure

> "In 15 years, there will be seamless technology with superior security and bandwidth to what we have today. Applications for wireless portability and faster access will drive the demand."
>
> —Richard Yee,
> competitive intelligence
> analyst, AT&T

characteristics (memory, processing power, access tools), but zero applications; all applications will come from the Net."

MOBILE DEVICES SEEN AS KEY TO GLOBAL CONNECTION

Hal Varian, dean of the School of Information Management and Systems at the University of California–Berkeley and a Google researcher, generally agrees with the scenario. "I think this could easily happen," he wrote. "Of course, some of the mobile access could be shared access (à la Grameen Phone) but, even so, I would guess that most people in the world could get on the network if they really wanted to by 2020." **John Browning**, cofounder of First Tuesday and a writer for *The Economist*, *Wired*, and other technology/economics publications, sees many improvements in networking and devices in the next 15 years. "[The system won't be] perfected and perfectly smooth, but certainly more, better, and deeper than today," he wrote. "The biggest change will come from widespread and reliable identification in and via mobile devices. The biggest source of friction will be copyright enforcement and digital rights management. There will be much innovation in devices to match form and function, media, and messages."

Marc Rotenberg, executive director of the Electronic Privacy Information Center, wrote, "The infrastructure for low-cost communications will be in place. Consumer products, particularly electronics, will be very cheap. But there will be widespread Net 'brown outs,' and gossip and advertising will overwhelm news and public debate."

Michael Reilly of GLOBAL-WRITERS, Baronet Media LLC, predicted that "mobile technologies facilitated by satellite" will reach out to all people.

> "Economies of scale make this possible and will dramatically increase in the years to come. The 'tipping point' in many countries already has been reached; as networks move to other countries, they, too, will reach and exceed that point."
>
> —Jeffrey Branzburg,
> educational consultant
> for National Urban Alliance,
> Center for Applied Technologies in
> Education, and other groups

"Sat-nets will be subsidized by the commercial lines of interest that promote all kinds of brand expansion," he predicted. "Nonprofits also will use these technologies to provide services and support as well as to help bridge divides such as the Islamic and Judeo-Christian worlds. The Rockefeller Brothers Foundation, to name one, is working on the first stages of this now."

CARRIERS AND REGULATORS MUST WORK TOGETHER

Rajnesh Singh of PATARA Communications, GNR Consulting, and the Internet Society for the Pacific Islands, qualified his agreement with the proposed scenario. "The issue governing whether this happens completely and really 'worldwide,'" he wrote, "will depend on the various telecom carriers and regulators around the world taking the necessary steps to effectively relinquishing control of their in-country networks. This may not be completely practical in developing countries, as it will severely impact the revenue model of the incumbent carrier that is typically government owned. For the 'developed' world, this prediction is indeed a reality we may end up experiencing."

Andy Williamson, managing director of Wairua Consulting in New Zealand, wrote, "The technical and social conditions for this will most likely exist…my hesitation is that I do not see a commitment from national legislatures and from international bodies to control commercial exploitation of networks. For your prediction to come true, global regulation of networks that privileges public good over commercial reward must occur."

Alik Khanna of Smart Analyst, Inc., in India, sees a low-cost digital world ahead. "With growing data-handling capacity, networking costs shall be low," he wrote. "The incremental efficiency in hardware and software tech shall propel greater data movement across the inhabited universe."

THERE ARE MANY WHO EXPRESS DOUBTS
ABOUT A "NETWORKING NIRVANA"

While 56% agreed with the positive scenario for network development, a vocal 43% disagreed, most of them providing eloquent answers questioning the ideas of interoperability and global access at a low cost, with many noting the necessity for government and corporate involvement in worldwide development and the negative political and profit motives that usually accompany such involvement.

"While society as a whole would be likely to benefit from a networking nirvana, the markets are unlikely to get there by 2020 due to incumbent business models, insufficient adoption of new cost-compensation methods, and insufficient sociotechnical abilities to model human trust relationships in the digital world," wrote **Pekka Nikander** of Ericcson Research, the Internet Architecture Board, and the Helsinki Institute for Information Technology.

Brian T. Nakamoto of Everyone.net wrote, "Companies will cling to old business models and attempt to extend their life by influencing lawmakers to pass laws that hinder competition."

Ian Peter, Australian leader of the Internet Mark II Project, wrote, "The problem of the digital divide is too complex and the power of legacy telco regulatory regimes too powerful to achieve this utopian dream globally within 15 years."

Peter Kim, senior analyst with Forrester Research, agrees. "Profit motives will impede data flow," he wrote. "Although interconnectivity will be much higher than ever imagined, networks will conform to the public utility model with stakeholders in generation, transmission, and distribution. Companies playing in each piece of the game will enact roadblocks to collect what they see as their fair share of tariff revenue."

> "By 2020, network communications providers will have succeeded in Balkanizing the existing global network, fracturing it into many smaller walled gardens that they will leverage to their own financial gain."
>
> —Ross Rader,
> director of research
> and innovation, Tucows, Inc.

WILL THERE BE A NEW OR DIFFERENT NETWORK BY THEN?

Fred Baker of Cisco Systems, chairman of the board of the Internet Society, posed the possibility that "other varieties of networks" might "replace" the current network. "So, yes," he wrote, "I suspect there will be a global, low-cost network in 2020. That's not to say that interoperability will be perfect, however. There are various interests that have a vested interest in limiting interoperability in various ways, and they will in 2020 still be hard at work."

One of the key actors in the development of another "variety of network" is **David Clark** of MIT. Clark is working under a National Science Foundation grant for the Global Environment for Networking Investigations (GENI) to build new naming, addressing, and identity architectures and further develop an improved Internet. In his survey response, Clark expressed hope for the future. "A low-cost network will exist," he wrote. "The question is how interconnected and open it will be. The question is whether we drift toward a 'reintegration' of content and infrastructure."

Robert Shaw, Internet strategy and policy advisor for the International Telecommunication Union and official advisor to ICANN's Governmental Advisory Committee, wrote, "Cross-border tensions on audio-visual policies will continue to rise in importance, and, with the ineffectiveness of national regulator regimes to deal with them, there will be a bigger push for both 'national walled gardens' and international cooperation."

Bruce Edmonds of the Centre for Policy Modeling at Manchester, U.K., expects that continuous changes wrought by the evolution of Internet architecture will remove any chance for a "perfected" or "smooth" future. "New technologies requiring new standards," he predicted, "will ensure that (1) interoperability remains a problem, and (2) bandwidth will always be used up, preventing smooth

> "The lack of a global society and the dominant capitalistic logic in the existing power structures work against smooth, low-cost availability for anyone."
>
> —Stine Gotved,
> cultural sociologist,
> University of Copenhagen

data flow. Billing will remain a problem in some parts of the world because such monetary integration is inextricably political."

CORPORATE AND GOVERNMENT RESTRICTIONS FORECAST

Many of the elaborations recorded by those who disagreed with the 2020 operating-environment scenario express concerns about the possibility that the Internet will be forced into a tiered-access structure, such as that now offered by cellular communications providers and cable and satellite television operators. **Mark Gaved** of The Open University in the U.K. sees it this way. "The majority of people will be able to access a seamless, always-on, high-speed network which operates by verifying their ID," he predicted. "However, there will be a low-income, marginalized population in these countries who will only have access to limited services and have to buy into the network at higher rates, in the same way people with poor credit ratings cannot get monthly mobile phone contracts but pay higher, pay-as-you-go charges."

Christopher Johnson, CEO for if People, wrote, "Current dominant market forces will further alienate themselves from 'open and accessible' by creating more proprietary and limited ways of acting online, continuing their ability to feed on the technology fears and ignorance of some people."

Some of those who disagreed with the scenario also saw government interference limiting online freedoms and access. **Mark Gaved** wrote that there will be "government-limited access in less democratic states." And **Scott Moore**, online community manager for the Helen and Charles Schwab Foundation, wrote, "New networks will be built with more controllable gateways allowing governments and corporations greater control over access to the flow of information. Governments will use the excuse of greater security and exert control over their citizens. Corporations will claim protection from intellectual property theft and 'hacking' to prevent the poor or disenfranchised from freely exchanging information."

Stewart Alsop, writer, investor, and analyst, commented that there is a chance for innovations to make a world-changing difference in the next 15 years. "This depends on technology standards exceeding the self-interest of proprietary network owners, like mobile operators, cable and telephony network owners, and so forth," he explained. "So timing is still open, but most likely by 2020."

Internet Society Board of Trustees member **Glenn Ricart**, a former program manager at DARPA now with PricewaterhouseCoopers, predicts a mix of system regulation. "A few nations (or cities) may choose to make smooth, low-cost, ubiquitous communications part of their national industrial and social infrastructure (like electrical power and roads)," he predicted. "Others (and I'd include the United States here) will opt for an oligopoly of providers that allows for limited alternatives while concentrating political and economic power. Individuals and businesses will provide local enclaves of high-quality connectivity for themselves and their guests. A somewhat higher cost 'anywhere' (e.g., cellular) infrastructure will be available where governments or planned communities don't already include it as an amenity. I believe that the Internet will not be uniform in capability or quality of service in 2020: There will be different tiers of service with differentiated services and pricing."

> "Patching tinkered, ad hoc solutions, regional/national/brand interests, and simple human egoism in general is the order of technology and design. This will never change, unless suppressed by some kind of political regime that takes control in order to harmonize technology, protocols, and formats by brute force. Does anybody want that in order to attain compatibility and smooth operation (even if possible)? No, of course not."
>
> —Mikkel Holm Sørensen,
> software and intelligence
> manager, Actics Ltd.

ADDRESSING ACCESS IN REMOTE AREAS AND THE DIGITAL DIVIDE

Another issue pointed out by many was the difficulties involved in bringing technology to remote regions and to people living in the poorest conditions.

Craig Partridge, Internet pioneer and chief scientist at BBN Technologies, wrote, "We tend to overestimate how fast technology gets installed, especially in Third World countries. One is tempted to say yes to this idea, given the tremendous profusion of cellular over the past 20 years or so. But it is far too optimistic. If one limited this to First and Second World countries, the answer would be more clearly 'yes it will happen.' "

ISOC's **Fred Baker**'s answer included a similar point in his elaboration. He wrote, "Mobile wireless communications will be very widely available, but 'extremely low cost' makes economic assumptions about the back sides of mountains in Afghanistan and the behavior of entrepreneurs in Africa."

Adrian Schofield, head of research for ForgeAhead and a leader with Information Industry of South Africa and the World Information Technology and Services Alliance, pointed out the fact that there may always be people left behind. "Although available," he wrote, "not everyone will be connected to the network, thus continuing the divide between the 'have' and 'have not.' "

And **Matthew Allen**, president of the Association of Internet Researchers and associate professor of Internet studies at Curtin University in Australia, echoed many respondents'

> "Technology will make access near global, yet economics will continue to create and even enhance a digital divide...We will see those with access gain even more advantage in knowledge, and the returns to such knowledge; while the low-income and/or rural will fall further beyond."
>
> —Ed Lyell,
> pioneer in issues
> regarding Internet and education;
> professor at Adams State College

sentiments when he wrote, "Fundamental development issues (health, education, basic amenities) will restrict the capacity of many people to access networks."

Alan Levin, chairman for ISOC's South Africa chapter, wrote, "The rich get richer and the poor get poorer, hence in 2020 there may be a thriving, low-cost network, but those in need of the basics will not be able to use it." **Alejandro Pisanty**—CIO of the National University of Mexico, a member of the Internet Governance Forum

Advisory Group, and a member of ICANN's board of directors—
boiled it down to numbers. "At least 30% of the world's population
will continue to have no or extremely scarce/difficult access due to
scarcity of close-by services and lack of know-how to exploit the
connectivity available," he predicted. "Where there is a network, it
will indeed be of moderate or low cost and operate smoothly. Security, in contrast, will continue to be a concern at least at 'Layer-8'
level."

Jonathan Zittrain, an expert on worldwide access and cofounder
and director of Harvard University's Berkman Center for the Internet and Society, also boiled it down to numbers. " 'Anywhere on the
globe to anyone' is a tall order," he responded. "I think more likely
80% of the bandwidth will be with 20% of the population."

A CALL FOR ALL CONCERNED TO COME TOGETHER FOR THE PUBLIC GOOD

Raul Trejo-Delarbre of Universidad Nacional Autonoma de México
urged collaboration among nations. "A significant reduction on the
digital divide only will take place in a new international environment, with a genuine multisector cooperation," he explained. "We
don't have a landscape like that now. In absence of that commitment,
we will see an irregular and inequitable development of the wired
and wireless resources."

Author, teacher, and social commentator **Douglas Rushkoff**
summed up the opinions of many respondents regarding the proposed
operating environment scenario for 2020 when he wrote, "Real
interoperability will be contingent
on replacing our bias for competition with one for collaboration.
Until then, economics do not permit
universal networking capability."

> "No. This will happen over the telco's dead bodies—literally."
>
> —Anonymous respondent

Scott Hollenbeck, director of technology for VeriSign and an
Internet Engineering Task Force director, wrote, "The technology
may exist to improve things greatly, but there will still be economic

barriers. Low-cost (even extremely low-cost) communications technology is still something that will have to be balanced against costs for food, shelter, and other basic necessities."

And **Marilyn Cade** of the Information Technology Association of America and the Generic Names Supporting Organization of ICANN expressed a common theme when she wrote, "I wish this [optimistic scenario] were true. And I want it to be true, and I want all of us to work very hard to make it as true as possible. First of all, we are at 2006, and we need to address connectivity and affordable access still for vast numbers of potential users on the planet Earth."

So, How Many People Are Online Now?

The total number of Internet users across the world now, in the fall of 2006, is a matter of debate. There is no one, efficient way to record this measurement. Some market-research firms have estimated the overall total in 2006 at more than a billion users, with 845 million using it regularly.

Statisticians at comScore World Metrix reported that more than 694 million people aged 15 and older were on the network as of March 2006—14% of the world's total population in this demographic. The comScore report indicated that the total Internet use in major Asian nations, including Japan, Korea, India, and China, constitutes 25% of the total worldwide online population (168 million users), a group 11% larger than U.S. users (152 million). The report noted that 10 years ago, U.S. users accounted for two-thirds of the global Internet population; now they represent less than a quarter of Internet users (comScore, 2006, p. 1).

Current Issues in the Network's Global Development

The continued innovation of the architecture of the Internet to support efficiently and securely the flow of more data to more people is no small order, but it is a given in most technology circles.

The innovation is expected. The most often-mentioned hurdles to a low-cost system with access for all are not technological. The survey respondents nearly unanimously said that the development of a worldwide network with easy access, smooth data flow, and availability everywhere at a low cost depends upon the appropriate balance of political and economic support.

The battle about political and economic control of the Internet is evident in the loud debate in the U.S. Congress and Federal Communications Commission in 2006 about "network neutrality" (with Internet-tech companies such as Microsoft and Google facing off against the major telecommunications corporations such as AT&T that provide the data pipelines) and in the appearance of a newly formed world organization inspired by the UN's World Summit on the Information Society—the Internet Governance Forum (http://www.intgovforum.org/), which met for the first time in October 2006.

The technology to make the Internet easy to use continues to evolve. World Wide Web innovator Tim Berners-Lee and other Internet engineers in the World Wide Web Consortium are working on building the "semantic Web," which they expect will enable users worldwide to find data in a more naturally intuitive manner. But at the group's May WWW2006 conference in Edinburgh, Berners-Lee also took the time to campaign against U.S. proposals to change to an Internet system in which data from companies or institutions that can pay more are given priority over those that cannot or will not. He warned that this would move the network into "a dark period," and said, "Anyone that tries to chop it into two will find that their piece looks very boring...I think it is one and will remain as one."

The problem of defeating the digital divide has captivated many key Internet stakeholders for years, and their efforts continue. Nicholas Negroponte of MIT's Media Lab has been working more than a decade to bring to life the optimistic predictions he made about an easily accessible global information network in his 1995 book *Being Digital*. He has said he hoped to launch his "one laptop per child" project (http://www.laptop.org/) in developing nations later in 2006 or in early 2007, shipping 5–10 million, $135 computers to China, India, Thailand, Egypt, the Middle East, Nigeria, Brazil, and Argentina. Partners on the project include the UN, Nortel, Red Hat, AMD, Marvell, Brightstar, and Google. The computers will be equipped with Wi-Fi and will be able to hook up to the Internet through a cell-phone connection. The developers hope to see the price of the computers drop to $100 by 2008, and as low as $50 per unit in 2010. "We're going to be below 2 watts [of total power consumption]. That's very important because 35% of the world doesn't have electricity," Negroponte said. "Power is such a big deal that you're going to hear every company boasting about power" in the near future. "That is the currency of tomorrow" (Spooner, 2006).

In responding to this survey's optimistic 2020 operating-system and access scenario, foresight expert **Paul Saffo**, director of The Institute for the Future, wrote, "My forecast is that we will see neither nirvana nor meltdown, but we will do a nice job of muddling through. In the end, the network will advance dramatically with breathtaking effect on our lives, but we won't notice because our expectations will rise even faster."

ADDITIONAL RESPONSES

Many other survey respondents shared comments tied to the scenario about the future of the global network. Among them:

> "This is the direction that technology and economics and markets are moving. However, the desire by large owners of telecommunications pipes (e.g., cable companies, DSL providers) to control traffic (i.e., by disallowing bits they don't approve from traveling on their part of the network) could balkanize the Internet." —**Howard Rheingold**, Internet sociologist and author

> "As a stubborn optimist/idealist, I hope this will be true. However, it will only occur to the extent that the power and

greed of massive private-sector conglomerates can be held in check, and the desire of governments to censor and control content can be restrained. It will obviously vary wildly, between nations. Also, one advantage that poor nations have, is that they often have no established infrastructure that will be threatened." —**Jim Warren**, founding editor of *Dr. Dobb's Journal*; technology policy advocate; futurist

"While we think of a portable radio with batteries as possibly the lowest cost medium, there are a lot of people who cannot afford this, or, as in Uganda, men take the batteries so their wives cannot use the radio (reflect-action.org is the source). I also worry about the problem of Net neutrality balkanizing the U.S. Internet, the walled gardens of the telco mobile services, and of course the Chinese setting up their own domains. However, in spite of these barriers, more people will be using the Internet on a global basis, but I can't forecast the percentage." —**Steve Cisler**, former senior library scientist for Apple; now working on public-access projects in Guatemala, Ecuador, and Uganda

"The network might not be perfect, but it will certainly be widespread. We already have a telephone network which reaches all over the world, and worldwide access to GPS. So it's not too much of a stretch to extend this to wireless. Though there may be artificial barriers at the country level (e.g., China may not interoperate for political reasons, even if it could at a technical level)." —**Seth Finkelstein**, anticensorship activist and programmer; author of the Infothought blog; EFF Pioneer Award winner

"Worldwide interoperability and that wireless will likely be free, at least in some form, to everyone. I don't understand what authentication and billing are doing in that sentence. I think it's perfectly plausible that identifying people reliably is impossible, full stop. As to billing—what if it turns out that the marginal cost of information and knowledge goods is too cheap to meter? Do we need billing? Couldn't we have blanket licenses, instead?" —**Cory Doctorow**, blogger and cofounder of Boing Boing; EFF Fellow

"This will be true for many people, but not for everyone." —**Esther Dyson**, former chair of ICANN; now of CNET Networks

"While costs will come down and accessibility will increase, barriers of literacy—both with written language and technology—will become the greatest barriers to access for 'anyone anywhere.'" **—Mike Kent**, professor of social policy, Murdoch University

"Mobile wireless communications will also be available at an extremely high cost (and all points in between). It will do you no good to have cheap wireless access if you can't live with less than 10 gigabits to the desktop." **—Fred Hapgood**, author and consultant

> **"A significant portion of the global population lacks food, water, sanitation, electrical service, and the like. Smooth data flow? Who cares?"**
>
> —Edward Lee Lamoureux,
> associate professor,
> Bradley University

"Three factors will impede the growth of interoperable networking: political resistance within some countries where elements wish to reduce citizen access; legal/economic issues that cause interoperability and access restrictions in the name of copyright protection, or protection of the underlying ISP's economic interests; and difficulties with authentication and traceback needed to provide access while also preventing fraud and identity theft." **—Eugene Spafford**, director of CERIAS (Center for Education and Research in Information Assurance and Security)

"There will undoubtedly be 'holes' in network coverage, even by 2020, in remote parts of the world. In parts of interior Africa or Asia, for example, wireless coverage is likely to remain expensive and spotty, if available at all." **—Gary Chapman**, director, The 21st Century Project, LBJ School of Public Affairs at the University of Texas–Austin

"The stride of development has been very evident in the time I have been working on the Net and related technologies. There is no reason to expect it to slow down, but availability will still be a major issue for billions of people. More people will have access, but for those who do not, the digital divide will grow and they will be left lagging increasingly behind. Some of the reasons will be infrastructure, but most will be political restrictions. Centers of power are shifting and transfer of information will be hampered to try to maintain stability." **—Amos Davidowitz**, director of education, training, and special programs for Institute of World Affairs; Association for Progressive Education

"Mobile wireless communications on the GSM platform will be the universal tool of engagement; even so, communications will still be localized in terms of networks and content." —**Tunji Lardner**, CEO for the West African NGO network: wangonet.org; agendaconsulting.biz; consultant to the UNDP African Internet Initiative

"Well, 'nearly' perfected, and available to 'almost' everyone." —**Reva Basch**, consultant for Aubergine Information Systems

"It's hard to fit this one into a Boolean logic, and given a choice, I'd select 'by and large.' Countries where mobile networks are broadly available today, and most of those in which that is less the case, will likely fit the definition. However, barring a revolution in wireless technology (that would basically flood the entire planet with wireless access), I'm afraid that countries at the poorer end of the spectrum in which most people today have yet to make their first phone call, while they will see improvements in their network infrastructure, will be nowhere near pervasiveness. 2020 is, after all, only 15 years away, and poverty today has not improved all that much compared to what it was 15 years ago." —**Robin Berjon**, W3C and Expway

"I agree that by 2020, a global network will thrive. However, market conditions may require that the charged cost will still be high for the poor in the world." —**V. K. Wong**, director of IT campus initiatives and CARAT (Collaboratory for Advanced Research and Academic Technologies), University of Michigan

"Network interoperability is only a question of connecting the missing dots to much already existing technology. The world today is already demanding this, and that demand and the very use of the technology is creating a forward synergy that will cause it to happen. This will evolve as providers of the integrated services needed to make it happen discover that there is a far greater potential for product and economic growth by working across platforms to cooperate rather than complicate." —**Tom Snook**, CTO, New World Symphony

"This statement reflects a continuation of the technology and interoperability development and cost declines already underway and evident. There are numerous examples within the communications industry that serve as an example, but consider that the per-bit cost of optical transport equipment has fallen by over 90% versus only a few years ago." —**Jim Archuleta**, senior manager, government solutions, Ciena Corporation

"I wouldn't say 'perfected,' and I don't know that it will be anywhere on the globe, but I mostly agree we'll see it be much more cheaper and accessible." —**Danny Sullivan**, editor-in-chief, SearchEngineWatch.com

"Global political pressures from some governments will continue to prevent total, open access to some of the constituents within geographical areas. There will be fewer Third World countries, but the ones that continue to exist will receive help from other countries as they build out their infrastructure. This will probably not be totally complete within this time frame." —**Mike McCarty**, chief network officer, Johns Hopkins

"Anywhere? No. Many places? Yes. Some countries will deliberately prohibit wireless Internet communications for political reasons. Others will fall behind (or remain behind) the curve because of business or government telecom monopolies trying to maintain their current cash cows at the expense of new services. Will all these things be technically possible by then? Sure. But deployment is a different issue." —**John S. Quarterman**, president, InternetPerils, Inc.

"The key will be the prosumer model where people pay or are paid for content at a microbyte level with some form of economic granularity that ends up a balancing of costs for production and consumption for an individual." —**Rich Ling**, senior researcher and sociologist, Telenor Research Institute, Oslo, Norway

"After 15 years, there still will be some countries where mobile communication will be unavailable due to economical or political situation. Smooth data flow still requires significant improvements across the countries and network operators in Europe. It would be silly to expect a better situation in Africa in 2020 than in Europe today." —**Wladyslaw Majewski**, OSI CompuTrain SA, ISOC Polska

"The technology supporting this kind of development is proceeding at full speed. In addition, there is now a political will in a number of countries to develop electronic medical records (EMR) nationally. It is only a matter of time when EMRs would be accessible worldwide." —**Rashid Bashshur**, director of telemedicine, University of Michigan

"I live in a so-called 'Third World' country and I have seen it happening that way. I remember I didn't get to know a conventional telephone until I was 4 or 6, now my 2-year-old already uses the cell phone and the digital camera of the family like any of his other toys. It just seems natural to me that by the time he is my age, he will have, what for me is now, 'the home of future.' 5 years ago, I had neither a digital camera nor a PDA, now I can't live without them! And I crave for wireless anywhere I go. And more important, it is not only my imagination— I read at least 20 tech sites daily and all news tends to go that way. The only thing that worries me is the parallel trend of, for example, conventional carriers that push to charge for every single thing related to the use of their connections." —**Claudia Cruz**, online editor of elPeriodico, based in Guatemala

"I don't see the economic motivation to deploy globally. Substantial parts of Africa and Asia offer little pull. A good comparison is rural America. Even with push from FCC and PUCs, rural America does not have access like the metroplexes." —**Willis Marti**, associate director for networking, Texas A&M University

"All aspects of our lives will be connected electronically so that we can pass personal data (music, voice, video) between devices and locations that are important to us. Kids, parents, teachers, friends, workers, colleagues—all of our personal associations will be available seamlessly and ubiquitously. At the same time, all of the traditional media that we access for information will be just as readily available." —**Michael Gorrell**, senior VP and CIO, EBSCO

"The Internet is a dynamic organism which is simultaneously evolving at every nexus, the 'computer,' the network protocol, the routers, etc. Complete uniformity and stability are anathema to the evolution of the network. One 'improvement' in software at a router can completely disrupt traffic. Fortunately, the systems will become more robust but there will never be a 'nirvana' or perfect network." —**William Kearns**, assistant professor, University of South Florida

"I agree that this would be possible but wonder whether the Third World and developing nations will really have the wireless communication networks posited by the question. The basics of life must take precedence over the technology in those nations." —**Jill O'Neill**, director of planning and communication, National Federation of Abstracting and Information Services

"Network neutrality and corporate control of networks will be major issues. Besides centralized corporate control, nations— China, India, Germany, and other countries—will control what their citizens can see and do online, and in some cases, who can get online." —**Nicco Mele**, U.S. political Internet strategist

"The digital divide will increasingly apply to communications. You can already see this with the varying degrees of broadband speed available. In the U.K., broadband is concentrated in the wealthier neighborhoods. Mobile voice connectivity will be quite widespread with 3 billion users worldwide—if not more. Universal service may apply to broadband by 2020, but this will be in rich countries only and for a basic degree of connectivity." —**Paul Lee**, a respondent who chose not to share further identifying information

"The actual challenge is about billing issues among countries and currencies as opposed to technical issues, which have already been sorted out to date." —**Fabio Sampaio**, Brazil; Internet user since 1994

"I am optimistic. The handheld devices used will become more and more like small computers. I do not believe that AOL's e-mail stamps will have a future. People will want such services for free. Older adults and those with chronic disease will have their vitals automatically monitored." —**Sturle J. Monstad**, University of Bergen, Norway

"The Internet will continue to grow and more devices (and individuals) will become interconnected. I don't think that all aspects of this will be 'smooth,' i.e., the security issues we are seeing are not easily solved and will not just 'go away.' However, significant progress toward the goal of a global, low-cost network will be achieved. This will be driven by the huge benefits of connecting people together." —**Thomas Narten**, IBM open-Internet standards development

"I seriously doubt interoperability will be perfected. I think the pace of change will increase and the amount of interoperability will be jagged. Up and down and up and down as disruptive tech comes and goes and is integrated." —**Mike Gill**, electronics engineer, National Library of Medicine

"I don't know if it will be perfected, but it will be as commonplace as plain, old telephone service used to be." —**Christine Haile**, chief information officer, University at Albany, New York

"Technology advances in fits and starts, so yes, networks will be faster and more interoperable, but issues will still remain and even newer technologies come to the fore and need standards and commercial acceptance. And new technologies make possible new threats and annoyances. Who had an issue with e-mail spam 10 years ago?" —**Joe Bishop**, VP, business development, Marratech AB

"It is merely a case of observing how other mass communications media developed over the 20th century: initially confined to the financially well off, and imitating earlier media before finding their own identity, their own language of expression, and their appropriate niches in the socioeconomic and cultural fabric of society…and just as cinema did not totally replace theatre, nor did television replace cinema, so electronic networks will never entirely substitute newspapers on paper, telephones, or conventional mail. There will simply be more options available. Just like modern buildings stand alongside ancient ones in Japan and other places, advanced networks in 2020 will have to share space with those deliberately choosing slower, simpler means of communication, not as a means of protest, mind you, but as a form of savoring experiences. Remember? Somewhere or other T.S. Eliot said something like, 'I had the experience, but I forget its significance.' Thoughtful people in 2020 will probably use high-speed networks for their everyday communications, but surely will use handwritten and snail-mail-delivered wedding invitations or tasteful thank-you notes for especially meaningful communications." —**Fredric M. Litto**, professor, University of Sao Paulo, Brazil

"This may seem utopian, but with due diligence and involvement from an active Internet Community of Users and NFPs, it is a possibility that we should aim for." —**Cheryl Langdon-Orr**, independent Internet business operator; director, ISOC-Australia

"Parts of this statement ring true, that a global network will be implemented that allows connectivity any time, anywhere. However, the prices will remain high enough that only citizens of well-off countries will be able to benefit from this connectivity. Attempts will be made to bring this connectivity to people traditionally without this access, but it will have limited success because of the many other aspects needed to make communications and computing work—access to computing devices, reliable electricity, and training/language issues. Interoperability will not be 'perfected,' as new innovations stand to make previous network incarnations obsolete." —**Philip Joung**, Spirent Communications

> "Nonglobal communication would be an exception. Anyone who expected the airplane to fly just to and from Kitty Hawk, NC, only had modified vision."
>
> —Stan Felder,
> president and CEO,
> Vibrance Associates, LLC

"Perfection will not be achieved, but I fully expect high-speed optical links through the air, and software should be more robust. Taxes will have kicked in by then." —**Michael Steele**, Internet user since 1978

"While it is probably technically feasible to provide the backbone capacity and local wireless access to achieve this goal, too many incidental barriers exist. There's the question of whether the world economy will support it (I expect disruptions), whether international political affairs will be healthy enough to permit it, and whether the designers of the network can fend off attacks." —**Andy Oram**, writer and editor for O'Reilly Media

"Low cost indeed! For all intents and purposes, the network will be free. However, people will subscribe, for a monthly fee, which will provide virtually all sorts of services including all telephone, television, music, radio, games, entertainment, Internet, etc. Advertisements will play a large role in allowing this low-cost service, but subscribers will do significant purchasing through this medium as well." —**Don Heath**, board member, iPool, Brilliant Cities, Inc., Diversified Software, Alcatel, Foretec

"What we are referring to as 'worldwide' will, however, mean a large—but not absolutely comprehensive—part of the world. The same occurs now when we say 'electricity is available worldwide.'" —**Suely Fragoso**, professor, Unisinos, Brazil

"'Extremely low cost' is relevant. What is small to those in the developed world is expensive to nonelites in the rest of the world." —**Barry Wellman**, professor and director of NetLab at University of Toronto, Canada

"While network interoperability may be perfected at a technological level, it is unlikely to lead to smooth data flow, authentication, and billing because it is to the advantage of organizations that make money off of these things to try and maintain monopolies. Likewise, providing wireless communications still requires building infrastructure, and it isn't clear that there will be sufficient funding to develop those networks in all parts of the world, or that satellite technology would come down enough in cost to meet the low-cost scenario. Launching satellites and building infrastructure costs money the Third World doesn't have—and private companies work for profit." —**Lisa Kamm**, has worked in information architecture since 1995 at organizations including IBM, Agency.com and the ACLU

"Although the network will be widespread, there will still be pockets of poverty where access to the equipment, energy, and knowledge will be limited. A ubiquitous network means ubiquitous electricity, computer equipment, and global literacy. That's a tall order." —**Karen Coyle**, information professional and librarian

"There will probably still be segments of the world that will deliberately obstruct true, unfettered interoperability for purposes of controlling the flow of information (e.g., China)." —**Jim Huggins**, associate professor of computer science, Kettering University

"There will be a global network but [people will] have less confidence that it will be low cost, given that access will often be in for-profit hands. I expect consolidation of companies providing access and a correlative increase in prices." —**David Elesh**, associate professor of sociology, Temple University

"The real question is what kind of wireless. It seems increasingly inevitable that we will be moving to pricing structures that will require a premium for higher bandwidth. So, ubiquity, but not at speed." —**Alex Halavais**, assistant professor, Quinnipiac University

"I doubt the necessary investments will be made in many of Africa's countries. I suspect commercial interests will continue to compete for dominance and that we will still have different standards (for example, the European and U.S. global positioning systems). Just trying to use my mobile in different countries of the Caucasus and Eastern Europe convinces me we have significant challenges." —**Leigh Estabrook**, professor, University of Illinois

"I doubt the issues surrounding proprietary standards and protocols will exist so long as they provide a perceived economic advantage. I doubt a single mobile data network will operate in Nigeria, East Timor, and Tasmania. In many cases, I expect it will be on the client side (tri-mode phone? Try oct-mode or duodeca-mode) that many of these issues will be addressed, and that many of these solutions will be hacks that try to integrate disparate systems underneath." —**Michael Cannella**, IT manager, Volunteers of America-Michigan

"It will be recognized by all that the velocity of knowledge, like the economic velocity of money, will enrich everyone." —**Charles Hendricksen**, research collaboration architect, Cedar Collaboration

"To build a system like that, you need not only worldwide technical solutions delivered by idealistic and perfectly honest providers, you also need world peace, to end famine and free education for all. That is too tough to deliver in 14 years." —**Torill Mortensen**, associate professor, Volda University College, Norway

"I'd be extremely surprised (pleasantly, of course) if there were universal access in the world's 50 poorest countries by 2020." —**Peter Levine**, director of CIRCLE (Center for Information and Research on Civic Learning and Engagement), University of Maryland

"When you say 'anyone anywhere in the globe,' you infer that all Internet users will have equal access. That isn't true now—why would we believe that it would be any more the case down the road? There are global disparities in income, geography, infrastructure, etc., that will continue to remain unaddressed." —**Christine Ogan**, professor, University of Indiana School of Journalism

"There will still be a global Internet, but intranets (localized networks) will be the core hubs for business and universities keen to keep their traffic in local bubbles, away from litigation and ever-increasing surveillance. The Internet at large will still be the share point, but e-mail and other protocols will be routinely encrypted, and prying eyes will have a much harder time in an era of informatic paranoia." —**Tama Leaver**, lecturer in digital communication, University of Western Australia

"With all the research in ubiquitous computing and ambient intelligence, it is very likely that RFID technology, systems interoperability, ubiquitous information and communication applications, and wireless systems will become part of our everyday lives. I wonder whether they will be available for anyone (since differences between First World and Third World countries will not be solved within 15 years), but do believe they will be available to large groups of people worldwide." —**B. van den Berg**, faculty of philosophy at Erasmus University, Rotterdam, The Netherlands

"Rural communities in developing nations will still lag substantially behind urban-dwelling, higher income individuals globally. This is one of the most important gaps that needs to be addressed." —**Kathleen Pierz**, managing partner, The Pierz Group

"I agree with parts of this statement, but not all of it. For instance, I think authentication will be improved, but there will always be sophisticated criminals who can 'crack' the system for illicit reasons. Additionally, I doubt that mobile wireless communications will be available anywhere on the globe at low cost. There will still be problems in mountainous areas, especially where population density is low. Some regions of the world with low population density will still have limited wireless access (e.g., rainforests of Borneo, Gobi Desert) and it will still be expensive to provide wireless communications over the ocean." —**Michael S. Cann, Jr.**, CEO, Affinio Corporation

"Interoperability won't be perfected, but attempts to regulate the network according to telcos' desire to implement QOS at the network layer will have failed because of international pressure." —**Kevin Schlag**, director of Web development and IT for Western Governor's University, BYU-Hawaii

"With the current rhythm it gives development and technological innovation, it is very possible that this is this way. Alone it is necessary to see, for example, the installation of nets Wi-Fi in the rural area of Peru that helps the Peruvian peasants to negotiate its crop. It is a remote and not well-communicated area, but that, thanks to the new technologies, is very competitive inside the domestic economy." —**Sabino M. Rodriguez**, MC&S Services

"While I think it will be better, 'perfect' is a pretty strong word. I wouldn't underestimate the tenacity of people who make money from proprietary networks to hang on to them." —**Cleo Parker**, senior manager, BBDO

"While we will have worldwide network interoperability, we will continue to be plagued by badly or inadequately written and documented software for most other applications. A fundamentalist movement toward rigorously designed, open-source applications might occur if we acknowledge that the lack of interoperability of these programs results in a huge drain on productivity. On the other hand, we may just continue to muddle along." —**Sam Punnett**, president, FAD Research

"Commoditization of telecommunications services, open standards for documents and server operations, and the expectations of access to the Internet and its successors will force businesses, universities, and governments to make this come to pass. While there will be a global, low-cost network, there will also be numerous large, but closed, networks attached to the global network. These networks will use their own domain-name-resolution servers. Both governments working with regional partners and multinational companies in cooperation with each other will develop their own alternative networks to satisfy security and political concerns." —**Sean Mead**, consultant for Interbrand Analytics, Design Forum, Mead, Mead & Clark, and other companies

"The technology may be available, but the business interests that drive technology will not be in a position to allow a perfected scenario by 2020." —**Nan Dawkins**, cofounder, RedBoots Consulting

"The greatest threat to this scenario is the increasing tendency of the telecom giants to 'privatize' the Internet by applying artificial and proprietary cost and access structures in an attempt to drive greater corporate profits. There will never be enough competition in broadband access in the U.S." —**Brent Crossland**, technology policy analyst

> "Already the cost of Internet access and broadband access is decreasing. In other countries, governments are working to provide low-cost computers and Internet access (India is one example). This lowers the barrier to get online. Interoperability is a necessity, though I'm not sure there will be a time when everything runs entirely smoothly."
>
> —Enid Burns,
> editor, ClickZ.com

"Global inequities are still going to exist in 2020. It is too short a window for a utopian ideal of universal access and use over the globe. By 2020, I believe that high-income users in large cities in rich countries will be able to experience the world this way. The downside is they may assume that's the case for everyone and fail to consider the way this draws more lines between haves and have-nots. What is 'low cost' to some is high cost to others." —**Caroline Haythornthwaite**, associate professor, University of Illinois at Urbana-Champaign

"Paranoia about spam, worms, Trojans, and viruses has caused people to look at the impact the Internet is affecting on their lives. Allowing more gateways is viewed as intrusive and will be rejected." —**W. Reid Cornwell**, director, the Center for Internet Research

"Copyright and other turf wars such as political censorship will lead to a fractured global information infrastructure." —**Richard Forno**, principal consultant, KRvW Associates, Infowarrior. org; CMU Software Engineering Institute

"Most people will be able to afford some sort of handheld apparatus for communication, but the cost of accessing the network will be high in some remote parts of the globe. I live in part of the world that has some of the highest jetstream costs in the world, and that is unlikely to change in remote island states, compared to large continental nations." —**Barbara Craig**, Victoria University

"It is hard to speculate on this issue, since technology does not exist in a vacuum but is dependent on, or rather operates in, its social, cultural, and political context. What I think is reasonable to say is that interoperability will be perfected in those parts of the world that will belong to the same political and economic context. This refers both to formal political and economic integrations or neocolonial conditions, which I expect to continue to develop globally. But the growth and advancement of technology will doubtlessly also play a part in a form these relations will take place." —**Mirko Petric**, University of Zadar, Croatia

"While interoperability may be perfected, the smooth data flow will not. Content providers will regulate/control/charge for the use of or access to their materials. It will require the establishment of a trusted 'digital identity'—a key to the source of information." —**Todd Costigan**, National Association of Realtors

"Internet access will increase in cost by 2020 as the use of video streaming, online games, e-mail, wireless networks, and high-speed access increases and overloads network servers and the Internet network itself. Access to and data transmission through the Internet is a business. By 2020, home users with high-speed access will be charged for bandwidth used, just like electricity or other utilities." —**Ted Summerfield**, president, Punzhu.com

"The economic benefits of a connected populace will outweigh other factors." —**Janet Salmons**, president, Vision2Lead Inc.; consultant on organizational leadership and development and virtual learning

"The technical achievements will come about, but they will only be 'low cost' to some people (i.e., those from affluent countries). Due to an enduring wealth gap, many people in developing countries will not be able to afford these services and technical accomplishments." —**Ben Detenber**, associate professor, Nanyang Technological University, Singapore

"Ahahahahahah! As this has not happened when there was a single controlling force, before 1991 privatization, how should it happen now? As to the mobile wireless, do we live on the same planet? Are you sure?" —**Wainer Lusoli**, University of Chester, U.K.

"I do believe that there will be a global, low-cost network by the year 2020, if not before. But I think it will also be at least a two-tiered system, maintaining the class divide." —**Michael Dahan**, professor, Sapir Academic College, Israel; Digital Jerusalem

"I disagree that it will be at low cost. I believe the relation between living and its respective cost will be almost the same in 2020 as it is today (2006)." —**Ivair Bigaran**, Global Messenger Courier do Brasil, American Box Serviço Int'l S/C Ltda.

"While we are moving toward virtually ubiquitous low-cost wireless communications, we won't get there by 2020, and there will be large populations of poor and disenfranchised groups to which the benefits of technology will not be available." —**Benjamin Ben-Baruch**, senior market intelligence consultant and applied sociologist, Aquent, General Motors, Eastern Michigan University

"The general use of the Internet will expand horizontally to include new media (TV, voice, etc.), and the fees that we currently pay for these services will shift to the Internet." —**Paul Craven**, director of enterprise communications, U.S. Department of Labor

"Initiatives such as Google Wi-Fi and open communal networks will launch a new phase of connectivity. Billing standards such as PayPal and payment-enabled 3G phones will complement credit cards to allow instant micropayments." —**Steffan Heuer**, U.S. correspondent, *brand eins Wirtschaftsmagazin*

"From a Western perspective, I guess the 'availability everywhere at an extremely low cost' prediction sounds possible and very inclusive. In practice, that which is supposed to be inclusive and cost very little is usually quite exclusive and costs a lot (not just financially, but culturally and socially) to those in other parts of the world. The prediction seems a little like 'Silicon Valley guilt-ridden idealism,' but as I know very little about the actual technology and its future direction, this answer is based solely on the failure of previous technological claims to meet the then-grandiose predictions to reduce the digital divide. But for countries that currently have poor basic telecommunications infrastructure, the idea of a 'low-cost' global network seems a little far fetched—there will have to be great cost in updating/creating the appropriate infrastructure to allow these nations to participate in the global network." —**Janine van der Kooy**, information management/librarian

"By 2020, devices for staying connected to the network will encourage people to remain 'always on' the network. The low-cost, always-on nature of this network will make it truly transparent, which means that choosing to remove yourself, even for brief periods, may carry penalties that make staying connected a more efficient decision than 'opting off.' I would look at the challenges of removing yourself from the electric grid in the developed world today as a model for the challenges of removing yourself from the 'information grid' of 2020. It is a possible, but not a practical, decision for the vast majority of humans who are not concerned with day-to-day considerations such as food, shelter, and clothing." —**Jeff Hammond**, VP, Rhea + Kaiser

"The use of technology, in my opinion, will increase in urban centers, but a bigger gap will be created with African countries (no profit there) and Middle East (religious reasons will restrict access to information)." —**Nuno Rodrigues**, 4EMESmulti-média, um ovo a cavalo

"There may be tiered access to many of the services, with restrictions being applied to free services." —**Suzanne Stefanac**, author and interactive media strategist, dispatchesfromblogistan.com

"Until vicious commercial infighting between competing companies for customers is sorted out with a clear winner, and major shifts in governmental positions take place, 100% interoperability is just a dream. Note also that there is substantial investment in hardware/software on the part of consumers. The decade-old WIN95 platform is still in use. Presence of these legacy systems may also cause adoption lag. The Asian model is seductive in its apparent success (Japan/S. Korea/ Singapore), but note these are geographically small countries with concentrated populations, a high level of industrialization, and the capital available to invest in infrastructure—I do not see this becoming available to anyone, anywhere, as remote and impoverished areas are likely to struggle. The model of the success of cell phones in rural India may yet prove me wrong." —**Cath Stoll**, Internet user since 1982

"I am not sure that I completely agree or disagree with this concept. The statement might be true, but what we are going to run into is still the state that we are in due to new emerging technologies that we are not able to predict right now. These technologies will always have a learning curve and a state of disruption until there is a universal adoption." —**Jeff Gores**, Internet user since 1994

"The network will be very expensive, and treated as a utility. The Global Network now is a mess; in 2020 the small, local operator will be a thing of the past. Where old infrastructure still exists, you will find inexpensive, possibly unreliable connectivity. Interoperability depends on Microsoft—almost everyone else is." —**Gordon MacDiarmid**, Lobo Internet Services

"There will be low-cost, widespread interoperability that will be widely available. Education, language, and values will affect whether and how people make use of this technology. Both voluntary and involuntary groups will specialize and separate by technology used, values, 'remembered and selected' demographics, and for competition and cooperation. In some cases, the use of differing primary technologies will engender quite different cultures." —**Mary Ann Allison**, chairman and chief cybernetics officer, The Allison Group, LLC; futurist

"The rise of proprietary internets will continue, and these secure, robust networks will become the primary means of distributing entertainment and

> "Mobile wireless communications may cover the geography consistently. The issues that may still require surmounting is the economic viability, social need for the same in the poorest and farthest regions. The need and potential needs to be translated into reality."
>
> —Syamant Sandhir, leader in experience design and implementation, Futurescape

video. The surprise: The open-source movement will become a cultural and political force, carving out a permanent niche on the free Internet and WWW. While media corporations will attempt to capture and control as much market share as they can leverage, open-sourcers will survive based on their proven ability to lead by innovation. Mobile wireless communications will be an urban utility, but not something available in all rural areas." —**Daniel Conover**, new-media developer, Evening Post Publishing

"I see no way that in a real, commercial world, wireless communications (mobile or otherwise) will be available to 'anyone anywhere' at an 'extremely low' cost, assuming any useful definition of 'extremely low.' —**Walt Dickie**, VP and CTO, C&R Research

"The current cooperative Internet will be subsumed by large corporate efforts trying (and succeeding) in controlling the network for profit, to the benefit of only the privileged." —**Cary Curphy**, operations research analyst, U.S. Army

"Mobile wireless communications will remain expensive." —**Pascal Perin**, futurologist, France Telecom

"By 2020, we'll be lucky to get 50% of the world connected. There are many more poor countries and poor individuals who can't afford advanced networking than there are those who can afford it, even with prices likely to come down." —**Rob Atkinson**, director, Technology and New Economy Project, Progressive Policy Institute

"Bandwidth will continue to increase, and the cost of sharing it will decrease dramatically over the next decade, giving rise to more free wireless initiatives like the one in Portland, OR. As a result, more and more power will shift toward communities that value open standards and cooperation, as opposed to closed networks designed to keep pricing power in the hands of large telecoms. That said, certain governments—possibly China, the newly independent states of the former Soviet Union, the more conservative Arab countries—will step up their efforts to create a segregated Internet in an effort to protect their culture and political systems." —**Kerry Kelley**, VP, product marketing, SnapNames.com

"While I do believe that smooth data flow at low prices will be achieved by 2020, I don't think that authentication and billing problems will be solved, nor that mobile wireless communications will be available to anyone, anywhere, at low price. The security problems of creating universal, reliable authentication and billing processes, now that it seems that quantum cryptography and other promises of the future are not the heaven we expected them to be, are only a part of what we have to face. Internet is consistently being regulated by nonneutral parts, specifically estates and supranational organizations with agendas of their own, and often contradictory with both the spirit and the needs of Internet culture (being data protection and domain regulations just two examples). It is much more than what it ever was in the short history of the Net, a matter of estate policies. Thus, it seems that the process will not be a pleasant, easy transition from the current flawed models. As to wireless technology, only liberating broadcasting air that would be possible, and then the problem of ISPs and state policies comes up. For global cheap wireless, we need a different, more open broadcasting regulation, which we don't have at the moment, and I believe we won't have due to the current obsession with a misguided concept of security." —**Miguel Sicart Vila**, junior research associate, Information Ethics Group, Oxford University

"Bandwidth barriers have consistently been removed in the 11 years of the commercial Internet world. There are no obstructions and, in fact, many change agents insuring that this trend will indeed continue to the point, perhaps well before 2020, that we will in fact see a completely ubiquitous, affordable network pipeline." —**Kevin McFall**, director, Online Products & Affiliate Programs, Tribune Media Services, NextCast Media

"There will still be people without access to this 'perfected' platform. The cost will be nominal except to those who are in extreme poverty or extreme ignorance. The Internet will not solve those issues." —**Gwynne Kostin**, director of Web communications, U.S. Homeland Security

"Interoperability itself will never be perfected since corporate alliances and other proprietary schemes will sector off some Internet services. The government(s) may be the biggest users of such 'private' approaches." —**Gary Arlen**, president, Arlen Communications, Inc., the Alwyn Group LLC

"Interoperability will only occur when those who benefit from the networks believe their value proposition will increase due to interoperability and low-cost access. I still believe access providers and content providers will try to hold on to control in order to gain value." —**Jeff Corman**, government policy analyst, Industry Canada, Government of Canada

"We're seeing the approach taken by 'walled gardens' (like the WELL [the first online community]) coming back into play as security threats (and perceived security threats) continue to evolve. I think 2020 is too soon to expect any particularly evened-out access of this kind, even in the developed world, let alone worldwide. Fits and starts in many places, pockets of utopian technology access—yes; perfect worldwide mobile access, cheaply, for all—not so much." —**Caitlin Burke**, Internet user since 1992

"Have corporations ever allowed anything to get nearly free? Will Taliban-like governments, sprouting everywhere, permit open access, smooth data flow? Will the disruptions of the Second Great Depression, caused by any number of near catastrophes that loom—water and fuel shortages, wealth imbalance, bankrupt empire collapse, nuclear bombs, weather gone berserk—open the world to interoperability and smooth, flat-earth flow; or will disaster build walls of noncommunication, isolation, and Dark Ages city and nation states?" —**Scott Keeney**, librarian, Albany Public Library

"There will be some world regions where reality will not be as mentioned on the statement." —**Georg Dutschke**, Universida Sevilla, Forum Criança, Cortefino

"Many cultures on earth live outside the potential of a technologically assisted lifestyle. People who develop these dreams lack real-world experience and perspective. There is no wisdom in their prediction. In an automated world, increasingly, people will spend time undoing automatic transactions. Overall, an automated world lacks a moral compass. If people in

Kansas understand this—they are the farthest away from either coast in this example, and cannot participate in an automated world to the levels enjoyed by those who live on both coasts—people in more established and remote cultures have no reason to participate in an automated culture. Broad acceptance of automation has always lagged behind the enthusiasm of early adopters. Implementing the infrastructure in remote cultures lacks a viable business purpose, and why else would the infrastructure be implemented." —**Elle Tracy**, president and e-strategies consultant, The Results Group

"The primary winner in this is the global supply chain. As goods and services become global commodities, tracking and managing those assets on a global level will be vital to every link in the procurement and delivery chain." —**Alix L. Paultre**, executive editor, Hearst Business Media, Smartalix.com, Zep Tepi Publishing

"With the widespread use of mobile-phone technology, the [proposed] scenario seems almost certain. Every less developed country I have visited features personal mobile phone use by some of the most humbly employed people. I have seen field workers with phones. Some of this use is status based, but much of it seems to be people scrambling to make connections/deals for more income." —**Anthony Hurst**, teacher, American Cooperative School of Tunis

"As a percent of household income, data communications, including phone, TV, and Internet, will continue to grow in cost." —**Rachel Thompson**, District of Columbia Advisory Neighborhood Commissioner

"In all honesty, when a person needs to worry about warring tribes, ethnic, and religious conflict, Web access is and should be a low priority." —**Doug Olenick**, computer technology editor, TWICE (This Week in Consumer Electronics) magazine

"Cultural disparities will always interfere with true global network interoperability, and it would be naïve to assume sufficient technological acumen will exist along with the necessary disposable income to assure global access to wireless communication." —**Al Amersdorfer**, president and CEO, Automotive Internet Technologies

"By 2020, there will still be many blind spots on this planet, many areas will be covered with low-capacity networks, and, more importantly, still a majority of people with no resources nor education that permit use of ICT. The 'extremely' low cost will still be excessive for many people." —**Michel Menou**, professor and information-science researcher

"There will always be 'a better way' and, as such, competing groups will be creating the 'cassette and 8-track' players. The competition will get to the point where one takes market share and becomes the new standard. There are too many bureaucratic agencies and the world governments that will work too slowly at resolving differences." —**Terry Ulaszewski**, publisher, Long Beach Live Community News

"I have two reasons for disagreeing with the proposal that worldwide network interoperability will be perfected by 2020. The first is that there are too many competing corporations involved, the majority of which do not see the interoperability of their products with those of other corporations as a significant goal. The corporate interest is directed towards tying customers to their brand, which is opposed to the interoperability agenda. This may be overcome in the long term, but not by 2020. The second reason for disagreement is that of the existence, or lack thereof, of communications infrastructure to cover the majority of the world. In Europe, North America, Japan, and maybe Australia and New Zealand, the infrastructure issue is not a problem. In South America, Africa, and Asia, there is a huge gap between the reality and the ideal." —**Robin Lane**, educator and philosopher, Universidade Federal do Rio Grande do Sul, Brazil

"There is money to be made from a smooth, global data flow, so I suspect it will happen. As to consequences? I doubt they will be favorable to a smooth, global flow of compassion or equality." —**Leslie-Jean Thornton**, researcher and educator, Cronkite School of Journalism and Mass Communication

"Government security, scammers, and greedy content aggregators will keep the Internet from developing into an integrated technological community." —**Martin F. Murphy**, IT consultant, City of New York

"A global network will thrive. However, I certainly do not believe it will be low cost. It is beyond commercial industry to ignore such an integral and popular vehicle such as the Internet and not exploit it." —**Rick Gentry**, acquisition coordinator, Greenpeace

"While I think the technology exists for such a network, I don't believe politics and business will allow it to work. The U.S. is a prime example where the expense of cell phones is far above that of other countries and the extent of the network is much less. This is primarily due to the fact that businesses have competing standards and are unwilling to open their networks up to subscribers of other networks without charging considerable roaming fees. In places such as Europe and Australia, there is one common system and it works much better. I suspect we will have the same issues with a data network." —**Rangi Keen**, software engineer, Centric Software

ANONYMOUS COMMENTS

A number of anonymous survey respondents shared comments tied to the scenario about the future of the global network. Among them:

"We will see portability take on new and more flexible dimensions, as technology and usability become increasingly an extension of ourselves."

"It's taken 40 years to get to this point, and things are still a mess. This is a holy grail."

"If the model of uniform utilities is followed, telecom will be as behind as ever. The major factor—all countries need to unite in one platform for telecom—the U.S. and Japan with 'special needs' platforms will drain the efforts of the rest."

"Companies are greedy; it won't be worth it to them to make it truly global."

"Such a system will be available for the 'haves' in the world, maybe 1.5 billion people. But poverty, terror, and government conflicts will limit the range of the network."

"New technology brings new bugs, and compatibility issues will not be resolved prior to the Second Coming."

"It won't be perfect. There will be bumps along the way, and the system may become overloaded at times."

"I don't trust the so-called captains of industry who have proven to be driven only by greed."

"Agree—this is assuming U.S. telecom companies don't get their way in double charging for pipeline use."

"A solar flare will have totally disrupted communications."

"While networks will continue to expand and become more reliable, the inevitable specters of government control and private-sector incompatibilities will keep prices artificially inflated."

"It's really an even-money bet whether the Net will be more open or less. There is a good chance that telcos and other carriers will have control of access and transport. There is a better-than-even chance that the Net will be filtered and firewalled by government for most users worldwide."

Predictions from respondents who chose to remain anonymous:

"Yes—it's a simple projection of looking how far we have come in just a few short years."

"National, political, and religious divisions will reinforce silos of thought and action."

"The technology will be so seamless, you won't even think of it as technology."

"The Internet will fragment into several networks operating independently."

"Unless Bill Gates is planning on funding this, I don't see it happening by 2020."

"Steps already being taken within the industry clearly indicate their preference for widening the digital/economic divide rather than allowing ICTs to become a tool for democratizing the world and reducing social inequities."

"The world is leaving the U.S. in the wake."

"The trend is toward an open and low-cost network. But there is the real threat of corporate control coming from major telecommunications resources."

"Companies will still disagree on standards for competitive reasons—and there will be insufficient reason to lower cost significantly."

"Wireless communications will be available to anyone anywhere on the globe, but I don't think the cost will be extremely low. While the prices for hardware seem to fall as technology improves, the service part—just establishing and maintaining the connection—doesn't. My Internet connection is faster, but $10 per month more expensive than it was 5 years ago. I have DirecTV, and the bill just went up $6 per month with no change in service. Why would I expect these service charges to drop dramatically in the next few years? So while the communications technology will be available to anyone anywhere, I still expect there will be a huge number of people who will find it unattainably expensive to take advantage of."

"Controls will get stronger and stronger, dataflows will be hacked, interrupted, and managed by big giants (political, commercial). Wireless will be available to many, but the same countries and regions that are left out right now will not have access. Even though availability will be ubiquitous, this still doesn't mean uptake will be."

"There will still be pricing issues for speed—the faster you want to go, the more you'll have to pay for it. In addition, extra services, applications, etc., will be premium services offered on top of the basic costs of the network access."

"The U.S. will be a sort of data ghetto, with slower speeds, heavy government surveillance and restrictions, and disconnected networks (sort of like the present-day U.S. banking system, which is not connected to the global system)."

"Commercial interests are increasingly taking control of the means of transport, walling off the Internet for the purpose of making a profit."

"There will still be lots of technical glitches to work out. And there are many people (and places) where computers will not be affordable. Even if school kids have computers, they can graduate and then not have access to computers."

"Some areas will have excellent networks while others will not. Unfortunately, I am concerned that if the telcos have their way, the U.S. will be in the 'have not' category on this one."

"Market forces will encourage specialization and differentiation of solutions, preventing a unified network."

"Technology will advance to the point where mobile communications will be ubiquitous and low cost, but 'perfect' interoperability will probably still be a challenge due to conflicting standards."

"Even if costs to the consumer do not increase, costs to those who have to deal with technological waste will continue to grow as they have been."

"Given how balky, incompetent, and shortsighted American telcos are—and how much influence they've bought in Washington—I suspect that Americans will not enjoy ready access to low-cost wireless technologies for quite some time. The rest of the world will develop them without us, often with the aid of American companies who are having their cake and eating it too."

"The financial cost might be low, but the cost of losing freedom because of Big Brotherization of our daily lives might turn out to be high if the trend of closing the openness of the Net continues."

"Companies will always attempt to keep the cost of services as high as possible to maximize profits. The difficulty that many have experienced with poorly designed, flawed resources and Web sites will be unlikely to be rectified even by this date."

"What we think of today as the nirvana of network interoperability will have changed dramatically

Predictions from respondents who chose to remain anonymous:

"This theory indirectly makes the claim that the digital divide will be bridged within 15 years. Such a claim seems ridiculous given that it's been over 100 years that we've had plumbing technology and there are still areas of the U.S. and other industrialized nations that have 'plumbing divides.'"

"Only anonymity permits freedom, which means no authentication and no individual billing."

by the time 2020 comes. And new issues that we have not dreamed of will afflict such a system and cause it to be less than our perfect vision of the future, today."

"Far too general and far too utopian. Companies don't necessarily want smooth data flow, they want to maximize profits; slowing down others' data (tiering) may be seen as beneficial (well, it is currently seen that way). There are constant security problems, ranging from Windows viruses to identity theft to personal-information theft."

"National governments will keep this from happening for a variety of reasons—censorship, fear of cultural imperialism, and corruption, among them. There will be an underground, black-market network as described, and it will largely be used with mobile devices communicating through satellite or other wireless technologies."

"Perhaps the technology will exist, but entrenched business interests and governments will team to thwart the network from reaching the promise that technology enables."

"The fear of terrorism and the use of the Internet as the means by which they communicate, pornography, and the lack of respect extended to individuals speaking something other than English have the potential for splintering the Internet."

"Much of this will be supported by advertising for free or almost-free networks. These lower cost networks won't provide the full range of functionality and features that can be found for more expensive versions of the network. Additionally, private networks will flourish as people wish to create 'safe' areas for data and people without access to the wider network. However, even with this worldwide network, some areas will have faster/slower access. There will still be differentials in poorer parts of the world as to who can access and use the technology."

"Unless we can get the world's cellular providers bypassed, there is never going to be 'cheap' wide-area wireless Internet access."

"National telecoms will prevent this by nation-by-nation regulations."

"The developing world will not have ubiquitous Internet access at reasonable data rates by then."

"This is all possible, but it will take much longer to happen."

"Peer-to-peer Wi-Fi meshes will be the ordinary connection to the Internet—better yet, there will be no 'access' as every node will be part of the Internet."

"I don't believe that rich/poor gap issues will be resolved, and remote places will not have access."

"Everyone with any brains will no longer be tethered to an office but will roam freely from country to country, conducting business effortlessly over the Web."

"Technology is human."

"The digital divide is, if anything, becoming more entrenched and especially exacerbated around axis of gender in developing countries. No sign that this is being taken seriously by policy makers, or being addressed on any major scale."

"The utopian vision is never achieved. There is always a further innovation, which creates additional disruptions and adjustments, which yields further benefits and costs."

"The differentials within societies will mean that, although MWC [mobile wireless communications] will, in theory, be available to everyone, the billing procedures will be likely to exclude people. What we may see, however, is the development of 'pay as you go' systems as used in the U.K. for cell phones, with the market keeping costs down for commercial services."

"Corporate control of the Internet will destroy its promise, leading to balkanized networks and devices that cannot interoperate with devices from other manufacturers."

"After nearly 100 years of telecommunication, we still do not have global, low-cost voice network. The evidence suggests that global haves will continue to have more and more and global have-nots may have some incremental increases."

"I expect variations in connectivity, bandwidth, and cost between countries, resulting from differences in economic power, education, and regulatory regimes."

"E-commerce will have at least one great crash. It'll be the equivalent of Black Friday and finally bring regulation to the Internet."

"Two processes will take place at the same time: increase in networks with higher efficiency for some participants, and no or restricted access for others."

"There will still be too many players (service providers, content providers, network vendors, etc.) for the network to be both global and smooth, even in 15 years. There will probably be pockets that might be, but where you have uniformity (i.e., fewer vendors in the mix or even just one), the price for the service will probably be higher due to less competition."

"The statement is a bit too optimistic, but on the whole, I expect steady improvement in networks over the next 15 years."

"The expansion of a global network will be hampered by territory disputes between public groups (NGOs, governmental organizations, quasi-governmental organizations, community networks, etc.) and for-profit organizations over market shares."

"There'll still be bugs, hacking, etc."

"A global, low-cost network will exist but will be pushed aside by commercial eyeball grabbers and spam/phish... concerns."

> *Predictions from respondents who chose to remain anonymous:*
>
> **"The honest, above-board providers will survive, and the greedy, self-serving providers will dry up. Perhaps I'm too optimistic here, but I think there will be a major shake out of bad seeds."**
>
> **"Firstly, developments are driven by profit and profits are not everywhere to be made. Secondly, issues like lack of electricity or literacy do have their consequences."**

"Even by 2020, there will not be good adoption in Third World countries."

"People want more and quicker access to information important to them, whether it's personal or professional, and business now sees and understands this interaction. Look at how cable channels and their adjunct Web sites offer similar video programming and, with some, the ability to transfer it to portable devices."

"Wireless communication will be available anywhere on the globe—that's already nearly true—but I do wonder whether 'extremely low cost' will be the case as long as there's a profit to be made."

"This is possible. However, it is incumbent on us to identify methods to ensure confidentiality and protect against hackers and others intent on doing harm to networks and e-communication channels. In other words, along with this global, low-cost network come new problems and issues that must be addressed and resolved in order to insure a seamless data flow."

"A number of politico-economic factors and policy outcomes are necessary for the realization of such a network. Recently, Vodaphone Germany has released its plan to disable access to its network from Voice Over Internet Protocol telephony, one of the most promising emerging technologies in terms of low-cost, networked communications. This example challenges the notion that we are inevitably and seamlessly transitioning in to a global network society and demonstrates that if such an end is truly a political goal, political means and policy interventions are necessary for its attainment."

"I agree with this statement—as long as 'mobile wireless communications' is meant to encompass unlicensed spectrum (Wi-Fi). I do not think that 3G networks will interoperate well with the rest of the Internet, but then again, I don't expect that most users will care."

"I think we'll be a long way toward this vision, but it won't be perfect."

"Communications companies will continue to keep the cost of Net access just out of reach for the lower class in order to maximize profits, subsidize free or lower cost access for the poor, and fund research."

"Interoperability will be good but not perfect; authentication will not be worked out yet; mobile wireless will indeed be in most places."

"There are still many parts of the world that don't have electricity."

"By 15 years from now, the U.S. will have caught up with the rest of the world, and most of the planet will have wireless connections."

"I largely believe this to be true, but I am skeptical that wireless will be 'extremely low cost.'"

"I agree on the whole, but there will still be areas of the globe that lag behind due to developmental problems. Cost is also relative to your social-economic standing."

"While I believe a global, low-cost network will thrive, I think extended geographic or temporal bubbles with very limited network connectivity will continue."

"Authentication and privacy will be the big issues."

"Although technology that provides clean drinking water has been available for many years, it is not currently available to everyone everywhere. Sadly, I don't see why the world would suddenly become fair in 14 years."

"Individuals will likely still be required to pay additional for access to content and for higher quality network connections."

"Poor parts of least-developed countries will still find it costly to connect to the worldwide network."

"The global situation is moving in that way. China, Korea, Taiwan, India are producing low cost technology tools. They are developing a lot."

"Technically, we will have achieved this. Socially, I am not as optimistic that we have enabled the network to flow across the barriers created by politics, socioeconomics, and the weaknesses of human beings."

"IP and the Internet have enabled the data networks the independence from the access network horizontalizing the networks. In addition, the horizontalization has taken away many old control points and value points from the network, adding cost to the network usage."

"The Internet's largest corporate beneficiaries will continue to retain enough power and influence to keep the Internet relatively secure for communication and commerce. In general, however, we must conclude that it will never be 100% safe—and not even 'mostly safe' for extended periods of time. We will also conclude—if we haven't already—that many of the threats serve as inspiration for entrepreneurial development as privacy and security tools become a wellspring of new product ideas and innovation."

"Low-cost wireless communications, yes, but I don't believe in global authentication and billing happening by then. Fifteen years is not enough for the governments to get this done."

"Increasingly, the tools that allow us to mine more information and leverage this information into discriminatory decisions and partitions will partially reverse the original effect of the Internet, which was to open up communication. Technical interoperability will exist; however, the corporate and governmental interests will intervene to partition the Internet by proxies, filtering mechanisms, and even personal firewalls to regulate information flows."

"Nothing we do ever gets 'perfected.' Technology always marches on; people always have new ideas and want to try new things. Therefore, I cannot agree whatever network we'll be using in 2020 will be 'perfect.'"

"Maybe not 'extremely' low cost, but affordable enough to be ubiquitous."

"Big Business will encroach upon the 'free' aspects of the Web, particularly wireless, and will continue charging for access to information. Further, more information will become password protected as organizations seek to achieve registration lists and control over their content."

"Yes, but content will be dominated by companies, not by individual users. Commercial speech will masquerade as personal speech."

"Yes, a global, low-cost network will thrive, but so too will half the world's population be left behind. Just like today, roughly half the world's population has never made a phone call despite years of progress. Many will be left behind in the digital world as well. On the one hand, everyone will probably be able to use some kind of networking, but there will still be haves and have-nots in relation to speed and access to particular content."

"This may be true for developed countries, but not for the rest of the world, which is the overwhelming majority."

"All hardware and connectivity costs are falling. Proprietary software costs are rising, but there are good free alternatives. Also, new technologies will push the costs of current technology down."

"The network will indeed be truly global by 2020 or even earlier. However, there are serious challenges in making it available to everybody at a cost that they consider as 'low.'"

"I am skeptical about interoperable authentication and billing on a global scale, unless the privacy issues can be resolved. It will depend also on how this is done, whether it is centralized (and there is the risk of governments accessing this info) or decentralized and works similar to global credit card use/ATM use around."

"The connection in the Pacific Islands will be still challenging. There is barely any satellite coverage at the moment, and the islands are very disperse and remote. Undersea cables are too expensive; satellite beam covering the Pacific Islands for high bandwidth are not economically viable due to lack of population density."

"Nothing is ever perfected. It will be great by our standards. By the standards of 2020, it will still have many flaws."

"At best, 15% of the world population now has access to the Internet. In 15 years time, this will no doubt have risen, but at the same time, [we] should realize that computers cannot overcome the 'social divide.' Technology can assist certain tendencies, but let's not overestimate its power."

"In some ways, we're already there, but in some ways, we are not. There is likely to be such network interop in a technical sense, but it is up to regulators, politicians, and engineers to permit deployment on a local scale."

"Given politics and government restrictions to free flow of information, it is hard to believe that this will happen on a global basis. What will happen is that interoperability will increase in the developed markets and, to a lesser degree, will improve in developing markets."

"Techniques for authentication and billing will be relatively easy to implement and ubiquitous, but I do not agree that anyone will have access. We will still be dealing with various kinds of 'digital divides' in this time frame."

Predictions from respondents who chose to remain anonymous:

"We are not focusing nearly enough research and development on the real issues. The U.S. is stuck with paying the world's bill for super-computing, and no matter how much we talk about Shared Cyber-infrastructure, it has been hijacked in the wrong direction. These aren't even the right answers to real problems."

"Commercial interests seem determined to fragment the Internet and to block integration of other Nets like mobile wireless."

"If the analogy for worldwide network interoperability is other types of 'utilities,' then the 'anyone anywhere' statement is a bit of a pipedream. Electricity and running water are still challenges in some parts of the world. If those basic utilities can be so slow in being available because of technical, ecological, or geopolitical issues, there is no reason to think that network interoperability will be any less challenged."

"It will definitely not be extremely low cost. There are substantial investments necessary to make this possible and companies will want to get that back. It will take until later than 2020 to get that done. For higher education and research, it will be the case. Not for other sectors, I'm afraid."

"2020 is a long ways off, and much can happen (negatively as well as positively) to direct whether this thesis is correct. But there is much evidence to suggest that decreased cost of deploying and owning telecom infrastructure will further encourage local build-out. It is hard to imagine that current inaccessibility in remote, developing regions of the world will still remain in 2020."

"Density of use is critical to efficient deployment of wireless communications; in areas with very low density of use, wireless communication will remain difficult to access through 2020. As a thought exercise, imagine attempting to support all of the water-covered areas of the Earth with mobile communications; this is possible only with specialized satellite gear, which is not interoperable with the commodity equipment available for areas with dense usage."

"The universality of these facilities is wishful thinking. Half of the people on earth still have no electricity after 80 years or more. The evolution of costs to end users is unpredictable, and low cost is a function of income. Millions of people will still have $1 a day or less for income."

"I do not foresee either political will to harmonize law and its enforcement (e.g., privacy, democracy rights) or commitment of the main players (including governments, but not only) to set up and maintain the 'international trustworthiness chain.'"

"Too many nation-states will think it best to control or limit access, and too much money can be made by hoarding data and information."

SCENARIO 2

ENGLISH DISPLACES
OTHER LANGUAGES

PREDICTION: *By 2020, networked communications have leveled the world into one big political, social, and economic space in which people everywhere can meet and have verbal and visual exchanges regularly, face-to-face, over the Internet. English will be so indispensable in communicating that it displaces some languages.*

Respondents' Reactions to This Scenario	
Agree	42%
Disagree	57%
Did not respond	1%

Note. Because results are based on a nonrandom sample, a margin of error cannot be computed.

CONSENSUS OF OPINION: English will be the world's lingua franca for cross-culture communications for at least the next 15 or 20 years; Mandarin and other regional dialects will continue

to expand their influence, thus English will not "take over"; linguistic diversity is good, and the Internet can help preserve it; all languages evolve over time.

Until translation technology is perfected and pervasive, people must find other ways to communicate as effectively as they can across cultures. A lingua franca is a common language for use by all participants in a discussion. At this point, the world's lingua franca is English—for example, it has been accepted as the universal language for pilots and air-traffic controllers. But English-speaking nations have an estimated population of just 400 million out of the 6 billion people in the world. People whose first language is the lingua franca often hold a political edge. If the pendulum swings to a different dominant language, or two or more overwhelmingly dominant languages, it would bring powerful change.

NEVER HAS THERE BEEN A LANGUAGE SPOKEN BY SO MANY

Linguist David Crystal has estimated in his research that the world has 140 languages in use by at least a million people each. He said there has never in the history of the world been a language spoken by so many people as English is today, adding that as many as 1.5 billion people speak English as a first or "added" language, and the number could exceed 2 billion by 2020 (2003, p. 6).

The respondents who agreed with the survey's 2020 language scenario generally noted that English is already a pervasive "second" language—used as a tool of diplomacy, education, and business around the world—and it is also the language of the originators of the Internet, and is thus most likely to continue to dominate.

"English will be well on the way to being the world's most popular second language (by 2020)," wrote **Hal Varian**, dean of the School of Information Management and Systems at Berkeley and a Google researcher. "Mandarin is a contender, but typewriter keyboards will prevent it from really taking over from English."

Tunji Lardner, CEO for the West African NGO network wangonet.org and a consultant to the UNDP African Internet Initiative, wrote, "English will maintain its linguistic hegemony of the Internet. But there will be parallel Internet universes, with English being the babelfish for metaverse translations."

Jim Warren, founding editor of *Dr. Dobb's Journal* and a technology policy advocate, agreed that the issue of interface construction plays a role. "English has already become the mandated standard language... most keyboards around the world are the ASCII character set," he wrote. "The accent characters of other Western languages require special finger contortions, and it seems certain that the world will NOT standardize on any of the more complex character sets of the East, much less the pictograms of Asia...it's only 15 years to 2020."

> "The leveling effect is already quite visible. It seems paradoxical that the Internet can be a powerful force for memorializing and evangelizing local languages and cultures and differences and still lead to a great homogenization as the thirst for knowledge leads one invariably into Chinese and English. In 2020 many more people will be bilingual, with a working Web-interaction knowledge of English to go with their native tongue."
>
> —Glenn Ricart,
> executive director,
> PricewaterhouseCoopers
> Advanced Research;
> member of the board
> of trustees of the Internet Society

Paul Saffo, forecaster and strategist for The Institute for the Future, responded that the scenario is actually a "present-tense description." He added, "Badly accented English is to global society today what Latin once was to Western society long ago. English will continue to advance, but the real question is whether this trend will peak in the next two decades, and I believe it will. English's acceptance will reach a certain high-water point not terribly larger than its penetration today. Then things will get interesting."

"English is going to be the common language," wrote Internet pioneer **David Clark** of MIT, "but we will see an upsurge in use and propagation of local languages. For many users, their local language will still be the only language they use on the Internet. And of course,

> "Yes, English will 'displace' some languages, but there will be, for example, much more Chinese. People pick their language according to whom they want to communicate with, and there will be many different communities with (still) many different languages."
>
> —Esther Dyson,
> former chair of ICANN,
> now of CNET Networks

for low-complexity uses, we will see more translation."

ENGLISH IS NOT THE BE-ALL AND END-ALL

Many of the 57% who disagreed with domination by English in this 2020 scenario generally acknowledged that English is a common "second language" of choice, but said they expect many users of the Internet will mostly use the language of their own cultures in online communications.

Many expressed enthusiastic support of another language—such as Mandarin Chinese—supplanting English within the next 15 years, or they agreed that English will be important but not dominant, or they speculated that by 2020, innovators will build some sort of translating function into the Internet to make it technologically possible for everyone to speak and write in their native languages while being easily understood by people across the globe.

"The Net of the future will very likely evolve more into a big assembly of micro Webs serving micro communities and their languages," responded **Thomas Keller**, a member of the Registrars Constituency of ICANN and employee of the Germany-based, Internet-hosting company Schlund.

Adrian Schofield, of WITSA and ForgeAhead in Africa, wrote, "It is only English speakers that see the dominance of English. Chinese is just as likely to be the dominant language."

Fred Baker, chairman of the board of trustees for the Internet Society, wrote, "To assert that we will therefore have a large English-only world doesn't follow; Mandarin, German, Spanish, and many other languages will continue to be important."

Robin Lane, an educator and philosopher at Universidade Federal do Rio Grande do Sul in Brazil, wrote, "First, the premise that networked communications will have developed to this point is false.

Second, it is a fact that English has been indispensable for international communications for the last century—a fact that has not led to English displacing other languages. It is, and will continue to be, layered on top of the native language of the user of intercultural communications."

And **Seth Finkelstein**, anticensorship activist and author of the Infothought blog, wrote that this scenario is "much too ambitious. There will still be plenty of people who will have no need for global communications in other languages, or who choose to communicate only within their local community."

INTERNET GROWTH IS COMING IN NON-ENGLISH LANDS

While Internet-usage demographics are inexact, most measurement experts agree that North American dominance in regard to Web-content building and total usage of the Internet ended a while ago, with only about one-fourth of Internet users hailing from the U.S. or Canada at this point in time.

While there are other nations in which English is a dominant language, including the U.K. and India (where Hindi *and* English are officially used), the nations where Internet growth will see the most progress in the next few years are situated primarily in Asia; the expectation is that China will have the world's largest Internet population within the next 5 years.

"Sure, English will displace some languages," wrote **Howard Rheingold**, the Internet sociologist and author. "But as the century advances, Chinese becomes more dominant, strictly because of demographic drivers." Former InfoWorld editor **Stewart Alsop** wrote, "English will not displace or replace the other major languages in the world, including French, Spanish, Japanese, Germanic, Hindu, etc." And communication technologies researcher **Mark Poster** wrote, "Chinese might be emerging as the new lingua franca."

Alejandro Pisanty, an ICANN leader and member of the UN Working Group for Internet Governance, wrote, "Agree and disagree. English will be the lingua franca and in some communities (more functional than local) displace other languages. But the overwhelming amount of communications over networks will occur in Chinese."

INTERNATIONAL DOMAIN NAMES WILL CHANGE THE LANDSCAPE

The Internet Corporation for Assigned Names and Numbers has been urged for years to find a way to initiate the use of non-English, top-level domain names—at this point in time, roots (such as .com, .org, .net) are only used in English (and the Roman character set). ICANN was established in 1998 to oversee technical details regarding Web addresses—the Domain Name System. It is an international body working at sorting out worldwide networking details for a technology established by English-speaking people. There has been some fear that other nations, frustrated with ICANN's slow progress toward opening its system to other languages, might split off into nation-state networks with their own naming schemes rather than staying tied to the global network. ICANN officials agreed in March to begin to test the use of international domain names written in local character sets in July of 2006.[1]

> "Two powerful trends will collide: English will become more prevalent as American culture and technology flow out across the world, but critical mass will also be achieved for global communications in Spanish, Mandarin, Japanese, and Arabic as new Internet protocols which support international domain names are more widely adopted."
>
> —Marc Rotenberg,
> executive director,
> Electronic Privacy
> Information Center

Scott Hollenbeck, IETF director and a leader for Internet-infrastructure-services company VeriSign, reflected the politics of root addresses in his survey response. "While I do believe English will continue to be the predominant language used for 'across-the-network' human communication," he wrote, "I do not believe that it will be ubiquitous by 2020. In 2006 there are efforts to localize Internet protocols in a way that will likely create islands of non-English-communication capabilities. These efforts will continue and will gain traction in communities where English is not spoken by a large portion of the population."

Bret Fausett, a partner with a U.S. law firm and producer for ICANN.Blog, wrote, "In 2005 we're at the peak of the English language on the Internet. As internationalized domain names are introduced over the next few years, allowing users to conduct their entire online experience in their native language, English will decline as the central language of the Internet."

Alan Inouye, a U.S. Internet policy analyst, agreed. "I would say 'displace' is not likely," he wrote. "English will continue in its role as the de facto international language. However, there are countervailing forces against English-language dominance on networks. Networks such as the Internet facilitate the development of communities of common interests and languages among people who may be widely dispersed geographically. Also, we will see a dramatic increase in Chinese-language content."

TRANSLATION TECHNOLOGY IS EXPECTED BY MANY

Some respondents who questioned the likelihood of the 2020 language scenario did so because of their belief that technology innovators will have found a way to bridge the gaps in intercultural communication.

One person with such confidence is pioneering Internet engineer and Internet Architecture Board and Internet Society leader **Christian Huitema**, who wrote, "Computer technology increases the frequency of communication, which creates a desire to communicate across boundaries. But the technology also enables communication

> "The overall proportion of English on the Internet will continue to diminish...Language consolidation and erosion of linguistic diversity will continue, but through multiple 'über-languages' (English, Spanish, Chinese, French, etc.)."
>
> —Luc Faubert,
> president of Quebec's Internet Society chapter; ambassador to World Summit on the Information Society

in multiple languages, using various alphabets. In fact, by 2020, we might see automatic translation systems."

Marilyn Cade, of the Information Technology Association of America and the Generic Names Supporting Organization of ICANN, wrote, "English may be the default 'universal' language, but we will see a rise of other languages, including Chinese, French (francophone Africa), and other languages supported by technological translation—at last."

At this point, computer-based translation is still in early development, and despite improvements, it lags far behind the ability of a good human translator. Among the companies working on perfecting it are Systran, Google, and Yahoo. Online translation is available, but it works best only for the occasional word or two; feeding a foreign-language phrase or an entire document into such a system for translation is not the way to accomplish a fully accurate communication.

THE INTERNET IS KEY TO PRESERVING LANGUAGES AND CULTURES

Many survey respondents pointed out that the Internet is actually helping to halt the complete disappearance of some languages and is even being used to revive those that were considered to be "dead."

Previous 20th-century communications technologies were principally responsible for what researcher Michael Krauss of the Alaska Native Language Center said in 1992 is "electronic media bombardment, especially (by) television—an incalculably lethal new weapon which I have called 'cultural nerve gas'" (pp. 4, 7). But today the Internet is being used for "RLS"—reversing language shift—projects. For instance, the Tlingit language of the Inuit people in southeast Alaska has been preserved in an online database used by schoolchildren in Glacier Bay. More places are seeing the development of indigenous-language projects and databases online. Broadband allows the use of richly detailed audio and video files on such sites—allowing depth of detail in pronunciation and in facial and other physical movements associated with the languages to become a part of the record.

Survey respondent **Steve Cisler**, a former senior library scientist for Apple now working on public-access Internet projects in Guatemala, Ecuador, and Uganda, wrote, "Indigenous languages will have a hard time changing to accommodate the impact of popular media languages, though more people will use ICTs to try to revitalize some languages or spread the use of them outside of local places."

Michel Menou, a professor and researcher in information science who was born in France and has worked in nearly 80 nations, replied that while linguistic diversity is increasing on the Internet, the challenges to their survival still remain. He added what the Internet will do is "offer new options for their preservation, teaching, and use." And **John Quarterman**, president of InternetPerils, Inc. and the publisher of the first "maps" of the Internet, wrote, "Internet resources will permit some languages to thrive by connecting scattered speakers and by making existing and new materials in those languages available."

> "**Ubiquitous communication capabilities don't bring homogenization. If anything, communities will continue to flourish, encouraging 'marginal' languages to gain wider use.**"
>
> —Ross Rader,
> director of research
> and innovation, Tucows, Inc.

WORKING TO PROMOTE A MULTILINGUAL INTERNET

Language authority Crystal projects in his book *English as a Global Language* that about half of the world's 6,000 known languages will fall out of use within the next century—he estimates that 96% of the world's languages are spoken by just 4% of the people, with nearly 5,000 languages with less than 100,000 speakers, and 500 with less than 1,000 speakers.

Why should the world care if "minor" languages are kept alive? One international, nongovernmental organization established to promote the protection of language diversity is the Linguapax Institute

(http://www.linguapax.org), created by UNESCO (the United
Nations Educational, Scientific and Cultural Organization) and based
in Barcelona. Its online site promotes the ideal that all people learn
several languages because "in a context of multiple linguistic contacts, language learning can become a way for intercultural understanding and peace."

The ITU and UNESCO convened a Global Symposium on
Promoting the Multilingual Internet (http://www.itu.int/ITU-T/
worksem/multilingual/) in Geneva in May 2006 after delegates who
met at Phase II of the World Summit on the Information Society
emphasized the role of multilingualism in successfully building the
global Internet and bridging the digital divide (2005, par. 53).

UNESCO's 2005 report, "Measuring Linguistic Diversity on
the Internet," includes research by Daniel Predo, Daniel Pimiento,
Jose Antonio Millan, John Paolillo, and members of the Language
Observatory Project of the Japan Science and Technology Agency.
It is nearly impossible to measure linguistic diversity on the Internet
because of the network's ever-changing content and the lack of a tool
to efficiently reach every corner of its influence. Many researchers
have counted on statistics assembled by Global Reach, a translation
services company that came up with its data by using ITU estimates
of user populations from each nation.

Using these statistics, Paolillo, of Indiana University, concludes
that "the Internet has not become linguistically diverse merely by
being global and interconnecting large numbers of people; other
issues need to be addressed in order to guarantee that languages of
the connected peoples are represented online" (UNESCO, 2005, p. 62).

As **Frederic M. Litto**, a professor at the University of Sao Paulo,
Brazil, wrote in his survey response, "Local languages are capable of
nuances, and a whole range of marvelous rhetorical devices English
and Chinese cannot hope to compete with. Portuguese, for example,
is a language that is highly expressive, mischievous, sensual, and
constantly open to delightful, 'politically incorrect' neologisms.
There's no way these local languages will be substituted. Rather,
people who have the opportunity to speak them will be able to 'wear

two hats,' switching between the local language and Chinese or English as the type and destination of the communications require."

Some of these researchers and others have estimated that while Chinese and other languages may gain great strength on the Internet, English will continue to be the Internet's lingua franca because it is a classic example of a positive feedback loop; English was the Internet's first language, new Internet users find it useful to learn English and employ it online, the language continues to gain and retain users, and it continues to dominate as a "second language" for crossing international lines in communication. The Chinese must see it that way—ESL courses are required nearly everywhere in China. Researcher Richard Rose of the Oxford Internet Institute also predicted an increase in the worldwide total of EFL-users on the Internet in a 2005 research report.

INFLUENCES WILL CHANGE THE ENGLISH LANGUAGE

Several respondents noted that English itself is likely to see some changes in the next 15 years, as globalization and new communications-content delivery systems alter cultural needs.

Bruce Edmonds of the Centre for Policy Modeling in the U.K. observed, "(1) Technology will allow considerable interoperability between languages, making a single language less necessary. (2) As in all evolutionary systems, very successful, dominant species spawn subspecies; English will continue to fragment into many sublanguages."

Bob Metcalfe, inventor of Ethernet, founder of 3Com, and

> "English will be a prominent language on the Internet because it is a complete trollop willing to be remade by any of its speakers (after all, English is just a bunch of mispronounced German, French, and Latin words). The lack of a language academy and the concomitant formality means that English is very competitive and well suited to morphing into other languages. That said—so what? Chinese is every bit as plausible a winner. Spanish, too. Russian! Korean!"
>
> —Cory Doctorow,
> blogger and cofounder
> of Boing Boing; EFF Fellow

now with Polaris Venture Partners, wrote, "Of course, a lot of 2020 English will sound Mandarinish." **Paul Saffo** of IFTF wrote, "Mandarin will of course grow dramatically, but I believe we will also see the rise of divergent English dialects."

Michael Gorrell, senior VP and CIO for EBSCO, wrote, "Some internationalized variation of English will evolve. Internet and instant messenger-based acronyms will grow into everyday use, fwiw [for what it's worth]. This new slang will be combined with new words and concepts—like blog, wiki, chat—to form a new 'Net dialect' of English."

ADDITIONAL RESPONSES

Many other survey respondents shared elaborations to the scenario about the future of languages in networked communications. Among them:

> "You hedged the question at the end by saying 'some languages.' There's always a process of changing languages, so some languages will disappear anyway. But the point is that English will not displace or replace the other major languages in the world, including French, Spanish, Japanese, Germanic, Hindu, etc. It is likely that English will become (as it already has in most domains) lingua franca, and a requirement that everybody learn English as a second language to have a common language to communicate with." —**Stewart Alsop**, investor and analyst; former editor of InfoWorld and Fortune columnist

> "I both agree and disagree—the heading 'English displaces other languages' will not happen, but the text 'English displaces some languages' is likely." —**Ian Peter**, Internet pioneer; Internet Mark II Project

> "English has momentum behind it, but I'm not at all sure that it will prevail in the long term—and 15 years out is long term." —**Reva Basch**, consultant for Aubergine Information Systems

> "The key element here is 'some languages.' English will not, alone, predominate. However, many smaller language groups

will give way to a general reliance on one of several large languages such as English, but also Spanish, French, and variations on Chinese. One specific note of caution, however, is that the Internet will enable some language groups to flourish through worldwide communication between diasporic members of that language group." —**Matthew Allen**, associate professor of Internet studies at Curtin University, Australia; president of the Association of Internet Researchers

"Indeed, some 50 or 60% of the world's 6,000 languages will be extinct by 2020, but it won't be just English that replaces them. The available selections will be fewer, but not exclusively English or American." —**Douglas Rushkoff**, author of many books about Net culture; teacher, New York University

"The world will be interconnected, but people as individuals and cultures will still seek and need differentiation. As someone who organizes international peace projects in over 30 countries and many more communities, English is the common tool and will be the tool in the future. But translation tools enhance the capacity of the trading of ideas and information and will allow maintaining multilingual interaction. For synchronous communication, English will be the tool. For interactive multiplayer content over the Web, English will be the language. Predictions of Chinese taking over are not serious. The cultural and cognitive differences entailed in learning Chinese will not allow most of Western society to be able to master it." —**Amos Davidowitz**, director of education, training, and special programs for Institute of World Affairs; Association for Progressive Education

"I agree to some extent, because I believe that communications will be universally translated, probably into English; however, I also believe that unless whole cultures disappear, some global integration of language made up of visual, aural, and written elements will emerge as the dominant means of communicating." —**Tom Snook**, CTO, New World Symphony

"This is not a prediction, English has already displaced some languages, and by 2020, our linguistic ecosystem will be infinitely poorer than it was 50 years ago. I don't believe, however, that the Internet is the primary cause of this. In fact, by making content in one's language more readily available, I believe it can be a counterbalancing factor, albeit not strong enough to outweigh the current steep loss of language diversity. I hardly doubt that the Internet will turn the world into one big political, social, and economic space though. Not in 15 years, at least!"—**Robin Berjon**, W3C and Expway

> "English has already become common as the default language for doing business, and that trend will probably continue. The Internet won't create a single political, social, and economic space—there will continue to be international divisions, and control over digital information and networks will emerge as a source of tension."
>
> —Nicholas Carr, independent technology writer and consultant

"I agree, but only to a point. It's more likely that English will evolve through linguistic contact with other tongues to have numerous variants that make it challenging to understand for persons not from that region. For example, consider 'Spanglish,' which is an amalgam of Spanish and English. It's probable that this will obtain for 'Chenglish' (Chinese English) and other hybrid languages after several years." —**William Kearns**, assistant professor, University of South Florida

"While I believe that English will remain the dominant or bulge language of the Internet, I think that many guilds of different languages will coexist with the modal English guild and flourish as long-tail guilds." —**V. K. Wong**, director of IT campus initiatives and CARAT (Collaboratory for Advanced Research and Academic Technologies), University of Michigan

"While I agree that English will be the predominant language of the Internet, I also feel that a number of countries will want to preserve their culture and insist on the use of their language. It is highly likely that products/services will be in place and widely available that will handle the translation as necessary. Think of the heritage and the desire of the persons living in Quebec City to maintain their use of the French language. As 'global' economies reach out and improve the world, I anticipate a renewed sense of tradition and patriotism." —**Mike McCarty**, chief network officer, Johns Hopkins

"English will continue to expand as the online language of the world. However, other languages might even flourish as more people get to know one another online and then follow their curiosity to learn about cultures and languages of those with whom they are communicating. Increased respect for multiple viewpoints and insight will follow expanded global communication." —**Ed Lyell**, pioneer in issues regarding Internet and education; professor at Adams State College

"English is already the lingua franca of technology. This will not change. On the other hand, real-time communications will facilitate language learning and proficiency for those who want to learn or perfect additional language skills." —**Joe Bishop**, VP business development, Marratech AB

"Language is tied to culture, national pride, and potential reach. I doubt that the rest of the world would simply succumb to English dominance." —**Rashid Bashshur**, director of telemedicine, University of Michigan

"Most non-English-speaking countries already teach English in schools because they recognize it as a common denominator language. Air traffic control worldwide is already standardized on English. This doesn't mean that other languages won't exist and there won't be social and economic spaces in which non-English languages continue to be used. However, I believe as more companies and industries become global, they will be forced to communicate in one common language just as the European Union now uses one common currency." —**Rangi Keen**, software engineer, Centric Software

"The same types of predictions were made about the telephone in the 1920s, but there is still a diversity of language spoken and used online." —**Robert Kraut**, Human-Computer Interaction Institute, Carnegie Mellon University

"This will not happen. If any language is to ultimately dominate, it's likely to be Chinese, where most of the future growth of the Internet will take place. English-speaking countries have a diminishing share of the presence on the Internet." —**Robert Shaw**, Internet strategy and policy advisor, International Telecommunication Union (ITU)

"I would like to see the preservation of some languages via use of the Internet as opposed to the displacement of any, with the possibility of global connections between language users and learners, giving a critical mass to keep even rare languages alive, blended with the possibilities of real-time translation. We should be able to talk/read in our own preferred language selection(s) from a vast variety of language sources." —**Cheryl Langdon-Orr**, independent Internet business operator; director, ISOC-Australia

"In many ways, this has already happened, with e-mail playing a significant role. English has become a nearly crucial language to use for Internet-based communications—but while it may dominate in 'cyberspace,' people will continue to use their native languages for everyday communications. This idea is a utopian vision that, while attractive in many ways, doesn't have much chance of happening in the next 15 years." —**Philip Joung**, Spirent Communications

"English is likely to become the common language; however, I am not so sure it will displace some languages by 2020. It will likely become the language of choice for interaction over dispersed networks." —**Rajnesh D. Singh**, PATARA Communications & Electronics Ltd., Avon Group, GNR Consulting, ISOC Pacific Islands

"English may well become more prevalent, especially as a second or universal language, but it will not displace all other languages." —**Thomas Narten**, IBM open-Internet standards development

"I think that politics will continue to play an important role. One cannot say anything to anyone anywhere because there will be censorship." —**Mike Gill**, electronics engineer, National Library of Medicine

"English will not be the predominant language as the Net/Web becomes more global." —**Sharon Lane**, president, WebPageDesign

"Though English is likely to be indispensable online in the future, the increase in connectivity around the world means that there is greater likelihood of regional, local, and national online communities forming and becoming vital. These communities would not need languages other than their native tongues, creating pockets of the Internet that are as localized as a vegetable market. In the broader scheme, English is likely to be rivaled by Chinese as the most common language, followed by Spanish." —**Christopher Johnson**, cofounder and CEO for if People, Inspiring Futures

"Online communication leads to more education and literacy, and nations that are more educated and literate learn to maintain their local cultures and languages while learning English and other key languages. It could well become a badge of honor for local communities to maintain their own local references and slang." —**Andy Oram**, writer and editor for O'Reilly Media

"The Internet will become more multilingual; however, English will remain the predominate language. I expect that English will become, for some, a second language rather than a replacement for their native tongue." —**Joel Hartman**, CIO, University of Central Florida

"Although English will be the lingua franca of international communication, cultural works are so intertwined with language that the only way that English could replace those languages is to replace the culture altogether. The creation of the Universal Character Set/Unicode should make it possible for cultural activity to take place using computing platforms. Science, however, has already moved to a single language (English), and will continue in that direction." —**Karen Coyle**, information professional and librarian

"English will continue to displace some languages on the Internet; some other languages will become more familiar to English speakers because they are frequently encountered on the Internet." —**Peter Roll**, retired chief system administrator

"English may be dominant; however, technology will allow immediate translation such that language (at least the several major languages of the world) will not be an issue—allowing one to hear/read in the language they want." —**Don Heath**, board member, iPool, Brilliant Cities, Inc., Diversified Software, Alcatel, Foretec

"English has the same network effects that made the Internet grow." —**John Browning**, cofounder of First Tuesday, a global network dedicated to entrepreneurs; former writer for *The Economist* and other top publications

"This is already happening. Since the 1990s, non-English pages on the Web often offered translations into English for at least some of their content, but the same is not as common for English-language sites. On the other hand, it seems clear that new global linguistic communities will thrive, and bonds between diasporic language communities (Mandarin, French, Spanish) will represent significant blocks of discourse online."
—**Alex Halavais**, assistant professor, Quinnipiac University

"English is and will continue to be an important 'bridging' language, but it will not displace other languages as 'bonding' languages." —**Hernando Rojas**, professor in the department of life-sciences communication at the University of Wisconsin–Madison; consultant for the UN Development Program

> **"Regrettably. At a recent conference of Nordic and Baltic countries with only two native English speakers, English was still the designated conference language—and would have been with no native English speakers present. I am not sure this is driven only by the Internet."**
>
> —Leigh Estabrook,
> professor,
> University of Illinois

"Emphasis on 'some languages.' English won't displace some major languages, which will actually enlarge their presence on the Net by 2020." —**Peter Levine**, director of CIRCLE (Center for Information and Research on Civic Learning and Engagement), University of Maryland

"The advantages of a common language will continue to give an advantage to English. This advantage is less important in asynchronous communications which grant those who are not facile with English the time to compose and reflect." —**Charles Hendricksen**, research collaboration architect, Cedar Collaboration

"English won't 'displace.' It will coexist. More will know/use English to access the Net's riches. Yet a great absolute number and percentage of the Web will be available in non-English."
—**Barry Wellman**, professor and director of NetLab at University of Toronto, Canada

"When you say 'English,' is that American, British, Australian, Indian, Singaporean? There is no one 'English.' I'd prefer we try to get decent education, jobs, living spaces, and health care for everyone before getting all excited about networking them. You're terribly discounting the very technology you say will advance, as well. If the technology is so advanced, why can't it translate on the fly? Maybe this will slow the adoption of English. Google language tools aren't perfect, and only do text, but if you're thinking that technology will improve, there's no reason to think it won't improve in this area." —**Nathaniel Poor**, lecturer, Department of Communication Studies, University of Michigan

"Displaces how? In nonnetworked usage? Network penetration will tend to increase and consolidate the position of English as the language of business and the language of technology, and thus the default second language for most. Off the network? The social and cultural functions of language, particularly in communities of a certain size, will keep local languages alive. Several forces will keep other languages strong. Competitive advantage in domestic markets + Community and identity issues + Personal need to maintain identity in postmodern world + Community size and isolation (economically, geographically, electronically) + Political motivation + Ease of maintaining communication with language community electronically. To sum up: English will displace where it already is doing so. Other languages may thrive as the 'small world' both eases personal and community communication, raises questions about culture and identity for the individual, and pressures language communities to (socioculturally) defend their existence." —**Michael Cannella**, IT manager, Volunteers of America-Michigan

"Individual cultures will be bolstered by making it easier to access culture-specific information online. Software will be increasingly internationalized and localized, and machine translation will be improved to the point where it can give the gist of a text in many languages." —**Simon Woodside**, CEO, Semacode Corporation

"English will become the language of choice simply because the technical aspects will drive it. Not only the U.S., Canada, British, and Indian nucleus, but the Chinese/Asian countries will adapt in order to sell their products to this market. Eventually, it will be adopted with the exception of some European and South American holdouts." —**Terry Ulaszewski**, publisher, Long Beach Live Community News

"English—especially American English—has already become the language of money." —**Martin F. Murphy**, IT consultant, City of New York

ANONYMOUS COMMENTS

A number of anonymous survey respondents shared comments tied to the scenario about the future of languages in networked communications. Among them:

> "There may indeed eventually be a global language, but it won't be English."

> "This is already the case for global knowledge workers and elites, and will continue, although indigenous languages will continue to serve more mundane purposes."

> "English will only be necessary for those who seek to communicate across those boundaries and those populations might increase, but they will not obliterate the nationalist tendencies of languages."

> "If information exchanges and interactions are to be globally ubiquitous they have to employ a universally accepted and used language."

> "This presumes that the United States continues to be the dominant political, economic, and military force on the planet. International backlash in the last 4 years has resulted in more foreign students abandoning the language for Asian and Eastern European languages."

> "Today, I am always surprised when I hear English spoken by people in Africa, Russia, South America. In 2020 it will be *the* international language of communication and business."

> "It pretty much already has."

> "The English language will change and absorb words from other languages at a faster rate than it has for the past 100 years."

"Not only English. There will be a division of five major languages used."

"There will be a flourishing of languages such as Chinese, enabled by the Net, not dissolved by it."

"It will not displace Chinese, even if the world conducts communication and business in English."

"By 2020, initiatives will be underway to have

> **Predictions from respondents who chose to remain anonymous:**
>
> **"Virtually everyone in the business world will be obliged to have English as either a first or second language; however, society as a whole will not have universally adopted it."**
>
> **"Local languages and cultures will show resilience. There will be a backlash. English at a low level will spread wider, but indigenous languages will be just as indispensable."**

other languages play a more relevant role online. Individuals around the world will be able to access content and communicate in their own language thanks to near-instantaneous translation services that exist."

"Improvement in language translators will make this less of a problem."

"Yes; however, a few other languages will also be quite common—Chinese and Spanish, probably."

"No, English will be the second language of choice, but people will continue using their own languages."

"The Internet is driving more people to use English. This has been the case with America's technical leadership and, probably now equally important, entertainment leadership that is becoming increasingly digital and transportable. India's emerging technical leadership will help reinforce this trend."

"It is utter folly to suggest such a utopian vision of the future (or dis-utopian, as the case may be). There will be shifts in the languages used—and some less frequently spoken languages (like, say, Hungarian) will largely disappear. We may also see more multilingual individuals."

"English will be indispensable for global communications but with the increase in localization of software and user interfaces

Predictions from respondents who chose to remain anonymous:

"Educational systems are designed to teach English today; there is nothing to change the course. Not even China."

"The importance of main languages in China, India, as well as Arabic, may increase significantly."

"So long as nationalism continues to be—if not on the rise, then at least stable as a powerful social force—I don't foresee English dominating."

as allowed by open-source software and other internationalization efforts. Local or regional languages won't disappear and may in fact strengthen. You will see an increase in the 'glocalization' trend."

"The era of the English-focused Internet is over. English is convenient as a last-choice/common way of communication, but most people prefer to communicate in their own language. Internet makes it easier."

"Yes, English will displace some languages for some people, but groups will be formed to create islands of language (Francophonie group which includes non-French-speaking countries, too). Also some languages will emerge—like Spanish, Chinese, and Hindi—on the Internet."

"English is already displacing some less widely spoken languages, and it is indeed the lingua franca of computing. However, there are other factors to consider in this analysis. There is wide support for languages other than English on the Internet. Consider Google's social-networking site, Orkut. The Orkut team was surprised to discover that a large percentage of their users hailed from Brazil, and these users communicated on the site almost entirely in Portuguese despite the fact that the user interface was in English. As they discovered, users adapt technology for their own purposes, and this includes making it linguistically accessible. Many current software programs have an option to render the user interface in the user's native tongue. Further, as machine translation technologies improve, language barriers will become less imposing. Finally, it should also be remembered that while English is currently the default language of the Internet, the number of people who speak Mandarin Chinese is double the number of people who speak English worldwide. As China continues to expand its efforts to achieve international competitiveness in science and technology, it would not be far fetched to think that Mandarin Chinese would maintain a foothold in global communication."

"I doubt that you will see English become the official language of China anytime soon."

> *Predictions from respondents who chose to remain anonymous:*
>
> **"Cantonese, Mandarin, Spanish, and Arabic will be the four significant languages."**
>
> **"The Internet affects culture —it doesn't transform it."**
>
> **"A text-message pigeon language will evolve as a common language just as something like that does in African nations with many languages."**

"English will be very significant. But language is cultural. To say that it displaces another language is to say that it displaces culture. The Internet has given a new lease on life to the Welsh language as the Welsh diaspora have connected online. The Internet empowers minorities. They may be minority in a physical location, but when they are connected they become a sizeable number. So it would not surprise me to see minority languages strengthened in numbers and use."

"Linguists can provide better statistics/evidence one way or another—but it is probably rather true that English will become an increasingly important language in an increasingly multilingual world."

"English will continue to move forward as a global language but new technologies will also emerge that allow fluent communication between people who do not share a common language."

"English will not culturally trump other languages to the point of extinction by 2020 or even far after that. English will become more prevalent as a second language, and we in the U.S. will become more multilingual."

"English has become a language of common use used not only in academic surroundings and science, but it also has been able to penetrate dissimilar and far away cultures, such as the Chinese. This makes English the natural language of this area to communicate and serve as a bridge to transport the knowledge and 'know how' of science and technological advancements."

"Just read the statistics. English is becoming less and less important the more people join the Internet. There is nothing inherently bad or worrisome about this tendency. Only 8% or so of the world population speak and read English (let alone write it). Should we somehow condemn this reality?"

"This has already started to happen. The use of one language to conduct business internationally will be the norm. Local languages will remain important within national borders, but to communicate with the rest of the world, especially in business, standardization—most probably through software—will become a crucial element in the success of an enterprise. I doubt that translation software will be perfected to enable use of different languages by 2020."

"Other nations want to keep their languages, and they are growing faster than we are."

"English is important, but so is Chinese (it will be used by most people online) and Spanish. I believe more in online, real-time translation software."

"English will be the dominant language in the Internet, and it already has and will also in the future continue to influence other languages. However, this is not only due to the Internet, but also in general due to Hollywood, PCs, and other material (books) in the English language and the fact that people who speak English are more globally mobile and generally more educated. However, the local languages (even small ones) have an important cultural and national importance. In addition, the education level, especially in developing countries, is not at the level where English is universally spoken or understood. On the contrary, there will be more localized content to attract local markets."

"English will not be indispensable, but I do agree that it might displace some languages—but none of the major languages in use today."

"So long as nationalism continues to be, if not on the rise, then at least stable as a powerful social force, I don't foresee this at all. Although, in a sense, English already 'displaces some languages' in particular contexts, it is highly unlikely to displace them on a nonpolitical or nonbusiness level."

"English has occupied the position that cannot be changed in the next 20 years, whatever the global situation."

"Chinese is the dominant language today, and by 2020, that is certain to be reflected across the network infrastructures."

"English will grow as the predominant universal language, but at the same time, the Internet will allow people with niche cultures and languages to find each other and thrive."

"While we'll see an increase in the use of other languages, it will become increasingly difficult to avoid English as a common denominator."

Predictions from respondents who chose to remain anonymous:

"New technologies will emerge that allow fluent communication between people who do not share a common language."

"India's emerging technical leadership will help reinforce this trend (toward English)."

"We may see more multilingual individuals."

"Groups will be formed to create islands of language."

"Virtually everyone in the business world will be obliged to have English as either a first or second language; however, society as a whole will not have universally adopted it. Nor will English have displaced any broadly spoken language."

"Local languages and cultures will continue to show resilience. There will be a backlash. English at a low level will spread wider, but indigenous languages will be just as indispensable."

"It has often been said that a language is a dialect that has its own army. Just as languages often spread through conquest, English will continue to spread through economic conquest. Not that English-speaking countries will necessarily rule, but the need for ever-bigger markets will force consolidation into those languages which already have the most speakers. English will be one of those languages, but not the only one."

"English currently dominates the Internet; that will continue to decrease irrespective of the fact that English will continue to grow as language of science and education. The Internet will become much more language diverse."

"It is the common language today. Educational systems are designed to teach English today. There is nothing to change the course. Not even China."

"Obscure or less prevalent languages will survive because of the Internet—but English will dominate the operational aspects of Internet life and other languages will suffer as a result."

"English will be a lingua franca, but will not displace many languages; rather, English-only speakers will be second-class citizens in these communities (e.g., Chinese speakers)."

"English will be the dominant language for online communications, but will not displace other languages. On the contrary, the importance of main languages in China (Mandarin, Cantonese), India (Hindi), as well as Arabic, may increase significantly."

"This is actually contrary to observed trends. The availability of the network for low-cost communication has enabled minority-language communities to connect and remain vibrant in ways that were not possible when relatively small numbers of speakers were geographically dispersed. English may remain as a dominant language of intercultural exchange, but that does not eliminate intracultural exchange in any way."

"The unification will only affect the rich countries. And even for them, electronic communications will continue to be hindered by physical factors. What we witness at this moment is the opposite: a growing linguistic diversification on the Internet."

"I generally agree with this statement within the First World, but there will always be a need to have support for other languages worldwide. There will always be people who are not

English-language literate. While more and more people will be economically incented to speak English, I do not think any language will be displaced altogether."

"The availability of advanced translations tools will have a more significant impact in the pervasiveness of Internet than the English as a lingua franca."

ENDNOTE

1. See "Internationalized Domain Names," available at http://www.icann.org/topics/idn.html.

AUTONOMOUS TECHNOLOGY IS A PROBLEM

PREDICTION: *By 2020, intelligent agents and distributed control will cut direct human input so completely out of some key activities such as surveillance, security, and tracking systems that technology beyond our control will generate dangers and dependencies that will not be recognized until it is impossible to reverse them. We will be on a "J-curve" of continued acceleration of change.*

Respondents' Reactions to This Scenario	
Agree	42%
Disagree	54%
Did not respond	4%

Note. Because results are based on a nonrandom sample, a margin of error cannot be computed.

CONSENSUS OF OPINION: Those who disagreed with this scenario generally said the humans who design technology will have no

difficulty controlling it—some noted a fear of *the people* who control it. Some who agreed with the scenario cited the increasing complexity of human-made systems and decreasing oversight and urged "human intervention."

Of course the responses to this scenario, as with all on the survey, were shaped by the way participants have been wired by their experiences and intellect to perceive its language. Many respondents—those who disagreed *and* those who agreed—were moved to react by comparing this proposed future to a science-fiction plot (*The Matrix, The Terminator, Frankenstein*). The answers were also shaped by how closely people read every word of the scenario. The group disagreeing included many engineers and computer scientists—many of them taking issue with the phrase "impossible to reverse"—while many sociologists, government workers, and network-policy makers found some of this scenario's points to be quite worthy of serious discussion. Again, the scenario was written to engender engaged discussion, not to propose what we see as the likeliest future.

Technology architects generally answered by saying that humans will retain control of any system they design. "Agents, automated control, and embedded computing will be pervasive, but I think society will be able to balance the use," wrote **David Clark** of MIT. "We will find these things helpful and a nuisance, but we will not lose control of our ability to regulate them." Internet Society board chairman **Fred Baker** wrote, "We will certainly have some interesting technologies. Until someone finds a way for a computer to prevent anyone from pulling its power plug, however, it will never be completely out of control." **Pekka Nikander** of Ericcson Research and the Internet Architecture Board responded, "As long as the everyday weapon-backed power systems

> "Completely automating these activities will continue to prove difficult to achieve in practice. I do believe that there will be new dangers and dependencies, but that comes from any new technology, especially one so far reaching."
>
> —Thomas Narten,
> IBM open-Internet standards
> development

(e.g., police force) are kept in human hands, no technical change is irreversible. Such reversion may take place as a socioeconomic collapse, though."

Author and consultant **Fred Hapgood** wrote, "The surveillance systems will themselves be surveilled by other systems, etc." **Robert Kraut** of the Human-Computer Interaction Institute at Carnegie Mellon University sees the development of automated systems running smoothly. "Certainly intelligent agents and distributed control will automate some tasks," he wrote. "But heavy automation of tasks and jobs in the past (e.g., telephone operators) hasn't led to 'dangers and dependencies.' "

The most dismissive reactions to the scenario were most likely to come from those who are involved in writing code and implementing the network. **Anthony Rutkowski** of VeriSign, during the past decade a leader with the Internet Society and ITU, wrote, "Autonomous technology is widespread today and indispensable. Characterizing it as a 'problem' is fairly clueless."

Programmer and anticensorship activist **Seth Finkelstein** responded, "This is the AI bogeyman. It's always around 20 years away, whatever the year." And **Alejandro Pisanty**, of ICANN and the Internet Society, wrote, tongue-in-cheek, "This dysfunctional universe may come true for several types of applications, on and off the network. We better start designing some hydraulic steering mechanisms back into airplanes, and simple overrides of automatic systems in cars. Not to speak about pencil-and-paper calculations to get back your life's savings from a bank." **Hal Varian** of Berkeley and Google wrote, "It's a great science-fiction plot, but I don't see it happening. I am skeptical about intelligent agents taking over anytime soon."

MANY SEE DANGERS OR PROJECT NEGATIVE IMPACTS

Elle Tracy, president and e-strategies consultant for The Results Group, suggested overconfident humans may allow this scenario

> "Human beings always have control, but they often choose to give it up. For example, when the airline agent tells me I cannot do something because 'the computer won't allow it.' Human beings have made choices to program that computer that way, to limit human abilities to override functions. I could also say I agree since we do seem willing to give up control to systems, and increasingly legislators and the judiciary have allowed surveillance, security, and tracking systems that would seem to me—and to many others—to be dangerous."
>
> —Leigh Estabrook,
> professor, University of Illinois

to unfold. "The only reason I can agree with this is because of my first-hand experience within the technology industry," she wrote. "The people who write this code are so proud of their work—and they should be—that the rational, real-world checks and balances that should be implemented on their results fall into a second-class-citizenry level of import. Until testing, bug fixing, user interfaces, usefulness, and basic application by subject matter experts is given a higher priority than pure programmer skill, we are totally in danger of evolving into an out-of-control situation with autonomous technology."

Marc Rotenberg, executive director of the Electronic Privacy Information Center (EPIC), sees extreme danger in the autonomous technology scenario. "This is the single greatest challenge facing us in the early years of the 21st century," he responded. "We are constructing architectures of surveillance over which we will lose control. It's time to think carefully about *Frankenstein*, the Three Laws of Robotics, *Animatrix*, and *Gattaca*." **Amos Davidowitz** of the Institute of World Affairs responded, "The major problem will be from providers and mining software that have malignant intent." His concerns about surveillance were echoed by many respondents, including **Michael Dahan**, a professor at Sapir Academic College in Israel, who wrote, "Things may be much worse with the increasing prevalence of RFID chips and similar technologies. Before 2020 every newborn child in industrialized countries will be implanted with an RFID or similar chip. Ostensibly providing important personal and medical data, these may also be used for tracking and surveillance."

Robert Shaw, Internet strategy and policy advisor for the ITU, had other concerns: "Even in today's primitive networks, there is little understanding of the complexity of systems and possible force-multiplier effects of network failures," he wrote. "The science of understanding such dependencies is not growing as fast as the desire to implement the technologies."

Some respondents pointed to the fact that certain technological systems are already suffering due to a lack of well-intentioned human input throughout the processes they are built to accomplish. "Systems like the power grid are already so complex that they are impossible to predictably control at all times—hence the periodic catastrophic failures of sections of grid," wrote author and social observer **Howard Rheingold**. "But the complexity and interconnectedness of computer-monitored or controlled processes is only a fraction of what it will be in 15 years. Data mining of personal traces is in its infancy. Automatic facial recognition of video images is in its infancy. Surveillance cameras are not all digital, nor are they all interconnected—yet."

Douglas Rushkoff, teacher and author of many books on Net culture, sees a need to take action. "If you look at the way products are currently developed and marketed," he explained, "you'd have to say we're already there: Human beings have been taken out of the equation. Human intervention will soon be recognized as a necessary part of developing and maintaining a society."

> "History has shown that as technology advances the abuse of that technology advances. History has also demonstrated that we do not control technology as much as we think we do."
>
> —Paul Craven,
> director of enterprise communications,
> U.S. Department of Labor

Gwynne Kostin, director of Web communications for U.S. Homeland Security, pointed out the inadequacies of an automated system during a recent natural disaster in responding to this scenario. "This is an extension of the current status," she wrote. "A suggestion for an XML standard for emergency deployments during Hurricane Katrina ignored the fact that there was no electricity, no Internet access, decreasing batteries, and no access to equipment that was swamped. Nontechnical backups will become increasingly important—even as we keep forgetting about them. We will need to listen carefully to people on the ground to assess—and plan for—events in which we have no (or nontrustworthy) technology."

There also were concerns about inequities created by computer networks. **Arent Greve**, a professor at the Norwegian School of Economics and Business Administration, wrote, "There will be a trend in this direction, not as extreme as displayed in [this] scenario, but bad enough that we will experience injustice; I think that some of those systems may be reversible, others may not. I would guess a probability of about 30% that such systems develop." And **David Weinberger** of Harvard's Berkman Center wrote, "DRM and 'trusted computing' initiatives already are replacing human judgment with algorithms that inevitably favor restricted access to the content on our own computers."

Alik Khanna of Smart Analyst, Inc., in India, responded that advances in nanotechnology and robotics will build an increasing reliance on machines. "Whether the development of AI will lead to self-awareness in machines, time will tell," he wrote. "Welcome, the Age of *The Terminator*."

SOME SAY ELEMENTS OF THIS WILL TAKE PLACE, BUT WE'LL SURVIVE

"I agree, but this is not a doomsday scenario," wrote **Mark Gaved** of The Open University in the U.K. "The development of these technologies will echo previous technologies with similar curves, unexpected developments, and unauthorized appropriations by grassroots groups."

Marilyn Cade, CEO of ICT strategies for MCADE, wrote, "We are (into this scenario already) aren't we? But can't we also be

> "We may come dangerously close to this point, but I think we'll still be able to kill Hal."
>
> —Buff Hirko,
> virtual reference coordinator,
> Washington State Library

into self-correction of this problem? Awareness is beginning to emerge, and technological solutions can develop for the technological challenges named *if* we self-govern as industry, and partner with governments to achieve some limitations of the surveillance powers of the 'states.' "

Charlie Breindahl of the IT University of Copenhagen wrote, "I agree that it is a very real danger. However, I think that our present thinking about how automation and distributed computing works is naïve. In the year 2020, the general public will be much more aware of how to utilize their agents and control schemes. We should see a much more 'AI-literate' population, if not in 2020, then in 2040."

Michael Reilly of GLOBALWRITERS, Baronet Media, wrote, "While a few activities could spin off course, most really problematic issues will be spotted early and repaired. Also, monitoring which alerts humans to problems will become a high-order business on its own, incorporating 'self-healing' networks equipped with alarms when boundaries are exceeded."

Robin Lane, an educator and philosopher from the Universidade Federal do Rio Grande do Sul in Brazil, wrote, "The desire for convenience, for ease of use, for the removal of tedious, laborious tasks is—in my opinion—inherent in us as beings. As such, we will continue to use and abuse technology to make our lives easier. The price for this is increased dependency on the technology."

> "The Internet will evolve like other pathogenic systems; at some times, the pathogens will hold the upper hand as they adopt to measures to counter them, and sometimes they will not."
>
> —Jeff Corman,
> government policy analyst,
> Industry Canada,
> Government of Canada

And **Jeff Hammond**, vice president for Rhea + Kaiser, responded that autonomous technology will have "benefits and challenges that individuals will have to deal with on a personal basis." He added, "The real danger is in autonomous technology that stifles interdependence among humans. I believe that human interdependence is the characteristic of our species that enables us to evolve and adapt to challenges we cannot foresee."

WORKING TO AVOID "UNINTENDED CONSEQUENCES"

Some respondents specified that humans must plan in advance to build the best outcome for an automated future. "I truly do agree that there will be nearly complete automation of such boring-to-humans activity as surveillance, security, and tracking systems," wrote **Glenn Ricart**, a member of the Internet Society Board of Trustees and the executive director for PricewaterhouseCoopers Research. "There will clearly be unintended consequences, some of which may endanger or take human life. However, I don't believe it will be impossible to reverse such things; indeed, we will continue to perfect them while undergirding them with something like Asimov's Three Laws of Robotics."

Rajnesh Singh, of the Pacific Islands section of the Internet Society, wrote, "This is likely to be so, but hopefully common sense prevails and necessary safeguards are put in place prior." And **Ben Detenber**, an associate professor at Nanyang Technological University in Singapore, wrote, "Organizations like CPSR [Computer Professionals for Social Responsibility] and EPIC will serve critical roles in revealing, understanding, and addressing these problems."

> "The fact that this question is being asked/asserted suggests that it will not happen. Enough healthy paranoia exists among the people on the inside—those creating the standards—that others who might purposefully, or accidentally, unleash these kinds of problems will be effectively neutralized."
>
> —Kerry Kelley,
> VP, product marketing,
> SnapNames.com

Henry Potts, a professor at University College in London, expressed concern over potential economic impact. "The use of standard decision-making software by stock market traders has already led to effects outside of what we planned or wanted," he wrote. "I don't fear robots looking like Arnold Schwarzenegger taking over the world, but unexpected and unwanted effects of distributed control are feasible."

Jim Archuleta, senior manager for government solutions for Ciena Corporation, wrote, "In some cases, reversal of the processes will be difficult and nearly impossible. There are scenarios where processes based on automation and intelligence based on rules and identities will miss 'outliers' and 'exceptions,' thereby resulting in mistakes, some of which will be life threatening."

Lilia Efimova, a researcher with Telematica Instituut in The Netherlands, wrote, "This is a possible scenario, so I believe there is a responsibility for Internet researchers in that respect to recognize those dependencies in advance and to act on preventing dangers." **Sabino Rodriguez** of MC&S Services responded that the European Commission is already assigning "studies, proposals, and invest-ments" into avoiding negative consequences of new technologies. And **Sean Mead**, an Internet consultant, wrote, "Science fiction has warned of nearly any threat that autonomous technology can raise. There will be problems caused by autonomous tech, but, like germs provoking an immune-system response, the eventual effect of the initial damage will be to install safeguards that protect us from long-lasting damage."

ALLOWING ANYONE TO PROJECT POWER

Several survey participants said this scenario also presents some positive aspects. **Ted Coopman**, a social science researcher and instructor at the University of Washington, sees the formation of a "new bottom-up, global, civil society" thanks to autono-mous technology "in the form of ultra-structure capabilities that allow almost anyone to project power with little or no cost."

He continued, "The reper-toires of individuals and groups will be readily available and successful, or attractive ones will spread and scale rapidly. The aggregate adoption will cause huge and likely

> "Autonomous systems will not become a serious problem until they are sophisticated enough to be conscious...As it stands now, they are simply tools—advanced tools, but tools nonetheless. True AI is still 50–100 years away."
>
> —Simon Woodside,
> CEO, Semacode Corporation

unpredictable shifts in social, political, economic arenas. People will no longer favor incumbent systems, but will move to systems that make sense to them and serve their needs. This will force incumbent systems to adapt quickly or fail. Governmental protection of incumbent corporate and social power will lose much of its effectiveness as a force of social control. These parallel systems to serve people's needs will arise via digital networks."

Mary Ann Allison, a futurist and chairman and chief cybernetics officer for The Allison Group, responded, "While this scenario is clearly a danger, we don't yet understand how powerful fully connected human beings can be."

Rob Atkinson, director for the Technology and New Economy Project for the Progressive Policy Institute, and formerly director at the U.S. Congressional Office of Technology Assessment, responded, "The more autonomous agents, the better. The steeper the 'J-curve,' the better. Automation, including through autonomous agents, will help boost standards of living, freeing us from drudgery."

And **Mark Poster**, an authority on the ways social communications have changed through the introduction of new technologies, wrote, "The issue will be how humans and information machines will form new assemblages, not how one will displace the other."

WHERE DOES "AUTONOMOUS TECHNOLOGY" STAND NOW?

Distributed control systems—those with remote human intervention—have long been used across the world to handle various tasks, including the operation of electrical power grids and electricity-generation plants, environmental control systems, traffic signals, chemical and refining facilities, water-management systems, and many types of manufacturing. Systems are becoming more automated daily, as pervasive information networks are being invisibly woven into everything everywhere, helping us manage a world that becomes exponentially more complex each year.

Many operations are being handled by small microelectromechanical systems—better known as MEMS. Billions of these devices are already woven into our buildings, highways, and even our forests and other ecosystems; they are found in personal devices, from our automobiles to printers and cell phones. The market for MEMS hit $8 billion in 2005, with a forecast for growth to more than $200 billion by 2025, according to Joe Mallon of Stanford University (2006).

Some programmable, remote information devices now in use are called "agents" or "bots." Agents automatically carry out tasks for a user: sorting e-mail according to preference, filling out Web page forms with stored information, reporting on company inventory levels, observing changes in competitors' prices and relaying statistics, and mining data to detect specific conditions. Bots are programmed to help people who play online games perform various tasks; they are also used online to aid consumers in finding products and services— these shopping bots use collaborative filtering.

MEMS, agents, and bots are self-contained tools designed and distributed by people who monitor them and replace or remove them from a network when necessary. They are autonomous to some extent in that they are capable of functioning independently to meet established, human-set goals. Most of them do not possess any artificial intelligence. Intelligent agents have the ability to sense an environment and adapt to changes in it if necessary, and they have the ability to learn through trial and error or through example and generalization. MEMS, agents, and bots are the reality today. In the near future, as computing and data storage become more advanced and nanotechnology and artificial intelligence systems are more nearly perfected, it is expected there will be far less direct human input in the day-to-day oversight of human-built systems.

WHERE MIGHT THIS TECHNOLOGY TAKE US IN THE FUTURE?

Many of the sophisticated operational systems developed in the next few decades will be invisible or nearly so. Nanoelectromechanical systems—10,000 times smaller than the width of a hair—are being developed, and thousands of nano-related patents have already been issued. Most experts who predict a future that sounds a great deal like a science-fiction plot are those who see the continued development and convergence of networked nanotechnology, robotics, and even genetics.

Among the seemingly "extreme" predictions by respected tech experts are the following:

- **Networked "smartdust" devices, or "motes":** These would be the size of a dust particle, each with sensors, computing circuits, bidirectional wireless communication, and a power supply. They could gather data, run computations, and communicate with other motes at distances of up to about 1,000 feet. A concentrated scattering of a hundred or so of these could be used to create highly flexible, low-cost, low-power networks with applications ranging from a climate-control system to earthquake detection to the tracking of human movement (Last, Liebowitz, Pister, & Warneke, 2001).
- **Advanced robots:** British Telecom futurologist **Ian Pearson** has said robots will be fully conscious, with superhuman levels of intelligence, by the year 2020. In a 2005 interview with the Observer, a U.K. newspaper, he said, "Consciousness is just another sense, effectively, and that's what we're trying to design in a computer." And, he added, "If you draw the timelines, realistically by 2050 we would expect to be able to download your mind into a machine, so when you die, it's not a major career problem" (Smith, 2005).

In order to prepare in advance for a future that is likely to be filled with accelerating developments related to autonomous technologies, select leaders have founded watchdog organizations, held conferences, and created research projects. Among them are the Center for Responsible Nanotechnology (http://www.crnano.org/index.html) and the Acceleration Studies Foundation (http://www.accelerating. org/). In addition, Battelle (http://www.battelle.org/) and the Foresight Nanotech Institute (http://www.foresight.org/) are two major nonprofit organizations conducting an ongoing technology-roadmap project investigating the implications of autonomous technologies.

ADDITIONAL RESPONSES

Many other survey respondents shared comments regarding the scenario about autonomous technology. Among them:

> "I believe that agents, automated control, and embedded computing will be pervasive, but I think society will be able to balance the use. We will find these things helpful and a nuisance, but we will not lose control of our ability to regulate them."
> —**David Clark**, Internet pioneer; senior research scientist at MIT

> "You can only automate so much, but will never get to the system having innate intelligence, i.e., the ability to make judgments and handle ambiguity." —**Stewart Alsop**, investor and analyst; former editor of InfoWorld and Fortune columnist

> "If this were true, the world would have blown itself apart in the 20th century." —**Adrian Schofield**, head of research for ForgeAhead, South Africa; leader in the World Information Technology and Services Alliance (WITSA)

> "'J-curve'? Yeah, but that's not the end of the world nor of human control. Man is characterized by adaptability and also by occasional denial of the obvious. To the extent the latter is manifest, we will face surprises. The law of unintended consequences will remain the most powerful law." —**Bud Levin**, program head/psychology and commander/policy and planning, Blue Ridge Community College; Waynesboro (VA) Police Department

> "We can always switch off what we don't like and which causes trouble. This will be no more or less of a problem than a malfunctioning cruise control or thermostat today."
> —**John Browning**, cofounder of First Tuesday, a global network dedicated to entrepreneurs; former writer for The Economist and other top publications

> "People will adapt to such changes rapidly, but in the process, there may be a new set of winners and losers. The 'turbulence' due to such new technology will cause some short-term problems. In the long term, it depends upon whether agents

develop to occupy the same economic/ecological/social niches as humans or different ones. In the former case, one or another will dominate, in the latter case, there can be coexistence."
—**Bruce Edmonds**, Centre for Policy Modelling, Manchester Metropolitan University, U.K.

"The key phrase is 'our control.' These robotic agents and surveillance technologies will be under control, but it will be controlled by others—not those who are being tracked and surveilled. This is already happening, and escalating—not only in government operations, but also in seemingly innocuous private-sector operations (e.g., RFID tags now track consumers as they carry products they are purchasing; truckers and delivery drivers are now tracked by GIS systems that report their position—and every momentary stop for an undeclared coffee break—to their supervisors). One of the greater hopes, however, is that it takes human/supervisor time and effort to utilize the results of such automated surveillance—no matter how much assistance 'those who are in control' have from machines." —**Jim Warren**, Internet pioneer; founding editor of *Dr. Dobb's Journal*; technology policy advocate and activist; futurist

"Resistance is futile. And saying this gives Luddites their intellectual cover. Everything will work out, like *1984* did."
—**Bob Metcalfe**, Ethernet inventor; founder of 3Com Corporation; former CEO of InfoWorld; now a venture capitalist and partner in Polaris Venture Partners

"The question has an overly dramatic spin to it, but the trend is correct. Now, fear of enslavement by our creations is an old fear and a literary tritism. But I fear something worse and much more likely—that sometime after 2020, our machines will become intelligent, evolve rapidly, and end up treating us as pets. We can at least take comfort that there is one worse fate—becoming food—that, mercifully, is highly unlikely."

—Paul Saffo,
director, The Institute
for the Future

"Yep, Big Brother on caffeine and steroids." —**Tunji Lardner**, CEO for the West African NGO network: wangonet.org; agendaconsulting.biz; consultant to the UNDP African Internet Initiative

"I disagree in the hope that humankind is responsible enough to understand that the flow of information

is far too sensitive to leave it solely to the control of machines."
—**Thomas Keller**, domain services, Schlund + Partner AG

"People are afraid of the Golem. Film at 11." —**Robin Berjon**,
W3C and Expway

"As a race, we'd never let that happen. One of the things
that the Internet has enabled is for the masses to collectively
monitor and expose, when necessary, misguided or dangerous
trends. Things won't be able to 'sneak' up on us, and freedom,
especially of ideas and one's ability to think, will be of paramount importance to individuals worldwide." —**Michael Gorrell**,
senior VP and CIO, EBSCO

"I must agree. Leaving our future in the hands of automated
systems is very risky. The algorithms are only as good as what
you put into them, and many have never been tested to the
fullest extent to determine their robustness under actual conditions (witness the strategic defense initiative's 'Star Wars'
guidance software that is charged with saving the American
population from holocaust but which has never been field
tested fully and the code is so complex some scientists doubt it
is capable of functioning as designed)." —**William Kearns**, assistant professor, University of South Florida

"Some people will feel they have no or less control, but people,
perhaps smaller groups than present, will remain in control,
using agents to leverage their power." —**Willis Marti**, associate
director for networking, Texas A&M University

"Certainly there is the potential for the autonomous 'Big
Brother,' self-enabling technology that is both the dream of science and the nightmare of science fiction. The need to explore,
do research, experiment, and examine should act as the greatest
deterrent to this. We have to be careful that while we are creating systems that automate and develop intelligent conclusions,
we are not also limiting our ability to go beyond the boundaries of what is possible in the moment by creating systems that
could limit that." —**Tom Snook**, CTO, New World Symphony

"While I agree that autonomous technology is a problem
and has dangers, I disagree with the subsequent prediction of an inevitable run-away phenomenon. I am hopeful
that interventions (perhaps by other autonomous agents)
will prevent a runaway 'J-curve.'" —**V. K. Wong**, director of IT

campus initiatives and CARAT (Collaboratory for Advanced Research and Academic Technologies), University of Michigan

"I agree that we can anticipate change and new experiences that we did not anticipate as well as change that we cannot easily reverse. I also believe this is already evidenced by today with a variety of issues facing the public and corporations (spam, phishing, identity theft, etc.). Security will be less of an issue, but it will be followed by other unanticipated results of technology change." —**Mike McCarty**, chief network officer, Johns Hopkins

"As Asimov predicted, we are moving toward a more 'intelligent' and robotic world. In a climate of global fear—promoted so much by USA President—we will accept increasing amounts of privacy intrusion. Like most large-scale movements, there are pros and cons to this trend. Whether we 'feel' overall better off in 15 years is yet to be seen. It is likely that everyone moves to more structured, confined, and socially limited behavior as fears of being an 'outed' outcast rise among even law-abiding people worldwide." —**Ed Lyell**, pioneer in issues regarding Internet and education; professor at Adams State College

"Personal freedom continues to erode beyond anything that our founding fathers could probably imagine. Outsourcing surveillance and security functions to organizations like ChoicePoint has already resulted in a fraudulent election of a president. And governments seldom ask for less power. This trend is not likely to be addressed unless a significant portion of the population comes to their senses and realizes that much of the authority being asked for in the name of national security does nothing to make them more secure, but does a lot to make them less free." —**Joe Bishop**, VP business development, Marratech AB

"No doubt. However, as recent events have demonstrated, human miscommunication of intelligence, both accidental and deliberate, remains a huge problem. Intelligence available to everyone without human intervention could help stop unnecessary wars by letting everyone see whether or not there are troop buildups, and could help stop some environmental problems by letting everyone see what companies are polluting or clearcutting. Maybe we won't want to reverse some of these changes because they will be beneficial." —**John S. Quarterman**, president, InternetPerils, Inc.

"Technology may create more opportunities at leisure, increased productivity, and enhanced efficiency in some operations. It will never displace human creativity." —**Rashid Bashshur**, director of telemedicine, University of Michigan

"Intelligent, automated, and distributed don't necessarily lead to uncontrollable, out of control, and dangerous. Very few, if any, technologies live beyond the control of its creators—everything has a chokepoint. This is almost a certain design inevitability—people build in control points, often subconsciously, as matters of convenience, safety, and elegance. Wholly autonomous is probably unworkable." —**Ross Rader**, director of research and innovation, Tucows, Inc.

"Not every society around the world is as uptight about issues of privacy and surveillance as is the population of North America. In Latin America, for example, for centuries the 'haves' had domestic servants circulating around the house, making any kind of privacy absolutely impossible; and even today, privacy and surveillance are not issues which concerns most citizens in this part of the world. Electronic surveillance and tracking systems in the streets and interiors of buildings will be absorbed by the population here just as traffic lights, seat belts, and metal detectors—as necessary evils, but only because they take extra time, not because they 'invade' someone's private space." —**Fredric M. Litto**, professor, University of Sao Paulo, Brazil

"We will cut direct human input in a variety of human activities and this will cause problems. This is already causing problems and we're not yet near the 'singularity' where we're likely headed. However, the notion of 'technology beyond our control' is an alarmist construct. While one might argue that we're already going to wars without informed consent and our children are burning up their adolescence in escapist technological dodges—this statement doesn't allow for a learning curve. In all of the above areas, we are learning as we are making mistakes. So while we are hell bent on acceleration of change, I believe we will also rethink and respond to those systems that seem to be running away from us. We have the time to understand our relationship with technology and I think we will not get lost on a dead-end 'J-curve.'" —**Barry K. Chudakov**, principal, the Chudakov Company

"Yes, with mandatory date retention in Europe and a demise of democracy in USA associated with voting right given to suppliers of 'voting machines' instead of people, it is already a very real problem." —**Wladyslaw Majewski**, OSI CompuTrain SA, ISOC Polska

"Yes, this will increasingly be a problem. But, hopefully, the importance of these feedback loops can be recognized and this problem can be managed in cases where it is important to do so." —**Greg Brewster**, associate dean, DePaul University

"We already have no way of predicting how new technologies will affect society, and we know that innovations are occurring more rapidly. That such difficulties will continue appears to me to be a 'no brainer.'" —**Alex Halavais**, assistant professor, Quinnipiac University

"Whilst this is a hypothetical 'risk scenario' that we might indeed be headed towards, there is no such thing as an 'impossible to reverse situation' whilst Internet users and public interests groups are actively involved." —**Cheryl Langdon-Orr**, independent Internet business operator; director, ISOC-Australia

"In many ways, this has happened already—some writers of Internet worms purport to have written a piece of code that they never expected to have as far reaching implications as they originally intended—others, of course, were completely malicious in their attempts to disrupt networks. Flight systems (space shuttle, commercial aviation, etc.) are susceptible to this as well, and poor results from these automated systems can have deadly consequences. However, this issue will remain isolated to certain instances throughout the next 15 years rather than being a widespread problem." —**Philip Joung**, Spirent Communications

"I agree; however, the problem is not simply with the technology, but also with people's tendency to comply with surveillance." —**Monica Whitty**, professor, Queen's University, Belfast

"Dystopian scenarios are always a good warning, but it seems to me that such a complete erasure of the human function in the process is an exaggeration. Lack of privacy and surveillance, which includes humans, or more precisely human decisions, seems to me to be a more serious threat." —**Mirko Petric**, University of Zadar, Croatia

"I disagree with such dystopian technology perspectives, if only because they ignore the fact that technologies don't suddenly become autonomous agents overnight—people are there in the process of their becoming more autonomous every step of the way and can respond to the issues arising in the moment. I do believe, however, that it is important to thoroughly think through the consequences of new technological developments and the accompanying social and political consequences they will have." —**B. van den Berg**, faculty of philosophy at Erasmus University, Rotterdam, The Netherlands

"This is a scenario out of a science-fiction movie; I doubt it will take place. There will be points at which more data is collected than we intended to, but I don't foresee 'dependence' in the sense it is laid out here." —**Randy Kluver**, director, Institute for Pacific Asia at Texas A&M University

"There may be pockets of uncontrolled (by humans/'victims'), but I would expect to see technology evolve that once again puts the person in control of the environment. While we may use intelligent agents, they will be utilized in such a manner allowing the user to define precisely how and when used. Further, others, using intelligent agents to perhaps get information on someone, will be unable to do so without the object person allowing it. In other words, I believe the hue and cry of privacy violations today will invoke systems to protect the individual and preserve privacy." —**Don Heath**, board member, iPool, Brilliant Cities, Inc., Diversified Software, Alcatel, Foretec

"This already happens with some technologies (and applications of scientific knowledge in general) and the more complex technology becomes, the more often it will be misinterpreted and trusted beyond reasonable levels. For examples of the same happening today, one can think of uses of technology for medical diagnosis—medical doctors already trust the results of laboratory exams and technically produced images of the human body much beyond what their patients report. One can also see that when technology is used in court—DNA exams and the images from security cameras appear to be misused and misinterpreted rather often." —**Suely Fragoso**, professor, Unisinos, Brazil

"While there may be occasional home-grown rogue technologies, these will be limited to small outbreaks instigated by people on the fringes of mainstream society (religious fanatics, anticorporate activists, and the like). Large corporations and governments are so concerned about maintaining control that they will be very careful about building anything that might self-replicate. We see this attitude playing out in the form of crop seeds that cannot replicate and attempt to force people to pay every time they watch TV, a DVD, or listen to music. I doubt a 125-year copyright system or the patent process will have significantly loosened its grip on the exchange of intellectual property in 15 years." —**Scott Moore**, online community manager, Helen and Charles Schwab Foundation

"I'm putting a positive spin on this by disagreeing. I suspect there will be examples where the prediction is true but that socially mediated expectations will lead to limitations on such technologies." —**Andy Williamson**, managing director for Wairua Consulting Limited, New Zealand; member of the NZ government's Digital Strategy Advisory Group

"That scenario will be real only in the technologically most developed segments in our countries. Maybe most of humanity will be under surveillance and control by the technological resources and its managers but not in real command of that means." —**Raul Trejo-Delarbre**, Universidad Nacional Autonoma de México

"There is a collision between individual security and commercial interests. There is a flood of research on technologies that exploits all possible vulnerabilities." —**W. Reid Cornwell**, director, the Center for Internet Research

"I don't trust technology as much as I trust human intelligence as input into decisions. Technology is changing so rapidly that there is no time to really nut out consequences that could be negative." —**Barbara Craig**, Victoria University

"This is already a problem. We have become so content with technology handling the 'little things' that we have lost a sense of perspective on the 'big picture.' We are outsourcing our privacy." —**Martin F. Murphy**, IT consultant, City of New York

"Aided by governmental policies like those of the Bush administration, 'the people' lose track of what the governments are doing. 'The people' insist on using credit and other trackable means. We all lose to the machine or its ghost." —**Edward Lee Lamoureux**, associate professor, Bradley University

"Unless we severely damage our physical environment, cultural and social structures have proved to be flexible. History shows that empires fall. If we get an empire of the Net, this will eventually fall too." —**Torill Mortensen**, associate professor, Volda University College, Norway

"Technology will not master the emotional elements that drive certain decision making. Of course, left unchecked, we could become too dependent on machines, e.g., using a calculator for simple math when one's own computational skills could be used." —**Richard Yee**, competitive intelligence analyst, AT&T

"Increased automation will be problematic, but not irreversible. We'll still have some control, though end users will be more frustrated when the automation fails and no backup plans are in place." —**Kevin Schlag**, director of Web development and IT for Western Governor's University, BYU-Hawaii

"For the most part, society has a self-adjusting mechanism. As dangers on the horizon approach, the relative importance society puts on them increases until the cost to not address them becomes too great. It's the issues that require us to anticipate far in advance that may give us a problem."

—A. White, a respondent who chose not to share further identifying information

"That, sadly, is the price of technology evolution—like it or not. No good technology goes unpunished." —**Stan Felder**, president and CEO, Vibrance Associates, LLC

"We have only begun to see the beginning of the acceleration. Convergence of technologies will present complications and scenarios not yet thought of." —**Todd Costigan**, National Association of Realtors

"This is one of the scariest consequences of our light-speed technological advancement. Hollywood fiction will become reality." —**Daniel D. Wang**, principal, Roadmap Associates

"Calm down. We are only talking 14 years from now. There are so many problems even with basic 'intelligent agents' that exist today that much skepticism exists and the standards for dependency will be very high." —**Ralph Blanchard**, investor, information services entrepreneur

"Dangers exist now as the Patriot Act is the start of the 'J-curve.' Illegal wiretaps by governments are already taking place and explained away using the 'lipstick on a pig' spin. A society based upon fear is not a free society." —**Ted Summerfield**, president, Punzhu.com

"The drive to make smart technologies with artificial intelligence means developers will allow AI unrestricted access to the Internet. Self-learning AI could theoretically teach itself to override all security measures and begin the 'J-curve.'" —**J. Fox**, a respondent who chose not to share further identifying information

"Barring interruption, that does seem where we're headed. People are accepting more and more of this type of thing, though I continue to hope they will revolt against it." —**Ralph Mueller**, self-employed; Internet user since 1977

"There will still be generations living in 2020 who are not willing to give up so much control. It also takes a long time to prove autonomous technology for mission-critical applications." —**Brian T. Nakamoto**, Everyone.net, a leading provider of outsourced e-mail solutions

"Although the political climate of the U.S. in particular appears to be shifting in this direction, in 2020 balancing voices will be heard that argue for moderation, limiting

technological progress but preserving privacy and control."
—**Peter Kim**, senior analyst, marketing strategy and technology team,
Forrester Research

"Not exactly in the way described. A kind of war between
intelligence will come true: We will always have 'people
against' what is on, i.e., intelligence against the way things are
at a certain moment." —**Ivair Bigaran**, Global Messenger Courier do
Brasil, American Box Serviço Int'l S/C Ltda.

"We have to be careful that we still maintain our rights defined
in our Constitution. I am already uncomfortable with how much
Big Brother is watching, thanks to technology." —**Beth Galla-
way**, trainer/librarian/consultant, Metrowest MA Regional Library System

"While intelligent agents and distributed control will replace
much of the direct human input required today, the human element will never be totally replaced. While technology beyond
our control may come frighteningly close to reality, machines
will never be able to replace the human conscience." —**Mitchell
Kam**, Willamette University, OR

"Soon people with parts of the knowledge about these devices
will be valued, like car mechanics of high-tech cars on a
lesser scale." —**Susan Wilhite**, design anthropologist, Habitat for
Humanity

"There may be some merit in the thought. However, the rate
of evolution required is far greater for a 2020 situation."
—**Syamant Sandhir**, leader in experience design and implementation,
Futurescape

"We're there already. Scott McNealy, CEO of Sun Microsystems, said in 1999, 'You have zero privacy anyway. Get
over it.'" —**Nicco Mele**, U.S. political Internet strategist

"I agree that this is a risk, but not a certainty. UCSD Prof.
Natalie Jerimenko's idea of 'legibility' and the 'human read-
ability' I call for in my story 'Human Readable' both present plausible answers to this problem. It's possible that future
commercial services, like search engines, that publicly expose
their 'secret sauce' sorting and ranking algorithms will out
compete their proprietary and secretive brethren. After all,
science improves when you publish." —**Cory Doctorow**, blogger
and cofounder of Boing Boing; EFF Fellow

"This prediction is too pessimistic and not in keeping with North American and Western European political sensibilities."
—**Ellen K. Sullivan**, former diplomat; policy fellow, George Mason University School of Public Policy

"This is simply too far-fetched." —**Mark Crowley**, researcher, the Customer Respect Group

"I think we're smarter than to let this happen. I think, I hope, we can use technology as a tool and not to cut human input out of the process." —**Lori Keith**, Internet marketing consultant for Mannington Mills

"This is a negative result, but I can't see either the commercial or political forces yielding on this one with so much wealth and power at stake." —**Jill O'Neill**, director of planning and communication, National Federation of Abstracting and Information Services

"I prefer to be optimistic on this one. There is a danger that some of those things will happen, but I think—at least in democratic states and regions—popular pressure and checks and balances will ensure that such developments are prevented."
—**Olav Anders Øvrebø**, freelance journalist based in Oslo, Norway

"This has already happened to some degree. But the combination of human/bureaucratic/governmental screw ups and technological complexity will continue to produce bloated, underperforming über-systems, and the NSA of the future will continue ineffectually spending megabillions of dollars blindly screening communications traffic and surveillance data while turning up thousands of wasted false positives to every genuine hit. Only in small, well-demarcated areas will intelligent agents prove cost effective. Some over-reaching system designs will become famous blunders and public jokes."
—**Walt Dickie**, VP and CTO, C&R Research

"These trends are already evident. Ironically, these trends are being escalated by those who tend to devalue science and science education in favor of antiscientific and antitechnological fundamentalist religious curricula." —**Benjamin Ben-Baruch**, senior market intelligence consultant and applied sociologist, Aquent, General Motors, Eastern Michigan University

"I'm not necessarily talking science fiction here, more like self-replicating, out-of-control viruses and DNS attacks that (1) lack author-derived backdoors and (2) reproduce like minks." —**Roger Scimé**, self-employed Web designer

"Sensing and monitoring is already a problem intimidating many people. It will only get worse as more and more devices and programs have that built-in capability shoved down consumers' or employees' throats." —**Steffan Heuer**, U.S. correspondent, *brand eins Wirtschaftsmagazin*

"We are already here. It's a common theme from literature about technology for the past 150 years: unintended consequences, loss of control, disassociation of functionality from the real costs incurred by organic life." —**Denzil Meyers**, founder and president, Widgetwonder, Applied Improvisation Network

"In 2020 the big decision that each human being will make about their cultural alignment will not be 'Windows or Mac,' or 'gay or straight,' but 'corporate or open-source?' Corporate, proprietary systems and Internets will provide better performance, ease of use, anticipatory agents, etc. However, corporate-system subscribers will be trading privacy and control for convenience and pop-culture inclusion. Open-source life will be for technological innovators, programmers, pamphleteer bloggers, artists, pornographers, content creators, citizen journalists, political dissidents, and hackers. Participants in open-source culture will be fierce defenders of privacy, human rights, and civil liberties." —**Daniel Conover**, new-media developer, Evening Post Publishing

"These are two separate statements. I agree that we will be on the vertical part of a 'J-curve' of continued acceleration of change, but I don't foresee that we will be so shortsighted as to completely lose control of the intelligent agents that we create and program." —**Michelle Catlett**, instructional technologist, Edubuilder, Apria Healthcare, Laureate Education

"This sounds like the scenario of *The Terminator* movie. I don't believe that is a likely outcome (although entertaining for a movie). I suspect there will be more autonomous technology and most people will be as unaware of it as they are about the computer in their cars. It may replace some people from their

jobs (as robots have on car assembly lines), but most people will just see the end product and not know the difference."
—**Rangi Keen**, software engineer, Centric Software

"The slippery slope of want of privacy plus want of security changes the balances and leaves open the possibility for abuse of the information (which will be tremendous) generated from surveillance, security, and tracking systems. This also leads to more people trying to live 'off the Net' which leads to distrust of this group (what are they trying to hide?). Some of whom may just be want of keeping privacy."
—**Chris Miller**, a respondent who chose not to share further identifying information

"Due to Homeland Security fear (and money), there will be way more development of sensors and surveillance tech, but it won't be 'beyond our control.' People will question the tradeoffs in ways they don't at present, i.e., they'll give up private info to join a contest or get a discount." —**Steve Cisler**, former senior library scientist for Apple; now working on public-access projects in Guatemala, Ecuador, and Uganda

"How 'intelligent' will these agents be is questionable, but the rise of automated surveillance without any real counterweights seems very likely. What does not imply that it will be impossible to reverse them like any other form of oppression?" —**Michel Menou**, professor and information-science researcher

"While I don't suffer from Pollyanna thinking, and I do recognize the nature of subtle control over the Web by those with less than sterling character, I believe we will be able and willing to create safeguards and public-opinion mechanisms that will drive the Internet to safe and humane standards without cutting our chance at creativity." —**Walter J. Broadbent**, VP, the Broadbent Group

"I believe such technology will exist in some venues but not throughout the world and definitely not throughout society. There will be dangers and accidents that will result in deaths of some individuals and populations in some geographical regions where technological disasters occur." —**James Conser**, professor emeritus, Youngstown State University

"Just read classic science fiction—it is 'the history of our future,' and I believe many of the issues related to automated systems will truly come to pass." —**Gail Ives**, executive director for institutional research, Mott Community College

"I think that we need to strive to educate our people so that human input is involved in the oversight and accountability of automated systems." —**Jeff Bohrer**, learning-technology consultant, University of Wisconsin–Madison

"We are slowly learning that we all have to live together, that there aren't 'others.' So we will learn new ways of living together, rather than continue old habits of putting up barriers to protect ourselves from 'others.'" —**Cheris Kramarae**, professor, Center for the Study of Women in Society, University of Oregon

"Wherever it has become technically possible for the powerful to covertly increase their control over others, they have been eager to do so, and wherever the unscrupulous have learned the techniques, they have not hesitated to use them for criminal ends. The majority of humanity has no protection from such exploitation but the law. The lawmakers are too often unfamiliar with the technology and too ready to believe what the experts claim: that anything that can be done, should be done—regardless of social and ethical considerations—and the laws changed accordingly, rather than that the social goals and protections written into existing laws should be updated so as to also govern the use of new technologies." —**Judyth Mermelstein**, Canadian writer, professional communicator

"Probable cause could take on a new meaning. Did 'intelligent agents' have probable cause to freeze your accounts, call for your arrest, prevent you from traveling, turn off your car ignition, etc.?" —**Mike Parker**, Internet user since 1994

"If there is one thing that I think that history has shown us in this area is that very few individuals, organizations, or governments are capable of visualizing the long-range results of changes in technology. Without the human capability of review, evaluation, decision making, etc., autonomous technology could easily create problems that we can barely anticipate at this time." —**Loretta Righter**, librarian, Montgomery County-Norristown Public Library

"HAL is alive and well." —**Celia Bouchard**, assistant professor, St. Louis Community College

"A new field of study and academic training will emerge to specifically address the particular issue of identity, control, and security of communication technologies. Finding a balance between automaticity and human-interface interaction will become an interest in research and in application." —**Clement Chau**, research assistant and program coordinator, Tufts University, Developmental Technologies Research Group

"Doomsday predictions have always followed technological advancements, and the Web is no different. The human element will always be needed to make judgmental decisions, something computers are unlikely to be able to accomplish." —**Doug Olenick**, computer technology editor, *TWICE (This Week in Consumer Electronics)* magazine

"Ha ha, this is simply third-grade science fiction. Dangers come in much more subtle (read: less anthropomorphic) issues." —**Mikkel Holm Sørensen**, software and intelligence manager, Actics Ltd.

"This is a wildcard since it involves so many interim political and social steps as well as technology development. Yes, converged applications of automated tech— such as face scans matched to databases— are already on the way and will be widespread before 2020. But depending on global political developments, this Big Brother scenario could happen well before 2020...or much much later (if ever). Does 2084 sound like a century-late benchmark?" —**Gary Arlen**, president, Arlen Communications, Inc., the Alwyn Group LLC

> "Technology can only serve mankind; it will never lead it. Certainly there will be opportunities for abuse, but the culture of technology development is fused with the rights of personal expression, and this alone will probably suffice to assure reasonable balances."
>
> —Al Amersdorfer,
> president and CEO,
> Automotive Internet Technologies

"The problem is not automated systems that resemble our behavioral patterns. The problem is biomimetic systems that develop behavioral patterns of their own, which we cannot understand. If we leave surveillance to an adaptive AI, there will come a moment in which we won't understand the processes behind its efficiency. Then it will be a problem. But as long as surveillance, tracking, and tagging are modeled after human behavior, and thus after human values, we do have issues but not unsolvable problems." —**Miguel Sicart Vila**, junior research associate, Information Ethics Group, Oxford University

"Technology will certainly provide the means for this scenario to take place, but I'm optimistic that policy makers in government will be able to craft the regulatory framework to prevent this from getting out of control. There will be bitter debates in the U.S. between civil libertarians and technologists, but in other countries and cultures, there will be no debates. The only reason this scenario will not take place in many countries outside of the U.S. will be the lack of technology infrastructure in LDC and Third World countries." —**Michael Conlin**, former legislator, currently an entrepreneur

"While potentially troublesome, I think that because of the sci-fi depictions of the impact that autonomous technology could have, such as the most renowned example depicted in *2001: A Space Odyssey*, HAL will certainly be managed by smart and 'administratable' measures to avoid a logarithmic and uncontrollable set of circumstances." —**Kevin McFall**, director, Online Products & Affiliate Programs, Tribune Media Services, NextCast Media

"The increased threat of terrorism, cyberterrorism, and financial security will drive new security and crypto systems." —**Terry Ulaszewski**, publisher, Long Beach Live Community News

"This autonomous tech scenario is overstated. There will be many problems, but more will occur as a consequence of human choice and intervention than machines run amok." —**Suzanne Stefanac**, author and interactive media strategist, dispatchesfromblogistan.com

"I hope to be wrong, but I believe the stampede towards such monitoring in the name of 'security' now creates an environment where autonomous technology seems a logical consequence. Now, with the emerging social consequences of even 'harmless' technologies such as mobile phone cameras, we need to be very cautious about more even more intrusive technologies." —**Jean-Pierre Calabretto**, PhD student, University of South Australia

"Incompetence in organizations is so high that, even if the technical components are in place, it may not happen." —**Timbre' Wolf**, songwriter and member of PG5YP (People's Glorious Five-Year Plan—a band in Oklahoma)

"Managing intelligent agents and distributed control will be a significant issue, but lessons learned from the stock market and other venues where AI is used remind administrators to build in controls." —**Alix L. Paultre**, executive editor, Hearst Business Media, Smartalix.com, Zep Tepi Publishing

"Not a prediction. It is a current reality. Do you know how your computer, cellphone or microwave work?" —**Gordon MacDiarmid**, Lobo Internet Services

"Are not we almost there? See NSF, Homeland Security, need to know." —**Joe Schmitz**, assistant professor, Western Illinois University

"We are already aware of these potential problems and will not allow the autonomous entities to dominate. The main fear I have here is the impact restrictive governments will have on freedom and flexibility of these networks." —**Jim (Jacomo) Aimone**, director of network development, HTC

"There is likely much truth to this, and a fair amount of the difficulty will arise out of the inaccuracy of these intelligent agents." —**David Irons**, VP, cofounder, AScribe Newswire

Anonymous Comments

A number of anonymous survey respondents shared comments tied to the scenario about autonomous technology. Among them:

"Complex systems always introduce unintentional consequences."

"Autonomous technology is already a problem. From hospitals to the highways, from the classroom to the bank, it is already dangerously loose."

"We're only talking about 15 years away—Big Brother won't be here for at least another 50 years!"

"Likely, but I don't see the system as terribly efficient. This makes it even more dangerous."

"This is possible. We are relying heavily on unmanned spacecraft and whatnot. I'm worried machines will be perceived as less error-prone than humans."

"Technology is never outside of human control. It just depends on what you mean by control."

"People seem ready to embrace technology and to use it to automate all sorts of tasks. It seems quite possible that important activities such as security-related activities will become more automated than they already are and less under the control of humans. As it is, when a name gets placed on a 'watch list,' it seems very hard for people to prove that they do not belong there. Also, many banking activities are already out of the control of human beings to the point that it becomes very easy for someone to steal a person's identity and use it to open lines of credit. This can destroy someone's life as it is very difficult to undo the damage that is done when someone else easily opens lines of credit in another person's name."

> *Predictions from respondents who chose to remain anonymous:*
>
> **"Technology will still be very much controlled by large corporations, governments (for which read the USA), and megabureaucracies. The problem will not be autonomous technology, but faceless human overseers who are not held accountable."**
>
> **"I think we'll have time to put on the brakes."**
>
> **"Maybe we really are in *The Matrix*."**

"The *Terminator* movies will not come to pass."

"It could happen, and might happen, just not that soon."

"These events are a possibility. However, the systems will have too many errors in them, such that breakdown will occur. Human beings create these systems, so monitoring them is the human problem."

"While I believe in the high rate of change, truly autonomous agents won't be intelligent enough to be a major risk."

"We're smarter than that. These are scare tactics."

"Human judgment will continue to play a major role as mistakes continue to be made in attempts to automate."

"To date, humanity has been able to identify these problem trends and work to prevent major catastrophes caused by these dependencies. However, the increasing centralization of power in a few global companies could increase the chances of it occurring."

"While I agree that we may not immediately recognize some of the dangers/dependencies, I disagree that we will not be able to reverse, or better yet, counter them with other intelligent-agent capabilities."

"I disagree only with the 'impossible to reverse them' portion. The problems are already appearing now. That it will be uncorrectable, I do not agree. Partially because competing software/hardware suppliers can use such things as controllable/customizable systems as a point of differentiation to consumers. Partly because some large institutions, such as governments, corporations, developer groups, hacker groups, educational institutions, have varying levels of 'control issues,' for lack of a better term. They will likely provide resistance, whether organized and legal, or otherwise."

"This sounds a bit paranoid, as if the human element of computing will suddenly disappear and create a world like *Terminator 2* or *The Matrix*, in which machines develop artificial intelligence and then go to war against their human makers. Intelligent agents and distributed controls will help eliminate human errors in cases where human beings slow down the system, but they won't eliminate humans or create dangers and dependencies."

"The definition of the word 'problem' is highly subjective. Is this questionnaire a survey (about) technology or philosophy?"

"Surveillance, security, and tracking may become a danger; but I think, over time, it cuts both ways in that these technologies will be better able to uncover illegal and dangerous uses of the technology."

"If this means beyond the control of most individuals, then I do agree. Policy making, surveillance, information gathering, and such, are already out of the control of most individuals. Placing as many of these activities into automated hands will certainly be done if it saves someone money or increases their power. I think we'll have time to put on the brakes."

"Agree in a general sense, but it is a longer-term issue: 40–50 years."

"The fear of computers replacing people has been around at least since the 1950s, and the reality contin- ues to be that we have more to fear from humans than from machines."

> *Predictions from respondents who chose to remain anonymous:*
>
> **"The difficulty will be cultural rather than technical since we'll be increasingly dependent."**
>
> **"The increasing centralization of power in a few global companies could increase the chances of it occurring."**

"I agree that there will be changes that we do not recognize now."

"Autonomous control will be increasingly available, but con- trols and overrides will be available, especially inside corpo- rations where IT experts will still exist. We'll see more of the automation, however, in consumer applications."

"This is already happening."

"Intelligent agents and distributed control will expand in irre- versible ways, insinuating ways, but I do not believe human input will be cut out of the loop. My somewhat darker view reflects the culture of central control and repression that seems to dominate power brokers right now. They have every inten- tion of controlling these agents and systems at choke points they are currently building into the systems, invisible to most people, just as the ways the voting machines are being rigged is also invisible and untraceable. These people have seen what happens when the wild horse runs, and frankly, it terrifies them. We are in the middle of an enormous backlash. On the other hand, this could be a good time for some McLuhan-esque media reversals. Or is the backlash itself the media reversal? I doubt it is anything so innocuous."

"Automation is a legitimate tool in security, but humans will be loathe to cut human thinking out of monitoring human behavior, which is notoriously difficult to reduce to algorithms."

" 'Impossible to reverse' won't happen."

"It's already a mess in some industries, such as the airlines; no reason to believe it will stop there."

"Giant technology companies in all parts of the world will endeavor to cut more people out of the loop to maximize their profits. Machines will begin to create more machines, driven by profit, and humanity will lose control of what is really being produced."

"It will be worse for users since the need for control of automatic agents will increase discrepancies. Users' time will be jeopardized by machines."

"We rush to convenience time and time again. Underestimating the power of convenience and time saving is a sure-fire way to missing the next wave. This autonomous nature of transactions will be a problem, but we'll rush into it anyway."

"Technology will permit more control or power to be concentrated in the hands of a relative few, but I do not envision technology on its own spinning out of control. Ever hear of a back door? Programmers can't resist inserting them. Every system can be exploited. There are no secure systems. And every developer knows that systems must be developed with fail-safes."

"Every attempt to automate generates a backlash. These attempts are usually subject to political developments. I don't think any of these activities will go ignored, especially with all the Internet communities that are on watch and ready to subvert such attempts."

"This does not mean we will be safer. We will just be more videotaped, documented, and data mined."

"We lose human control because we try to create machines that do the procedures for us."

"To some degree, I think we're already there. Just look at the recent NSA/telecom carrier situation where, apparently and allegedly, millions of voice and data communications were tapped and analyzed. The dangers aren't always physical but can be financial or emotional, as in the case of identity theft."

"Sounds like a Philip K. Dick story...I'm not sure I'm behind this statement. I do think that technology will be enhanced so much by 2020 that human interactions will be even more limited than today, but I don't think it will be as bad as described above."

"Too much hype over something that shouldn't matter, just like Y2K."

"It could go this way, but I suspect that governments will be forced by their populations to legislate to prevent this."

> *Predictions from respondents who chose to remain anonymous:*
>
> **"Made by humans, run by humans, deactivated by humans."**
>
> **"While we *are* on a 'J-curve' of accelerating change, the time frame of 2020 is premature. 2050 is more likely."**
>
> **"There will be a minor scare and some moral panics, but we'll be all right. Won't we?"**

"Technology is making us increasingly vulnerable."

"I am optimistic that the public will reclaim our right to privacy and to space."

"Sounds like a good movie but not reality. Machines are and always will be just machines—only as valuable and dangerous as the people who run them."

"I think enough people are worried about this type of thing happening that there will be plenty of watchdogs."

"Technology is so interconnected that I believe it is humanly impossible to predict all the outcomes of the choices we are making. Civil liberties hang in the balance. I predict a backlash against technology."

"I disagree because autonomous technology, and the resulting 'de-skilling' of humans, is already considered a problem in some circles. Also, this sounds like a *Frankenstein* scenario—things would have to proceed perfectly according to plan for this to happen, and given the law of unintended consequences, they almost never do."

"Autonomous technology will be somewhat of a problem, although nothing created or tracked electronically is impossible to undo. There will always be loopholes, and the developers of these systems will need to account for that or the backlash will be incredible. Unless, of course, people just don't know its happening."

"Paranoia, pure and simple."

"Human intelligence will still be the key driver of the Internet, and user control tags, Web 2.0, etc., will be the norm."

"Yes, as falls in the cost of processing power, monitoring devices, connectivity will make this increasingly economically feasible."

"Every major change in technology has come with the same predictions. The result is that additional opportunities have always opened up."

"Too much regulation will completely alter the beauty of the Internet, which is its ability to connect people from all around the world, provide information sharing, promote free speech, all for a low cost. Too much control will alter the WWW for the worse not for the better."

"Possibly true, but this looks suspiciously like one of those 'overrun by robots' scares."

"Always have to be mindful of what the effect might be."

"A lot of danger lurks with intelligent agents, data mining, and how information can be used against someone. It is creepy to know that everything can be tracked electronically today and that the faster computer processors will be able to compile and comb through mounds of data and sometimes those smart agents will draw incorrect conclusions. That is the scary part."

"What is likely is that technology will continue to widen the gap between the haves and have-nots. Those with high education will continue to be able to use technology to advance. Those without will benefit from a higher standard of living but will not be able to take advantage of the technology to its fullest extent. Tedious tasks will be automated, but ultimately, anything that requires a 'judgment call' will be left in human hands."

"I don't think that we'll be subject to intelligent machines. I do think that the ease of surveillance will continue to provide leaders and other resource-rich individuals with too much power and not enough oversight. I am not as worried about machines as I am people using machines."

"Such trends will be recognized, but not by the larger public until it is very difficult to rein them in."

"There is not a lot of discussion going on regarding the future of technology (e.g., what about privacy in the Internet?). If you look at myspace.com, you see how irresponsible children are using this social software, not thinking about the possible impact in the future on their lives. Technology and personal life become more and more interchangeable."

"We are already hyper-dependent on technology we don't understand. Can any of your friends fix a TV or a mobile phone?"

"Too many people are control freaks, and time and time again law enforcement and the intelligence community have learned that nothing can truly replace human intuition."

"We're on the look out and will roll back things that get too dangerous."

"Consequently, we need to proceed with caution in the designing of such autonomous technology that compromises integrity over convenience."

"The areas in which autonomous technology will be a problem by 2020 will be limited. Regrettably, the signs of society's willingness to give up privacy through acceptance of the proliferation of security systems that pervade contemporary urban (and increasingly nonurban) areas portend this development."

"Free societies still place limits on technology. Repressive ones can't muster the innovation it takes to implement 'Big Brother.'"

"While human input will not be involved in the direct actions, it is only the human programming that will direct the issues and opportunities for tracking and surveillance. It will be the human inefficiency and poor planning that will be problematic, rather than any notion of not being able to reverse things put into action."

"General awareness of this crossing of the Rubicon will be limited. Top-down control of information will have become greater."

"People are creative, for better or worse. Technology can react, but rarely anticipate, human invention."

"I agree with the idea, but I disagree with calling it a 'problem.' It will be a problem in the U.S., where information is typically misused for political or socially abusive activities."

"Already today the most significant security threats to the network are automated. There is no reason to suspect it will be any less of a problem in the future, and it will likely be much worse. It's not much of a leap for an automated process once unleashed on the network to become uncontrollable by its creator, especially if there is malicious intent."

"Your 'key' activities represent only part of Internet usage."

"By 2020, technology will be developing itself, possibly at a rate beyond human capability. The unbridled quest for an edge in technology that we see today will accelerate and result in systems that will lack proper safeguards. It will not be a Y2K or *Terminator* scenario—systems will still be able to be unplugged—but there will be data and security disasters that will dwarf the ChoicePoint and other scandals seen thus far. A major banking system will collapse, perhaps a military system fold under pressure. The subsequent public outcry will result in legislation intended to insert safeguards—but they will likely be crippled by political and Johnny-come-lately pressures. Given time, however, the problems will be ironed out, but only at great cost."

"We are already there in some regards."

"I think we're further away from dependable AI than 2020."

"This is the nature of system effects."

"The trend is based on fear and it's rampant, at least in the U.S. People are willing to give up civil liberties in order to have the illusion of safety. This will accelerate the move."

"Humanity will remain in control of its own technology. But the control might end up in the hands of a relatively closed oligarchy."

"Just seeing how worms get out of control, and how some worms have been created by mistake, there's no doubt that today's 'spider' could be tomorrow's worm."

"Although I am unsure of technology getting out of our control, I do believe that 'intelligent agents' will take over many tasks that humans can do."

"Science-fiction scenarios are always true."

"In an increasingly automated world, the human touch will become more valuable. Things that do not need the human touch will be out of sight and out of mind (not unlike the electric company)."

"Look at the Echelon project and other governmental initiatives to monitor U.S. citizens with little to no human interaction. How successful have they been and how do we know that what successes have been pointed out are not the only successes?"

"Human bureaucracy will be replaced by e-bureaucracy. Just give me a live person. Help!"

"Tracking systems beyond any individual's control are already somewhat in place, but we can count on the presence of operator error, an excitable, omnipresent media, and enough privacy-hungry humans to keep us from advancing too far down the 'J-curve.'"

"It will get better, but I think there's a long way to go before tech is truly autonomous enough to trust it for such key activities."

"I believe this will be so. But I can't refer to specifics other than an underlying sense of the direction our technology is going."

"Most of the world will not be a party to this, but it could be a problem for technologically advanced nations with large intelligence machines. Without adequate checks on these systems, we could set ourselves up for a Judgment Day scenario as played out in the *Terminator* movies."

"I agree that autonomous technology will thrive but not that it will become the problem described. The 'J-curve' will hit a turning point or a newer overarching technology."

"Technology is clearly getting more and more sophisticated and autonomous every day. It is dangerous, but I don't believe we will ever see the threat of Neo's 'Matrix,' or Sara Conner's 'SkyNet' (but then again, I do believe that people are already inventing and deploying systems that would scare me if I knew about them)."

"We have a substantial track record of making choices without reckoning the consequences."

"These are important advances but must be developed taking caution into account. How does this not become 'Big Brother?' How do we ensure the human element always remains a part of the mix?"

"If by this statement you mean that there will be one or more significant 'accidents' due to use of autonomous technologies— yes, I agree."

"This is already a problem today, where organizations rely more on machines or software to manage tasks than people."

"I agree with trend but not that autonomous technology will be irreversible: If we're smart enough to get it there, we're smart enough to bring it under control. Man will continue to advance technology and control it."

"Agree—to the extent that some instances of unanticipated and detrimental consequences will occur."

"While change will continue and accelerate, humans seem to have the ability to keep themselves in the loop, either explicitly by preventing technology from becoming self-sustaining, or inadvertently by creating flawed technology."

"What we do with the results will be the problem, not the automation itself. We will continue on a 'J-curve' of accelerated change in this space though."

"Actually, I think this is already happening."

"Agree, for the most part—dangers and dependencies will be generated—but not to the extent that they are beyond our control."

"Please, we'll be lucky if our cars have GPS-enabled agents that can find the cheapest gas price within 'n' miles from its current location. That's possible now—but it'll probably take more than 15 years for a business model to make it work, get all aspects of society to 'plug in,' etc."

"We will become a world of 'mere subjects' rather than free citizens due to pervasive surveillance and monitoring. It's unlikely that this trend can be reversed. The human factor will remain vital no matter what because human error will be part of the autonomous technology. We who will not be part of that part of society will learn how to maximize our protection from all that activity in order to not become a victim."

"I agree that intelligent agents will control most of certain key activities—disagree that the technology will be 'out of control.' And we have been on the 'J-curve' for some time."

"Advanced technology, as with anything else, brings new issues and makes some jobs obsolete. However, as with everything else, change also brings opportunity. This means that people will need to be willing to adapt and change to keep up with a faster pace. Learning will need to be life long, and I believe universities will need to teach more about how to learn and adapt, rather than basic facts and skills, which are apt to quickly become obsolete."

"It will be possible, though not necessarily easy, to reverse."

"As more and more IT knowledge is commoditized and taught at ever-lower levels of education (elementary school, perhaps), more people will do more things, including the creation

Predictions from respondents who chose to remain anonymous:

"I expect technology will be developed that could affect the problematic possibilities described above, although I think that human input will continue to influence the choice to exploit and implement those possibilities."

"Beyond our control? Are you being serious!?"

"I am not a Luddite, so I cannot accept this. Yes, human-machine paradigms will change, but the human brain will adapt and supersede in many ways."

of bots or automated processes. Among those will be people of malicious intent."

"No, it will not be impossible to reverse dangers and dependencies. Dangers and dependencies break as we respond and adapt. Any 'irreversible dependency' is by definition life sustaining and will not likely be regarded as a problem. People will still carve out spaces for production, expression, and dissent. While there are certain technologies that put us at risk, there is little experience in history to suggest that our worst fears (or our most fantastic dreams) will all come to fruition. The idea that we can even produce an IT project that is 'irreversibly self-sustaining' is a science-fantasy concept that no one has ever been able to successfully pull off. No prognosis for this anytime in the near future (certainly not by 2020)."

"It has already happened. I don't know about the 'J-curve' stuff, but I agree with the rest."

"Clearly, we will see some 'beyond our control' technological failures; however, they will not be the norm. We will hopefully learn from early failures and ultimately integrate human and technological solutions into a working solution in most cases."

"Autonomous technology will be a problem, but not by 2020—that issue will come about a decade later."

"This is a difficult question because of the extremes it projects. I do think some aspects will get out of control, definitely to dependences, but not necessarily to dangers. Automated monitoring, database interoperability, etc., make us visible in ways we have never been before. If you see a danger to that, then you see danger coming."

"To a large extent, this already is the case. It's increasingly harder to get around or undo computer-based decision making."

" 'J-curves' of technological adoption are rarely followed, and 2020 is too soon to have fully autonomous systems."

"I agree to the extent that most people will not be able to influence technological development. A small group of elites, however, will continue to have some influence."

"Today, many of our research and applications only care about the outcome and neglect many issues, such as privacy."

"A system of checks and balances needs to be implemented as technology becomes more widely used."

"There will always be a human behind the technology implementation and maintenance."

"It won't be a 'J-curve.' It will be sporadic, increasingly erratic ups and downs."

"Agree with the principles, but disagree that it will be 'impossible' to reverse such changes."

"And if the kinds of hooligans now occupying the White House continue to be in power, it will happen much sooner than 2020."

"We'll recognize this happening and take steps to counter it."

"We have been on a 'J-curve' since humanity started thousands of years ago. I don't buy into agents. They were hyped a while ago and went nowhere. It's important to have human input and control."

"There will be dangers and dependences that will not be anticipated; however, there is little to no historical evidence that matters are ever completely outside the control of humans, and none to suggest that the current nature of technological innovation will be substantively different than earlier periods of innovation."

"Not gonna happen as soon as 2020."

"The human potential for subversion will make sure that this trend is undermined. I hope journalists will keep this from happening (by working to illuminate the issues in a timely, accurate fashion)."

"I disagree with the statement with respect to the complete 'cut out' of human input. This seems to me too over optimistic and also does not take into account that social and political movements might create countermovements against a total-surveillance scenario."

"Wherever there is intrusive technology, there is also the will to bypass it."

"Some corporations or individuals may engineer technology to cut direct user input out; however, the norm will be that technology will augment human intelligence and feedback rather than exclude it."

"The human aspect of technology will always be important. We might take some shortcuts, but ultimately, we have the control."

"Facial-recognition technology will be used for such purposes. However, interpersonally, pseudonymity will emerge in the mainstream, thus allowing for layers of anonymity and recognition—identity control."

"This may occur locally, but I also believe that developments will go different ways. Intelligent agents will not be used everywhere; there will be anonymous servers; U.S. regulation will not affect all of the globe."

"Technology is never outside of human control. It just depends on what you mean by 'control.'"

"This is already a problem, and as 'labor' becomes even more expensive in a relative sense, the problem will be exacerbated. However, I do not believe that it will get as bad as the explanation above seems to portray; there will be counterbalancing factors of a legal nature once this problem is 'big enough' to warrant Congress' attention."

"This is partially true but precautions must be taken earlier."

"This seems almost unavoidable."

"The *Brave New World* syndrome has been mooted before but doesn't seem to occur as predicted."

"There is a pendulum swinging here—and, as likely as it is that some of these activities will swing beyond human control, it is as likely that humans will manage the change after a sufficient segment of the human population recognizes the risks."

"The big problem will be to adjust wrong choices made now. In 2020 the 'solution' direction will be somewhere else."

"These systems will be significantly improved, but they will not generate irreversible dangers and dependencies."

"We are on a dangerous course regarding surveillance and tracking. The political climate will influence how this evolves in the future."

"We have seen these predictions before—there is always a need for human involvement."

"This possibility really concerns me."

"Science fiction."

"Sure, it could happen. It may be happening already now."

"This scenario is certainly possible, and elements of it will probably happen, but the level of concern about these problems now is such that I think sufficient safeguards will be implemented, although never completely or perfectly."

"Too many different thoughts here…agree with some of them."

"We are already on that path."

"Humans are always smarter than computers."

"Using the word 'impossible' biases this question, since nothing is impossible. As phrased, this question should generate a resounding nonconfirmation of autonomous technology."

"Anything man made can be reengineered, reversed, and given another useful meaning by the human intelligence."

"Autonomous technology will be a problem, but not an unmanageable one. We will adjust and the technology will adjust. Intelligent agents are overhyped anyway."

"This is a typical catastrophic scenario for bad journalism which historically never materializes."

"There is a clear danger of this happening, but the fact that it is already being identified as a concern, while there is still time to do something about it, suggests that it is far from being a certainty."

"There'll be problems, but this doomsday scenario of irreversibility is too hysterical."

"Only those with enough money can afford to not be online. To not be bothered with Internet and mobile devices is the ultimate status symbol."

"Their software never seems to work as well as they say, with clever programmers and hackers always finding weaknesses, therefore human programmers will have to continue to be involved in the updating and evolution of the software needed."

"I do have a general fear of relying too much on computers and then being subject to technical errors (as opposed to human error) and vulnerability to technical complications."

"Most kinds of surveillance, particularly ones involving, for example, face recognition, are too difficult for technological solutions, and while I do think this prediction may come to pass, I do not think it will happen by 2020."

"Irrespective of the policy issues, I am not so optimistic that technology will advance to support this scenario."

"For every new technology, there will be technology that will reverse its effect. Take the example of current security devices for which people manage to create a decoder. This vicious circle makes cutting direct human input out of any scenario. No, we've already seen some of these extremes, so future systems will be set up to be governed by human control. Things will change and we will be assisted by automated controls, but not too late to reverse them."

"We already have technologies that are (temporarily) out of our control, e.g., automated trading systems that have brought about precipitous stock-market readjustments until their behavior was reined in, and medical systems that give lethal dosages until they are found out. Similar scenarios will undoubtedly continue, and countervening actions will be necessary. But, the situation will be no more dire than it is now."

"This is happening already. Surveillance and security mechanisms are increasingly automated and they can cause 'false alarms' or behavior that will guide the human interaction to be incorrect."

"With new technology come new fences. Those new fences will be overlooked by some, as today backups are overlooked until you lose 1 year of work. But I see no reasons why such isolated mistakes would put the rest of the community in danger; the fact that an agent is autonomous doesn't make it a better invader than when its actions are controlled."

"This fear of losing control over the machines will prevent developers from relinquishing that much power to 'intelligent agents.' At least by 2020, humans will still have control over these elements."

"To an extent, we are considering a threat rather than the likely state of affairs in 2020. Modern history is dominated by ill applications of all sorts of technologies. That scenario could happen only if power (legislation, executive) is taken by nondemocratic groups."

"Freedom wanes as surveillance increases, eliminating the only freedom, anonymity."

"Putting systems online with 'dangers and dependencies that will not be recognized until it is impossible to reverse them' does not seem prudent, unless legal precedents are created so that somebody can get away with such a system. Having said this, the increased use of surveillance, security, and tracking systems may lead to an alienation of the general population from technology."

"There will always be problems with too much delegation or too much distraction. But it will be human error, not computer error. Technology will always give humans more and more control over our world."

"I would quarrel with your characterization of 'intelligent' agents here. Stupid agents are more likely, but governments and others will cheerfully assign them responsibilities in areas like surveillance and security."

"We are pathologically drawn to convenience, it would seem. We will mortgage important principles of privacy, security, finance, and morality for convenience—in many instances without even knowing it."

"This is a very real danger, and given that we are doing a lot of things so poorly in cyberspace, we are going to be in a world of hurt. My sister just spent considerable time trying to get her real birthday back—the IRS said it was June 31! Computer matching between government agencies is a total disaster— my sister's real birthday is June 3, but Social Security and IRS worked together to get it wrong. I worked in federal government for years—I fear for my grandson."

"I take this to be a two-part statement: one, that technology will have been deployed and is being assumed to be working properly; and two, that it's not working properly. I believe both will be true."

TRANSPARENCY TRUMPS PRIVACY ISSUES

PREDICTION: *As sensing, storage, and communication technologies get cheaper and better, individuals' public and private lives will become increasingly "transparent" globally. Everything will be more visible to everyone, with good and bad results. Looking at the big picture—at all of the lives affected on the planet in every way possible—this will make the world a better place by the year 2020. The benefits will outweigh the costs.*

Respondents' Reactions to This Scenario	
Agree	46%
Disagree	49%
Did not respond	5%

Note. Because results are based on a nonrandom sample, a margin of error cannot be computed.

CONSENSUS OF OPINION: Some level of privacy must be retained— there is disagreement over whether this should be by law or by social contract. There is an expectation that governments and corporations

will continue to escalate surveillance and "own" access to information; the powerful and privileged will find growing transparency more to their advantage than others in society.

This was the proposed future that finished closest to a dead heat in regard to the agree/disagree percentages. "We will continue to have very mixed opinions about the effects of transparency and the loss of privacy, just as we do today," predicted **Gary Chapman**, director of The 21st Century Project at the LBJ School of Public Affairs at the University of Texas–Austin. "These mixed opinions are likely to intensify, meaning that there will be passionate extremes on both sides of the issue." In this 2006 survey, while the answers were nearly evenly divided, the passion was most deeply expressed by those who disagreed with the scenario. Those who agreed generally hedged their agreement with qualifications indicating that the world would have to find ways to deal with privacy issues. "Things have never been private anyway," wrote writer and teacher **Douglas Rushkoff**. "The most important thing about transparency is it shows how transparent things have already been all along to the institutions that mean to control them."

Several top leaders of the Internet groups surveyed took the view that in a transparent world, the benefits will outweigh the costs, but they noted that privacy must also be protected in some manner, formal or informal.

"I generally agree," wrote Internet Society Chairman **Fred Baker**. "However, privacy remains important, so I tend to think that we will find ways to limit the invasion of it. Data-mining techniques and other kinds of analysis will make the globe more similar to a small town than it is now, in much the same way that the deployment of the Internet has pushed the development of McLuhan's global village. One characteristic of a small town is that 'everybody knows everybody's business,' which is to say that gossip and other activities betray confidences and otherwise invade the privacy of the people in the town. That will be one side of the global village."

Thomas Narten of IBM, who also works as the Internet Engineering Task Force liaison to ICANN, wrote, "I generally agree, but legislation will be needed (and is probably inevitable) to curb abuses. The incentives for abuse are simply too great."

Glenn Ricart, a member of the Internet Society Board of Trustees, wrote, "There *will* be higher degrees of transparency, but this will arise from a change in social norms and ultimately come from voluntary compliance...Look at taking cell-phone calls. A decade ago, no one would have interrupted a personal conversation to answer a ringing desk telephone. Today, however, people provide lots of transparency into their lives by answering their cell phones anywhere and everywhere. It's being done so often that it's becoming culturally acceptable. And, even if you don't answer your phone, it's still OK to SMS someone even while your attention was assumed to be elsewhere. IM 'away' messages and more...all make me believe that people will continue to surrender certain parts of their privacy for what they perceive to be benefits of interaction. However, I'm a staunch believer that we need to retain the 'off' button. People should be able to opt out of transparency, and I believe they will do so increasingly as a form of vacation or holiday or decompression. Some new name will attach to this phenomenon. ('Turning-off'?)"

> "Between 'agree' and 'disagree,' I'll pick 'agree,' but I think it's more accurate to say it *could* make the world a better place overall. The difference between the Open Society and the police state is political, not technological."
>
> —Seth Finkelstein,
> anticensorship activist and programmer; author of the Infothought blog; EFF Pioneer Award winner

Matthew Allen, president of the Association of Internet Researchers and a professor at Curtin University in Australia, tackled today's definition of the concept of privacy in the world's democracies. "Privacy has been asserted as a right within the modern Western paradigm that has come to dominate our perceptions of what 'ought' to be," he wrote. "In fact, privacy is not a right but a state of engagement with the world. Technologies that interlink people (whether they be telephones, ships, or computing and the Internet) bring people into proximity and thus into a realm of less privacy."

Australian Internet pioneer **Ian Peter** wrote, "The benefits are enormous in enabling communication across an interconnected planet. The potential problems this may give rise to in areas such as privacy do need to be addressed carefully,

> **"The trick is not to do anything you're ashamed of."**
>
> —Bob Metcalfe,
> Ethernet inventor;
> founder of 3Com Corporation;
> former CEO of InfoWorld; now a
> venture capitalist and partner in
> Polaris Venture Partners

though, and the benefits will only be as great as our governments and societal attitudes allow. If we do not learn to behave more compassionately and sensibly as global citizens, no amount of connectivity will make up for this (although it may help to bring it about)."

Chris Sorek—former director of global communications for Red Crescent and Red Cross, now with SAP—wrote, "Without transparency, there can be no 'level playing field'; competitive and open environments build economies and communities. This, in turn, enables everyone to have a fair chance to succeed and prosper." **Tiffany Shlain**, founder of the Webby Awards, wrote, "Giving all people access to information and a context to understand it will lead to an advancement in our civilization."

And **Christopher Johnson**, cofounder and CEO for ifPeople, wrote, "I am optimistic about the ability of the public to maintain control of the information that is generated, despite the current trend in secretive government information control. If the public has control, the benefits will outweigh the costs. If powerful groups have control and use of the information, it will further greed, discrimination, and infringement of privacy."

PLENTY OF PESSIMISM ABOUT PROSPECTS FOR TRANSPARENCY

Some respondents expressed deep concerns about losses of privacy; naturally, many of them are deeply attuned to the issues involved because they represent civil-liberties organizations.

The answer was a clear "disagree" for **Marc Rotenberg**, executive director of the Electronic Privacy Information Center. "The cost of unlimited transparency will not simply be privacy," he wrote. "It will be autonomy, freedom, and individuality. The personal lives of prisoners are transparent. So, too, is the world of the Borg." **Sharon Lane**, president of WebPageDesign, was also forceful in her reply. "It will NOT be a better world," she wrote. "It will be an Orwellian world! The benefits most certainly will not outweigh the costs."

Robin Gross, executive director of IP Justice, a civil liberties organization that promotes balanced intellectual property law, wrote, "The cost to privacy will be greater than we expect." **Barry Wellman**, a researcher on virtual communities and workplaces and the director of NetLab at the University of Toronto, responded, "The less one is powerful, the more transparent his or her life. The powerful will remain much less transparent." **Lisa Kamm**, an IT professional who has worked for IBM and the ACLU, wrote, "Privacy should remain a critical value and a right, and while there are benefits that come with increased transparency, they do not outweigh the costs."

Alejandro Pisanty, vice chairman of the board for ICANN and a member of the UN Working Group for Internet Governance, built his own scenario: "Transparency builds a much-worse world, at the expense of privacy and security. The benefits will not, or hardly, outweigh the costs. The situation will be dramatically worse in societies (countries or not) in which democratic governance is weak."

> "There are bad guys out there ready to exploit these vulnerabilities. There may be a giant technical step backward caused by privacy concerns."
>
> —Gwynne Kostin,
> director of Web communications,
> U.S. Homeland Security

Forecaster and strategist **Paul Saffo**, director of The Institute for the Future, said the scenario is "a utopian overstatement." He explained, "It underestimates the intrinsic flaws in the technology, and the capacity of clever people to subvert the system for selfish ends. The sensor society will be a mixed bag of real benefits and real cost in terms of lost freedoms. That said, we must press for transparency at every opportunity. The only way to control Big Brother is for all the little brothers to watch back. The most we can hope is that we will be able to find a reasonable balance between privacy and the need to know."

Michael Cannella, a member of Computer Professionals for Social Responsibility and an IT manager for Volunteers of America, wrote, "This 'transparency' will result in loss of liberty and privacy for individuals but will not give the individual human any more information about nor control over the consolidation of power in nongovernmental hands, such as multinational corporations. This will partially be a result of misinterpretation (by governments already beholden to these powers' and their interests) of the power of free markets to maximize all possible goods (including social and cultural). This outlook ignores the reality of collusion, market manipulation, and other limitations; overlooks the power money holds over politics (bribery, lobbying); forgets our historical lessons about relying on the 'invisible hand of the market' and the strengths of putting other values before money in market management."

MANY EXPECT THE INFORMATION WILL OFTEN FLOW JUST ONE WAY

Some respondents reflexively mentioned "Big Brother" and *1984* in their answers in reference to George Orwell's dystopian novel. Most just predicted that transparency will not be equitably applied. **Esther Dyson** of CNET, founding director of ICANN, wrote, "The world is not average, and the benefits and costs will not be evenly distributed." **Alex Halavais**, an Internet researcher and professor at Quinnipiac University, responded, "Recent events seem to indicate that reciprocal transparency is hardly an obvious future." **Suely Fragoso**, a professor at Unisinos in Brazil, wrote, "I do not believe everyone will be under the surveillant eye. Those...in the hidden corners that the panoptical eye cannot reach will have great advantages over the majority living 'transparent' lives (independently of them having chosen to do so or not)."

Denzil Meyers, founder and president of Widgetwonder, responded, "The general populace will have the experience noted above, but there are always ways to commit subterfuge for those who are so motivated. We will get lulled into a sense of false security and transparency, allowing the unethical to operate even more quietly than they do now; corporations will be the biggest offenders/danger."

> "Certain groups that have maintained secrecy to guard their power (shamans, governments that are autocratic or kleptocratic, criminals) will continue to do so. There may be double bookkeeping of sorts: a private face and record, and a supposedly open and transparent spin for public scrutiny."
>
> —Steve Cisler,
> former senior library scientist for Apple; now working on public-access projects in Guatemala, Ecuador, and Uganda

And **Michelle Catlett** of Edubuilder wrote, "The loss of individual privacy will be controlled by the companies and governments that can afford to utilize the massive resources to manipulate the information. This won't be used to benefit the individual. Transparency isn't going to be 'two-way': individuals will not have access to information about governments or large companies in the same way."

Joe Bishop, a vice president with Marratech AB, wrote, "The average person's life will become an open book to governmental agencies, financial service companies, etc. But the rich and powerful will always find ways to be less transparent." **Daniel Wang**, principal partner of Roadmap Associates, wrote, "With such widespread transparency, not only will privacy be sacrificed, but competitive edge will be dulled, especially for small- to medium-sized businesses. Only big businesses will have the capacity and resources to leverage transparency. And the keepers of the network will be the ultimate winners."

David Elesh, a sociology professor at Temple University, was one of several respondents to propose that people will be able to hide their information for a price or buy an identity. "What will happen," he wrote, "is that those who can afford to do so will create 'managed lives' to convey the impressions that they wish to. This is true now for a thin elite, but it will diffuse." **Hernando Rojas**, a Colombian and consultant for the UN Development Program, agreed: "Privacy becomes commodified, so yes, maybe more transparency, but not overall transparency."

In reaction to the prevailing assumption that those in power will try to escape being open to scrutiny, **John Browning**, cofounder of First Tuesday, a global network dedicated to entrepreneurs, wrote, "The global village metaphor holds true here. In villages, everybody knows everybody else's business. The security lies mainly in that, in a village, you know who's trying to find out about you. Governments and privacy advocates need to work to ensure mutual transparency."

THERE OUGHT TO BE A SOCIAL CONTRACT...
OR A BETTER TECHNOLOGY

Internet policy makers are already thinking along the lines Browning suggested in his response. **Robert Shaw**, Internet strategy and policy advisor for the International Telecommunication Union, said there will be a worldwide movement to protect privacy. "Privacy will be seen more and more as a basic human right," he wrote, "and there will be growing pressure to define this in an international instrument or convention and to have states enforce it through national legislation and regulation."

Marilyn Cade, CEO of MCADE and an active participant in Internet policy making, wrote, "We can devise a world that allows privacy, while also allowing transparency...Hiding the information about who has registered a domain name only

> "European and most other market economies have much stronger controls over the collection, use, and transfer of personal information... and the U.S. will increasingly move toward EU-style privacy protection, rather than the other way around. It will only take a few major incidents of theft of personal records and graphic stories about identity theft before voter outrage will compel Congress to pass strong privacy protection measures, over the strong objections of the U.S. business community."
>
> —Michael Conlin,
> former legislator, now
> an entrepreneur

makes it critical for law enforcement to have powers to investigate who that is. Making the data public, but limiting its use can achieve the goal of transparency...My personal perspective is that I want the choice. And I want it to be informed choice. So, we have some work to do to understand privacy in an always-on, always-connected world—and to devise informed choices."

Boing Boing blogger **Cory Doctorow**, an EFF Fellow, wrote, "Transparency and privacy aren't antithetical. We're perfectly capable of formulating widely honored social contracts that prohibit pointing telescopes through your neighbours' windows. We can likewise have social contracts about sniffing your neighbours' network traffic." And **Hal Varian** of Google and the University of California–Berkeley wrote, "Privacy is a thing of the past. Technologically it is obsolete. However, there will be social norms and legal barriers that will dampen out the worst excesses."

Robin Berjon, a technology developer working with the World Wide Web Consortium and Expway, wrote optimistically about the development of technology solutions to protect privacy: "I am convinced that as transparency becomes increasingly visible as an issue to the general public, solutions will be developed to handle the problems it causes, while at the same time maintaining as much as possible of the information infrastructure. This relies on a number of technologies such as identity, Web of trust, etc., that we have a crucial need to create very soon."

COSTS VERSUS BENEFITS, OPEN-SOURCE, AND WATCHDOG VALUE

Jeff Hammond, a vice president with Rhea + Kaiser, responded, "There will be clashes of sensibilities as we already witness with global access to every story or point of view as it happens. This will not change. A cost: A new sensibility of tolerance may emerge that homogenizes individual choices and responsibilities, as information is no longer a practical means of achieving competitive advantage over another. A benefit for some, a cost for others: Most individuals will

> "I worry about a system with too much public-domain info about individuals. It will limit the type of people who enter politics to those who grew up in convents and abbeys."
>
> —James Schultz,
> principal partner, Pretty Good Consulting; Institute for Work and the Economy

remain anonymous by virtue of the plainness of their lives. In this sense, the ego drive of the individual may push many more toward a supernatural domain for expressing their individualness. A benefit: The mass of humanity will still look to the 'performers and portrayers' who embrace the cost of having every movement being documented, tracked, and paid attention to. A benefit: If the cost also includes that all individual human ego must be subordinated to the mass sense of equality, then any temporary benefit will be outweighed by the loss of the adaptability embodied in billions of individual egos trying out ideas.'"

Daniel Conover, new-media developer for Evening Post Publishing, responded, "The future of intrusive informatic systems will allow participants in private corporate Internets access to all sorts of wonders, but their lives will be wide open to paying vendors. Most people will choose this lifestyle and will continue to choose this lifestyle so long as the tradeoff between 'smart suggestions' and 'intrusiveness' breaks in their favor. Most people will not care to look back through the glass so long as their luxuries and entertainments continue to flow in ever-improving streams. Meanwhile, on the open-source side of the culture, two-way transparency will change expectations of privacy and public life. Some aspects of life will become more guarded, and laws will require that specific permission be granted before certain types of information can be added to the data stream (think HIPAA). Most Americans, however, will trade waivers of those privacy rights for 'better' products and free access to media. And while open-source culture will be a minority culture, it will include a vibrant mediascape. Because of its innovative and creative power, the two-way transparency of the open-source networks will continue to influence the larger culture, even as expressed in the proprietary nets."

Lynn Schofield Clark, director of the Teens and the New Media @ Home Project, predicted that viable oversight groups will continue to be vital to the successful protection of privacy in the coming years of increasing transparency. "I am not sure that we as a society will place enough value on this watchdog role to underwrite the costs to continue to pursue lengthy investigations and legal action. It is incumbent on those of us in education and public life to continue to place a value on this watchdog and investigative role...and to continue to push for increased accountability structures, understanding that these must be continually updated so as to keep pace with the changes that technology allows."

> "We are facing a tidal wave of new thought on this issue. That is, people who are now, and will be coming into their maturity in the next 15 years, live in a very different technological environment, and the old meanings of such concepts as privacy are rapidly changing. Younger people seem to be less concerned with keeping private things private!"
>
> —Martin Kwapinski,
> senior content manager for
> FirstGov, the U.S. government's
> official Web portal

THE STATUS OF SURVEILLANCE TODAY

Our lives are being recorded in various ways today. Your cell phone is a tracking device. Your personal life and financial status are recorded in various databases. Anyone in the world can find out the tax-assessed value of your home with a 10-second Internet search. And, with the further development of "IP on everything"—the concept that people and goods will be tagged and trackable on the network through the use of sensors—things are becoming more complex and more transparent simultaneously.

Thanks to their growing adoption by retailers (such as Wal-Mart) and government agencies (such as the U.S. Department of Defense), the number of radio frequency ID (RFID) tags in use across the world is already numbered in the billions. The fairly inexpensive, nearly invisible devices are used as a means to improve efficiency. The devices can be used to track inventory, equipment, and personnel; they may replace bar codes. One estimate finds that corporations making RFID devices will make more than $24 billion a year by 2016.

At this point in their development, the information that is captured or transmitted by these tiny devices has little or no security—no screens or firewalls. A report released by researchers at Vrije University in Amsterdam in March 2006 raised concerns that RFID tags might be altered without a user's knowledge and utilized as a transmission medium for computer viruses, noting that the limited storage buffer of such tags (ranging from 90 to 100 bytes) could allow bad code a place to lurk and then enter the network.

A bigger concern is the surveillance applications implicit in the devices. In late May, the U.S. Department of Homeland Security issued a 15-page draft report that expresses concerns over the potential use of RFID in identification cards or tokens for illegal tracking of people. "Miners or firefighters might be appropriately identified using RFID because speed of identification is at a premium in dangerous situations," the report reads, "...but for other applications related to human beings, RFID appears to offer little benefit when compared to the consequences it brings for privacy and data integrity."

Bills regulating RFID tags have been proposed in at least 19 states, and Wisconsin passed a law that took effect in June stipulating that no person may force another to have a microchip implanted in his body. Several nations have begun to embed RFID devices in passports—the U.S. has tested this and is implementing it this summer and fall, despite complaints that the passports can be "read" by anyone with special equipment from 30 feet away.

Concerns have been raised because, at this point, it is easy to steal or modify data contained on most RFID chips. It is expected the RFID signals sent by U.S. passports will be encrypted (Newitz, 2006).

THE INTERNET IS NO LONGER A PRIVATE, BORDERLESS NETWORK

The governments of China and other nondemocratic nations are exerting more controls and surveillance all the time over the Internet—once considered to be a perfect conduit for anonymous communications. This is explained extremely well and in great detail in the book, *Who Controls the Internet?* by law professors Jack Goldsmith and Tim Wu. In it, they write, "[China] is trying to create an Internet that is free enough to support and maintain the world's fastest growing economy yet closed enough to tamp down political threats to its monopoly on power" (Goldsmith & Wu, 2005, p. 89).

They cite the example of Liu Du, a 22-year-old university student whose 2002 online essay, "How a national security apparatus can hurt national security," caused her to be jailed in a cell with a convicted murderer. When concerned supporters protested on her behalf, five of them were arrested. Liu Du was held for a year and released, but she is not allowed to leave Beijing, she is not allowed to speak to foreign journalists, and she is now under permanent surveillance. Alaa Seif al-Islam was arrested in May 2005 for protesting the beating of women at a prodemocracy rally in Cairo. Seif al-Islam is still in jail, and at least six additional bloggers were arrested for protesting Egyptian government policies in May 2006 (Williams, 2006, p. A10).

China reportedly employs as many as 50,000 Internet investigators who conduct online surveillance, erasing commentary, blocking sites, and authorizing the arrests of people for any communication that is seen to be unpatriotic. In addition, it has begun to employ thousands of university students as volunteer Internet monitors—the project is named "Let the Winds of a Civilized Internet Blow," and it is part of a broader "socialist morality" campaign, known as the Eight Honors and Disgraces (French, 2006). Records from a court case in China showed that Yahoo may have been involved in identifying the e-mail account of a dissident writer; Reporters Without Borders announced in April that this is at least the third incident of this type involving Yahoo. Google cofounder Sergey Brin acknowledged in June that his company has compromised its principles by accommodating censorship demands from the Chinese government. Brin told reporters in Washington, DC, that Google agreed to the censorship only after Chinese authorities blocked its service. The popular search service is now accessible only through the censored site Google.cn (Bridis, 2006).

China is not the only nation convincing people to participate in voluntary spy service. In another instance of a government recruiting people as active participants in surveillance, Texas governor Rick Perry announced a $5 million plan in June to install hundreds of night-vision cameras along the Mexican border, run live the video feeds on the Internet, and encourage anyone with a computer who spots illegal immigrants trying to enter the U.S. to call a toll-free number and turn them in—it is called a "virtual posse."

In these and other less public cases, governments and corporations are working—sometimes in league with one another—to spy on people, some of whom are being arrested and jailed. In order to convince Internet companies to help, in many cases (China for one) governments threaten a loss of access (this equates to a loss of corporate income) if the companies do not follow their wishes in regard to censorship, the sharing of the personal computing records of protesters, and the sending of "tracing" packets out on the network to identify the location of wanted users.

Filtering, network-tracing technology, and geo-identification were developed to help all nations fight online fraud and other crimes, to help certain nations retain their cultural identity (France is a leader in this regard), and to help corporations and other groups share information selectively on a regional level. Goldsmith and Wu (2006) wrote in *Who Controls the Internet?* that the firewalling of nations is becoming more sophisticated as the newest Internet geo-ID technologies are allowing companies to tailor content by geography and avoid sending content to places where it is not legal.

CORPORATE CONTROL OVER DATA IS AN ISSUE EVERYWHERE

Surveillance issues are not limited to nondemocratic nations. In a May 2006 preliminary discussion, the FBI suggested that U.S. Internet providers consider putting the storage capacity in place to retain their customers' Web-use records for up to 2 years in order to aid investigations into terrorism, child pornography, and other crimes. FBI and U.S. Department of Justice officials met formally with top Internet executives from Google, Microsoft, AOL, and other companies in an initial discussion of the request. At this point in time, Internet companies generally keep such information as sites visited, e-mail contacts, and downloads

> *Predictions from respondents who chose to remain anonymous:*
>
> "There will be an anonymity backlash online, and people will endorse a surveillance society with the idea that so long as everyone's activities are accessible, nobody's being violated."
>
> "By 2020, people will probably be required to have automated everything...I don't see this as a positive thing."

for a period of a few days to a few weeks, and the government generally does not have any access to these records. Internet providers have cooperated by opening records in specific government investigations of pornography and terrorist activity when subpoenaed in the past.

Earlier this year, the Department of Justice and National Security Agency were heavily criticized by privacy proponents for allegedly requesting access from U.S. companies to the phone and Internet records of virtually all U.S. customers.

U.S. law currently holds that court orders can be issued to require Internet companies to turn over records when they have them, but the Internet records needed to prove a case are generally erased before they are of use in court.

In March, Google was ordered by a U.S. District Court to give the U.S. government a randomly generated selection of 50,000 indexed Web sites to test Internet filters. The Department of Justice had originally asked for several months of keywords and search results; Google refused, spurring the court action that led to a reduced request, but one that was fulfilled.

Many threats to privacy have been initiated in response to the 9/11 attacks on New York and Washington. For instance, the U.S. Information Awareness Office (IAO) was established by the Defense Advanced Research Projects Agency in 2003 to apply information technology to preserve national security.

Through its Total Information Awareness program, it was expected to aggregate data and mine it to identify potential terror threats. After privacy concerns killed the IAO soon after it was formed, some aspects of the TIA program were reassigned to other government agencies, where they still exist.

Security expert Bruce Schneier goes so far as to say that thanks to corporate self-interest and greed, individuals do not really "own" their computers—the companies providing the software and hardware and Internet access do. He wrote in a recent column for *Wired* that "external control systems" influence your use of the Internet, pointing out that adware, automatic software updates, digital-rights-management technologies, and Google Desktop Search are examples "of some other company trying to own your computer." He adds, "There is enormous political and economic power behind the idea that you shouldn't truly own your computer or your software, despite having paid for it" (2006).

> *Predictions from respondents who chose to remain anonymous:*
>
> **"Rich people will be able to shield their data, at a price. Poor people will exchange their privacy for services. They'll be open books."**
>
> **"Watch teens and their style of computing—you see a future generation that questions our need for privacy."**

Data exposure makes headlines weekly and nearly daily, as personally sensitive data collections stored in corporate and government databases and on digital media are lost or stolen on a regular basis. In a famous example, privacy advocates made public the Social Security numbers of then-representative Tom Delay and Florida governor Jeb Bush, both found easily online on county Web sites.

Sometimes the data is not stolen or lost by accident. Many companies have been caught sharing it for a profit. Gratis, a Washington-based company, was sued in March 2006 by the state of New York for selling the personal information of millions of people to e-mail marketers.

ADDITIONAL RESPONSES

Many other survey respondents shared comments tied to the scenario asking, does transparency build a better world despite the loss of privacy? Among them:

> "Imagine a scenario where everything about you is presented in stats: (a) 55% probability of Mr. X being bald by 30 years, (b) 40% probability of Type II Diabetes by 40 years, (c) 80% probability of being suicidal. Would you want designed babies? (Wonder if you shall be able to relate to them like your parents to you!) Would you want the System to know everything you've done since the day you were born? Would you like to be File AK-IND-79? Would you want to be in the *Minority Report* world?" —**Alik Khanna**, Smart Analyst Inc., a business employing financial analysts in India

> "Privacy will become a luxury, not a right. It will be 'transparent' who the have-nots are." —**Kerri Karvetski**, freelance writer and advocacy specialist

> "We are headed towards control by those who control the technology. We are headed towards losing autonomy and privacy. These trends will be justified by appeals to our fears." —**Benjamin Ben-Baruch**, senior market intelligence consultant and applied sociologist, Aquent, General Motors, Eastern Michigan University

> "I agree, but the black market of hacker services to erase or change some personal information will be an option too." —**Mario Rios**, TDCLA (Tecnologías del Conocimiento, an e-learning group), Chile

> "The global statement that 'everything will be more visible to everyone' is extreme. But the value of the system knowing your preferences and activities will definitely moderate people's interest in keeping everything private and will incent users to want the system to store and act on private information. The issue will be much more about controlling the use of private information and learning a new set of rules for respecting individual interests in such an integrated environment." —**Stewart Alsop**, investor and analyst; former editor of InfoWorld and Fortune columnist

"Transparency does indeed build a better world. However, the statement needs to be qualified, since the same technology allows the dissemination of propaganda on a vast scale. Society needs to understand that successful communities are based on trust—trust in leadership, trust in information, trust in neighbours. Technology must be developed to reinforce that trust."
—**Adrian Schofield**, head of research for ForgeAhead, South Africa; leader in the World Information Technology and Services Alliance (WITSA)

"Yes, there will be greater transparency in some areas (especially in the short to medium term). However, technologies to create privacy/observation will also be developed as a response. The world will not necessarily be a better place—in place of secrecy, there will be massive information pollution. That is, finding relevant and correct information will be difficult due to the large amount of irrelevant and incorrect information around." —**Bruce Edmonds**, Centre for Policy Modelling, Manchester Metropolitan University, U.K.

"What do you mean 'better'? The marginalized will be even more marginal and those people with genetic 'defects' will not have health care available unless rich. Conformity will be de rigeur because any deviation will be noted in the nets, even nonparticipation will be something that will be data-mineable." —**Alec MacLeod**, associate professor, California Institute of Integral Studies

"The collection of information does not automatically translate to a loss of personal privacy. I don't believe the perceived erosion of privacy is a data-collection issue. I think it's more of a reflection of the general erosion of trust in public and business institutions, and the fact that legal guidelines are often years behind the abilities of current technologies. The primary threat to privacy is not due to technological advances; its more attributable to the erosion of ethical principals. Yes, technology might allow me to read someone else's mail. However, I don't do that because I know it's not right." —**Robert Lunn**, Focalpoint Analytics; senior research analyst on the 2004 Digital Future Report

"The costs unseen will outweigh the benefits perceived. Included in those unseen costs is an emphasis on 'sameness' for fear of being perceived as different, fueled by increasing government intrusion into private lives." —**Michael Castengera**, teacher and consultant, Grady College of Journalism, University of Georgia; Media Strategies and Tactics, Inc.

"Transparency is likely to good for the society only if the ability to peruse the collected information is evenly distributed. Given that data mining is likely to remain relatively expensive, increasing transparency is likely to shift power even more towards those that have more power already now. A crucial aspect would be to empower people to control and 'correct' any information collected about them. This is currently a pressing problem in the U.S., and a potential problem also in the EU." —**Pekka Nikander**, Ericcson Research, Helsinki Institute for Information Technology; past member of the Internet Architecture Board

"I agree that 'public and private lives will become increasingly "transparent" globally,' but I disagree that the benefits will outweigh the costs. Once lost, personal privacy is difficult to reclaim." —**Scott Hollenbeck**, director of technology, VeriSign; active director, Internet Engineering Task Force

"I disagree only because the statement is worded with such certainty. I think this issue is very much up in the air. I don't subscribe to very much technological determinacy—what humans do with the tools they find themselves using will matter. And unpredictable events will matter. If the Chinese model of censorship at the level of the router proves viable and is adopted worldwide, then the asymmetry of transparency will greatly favor centralized state powers. Will they use it in democratic ways?" —**Howard Rheingold**, Internet sociologist and author

"It's often said that the desire for privacy is a mile wide…and an inch deep. Everyone wants it, but few are willing to give up anything—e.g., access to credit, credit cards, etc.—to get it. We lost our 'privacy' as soon as government and company agents learned how to keep citizen and personnel records. What's important is to make sure that the government and corporate leaders have no more privacy than private citizens and employees! People don't want to a phone's caller-ID to give their identity to anyone they're calling. But they want to see who's calling them on their bedroom phone. They can't have it both ways. We lost our privacy to computers, the first time the neighborhood gossip got online. A case can be made for the proposition that, increasing lack of privacy has BEN-EFITTED diversity and tolerance. After all, when you know that 20% (or 80%!) of the others in your community are doing something, it becomes more acceptable." —**Jim Warren**, Internet pioneer; founding editor of *Dr. Dobb's Journal*; technology policy advocate and activist; futurist

"It is hard to say—tremendous amounts of pure trash flow within the Net and other communications systems. On the other hand, it allows people to verify information much quicker than anytime in human history. In a very complex, ever-changing world, the individual will have a much harder time creating a world view and be ever so more jealous of keeping it once created. All information will be filtered to support the world-view armor and thus, even though the information is out there, it will not be accessed. Overflow of information creates anxiety, not knowledge. Fear and ignorance are the cornerstones of hatred; ignorance can be overcome by information technologies, but not the fear—and the rapidly changing world will exacerbate the fear." —**Amos Davidowitz**, director of education, training, and special programs for Institute of World Affairs; Association for Progressive Education

"The truth(s) shall set you free?" —**Tunji Lardner**, CEO for the West African NGO network: wangonet.org; agendaconsulting.biz; consultant to the UNDP African Internet Initiative

"I might be more sanguine about a transparent society if the current U.S. political climate were less threatening." —**Reva Basch**, consultant for Aubergine Information Systems

"I think that privacy will remain important to people all over the world, but they will have many more choices as to what they are public about. Information will be more readily available, but as those windows into personal information are opened, new gates and barriers will be designed. So while a lot will be more visible to everyone, it won't be 'everything.'" —**Michael Gorrell**, senior VP and CIO, EBSCO

"My largest issue with this prediction is that it smacks of the phrase, 'Those who have nothing to hide have nothing to fear.' We wear clothes for a reason; there are some things we shouldn't know about each other and which, for our own mental health, should remain private. Unless one's intent is to be an all-knowledgeable god, having access to the 'what' doesn't necessarily give you access to the 'why.' The fallacy is that by using your network to find out what I've bought that you automatically think you know WHY I bought it. For example, was he just buying fertilizer for my farm, or was he building a weapon?" —**William Kearns**, assistant professor, University of South Florida

"While there may be more transparency, it is not clear that this will always be a better world because of it. The world will be better, but there needs to be continual protection and advocacy of privacy." —**Jim Archuleta**, senior manager, government solutions, Ciena Corporation

"People will have less privacy, but may regain anonymity through the sheer volume of data. There will be conflicts with people/groups who wish to use knowledge to control and people who wish to expand their capacity to choose." —**Willis Marti**, associate director for networking, Texas A&M University

"I agree only if a new radical democratic politics emerges which removes the risks of such transparency, such as not being disadvantaged because of sexual preferences." —**Mark Poster**, professor of film and media studies, University of California–Irvine

"Governments can already do it. Wider transparency will serve as a check on governments and on business." —**John S. Quarterman**, president, InternetPerils, Inc.

"Technology will only make the world a better place if it can also allow us to solve the more important problems of overpopulation, imbalanced distribution of resources, and global warming." —**Cliff Figallo**, online communities architect, SociAlchemy

"The 'little village' notion of privacy is attractive, but unproven. While I'm quite comfortable with it, I'm not sure that the world will be interconnected enough in the next 13 years to make this happen effectively and positively." —**Ross Rader**, director of research and innovation, Tucows, Inc.

"The phenomenon of social computing tears down geopolitical boundaries and this helps open up dialogue between nations and religions. Racism in the U.S. is greatly reduced as individuals find common bonds, but a new rift becomes unavoidable from an economic lens, as the retirement of the baby boomers has exhausted the nation's resources." —**Peter Kim**, senior analyst, marketing strategy and technology team, Forrester Research

"Of course, there will be winners and losers. Information about individuals may threaten some individual liberties." —**Rashid Bashshur**, director of telemedicine, University of Michigan

"A revolution will occur pushing this type of knowledge of an individual out for a number of years. As a result, it may happen, but it is unlikely that it will happen before 2020." —**Mike McCarty**, chief network officer, Johns Hopkins

"Answer is almost a test of optimism versus pessimism. Individualized GPS means that we will be less likely to die lost in a frozen tundra—however, we will not be able to 'get lost' for awhile either. Fudging or embellishing our past will become more difficult as video and digital records are available to show actual events, not transmitted stored memory with negative or positive enhancements that are common to the human psyche." —**Ed Lyell**, pioneer in issues regarding Internet and education; professor at Adams State College

"Yes, just as many people (myself included) have no interest whatsoever in reading the 'blogs' of other persons, almost all of whom lead very dull lives, so, too, will a high degree of 'transparency' about who's doing what with whom will soon tire most people. Until just a few weeks ago, practically no school or university in Brazil ran censoring software on the institutions' main server, the belief being that if adolescents have free access to pornographic sites, they quickly discover just how dull that type of content can be, and they, of their own volition, soon stop visiting such sites. Prohibiting access to pornographic sites only stimulates surreptitious procurement of them. Unfortunately, legislation requiring such censoring in educational institutions has just been introduced into the Brazilian Congress and may even stand a chance of being approved, which would reduce transparency and augment negative behavior patterns." —**Fredric M. Litto**, professor, University of Sao Paulo, Brazil

"The analog here is credit information. People give up some personal privacy for the convenience of more convenient or automated transactions." —**Robert Kraut**, Human-Computer Interaction Institute, Carnegie Mellon University

"Giving all people access to information and a context to understand it will lead to an advancement in our civilization." —**Tiffany Shlain**, filmmaker; founder and ambassador of the Webby Awards

"This is an illusion typical for Stalinist totalitarians and their contemporary followers from post-democratic, Bush-era USA. Bush administration is known for their Orwellian dreams of total surveillance, tortures, and concentration camps to keep people in detention without any form of judicial trial, but for people such ideas give no advantages over privacy, truth, and democracy." —**Wladyslaw Majewski**, OSI CompuTrain SA, ISOC Polska

"Without transparency there can be no 'level playing field'; competitive and open environments build economies and communities. This, in turn, enables everyone to have a fair chance to succeed and prosper." —**Chris Sorek**, senior vice president of public communications, SAP

"Privacy is already highly compromised and, in the name of the 'greater good,' no doubt will continue to be so. How we manage our privacy and rights to redress misuse and error in data collected/filed/misused/abused etc., is a critical issue to be continually monitored and redressed locally and globally; a set of digital 'human rights' will need to be formed perhaps. That said, I do prescribe to the school of thought that says if I don't want something I do/say to become public, then I really shouldn't do it." —**Cheryl Langdon-Orr**, independent Internet business operator; director, ISOC-Australia

"Disagree. Privacy will be seen more and more as a basic human right and there will be growing pressure to define this in an international instrument or convention and to have states enforce it through national legislation and regulation." —**Robert Shaw**, Internet strategy and policy advisor, International Telecommunication Union

"It is true that lives will likely become more 'transparent.' Primary amongst the pros is the fact that corruption and corrupt practices (be it at the governmental or corporate level) could be severely affected by more transparent lives. What does concern me, though is, the expense of privacy—it may take a bit of the fun out of life." —**Rajnesh D. Singh**, PATARA Communications & Electronics Ltd., Avon Group, GNR Consulting, ISOC Pacific Islands

"This one is hard to disagree with—there can be many advantages to having this transparency for many individuals. And in many ways, this is happening, certainly on the Internet and the Web, but even at brick and mortar stores. Time is certainly something that people value (and often lack), and transparency can save time, but most people are unwilling to give up privacy to save time, and I expect legislation to be enacted to further define and protect our privacy should we desire it." —**Philip Joung**, Spirent Communications

"This is clearly a trend. But there are checks and balances built into our societies that will mitigate more extreme forms of transparency; I believe these will cause the net result to be positive in most cases, the majority of the time." —**Peter Roll**, retired chief system administrator

"I think we'll have not so much transparency (though it would be desirable) as wrenching and scandalous revelations. Look at the NSA wiretapping scandal that broke in December 2005. Echelon was publicly revealed as far back as 1998 (perhaps even earlier), and *The New York Times* knew of George W. Bush's secret orders in late 2004, but there was no transparency and very little public debate. But truth will out, and modern electronic media allow it to spread faster and be harder to suppress once the spark flies. The cycle of secrecy and scandal could prove very disruptive." —**Andy Oram**, writer and editor for O'Reilly Media

"Privacy is a chimera, and has been for some time. The major problem isn't just sensing, storage, and communication technology, but rather faulty software and operating systems, a 'trusting' Internet, the susceptibility of innocent users to social engineering, and at its core 'bad guys' who exploit known weaknesses for thrill or profit." —**Joel Hartman**, CIO, University of Central Florida

"It will be a tradeoff between benefits and loss of privacy/freedom." —**Terry Irving**, producer, CNN

"Those who choose to retain a large degree of privacy will do so only at loss of connectivity with the community. Opt-in choices will be ubiquitous." —**Charles Hendricksen**, research collaboration architect, Cedar Collaboration

"This is difficult, but I think that overall transparency is a positive. It will be interesting to see if the line of what is public or private gets redrawn (or retrenched). Blogs are probably the greatest example—tell someone 15 years ago that they would write their diary in public every day and they'd laugh. Well, guess what happened!" —**Andy Williamson**, managing director for Wairua Consulting Limited, New Zealand; a member of the NZ government's Digital Strategy Advisory Group

"The most striking thing will be the change in our perception of what is private, or an infringement of that privacy." —**Florian Schlichting**, PhD candidate and researcher, University College, London

"While I do believe that more will be known about individuals, it will only be divulged and used by a 'trusted' authority who will use the information gained for the benefit of those affected. People will voluntarily consent to allowing certain information (probably in conjunction with the service they subscribe to) regarding their likes and dislikes, preferences, etc., to be gathered—but, as I said, only within the bounds predefined by them and held in trust by an entity renowned for trust. In so doing, they should expect to benefit from better rates for insurance, healthcare, buying leverage, etc." —**Don Heath**, board member, iPool, Brilliant Cities, Inc., Diversified Software, Alcatel, Foretec

"Automatic and compulsory transparency holds more dangers than benefits, because of essentially uncontrollable possibilities of criminal, terroristic, and governmental misuse." —**Gisela Redeker**, professor, University of Groningen, The Netherlands

"Better for control junkies? What about respect for individualism?" —**Mike Gill**, electronics engineer, National Library of Medicine

"Eliminating privacy changes human culture in such extreme ways that (1) 2020 is much too early for such a change to be in effect; (2) we have no idea whether this will be better or worse. Part of the issue here is that technology changes much faster than culture does. Culture requires generations to pass because it needs new members to grow up with new assumptions. This is the essence of the clash between culture and technology." —**Karen Coyle**, information professional and librarian

"Strong disagree." —**Leigh Estabrook**, professor, University of Illinois

"The open conversation on the Internet is a good thing. But the individual should have more control over the amount of personal information that is disclosed." —**W. Reid Cornwell**, director, The Center for Internet Research

"There will, however, be a similar rise in the ability to carefully protect certain aspects of your own information. Cryptography will become a huge business." —**Tama Leaver**, lecturer in digital communication, University of Western Australia

"There are few technologies out there not willing to be exploited for commercial means—and if even ethical companies draw boundaries for privacy, there will be plenty of companies unconcerned about such scruples." —**Jon Bonné**, MSNBC.com columnist

"I fully agree on this issue. Transparency is essential to rich and poor alike to avoid conflict." —**Prof. Lutfor Rahman**, executive director, Association for Advancement of Information Technology; vice-chancellor, Pundra University of Science and Technology, Bangladesh

"No, we will definitely find new ways to create opacity into the system. Certainly, a few people will have lots of information about us, but it certainly won't make 'everyone visible to everyone.'" —**Randy Kluver**, director, Institute for Pacific Asia at Texas A&M University

"Privacy is too fundamental a right to give up easily for the sake of transparency." —**B. van den Berg**, faculty of philosophy at Erasmus University, Rotterdam, The Netherlands

"'Transparency' cuts both ways. While I think it is very good that political and other public domains are becoming more transparent, protecting privacy of an individual should be made a priority in the context of a new technology-enabled 'transparency.'" —**Mirko Petric**, University of Zadar, Croatia

"As long as market forces are not given free rein, the benefits should outweigh the costs." —**Ben Detenber**, associate professor, Nanyang Technological University, Singapore

"Only if the private information that is collected actually become freely available. That means that corporations and governments would have to be willing to release the information they collect. I have my doubts that this will happen by 2020, as both corporations and governments view secretly held personal information as more valuable than completely free personal information. Corporations derive marketing and sales information from our personal data, and governments feel safer when their citizens do not know how much information is being collected about them." —**Scott Moore**, online community manager, Helen and Charles Schwab Foundation

"Loss of privacy is not better. I don't need my own software in the network that bad. Total connectivity is very, very bad for liberty." —**Edward Lee Lamoureux**, associate professor, Bradley University

"First: 14 years to make the world a better place is not a lot. Second: Transparency is one thing; information overload is another. Third: People will learn how to treat the Net and protect what they feel is important private information. So-called dysfunctions to a lot of software is exactly this kind of resistance: By not using the shared calendar, you easily avoid to be supervised by others." —**Torill Mortensen**, associate professor, Volda University College, Norway

"I believe that, increasingly, we will have the options on transparency. Most of the time, we opt for the 'providing more information.' But, sometimes not." —**Jim Jansen**, assistant professor, Penn State University

"I think that our online identities will grow to become an even more important part of our lives. A 'vanity search' will become absolutely necessary for anyone in a position of power. This development opens a plethora of opportunities for spin doctors and the like." —**Charlie Breindahl**, external lecturer, University of Copenhagen, IT University of Copenhagen

"Again, it is too easy to cook it down to better or worse. If the changes come as described here, some will win and some will lose. A total accounting is next to impossible." —**Rich Ling**, senior researcher and sociologist, Telenor Research Institute, Oslo, Norway

"People will continue to resist the erosion of privacy online. Corporations will be forced to conform to consumer demands in this area." —**Simon Woodside**, CEO, Semacode Corporation

"Transparency requires the concomitant skills and knowledge in terms of how to interpret and interact with the information that transparency creates. There is a crisis of learning at present, and if that is not addressed transparency will still remain a tool or surveillance for most." —**Jason Nolan**, associate professor, Ryerson University, Canada

"This is a hard call, but I wouldn't bet on the benefits outweighing the costs. Information is power, and power tends to concentrate—where one is in the food chain in 2020 will likely determine one's perspective on whether benefits really outweigh costs." —**Nan Dawkins**, cofounder, RedBoots Consulting

"Governmental and corporate interests benefit most from 'transparency' at the expense of individual privacy and the liberties that are integrated with those privacies. More transparency isn't always better—but a greater ability of individuals to exert control over the degree of self-transparency is better. The tradeoffs—e.g., ongoing abuse of degrees of anonymity to take advantage of others—will continue as it does now." —**Patrick B. O'Sullivan**, director of the Center for Teaching and Learning, Illinois State University

"I only hope that the 'transparency' will not be an instrument of control by governments, politicians and big businesses." —**Lilia Efimova**, researcher, Telematica Instituut, The Netherlands

"Privacy will be more selective (area specific) and become a lifestyle choice. Most people will not care and simply accept having every aspect of their lives open and catered to capital." —**Ted M. Coopman**, activist; social-science researcher; instructor, University of Washington–Seattle; member of Association of Internet Researchers board of directors

"Not everything will be transparent to everyone. In fact, while lots more true and previously hidden info will be out there, there will also be a lot of mistaken info as well. I can't say we'll be that much better off because of it. A little, yes, but not enough to agree strongly." —**Danny Sullivan**, editor-in-chief, SearchEngineWatch.com

"I agree with the prediction that public and private life will be more transparent, with privacy a purchasable commodity. I'm not convinced that the benefits for the majority of people will outweigh the costs." —**Elizabeth Spiegel**, consultant and publisher, Australian Tax Office

"There are things that should be left unsaid or unknown. People will lose their individuality if there are no mysteries left about us." —**Richard Yee**, competitive intelligence analyst, AT&T

"I don't think we could assume that more information is better and it will make the world a better place. Could have the opposite impact." —**Jean Lubbert**, manager of marketing research, Guaranty Bank

"Hard to agree or disagree with this one without spending hours in thought. I'm leaning towards disagree as I think in the end we will be more annoyed by the privacy intrusions than we will feel benefited by the streamlining of services associated with complete transparency. I don't really understand the 'big picture' mentioned in the prediction and wonder how complete transparency alone can make the world a better place." —**Janine van der Kooy**, information management/ librarian

"I think the premise of transparency is true, but I'm not sure that will make the world a better place. One of my fears is the devolution of unique cultures. Cultures are built by limiting communication with other cultures. As communication becomes more and more global, we see many cultures begin to fade away." —**Carter Headrick**, director, grassroots and field operations, Campaign for Tobacco-Free Kids

"I would have marked agree if the date were 2040. But I don't think that will happen in less than 14 years." —**Stan Felder**, president and CEO, Vibrance Associates, LLC

"This is a very 'American' way of looking at things because as a culture we value transparency more than many others. Transparency will increase but governments in some countries will continue to (successfully) prevent complete transparency, sometimes with the support of their people, and sometimes without it." —**Michael S. Cann, Jr.**, CEO, Affinio Corporation

"For the past century or more technology has continued to 'shrink' our world; however, the global 'village' is still much larger than that small town where everyone knows you...and you have to care what they think!" —**Brent Crossland**, technology policy analyst

"People's personal and professional lives are already FAR more transparent than most realize. Increasingly, technologies are being used to link disparate pieces of personal data into powerful profiles. In the short term, the costs may outweigh the benefits; in the long term, the benefits should outweigh the costs." —**Kathleen Pierz**, managing partner, The Pierz Group

"Whether benefits outweigh the costs is going to depend on how much people value privacy in the future. If attitudes change and people become more accepting of a less private world, then clearly benefits will outweigh costs." —**Heath Gibson**, competitive intelligence manager, BigPond, Australia

"This is a typical instance of 'cyber-tarianism'—when cyberspace utopics meets libertarianism. Transparency matters as a means of revealing centers of power—not ordinary people." —**Toby Miller**, professor, University of California–Riverside

"Privacy is undermined (in the U.S.) on two fronts: from the government in the guise of Homeland Security; and from commercial interests in order to aggregate and exploit marketing information. The majority of advances in transparency will benefit large players who know how to use technology to their advantage, less so the average citizen who can barely configure his computer." —**Steffan Heuer**, U.S. correspondent, *brand eins Wirtschaftsmagazin*

"Transparency has the ability to bring us much closer to a better world. However, it unlikely that privacy would suffer as much as outlined in the scenario above. In many ways, privacy will be the 'new currency' in 2020. 'I will trade pieces of my private life for something of value.'" —**Howard Finberg**, director of interactive media, The Poynter Institute

"Much of what we do today in our online and even offline worlds is not private, even when it is perceived to be private. Data is there; however, it takes an extra step to be tracked or recorded. The realization that there is no privacy will happen. Tools to track and report activities will also advance and become more persistent." —**Enid Burns**, editor, ClickZ.com

"Individuals inherently desire a zone of privacy and will be resistant to technologies that create total transparency in personal areas." —**Mitchell Kam**, Willamette University, OR

"At some point, many will retreat or refuse further intrusions into their personal lives." —**Todd Costigan**, National Association of Realtors

"This is the big question. Who, after all, guards the guards? Whilst we generally agree that the ability to have all required data at easy reach would assist in any form of business dealings, it does also open the path to data abuse. Data security will be a major issue as will be identity fraud. An overload of data does not mean that things will be more visible. They may be less so due to the shear amount of data available. The average citizen will have little choice but to accept what corporations and governments enforce. Privacy at least allowed you to choose not to partake in issues that may be forced upon you. We predict a continued erosion of democracy per se and the establishment of a newly tiered society that is made of

technos and nontechnos." —**Robert Eller**, Concept Omega, Media &
Verteiler, Celler Blitz

"Without attacking the burgeoning information-crime problem, the aggregation of information may result in large sys-
temic costs. For example, mass vulnerability of Social Security
numbers may force us to create an entirely new structure of
identification for purposes of government benefits." —**Andrea
Matwyshyn**, executive director, Center for Information Research; assistant professor of law, University of Florida

"A balance must be struck. I admire the goals of organizations
like the EFF. We must gain more control over who has access
to our personal information and what can be done with it. We
need to shift much more aggressively to an 'opt-in' society
than one where every individual is forced to know who/what/
where/when and how to opt out. However, in many types of
exchanges (e.g., commercial transactions, juvenile chat rooms)
you should not be able to act anonymously. In order for the
benefits of global interconnectivity to reach their true potential, we must be able to verify the true identity of the sender."
—**Kerry Kelley**, VP, product marketing, SnapNames.com

"Transparency makes the world a better place for marketing and banking professionals, as well as government bodies. For the common people, it provides at best a good way
to be securely identified for transactions and such." —**Nicolas
Ritoux**, freelance technology reporter for La Presse, Montréal, and other
media outlets

"Yes, yes. We have romanticized our history. Many of the
worst excesses of our past have come because the truth was
hidden from us, shrouded by a smokescreen of religious and
political cant." —**Barry K. Chudakov**, principal, The Chudakov Company

"I agree. The good will result in untold changes for the better in health care, longevity, happiness in life, and a general
sense of fulfillment." —**Jeffrey Branzburg**, educational consultant
for National Urban Alliance, Center for Applied Technologies in Education,
and other groups

"Transparency will have a greater effect on governments and
businesses than it will upon individuals." —**Sean Mead**, consultant

for Interbrand Analytics, Design Forum, Mead, Mead & Clark and other companies

"Privacy is important to people. There is a reaction building to misuse of personal data which, when transferred to the Web, may enhance some shopping experiences but which creates vulnerabilities that we are only now just beginning to understand. People are beginning to demand Web privacy and will make Web-use decisions that reward those companies and services that can guarantee it. And as the MySpace.com crowd gets burned, one by one, they will come to understand and demand online privacy and security as well." —**Ralph Blanchard**, investor, information services entrepreneur

"The benefits outweigh the costs, but this is tempered by education and money. Smart people will be able to obscure or control their personal information well enough to protect themselves, but the poor and undereducated will be open books, ripe for exploitation." —**David Kluskiewicz**, senior account executive, First Experience

"I agree this is a trend, but I already see people (even young people) who work at being off grid and are proud of it. Ability to be and stay mostly off grid will be as valued, even elite, as New England folks with a tan in January. Living in places where satellites can't photo your house will be treasured." —**Susan Wilhite**, design anthropologist, Habitat for Humanity

"I disagree because I think we're already there. When you have a satellite picture of your backyard and your entire neighborhood's backyards on the Internet, you have lost all your privacy. It's a fallacy to think that we have any privacy at all, right now." —**Judi Laing**, Southern California Public Radio

"I agree that transparency can foster honesty, which theoretically makes the world a better place. However, how do we authenticate the information to make sure it's honest in the first place?" —**Brian T. Nakamoto**, Everyone.net, a leading provider of outsourced e-mail solutions

"The social contract is continuously renegotiated and reinterpreted as circumstances change and new technologies arise. I do believe there will be a privacy-efficiency trade in the predicted direction. It will be the people and not the corporations that determine the extents of the trades, and it will not be solely based on the economic criteria presumed under the 'cost/benefit' rubric." —**Ellen K. Sullivan**, former diplomat; policy fellow, George Mason University School of Public Policy

"Access to information can help us build understanding and new knowledge. Fairness will be more possible, and entities that have been unfair in the past will know their behavior is public." —**Janet Salmons**, president, Vision2Lead Inc.; consultant on organizational leadership and development and virtual learning

"Hogwash. Transparency is the buzzword of the day, but it only works for governments intruding upon individual freedoms and not an individual seeking government transparency. Privacy of the individual is paramount and is why laws were passed many years ago to protect the individual against the very abuses that are occurring today. 'Freedom of Information Act,' 'Patriot Act'—these type of Acts rip apart transparency. Getting critical government information in 2020 will be more difficult than it is now." —**Ted Summerfield**, president, Punzhu.com

"Strongly agree, also because people will find ways to deal with the 'transparency.' Companies that go too far in harming privacy will be punished by consumers." —**Olav Anders Øvrebø**, freelance journalist based in Oslo, Norway

"I agree that the world might be a better place, but privacy is not that hard to protect. Private lives can be kept private with some simple precautions." —**Mark Crowley**, researcher, The Customer Respect Group

"The future is unsure on the balance of the bad and good. Privacy had been repeatedly infringed even when we were at the beginning of the Internet era." —**Yiu Chan**, Internet user since 1995

"I agree with the statement but I'm not sure this will make the world a better place. It will make knowledge more accessible and more networked, for better or worse." —**Jonathan Sills**, SVP (strategy and corporate development), Provide Commerce, Liberty Media

"The benefits may initially outweigh the cost, but history has taught us there is always a group or an individual with their own agenda who will attempt or succeed, in manipulating the transparency for their own ends at the expense of 'the masses.'" —**J. Fox**, a respondent who chose not to share further identifying information

"The debate between transparency and privacy will shape the future of communications, as organised groups will fight against giving up private privacy. On the other hand, networked world will increasingly put pressure on worldwide organisations, whether state, NGOs, companies." —**Sylvain Grande**, Internet user since 1995

"Your public and private life is too valuable to corporate retailers for complete transparency." —**Nicco Mele**, U.S. political Internet strategist

"Again, this is entirely likely, but I do see it as a negative result even if there are tremendous benefits to the transparency (as I can see there might be)." —**Jill O'Neill**, director of planning and communication, National Federation of Abstracting and Information Services

"The only expectation I have about the effects of technology on privacy is that they will be unexpected. Through history, technological change has affected our privacy: We have more privacy now then we did in the largely agrarian societies with limited transport options of 200 years ago. Modern technology makes our lives more 'transparent' in some ways, yet it is also easier to ensure privacy too. E-mail and mobile phones make having an affair much simpler!" —**Henry Potts**, professor, University College, London

"The benefits to improving the distribution of goods and services and managing environmental changes/stresses outweigh the downside." —**John Pearson**, a respondent who chose not to share further identifying information

"Remove the word 'transparent' and I might have agreed; however, because the word is usually used in the context of government, it is a somewhat disingenuous construction. Granted, at the moment I am unable to come up with a better word for it—Asimov's 'goldfish bowl' comes close—but human beings need some measure of opacity in their lives and affairs if they are to be such." —**Roger Scimé**, self-employed Web designer

"I like being a Delta. I wouldn't want to be an Alpha or a Beta. They have too much responsibility." —**Walt Dickie**, VP and CTO, C&R Research

"Even with much more information being in digital form, there will still be significant levels of privacy. Laws determine privacy, not technology." —**Rob Atkinson**, director, Technology and New Economy Project, Progressive Policy Institute

"Human nature has always had a negative side when it comes to managing confidential information. What is paramount is the role of privacy in an ever-transparent world that can misuse confidential information. One can't wait for safeguards to evolve. They are the first step." —**Syamant Sandhir**, leader in experience design and implementation, Futurescape

"Our ideas of privacy coevolved with the gesellschaft environment. New concepts of privacy are already arising." —**Mary Ann Allison**, chairman and chief cybernetics officer, The Allison Group, LLC; futurist

"With such widespread transparency, not only will privacy be sacrificed, but competitive edge will be dulled, especially for small- to medium-sized business. Only big business will have the capacity and resources to leverage transparency. And, the keepers of the network will be the ultimate winners." —**Daniel D. Wang**, principal, Roadmap Associates

"Those with the most power in business and government will also be 'beyond sensing'—they will pay major dollars to protect their privacy from the public eye. Others will not have this privilege." —**Peter Samis**, program manager, interactive educational technologies, San Francisco Museum of Modern Art

"I agree with the scenario, but no benefits should or could ever outweigh individual rights, ever." —**Gordon MacDiarmid**, Lobo Internet Services

"Agree—with reservations. The possibility for abuse is incredible, and even well-meaning governments and private security systems will not be able to provide 100% security for our personal information." —**Bobbi Foutch-Reynolds**, VP, marketing, Interact Communications

"I agree, but only partly. Some services may benefit from this transparency, for instance, medical records that are kept on the Internet and available for all doctors, so your treatment can be improved. On the other hand, I don't think it is wise to put so much private information on the Internet since others may misuse such information." —**Jascha de Nooijer**, Universiteit Maastricht, The Netherlands

"Transparency also creates a homogeneity among people, cultures, etc. Think France and why they want to keep their country French. Transparency also leads to more people acting alike out of fear of being different. They may make the world safer but may not make it a better place. After all, sometimes it's the rub that sparks imagination, curiosity, etc." —**Chris Miller**, a respondent who chose not to share further identifying information

"When we are exposed as all too human by increased surveillance of our private lives, we will lose a great deal of our personal dignity and respect for ourselves and others." —**Martin F. Murphy**, IT consultant, City of New York

"Strongly disagree. The growth of information capture will be a leading force behind the commercialization of the Internet. This will hold little benefit to the average user." —**Rick Gentry**, acquisition coordinator, Greenpeace

"Transparency can build a better world but won't by 2020 if the transparency is only of the individual. Such transparency must include governments and corporations in order for individuals to trust more/be willing to allow or participate in a more transparent world." —**James Conser**, professor emeritus, Youngstown State University

"The privacy is a very ingrained right in the developed societies. For that reason, I believe that the citizens that live in developed societies avoided to lose their privacy. In Europe are discussing standards it has more than enough retention data in telecommunications, so much phone as by e-mail, that are rejected from numerous civic forums or the standards that they were tried to implant in United States and that the many citizens' associations have been rejected. I believe that it is

necessary to look for an intermediate point in the balance."
—**Sabino M. Rodriguez**, MC&S Services

"It's too easy to find ways around behaving like a decent adult. Nothing about the Internet, transparency, or voyeurism into other people's lives will change this basic human fact. Witnessing 'goodness' may ratchet up an encounter or two, but these influences will remain in the minority." —**Elle Tracy**, president and e-strategies consultant, The Results Group

"If this happens, it will not—clearly—be a better world. It will be interesting to see how the European model of mainly government having access to your private data versus the American model of corporations more freely owning it plays out (with China being the wild card)." —**Cary Curphy**, operations research analyst, U.S. Army

"Intimacy will become ever more precious." —**Dan McCarthy**, managing director, Neuberger Berman, Inc.

"I am not convinced that giving up the personal right to privacy is a price worth paying for the development of networked technology. I think people will gradually become more aware of the gradual erosion of their privacy and this could eventually provoke a backlash against this trend." —**Brian Power**, NHS hospital in the U.K.

"Transparency of each individual allows people to self-evaluate, and transparency of a corporation, a nation, and of the public as a whole allows people to better participate democratically. Transparency of both public and private lives, of common citizens and social figures, will have the greatest impact politically across the globe. It will encourage democracy." —**Clement Chau**, research assistant and program coordinator, Tufts University, Developmental Technologies Research Group

"I think that this prediction will come true, but I disagree that the benefits will outweigh the costs. We will be convinced that the loss of privacy and the increased transparency of our personal information will be a good thing, but will be a result of our perspectives being 'rewired' by technology, which has resulted in our placing less value on human dignity, individual rights, and privacy." —**Robert Rehn**, Internet user since 1986

"Except in cases of national security, privacy issues should always have the highest priority. I do believe sensing capabilities will improve, and if a person is not careful, it will become easier for their private information to be snapped up by criminals on the Web." —**Doug Olenick**, computer technology editor, *TWICE (This Week in Consumer Electronics)* magazine

" 'Transparency' to the levels described is only a good thing if your ideal society is Huxley's *Brave New World.*" —**Alix L. Paultre**, executive editor, Hearst Business Media, Smartalix.com, Zep Tepi Publishing

"How does one define 'better'? If we mean that everyone gets fed, then maybe. If we mean 'quality of life,' then I doubt it. Contemplatives, saints, shaman, holy men, and other types of spiritual people need privacy. A complete lack of privacy will render the world without a conscience." —**Timbre' Wolf**, songwriter and member of PG5YP (People's Glorious Five-Year Plan—a band in Oklahoma)

"I moderately agree, but there are a number of social and psychological issues related to such pan-transparency, which might leave us worse in a number of unforeseeable respects. Besides, the bad guys always found a way to avoid exposure, so they probably still will." —**Mikkel Holm Sørensen**, software and intelligence manager, Actics Ltd.

"The more information is linked, the easier it becomes for individuals as long as that information is not compromised or incorrect. We've seen this with credit reports and need to make sure we build in the necessary safeguards. On the positive side, if a system could uniquely identify me anywhere I go, I wouldn't have to carry cash, driver's license, passport, etc. The system would need to use two-factor authentication to avoid cases where someone may use the technology to debit my account without my approval, but if done correctly, it could greatly simplify our lives." —**Rangi Keen**, software engineer, Centric Software

"Although the information on everyone will conceivably be available to everyone, there will need to be some conscious reason for searching this out—bad or good." —**Jeff Corman**, government policy analyst, Industry Canada, Government of Canada

"Again, I'm wondering about political factors or consumer pushback. At some point, there may actually be a massive consumer opt out of these transparency schemes. The best target audiences will not be available, i.e., their private info will be at least partially hidden, thus making it less valuable." —**Gary Arlen**, president, Arlen Communications, Inc., The Alwyn Group LLC

"There is a problem with this formulation: What do you mean by 'transparency'? What is the 'everything' that will be visible? Because if it is my personal data, then it is not a better world. The benefits from collaborative, networked societies are only visible if we do have the moral grounds to achieve that visibility and yet respect privacy and individuality. In the utopia this question suggests, that world seems to be a data-hive world of collective consciousness, which is ineffective and immoral. Let us decide what is transparent and how we shall show and perceive: It should not be a matter of transparency vs. opaqueness, but a matter of degrees of clarity, of understanding the uncertain clarity of a networked world." —**Miguel Sicart Vila**, junior research associate, Information Ethics Group, Oxford University

"Transparency, as a requisite for accountability, is not the necessary result of 'visibility on public electronic spaces.' While the effects may indeed have a wide reach, this is not going to change the balance between positive and negative aspects. More transparency requires cultural, ethical, and behavioral changes far beyond the use and abuse of ICT." —**Michel Menou**, professor and information-science researcher

"Benefits of privacy loss will not outweigh the costs. Privacy loss will drive some people away from using technology, but new privacy-protection technologies will develop and make the creators wealthy." —**Mark O. Lambert**, former utilities commissioner, State of Iowa; consultant; futurist

"Here I think that our political and social institutions have lagged and often failed in keeping pace with technical advances. Given the vast disparities in resources, abuses of power, coupled with unprecedented capacity to harm, I am greatly troubled by the intrusions into privacy by governmental and commercial interests with limited agendas to serve public goods." —**Joe Schmitz**, assistant professor, Western Illinois University

"Perhaps the greatest opportunity to be had from the advancement of the 'Global Network' is the opportunity for individuals to become true 'citizens of the world.' Communication has always been the greatest threat to ethnic and cultural bias. The opportunity for individuals to communicate reasonably freely with others outside of their culture and national community should provide a better understanding of previously foreign cultures, which may help to overcome the biases of uncertainty." —**Al Amersdorfer**, president and CEO, Automotive Internet Technologies

"One still has the ability to manage ones use of these communication tools. If the technologies provide true transparency the costs will be minimal. True transparency assumes Governments/Criminal action or inaction are also transparent to all." —**Jim (Jacomo) Aimone**, director of network development, HTC

"But I could easily see it going the other way. The biggest gain could be in productivity; the greatest nightmares seem to be in all that will transpire around lack of privacy." —**David Irons**, VP, cofounder, AScribe Newswire

"This is troubling, but inevitable. Transparency is good and necessary to a great number of new tech developments, but it always comes at a price. We will need to more carefully define privacy issues and work to ensure that personal rights are not sacrificed to a phantom good of total transparency." —**Suzanne Stefanac**, author and interactive media strategist, dispatchesfromblogistan.com

ANONYMOUS COMMENTS

A number of anonymous survey respondents shared comments tied to the scenario, Does transparency build a better world despite the loss of privacy? Among them:

> "Privacy will be a commodity hoarded by those who can afford it."

"Losing one's privacy and security is never a benefit."

"The benefits don't outweigh the costs."

"I just know I wouldn't want to be in that world."

"The need—and right—for privacy will assert itself in the face of government and corporate efforts to use personal data widely. There is room for an effective detente between transparency and privacy, but it will take political will, wisdom, and some economic incentives to make it happen."

"The way things are perverted in 2006, I believe the opposite. Distortion will hold an unfortunately negative place in communication and lives will be negatively affected due to a culture that continues to move farther and farther away from God."

"Personal privacy seems expendable. It will only be valued when it's been lost by some people. By then, it will be too late."

"The private sector will charge for every fact they learn, every genome they decrypt and find advantageous to extract profit from. The irritating rash that is identity theft in 2006 will reach plague proportions in a decade. Gated virtual communities will be offered to those who can bank, e-mail, and surf the Net within their restricted, protected, and costly confines."

"We need to keep information more private and protected than we do now. It will not make the world a better place if we continue down this path of ease of use and transparency with regard to personal information."

"Definitely. The government already knows everything about us; it's just a question of time."

"Transparency would build a better world if there would be an ethical use of the information, which is not always

---

Predictions from respondents who chose to remain anonymous:

"Let's believe that the human being is, by nature, good."

"This trend will facilitate friendliness and relationships based on individual preferences."

"Transparency will fail to extend to government; prevent...the possible better world it could produce."

the case. Using terrorism as an excuse, lots of misuse is possible."

"Transparency can build a better world, but governments and corporations and others that wish to hide 'dirty' truths will continue to take effective steps to protect their secrets."

"As technology develops, people will learn how to keep private portions of their lives private. Much of the global learnings may even promote increased spirituality!"

"Review carefully the various privacy and personal-information-control laws being passed in various places around the world. If anything, the pace is accelerating towards stronger privacy and control, driven by misuse of individual personal information whether accidental or deliberate. I do not think people are convinced that benefits outweigh the costs and this will stall certain forms of data transparency. Legal challenges may control others."

"Those who have something to hide and for whom exposure may threaten their revenues will invest a lot in their 'security.'"

"Transparency rightly frightens many. However, I expect legal changes will be made to better help victims of identity theft and otherwise support online security. I think it's overstated, but true. Rich people will be able to shield their data, at a price. Poor people will exchange their privacy for services. They'll be open books. Not sure if the benefits outweigh the costs."

"Privacy is still required by the majority—we don't really want a 'naked' society. How can losing our privacy be a good thing? Unscrupulous types will take advantage of this."

"It is hard to disagree with this, because it is inevitable."

"While I do think that computers and other new technologies are working to facilitate rather than hinder communication, I don't think that real transparency is the result: We have, instead, the illusion that everything's out there, when the reality is that probably more and more is being hidden away."

"I cannot fathom how it will 'make the world a better place.'"

"I do believe that transparency will produce better, more socialistic lifestyles for everyone. However, I don't believe this will happen."

"There is no more privacy. We need to let go of the concept."

"The intrusion on our daily lives in this country and eventually internationally is at best frightening. The means does not justify the ends."

"This is historically obvious."

"This is still up in the air—privacy, identity theft, job loss, inflexibility, terrorism, and other threats may create as much negative effect as positive."

"The reversal on this feature has begun and the pendulum is swinging back. Example: Why was 'push' a flop, and RSS a success? One could argue they are the same thing, but that's a shallow view. The primary difference is that RSS givers users more interactive control, AND privacy. The way push was initially conceived, it was all to benefit the pushers. The users have won out."

"There is a definite struggle going on between the increased ease with which consumers can identify alternative suppliers (a much more fluid market) with value transferred to consumers but at the same time the data available to companies and the sophistication of the tools to use it (plus the winner takes all network effects) mean that there are potential downsides."

"Transparency is essential to progress. In my experience, keeping technology secret hinders improvements and, more importantly, inhibits our ability to predict potentially disastrous consequences."

"Offline systems will become the norm for key info—it will seem like a step back but will be a side step."

"If you watch teenagers and their style of computing (despite repeated warnings and suspicion of their parents) you see a future generation that questions our need for privacy. They are growing up street wise and don't hide from information. Their in-your-face computing is a more direct way to handle any fears than hiding behind encryption and passwords. There are lessons to be learned here if we adapt."

"Our world will need to deal with the excessive competitive pressures this puts on individuals. We see this issue already with the increased awareness and pressures involved in the measurement of children's academic and personal growth. We will need to learn what remains personal and noncomparative."

"Already we see that information is becoming more sensitive and more sought after. Everything is becoming more and more visible—at the expense of privacy. Even legislation will not eliminate the immense growth in the value of information."

"I think things will be more transparent. They already are far more so than I'd like. But I don't think this is a good thing. The potential costs are huge."

"Privacy evaporated in the '60s, and was gone by the '80s. People just didn't realize it. The focus on privacy that has occurred as a result of the Internet will actually cause information to become more private, thanks to higher awareness and better authorization and access technology."

"Technology advances have slowly eaten away at privacy since the beginning of time, and the increasing use of the Internet to showcase a person's life only continues that trend. Witness the social networking, blogging, and the trend of 'putting everything out there for the world to see' that today's younger generation embraces. I don't see that changing by 2020; in fact, more information is likely to be on display, but only by those people who either don't care about their privacy, or don't know any better. I'm not sure whether this will make the world a better place or not, as any advances in new technologies that have a 'benefit' also have a 'risk,' in that people are always out there to try and exploit that for their own uses."

"Transparency will continue, though there will be a major backlash if ubiquitous technology is thought to threaten personal safety (witness the current backlash against teens using MySpace and other personal Web sites)."

"If access to technology is ubiquitous, then it could have an amazing impact on social movements and change. I also think that antitechnology sects will also be a natural reaction to this transparency—much like the modern Mennonites. Some will yearn for simpler, more private lives."

"As information is communicated, the question remains about its accuracy, relevance, and use."

"In general, I agree, but I do think that people will have some control over their privacy, albeit with some effort. The benefits, however, will probably go to commercial organizations while the costs will be spread among everyone. How worthwhile people will perceive this to be will vary dramatically."

"From outside the U.S., this looks both scary and unlikely. Data protection is too institutionalised in the EU, at least for this to look probable this side of the Atlantic."

"People will choose what level of privacy they will trade off for convenience."

> *Predictions from respondents who chose to remain anonymous:*
>
> **"The self-serving nature of Americans will work against the world being a better place."**
>
> **"I don't believe losing my privacy makes the world a better place."**
>
> **"There will be a growth industry (more likely starting by 2010) providing 'privacy protection services.'"**

"I am nervous about the future."

"I agree that there will be a loss of privacy. I do not agree that this will make the world a better place. The benefits will not outweigh the costs, since one cost will be personal freedoms."

"We're already here. And yes, the benefits outweigh the costs."

"The more we know about other people, the more irrational fears we are developing, and the government beast is feeding these fears. Familiarity does breed contempt. It would be great if we could all learn from, and respect, everyone else's differences, but that doesn't seem to be the way that human nature works. We are just too lazy to care, and we feel threatened by everyone else."

"While police and security forces will probably welcome this transparency, it can easily become a costly 'enhancement' of our society. Our own history has shown us numerous instances of technology used in inappropriate instances. When medical records and purchasing information are available, what privacy does the individual have a right to expect? Does an employer have the right to expect to garner medical information concerning a staff member's medical condition if that medical condition is not adversely affecting their performance? Should an individual's purchasing of certain books or records be available to other commercial establishments or family members or their employers?"

"2020 is far off, and putting into practice user protection of privacy is a tedious task against marketing specialists. Much more difficult than protection against terrorists or viruses. The benefit will come but with more hardships for both developers and users."

"Nothing good can happen out of 'selling' one's privacy."

"There are many pitfalls to transparency. It is desirable in government but not in personal lives."

"While I may not disagree with the premise that 2020 will bring new intrusions, I cannot agree that we will be the better for it."

"Everybody has something to hide. Or something they like to hide. So, no."

"I would agree if transparency applied equally to governments, but this appears highly improbable."

"Don't believe people will allow it to get to that point unless 'terror' politics continue (both terrorist and politicians)."

"Loss of privacy, yes—better world, not necessarily so."

"It is impossible to weigh the cost benefit situation from 2006. As long as there is an active and free press and regular elections in the important countries of the world, we may be okay for a while."

"Transparency of organizations and political bodies in the sense described here will never happen as long as those in power want to stay in power."

"The more transparent, the easier to see problems as they are occurring and thereby stop them early in their tracks."

"Governments know more and more about us at the same time as our possibilities to gain access to information that should be in the public domain diminishes."

"Not in the United States; the public values of individuality, freedom, and privacy are too strong."

"Transparency of individuals will not result in a better world, but transparency of corporations and government will. That benefit will outweigh the cost of a loss of some privacy of the individual."

"Generally, I agree with this. We've already given up some privacy by using things like credit cards and EasyPass transponders. The information is out there, and a person's life and recent activities could be reconstructed relatively easily. The benefits will likely outweigh what we have to give up to achieve them.

"Increased transparency is better for the whole but more costly for the individual—interesting trade off."

"Unless there is a mindset change, no one will welcome nor appreciate intrusion of privacy especially in their personal lives. There will be benefits to consumers if businesses become more transparent."

"I think it is better to have an open society with the free flow of ideas and information. But I still think people need privacy to ensure that we stay human. Everyone doesn't need to know everything about everyone."

"I cannot agree that ceding privacy for transparency can or will be beneficial. One has only to look at past and present repressive societies to see how damaging and costly invasion of privacy has been. Privacy is a basic human right for good reason."

"It will take concerted efforts to make sure the benefits continue to outweigh the costs. When the balance shifts, problems will begin."

"The mass will move to an enlightened POV [point of view]."

"Transparency of corporate and government entities will be good, and citizens will need to work hard to protect and manage personal privacy."

"People's happiness is something very vague."

"A more personalized world can be more comfortable, but maybe less interesting. If it will be good or bad will depends on political state of the world in 2020, too."

"Transparency online is like looking at a person just on paper—there's a lot of missing pieces; the Internet can only go so far."

"Not sure the benefits will outweigh the costs. By 2020, people will probably be required to have automated everything, and perhaps a chip of some sort which would make personal information more transparent. I don't see this as a positive thing."

"Yep, big time. We've already started sliding down this slippery slope, with Google, Microsoft, and our government. There will be enormous amounts of data collected, archived, analyzed, and used to predict behavior of all of us. The danger comes when the data becomes personal and individual, tracking you specifically vs. an aggregate, and if all these sources of info about you are linked to a profile/identity. It's a bit scary, and we don't have laws to govern it yet, and people don't seem to be much interested in finding out about what's happening or how to protect themselves."

Predictions from respondents who chose to remain anonymous:

"Transparency and privacy are both myths and ideals. Since neither can ever be truly achieved, the tension between them will continue."

"Privacy is the one issue that could be the undoing of the Internet."

"I don't believe losing my privacy makes the world a better place."

"There will always be ways to be 'off the grid.'"

"A general rise in the living standard for the world is expected."

"An open environment ultimately will mean more democracy and transparency—a good thing."

"I totally support transparency regarding business relations, but where does it end? We should start a discussion in this country to understand the impact of a 'public life' on the Internet. All people have the right to live a private life, and they should be able to choose on their own how public they want to live. This should not be enforced by laws, etc. I can accept that there might be security issues that come first sometimes, though."

"We won't see complete transparency. The Internet will continue to facilitate the spread of hostile, violent groups that operate 'below the radar' because of the sheer magnitude of activity on the Web."

"We certainly need transparency with respect to the governments that rule us, so that seems good. It may also alleviate some of the problems with human trafficking too."

"There will be an anonymity backlash online, and people will endorse a surveillance society with the idea that so long as everyone's activities are accessible, nobody's being violated."

"This is a tough one. I think that transparency is key to democracy. But, privacy and anonymity are key when citizens are concerned about the powers of governments or large, powerful companies."

"I still see a very unequal access. While I'm uncertain that the advantages of personal communications 'transparency' would truly outweigh the hazards, I'm not sure that it will be ever be global. People without sufficient means may be pushed further outside the 'global' economy than they already are."

"If we vote for transparency, we can retain the controls necessary to avoid self-destruction. The downside is that so much value (which, heretofore, has always required the ability of some to pull the wool over the eyes of others) will be lost, or exposed. The thing that marketers will have to recognize is that no one stops to read the gas mileage on their new car now anyway—why should we be intimidated by a time when every aspect of a product or service is published for consumer appreciation? Unfortunately, a majority of the people want to be told what to do and what to buy."

"There are too many variables, and the results of these surveys will unfortunately move the stock market and hit the newspapers where hegemony reigns. It will be better, but I'm not sure the benefits will outweigh the costs. It is too complicated to predict."

"In general, I agree, though I think we can still have a balance and retain some privacy. Privacy and technology are not necessarily mutually exclusive."

"We have a challenge to find the line between helpful transparency and intrusion."

"The benefit will not replace the costs when that which was once public—respect of one another's privacy—has become privatised and controlled by profit motive."

"Agreed that public and private selves will be increasingly transparent, but disagree that the benefits will outweigh the cost. U.S. residents have an unrealistically heightened sense of entitlement to privacy—and this will be offended by the increasing transparency. The benefits (and there will be some) will reduce this to a degree. However, the problems of identity theft will continue to be a problem—as will a new threat, newly created identities."

"I don't believe that 'visibility' and 'transparency' is automatic. Commentators already speak of 'googlearchy' i.e., multinationals occupying pivotal power. The medium may change (i.e., Internet), but the message may also remain the same—the concentration of power and influence in the hands of the few."

"As a society, we are better off. Knowledge trumps ignorance. The more we know, the better we can cope with the problems we face. If someone with bad intent seeks to invade my privacy, then I want the power of transparency to shed light on that, too. One interesting consequence of the 'data everywhere' phenomenon is that many more criminals are being convicted with evidence culled from their own computers and their data trail across the network."

"This is a worthy vision of the future that hopefully will be realized over the objections of governments trying to control information and communications to hide something."

"The truth is what world communities want—truth and transparency from their politicians, clergy, and corporations. This will eventually force transparency. We'll probably have a more transparent world, but I'm not sure that's a good thing. There are things I don't really want to know about some (many!) people."

"The vision of such an information-dominated future is appealing; the reality is that we're not quite that rational. Nor will the technology be marshaled toward the 'common good.' Too much emphasis on short-term profit making will creating political, cultural, and marketplace dampers on full-scale digital living."

"There will be new pockets of freedom, but they will be available mostly to the existing privileged classes. This 2020 might turn out better for some, worse for the others."

"I am sad to see my unlisted telephone number splashed on the Internet. As a single mother I wanted anonymity and privacy—but I was not allowed to have this. I felt a little frightened to know that my name, address, and phone was published, and I was alone."

"New crimes will develop and there will be greater infringement on rights and freedoms. I think that in 2020, in hindsight, that we will find that the benefits do not outweigh the costs."

"Social conventions must be established to retain the balance."

"Transparency = accountability."

"The value of sensing, storage, and communication technologies is not proved by becoming 'cheaper' and 'better' (I read this to mean more efficient, faster, more precise, etc.). Higher visibility of some things does not in itself lead to better quality of life. People lead lives from a personal-experience perspective, therefore 'all of the lives affected on the planet in every way possible' is a poor measure of 'the' big picture. People differ in their hopes for the future of humanity, and there is no consensus on this benefit. In some ways, life would improve if communication technologies ceased becoming cheaper and better and, instead, people were more inclined to sense room for improvement in the quality of what passes through those communication channels. The facility of technology does not alone deliver a higher quality of life."

"I agree with the first part—that our private lives will be more transparent. I'm not sure what this lack of privacy will lead to—I think we are headed for a Big Brother scenario—albeit not one as dark as most science fiction would have you believe. I think as long as there is not overt effort to control using this information (as opposed to influence) that we just accept the gradual transition."

"There will assuredly be benefits from transparency, but individuals must retain some control over their own privacy. Big Brother will be resisted."

"No one will absolutely give up privacy. Perceived anonymity is what encourages people to play on the Net. Loss of anonymity will result in loss of play."

"The detriments will FAR outweigh the benefits."

"Transparency frightens me. I think we need to have mechanisms in place to protect privacy and individuals. Transparency, while it has its benefits, can also be misused in the wrong hands, thereby creating havoc on the lives of many if tight controls, systems, and protections are not put in place to guard against this danger."

"Our public/private lives may get more transparent, but results will be better for the resource rich and worse for the resource poor."

"Privacy will become more important than ever before."

"I expect that people will attempt to retain (or gain) control over personal information, despite or even in response to technological efforts (or capacities) to increase transparency."

"The consequences of increased visibility are not enough understood yet and deserve more research. Greater visibility not necessarily leads to more democratisation, and even if so, can lead to increased pressure on individuals to comply to standards."

"With the caveat that transparency shouldn't replace a moral code, but will help insure that we follow on one. It's going to be harder to do the back-room deal. I agree with all except the last line: The benefits will not outweigh the costs."

"It will be easier to be known, make purchases, verify identity, seamlessly work between systems, etc. But, privacy will—and already is—compromised."

"I agree in the public areas of the Net. In the private networks of governments and corporations, we will have neither privacy nor transparency."

"This is one that I would say I neither agree nor disagree... Too much depends on the people who have access to the information and the uses they make of it."

"These technologies could build a better world, but our world will not be better if conveniences come at the expense of privacy or if control of the Internet is too highly concentrated in the hands of a few large corporations. If the future of the Internet is shaped by democratic means, the future will be bright. If the future is shaped by commercial interests, where things like privacy, choice, and 'Net neutrality' are externalities, then we're in trouble."

"I disagree with the benefits outweighing the costs, but not the transparency assertion. I expect the adverse effects to disproportionately affect those who seek to lead. I expect candidates for leaders to become homogenous and bland because they must avoid leaving any trail of 'misbehavior' that must be explained."

"Transparency by itself will not make the world better. There are levels of transparencies. The full-range technological aspects of possibilities are not known."

"This is a characteristic of totalitarian systems (Stalinism, China, Nazi Germany)."

"The Panopticon theory, huh?"

"Tools of supposed transparency become tools of control."

"I am on the fence on this one...transparency creates a ton of information which creates information overload which can create paralysis. Technology can and should be an enabler for people; how do we determine how far is too far?"

"Privacy issues must be addressed to counter the 'Big Brother is watching' feelings generated by an increasingly transparent globe."

"The problem with this view is the differentiation of data that can/should be transparent and data that should not. Complete transparency is not a solution to solving issues relating to balancing personal privacy with public use."

"This is basically the question of panopticism. Is the self-censoring that comes of believing every action and statement is being monitored worth the 'good behavior' it creates? See what happens in communist Cuba or North Korea for the answer."

"Transparency, in my view, is only weakly related to the quality in this respect. Who wrote this questionnaire? There are two questions in here that should be separated: Will it happen? Will it be good?"

"Better world does not necessarily require a loss of privacy. It is possible to have the former without the latter, although achieving that will require considerable diligence—that I'm not sure society as a whole has."

"Public and private spheres need to be kept that way. If all the information in the world was available to everyone, we would have people, corporations, and governments that would take advantage of this."

"Security is huge. I believe that this will be on a country-by-country basis. Consumers are currently pretty innocent about information security. I believe that, as knowledge about security grows, that we will fight to protect this as we fight to protect freedom of speech."

"The world a better place for whom...who benefits?"

"Transparency is a human-controlled activity and does not necessarily lead to a 'better world.' There will certainly be more information available—but that does not necessary add up to 'transparency.'"

"The pattern of privacy will be reconfigured, but most of life will still (thankfully) be invisible."

"While the benefits are obvious, this projected outcome may stifle creativity, wrap things in increasingly obtuse red tape, and drive 'undesirable' elements further underground."

"Yes, the 'Big Brother' phenomenon from Orwell's *1984* has always seemed a scary picture of what our future could bring. I do agree that with the transparency of information, there will be good and bad results. I do hope that the benefits will out-weigh the costs."

"Although I do agree that individuals' lives will be increas-ingly transparent, I do not believe this will 'make the world a better place.' Personal freedoms, especially when it concerns dissenting ideas, will become more limited in this scenario as the sensing and storage technologies can be used to exert greater control."

"I don't know what the 'good' part of this is."

"I am happy to see national and world political processes become more transparent but find the idea of individual lives being transparent to total strangers in other parts of the globe rather frightening."

Predictions from respondents who chose to remain anonymous:

"The definition of privacy will change, becoming polarized at the high and low ends of society. Pri-vacy will become a selling point for real estate, travel, etc."

"The benefit will not replace the costs when that which was once public—respect of one another's privacy—has become privatized and controlled by profit motive."

"Transparency, follow-ing David Lyon and Mark Poster's ideas, has deeply worrying implications, especially given government's antiterror measures."

"As long as all nations in this world have adopted the similar pro-tocol among nations."

"I'm not sure that the benefits will outweigh

the costs. There's too much potential for abuse, and it's unclear at this point that these technologies are making people's lives 'better.'"

"I disagree that everything will be transparent and disagree even more that this will make for a better world. What have you been smoking?"

"I find it impossible to decide on this one. Given my age (60), I certainly was raised to prefer the values of privacy over those of visibility, but new generations may either adapt or revolt against increasing visibility, and their value systems will develop differently."

"Wow, the 'benefits outweigh the costs' is quite a bold statement. I do believe we'll have more transparency, but I bet that new tools to mask things will develop as well. And 'benefits vs. costs' will be determined on an individual basis, not society wide."

"George Bush's White House manages to keep lots of things secret, even illegally, and delete e-mail. Transparency, pah!"

"Transparency is not a goal in itself. For some processes, one might not want to have transparency, for others, interest groups will secure their information against transparency. Some information might become as already now more easier retrievable, but not in all areas."

"Everything will not be available to everyone; everyone will not use the Internet; there will be possibilities for privacy and for not disclosing personal information for public access."

"Transparency will continue to increase with mixed results. Sheer amounts of data will lead to the need to incorporate more and more anonymous and mechanized data mining, which will have significant and negative effects. Our human capacity to make sense of the data will help mediate some of these effects, but will also increase their impacts in certain cases."

"I am very concerned about this trend and I disagree that the benefits outweigh the costs (which is why I answered 'disagree'). Increasing data collection (and socially unacceptable uses) is likely to chill behavior and cause a huge change in society that is not a benefit."

"The bad results will be featured in the news, and we won't even see the worst of it by 2020."

"Privacy issues will become the most important concern— encryption and access control will have to become default and accessible in order to balance usefulness of networked communications without giving up freedom and human rights."

"The whole idea behind modern bureaucracy is to create even standards and thereby transparency. Does it work? You might be able to track a certain person through the details of life, but the so-called transparency will drown in the noise."

"Governments and companies will continue to undermine the transparency potential."

"We will lose privacy, and this will be overall a bad thing."

"Most of the time honest people have little to hide."

"Unfortunately, I'm afraid the haves are going to be able to spy on the have-nots. The haves will be the ones in governments and large orgs. The rest of us will be denied the power to spy on each other, or on the big guys."

"This is already the case, and will continue to be so, through 2020."

"Human beings can construct a better society by showing a crystal view of themselves, showing 'transparency' of their own attitudes, and ideals on the Web sphere will contribute to gain a deep understanding of each other, therefore there is nothing to lose, something to gain."

"We never really had privacy anyway. It was a social construct that served a very specific cultural engineering purpose for a few hundred years. If human beings are collective or tribal at base, then privacy seems moot."

"All I can say is I have a general feeling of optimism about the effects of technology."

"The 'better place' will be a matter of individual perspective… possibly yes, but equally possible that it will adversely impact individual freedoms and privacy to the extent that it does more harm than good."

"Everything will not be more visible to everyone. Any notion that access to the kinds of information that surveillance technologies produce will be equitably distributed are dubious at best."

"Notions of First World 'privacy' are maintained and 'protected' at too high a cost to the rest of the world, in relation to such matters as corporate accountability, conflicts of interest, etc. I like privacy but, on balance, would sacrifice some of it to achieve a fairer and more equitable society."

"Though more information will be available online, information will still stay private. Those in developing countries will have less of an ability to stay private. I can easily see that the transparency will come about, some by choice, some by dictate."

"I am very skeptical that benefits will outweigh costs. We will need to be vigilant and protect privacy."

"This is the worst kind of Orwellian logic."

"Orwellian society is not better."

"Society will revisit the issue of privacy in the coming years and develop new standards regarding what is appropriate and what is not. At the same time, information very much wants to be free, and greater transparency in the public spheres of government, commerce, etc., is essential and will be easier to achieve through emerging technologies."

"There are some benefits to a 'transparent' society, but there are some definite drawbacks that make me think that the benefits will not outweigh the costs. The social impacts of transparency must be considered. Easy access to private information raises some serious concerns about how that information will be used—true, it may seem easy to get lost in the cracks, but data-mining technologies are making it simple to extract relevant information from gigabytes of data. The potential for abuse is quite high. Consider the case of Chinese journalist Shi Tao, who was sentenced to 10 years in jail for 'leaking state secrets.' His crime was sending notes regarding the government's instructions on handling media coverage of the 15th anniversary of the Tiananmen Square protests to a U.S.-based Web site. Web portal company Yahoo played a key role in Shi's conviction by revealing that he was the owner of the e-mail account used to send the message. Dissidents like Shi and other anonymous informants (corporate whistleblowers, for example) depend on their anonymity to protect them from the consequences of disseminating sensitive information. Similarly, although less grievous, cases of people being fired (or not being hired at all) based on the content of their personal blogs have been in the news quite often in the past few years. As more and more information becomes searchable online, it seems likely that incidences of these sort of sanctions will only become more prevalent. Once something is posted on the Internet, it is likely to remain there indefinitely."

"There is no hiding from the past. One poor judgment call can follow you for the rest of your life."

> **Predictions from respondents who chose to remain anonymous:**
>
> **"Transparency will be applied selectively."**
>
> **"There must be a bias in favour of protection of individual privacy and against government/ market privacy. As it stands now, the trend is the other way."**

"Transparency would help to solve some problems of today. However, when we lost our privacy, we are living in an insecure world and the psychological impact may be more serious."

"What you write here will happen anyway. It is not a 'position' in a debate."

"The privacy genie is out of the bottle. People want privacy for themselves while demanding transparency for the organisations they work with."

"Yes, this is already happening."

"The direction is benefit driven, so benefit will be there and always outweigh costs. This is just too easy to predict."

"The transparency will penetrate on everything both private life and public life. However, more transparency gives less possibility for corruption."

"I don't fear that a program knows what I'm saying in private conversations. Thinking that human beings are actually spending time studying my private life is either paranoia or hubris."

"I believe strongly that the increased cultural exchange made possible by global telecom infrastructure will lessen the chance that we destroy each other via explosive warfare. In that sense, the new global community that emerges is essential to preventing holocaust of many sorts. But, there are corresponding risks (well documented but perhaps not yet largely known to larger public) to privacy that, given the propensity of governments to abuse power over privacy for 'good reason,' will demand that citizens use the new openness to maintain openness."

"This has been in every scenario developed for the past 5 years already and will continue to be there in new scenarios. And yes, I do believe this will happen. Connecting it to the previous statement: There will be a way to govern it and stop some of the outwashes."

"Agree on the antecedent (transparency will occur), but not the consequence (it will make the world a better place). It will have some very strong benefits, and other very large costs. People will appreciate the benefits and be resigned to the costs."

"International communications will significantly improve; feelings and sensitivities will not become more 'visible.'"

"I believe we are currently overdoing the 'privacy' part. We should distinguish between the need of confidentiality on one hand and privacy in general."

"This will happen. The big question is, will it be better?"

"Transparency in public services does produce a better world. But not on the individual or private level, so it will not necessarily make a better world. Ways to circumvent 'Big Brother' will also improve in the form of more complex encryption methods, etc. As far as the benefits outweighing the costs, I disagree—a balance must be sought."

"You should put 'covert' transparency at the beginning of this statement—this is a question about elites. I am a big fan of BOTH transparency and privacy, but not as discussed here or in the direction things are currently going. Selective manipulation is a HUGE issue!"

"Although there will be downsides to being so exposed on the network, nefarious activities tend to take place in secret, so transparency is necessary."

"Those with money and political clout will continue to exploit differentials in access to private information. Citizens will have more exposure in the name of law enforcement (or 'counterterrorism') but not enjoy similar transparency of the governments. There will be a lot of people who are more uncomfortable with the technology pervading their lives, perhaps to the point of spawning a political antitechnology movement."

"Somewhat—the level of impact is undetermined, and 'the world a better place' is a subjective term that can be interpreted very differently by different people."

"Transparency for accountability of governments and other powerful institutions is good. For private citizens, who wish to remain private, coercing transparency is not good. That seems a more likely scenario."

"There is a very strong privacy movement on the Internet, one that is backed by legal requirements in Europe as well as other countries. If anything, expectations of privacy are gathering steam."

"While I agree that the prediction will come to pass, I disagree with the juxtaposition of transparency and privacy, as if this is a zero-sum game and having more of one will automatically reduce the other."

"Transparency presumes that the data being made transparent are verifiable, so that inferences made from them can be supported. While I believe that the trend to provide data online will continue, perhaps with some levelling off, I strongly suspect we will not see increased verifiability in this time frame. The side effect of this lack of verifiability is that communities selectively credit particular data points and throw out data that does not match their existing worldview. More transparency does not help this."

"First, there is no evidence that more control will end up in more transparency. Second, there is no link between such forced 'transparency' and a better world. Third, the mighty ones will continue to escape any form transparency, dominate the media, and manipulate public opinion."

"Transparency refers only to public responsibilities and never should go beyond the legitimate limits of privacy law. International law-enforcement agreement should guarantee individual privacy rights."

"I'm not sure it will be a 'better' world; I'm more sure that it will be a 'different' world."

"I believe that the benefits will outweigh the costs—but not in this time frame. I think we'll still be wondering if we're going to survive this transition at this time. It will take many more years for many cultures to accept and adapt to the pace of knowledge acquisition and cross-fertilization."

"Only bad results come from making our private lives public—freedom exists only when one can remain anonymous and not surveilled."

"Note that the U.S. government is on a determined campaign to roll back 50 years of progress in transparency."

"The definition of 'benefits' and 'costs' are in the eye of the beholder. There are intuitive limits on the benefits of 'global transparency' of private data (e.g., financial information, time when residence is vacant, location of children). The availability of private information that can be globally accessed may create the need for legislated protection of 'digital privacy.'"

"Technically, there will be some solutions that will be available but that people may not use: PGP, onion router."

"The good and the bad are there today. The technology will only accelerate what is done today."

Virtual Reality Brings Mixed Results

Prediction: *By the year 2020, virtual reality on the Internet will come to allow more productivity from most people in technologically savvy communities than working in the "real world." But the attractive nature of virtual-reality worlds will also lead to serious addiction problems for many, as we lose people to alternate realities.*

Respondents' Reactions to This Scenario

Agree	56%
Disagree	39%
Did not respond	5%

Note. Because results are based on a nonrandom sample, a margin of error cannot be computed.

Consensus of Opinion: Those people who have technology available to them will spend more time immersing themselves in more sophisticated, networked, synthetic worlds for work and

entertainment and thus will be experiencing "virtual" reality more. "Addiction" is likely for some people.

What is virtual reality? Professionals in the field of VR research today say it is the immersion of human sensory channels within a computer-generated experience. This can also be explained by saying VR allows one to be in a place without *really* being in that place. Tech-savvy individuals define it in various ways; some people who "lose" themselves in today's online role-playing games and even in online chats consider this to be an experience in VR and even "full-immersion VR" because it envelops their minds to the point where they are not conscious of anything else; others do not see this as true VR.

In this survey, respondents' replies reflect the full range of current popular definitions of VR—from the point of view that "it's already happening" (mostly in people's full-scale immersion in today's massively multiplayer online role-playing games—MMORPGs) to the idea that the only true VR includes a full-scale, 3D, touch-sight-sound experience, generally using highly specialized equipment to shut out "reality" and give one a virtual "presence" in another place.

A majority of survey participants agreed with the proposed 2020 scenario, with many declaring it is already a reality. Most who disagreed with the projection defined "virtual reality" in a more formalized, 3D, all-senses format that has yet to be perfected. Some respondents also took issue in various forms with the use of the terms "reality" and "addiction."

Only a few respondents chose to focus their elaborations on the idea that VR work will allow more productivity than work in the "real" world. **Richard Yee,** competitive intelligence analyst for AT&T, wrote,

> "People who go off the 'deep end' will have done so NOT because of the technology but because of their own individual psychological configuration."
>
> —Frederic Litto,
> professor, University of Sao Paulo, Brazil

"By 2020, the term 'virtual reality' will be outdated. The Internet will become more sensory, attracting more applications that will appeal to end users.

The Internet will be surrounded by more applications, where it will become more stimulating. In turn, more productivity will be driven from the new ideas originating from such stimulation." **Ben Detenber** of Nanyang Technological University responded, "VR will only increase productivity for some people. For most, it will make no difference in productivity (i.e., how much output); VR will only change what type of work people do and how it is done."

Glenn Ricart, a member of the board of trustees of the Internet Society, wrote, "Various kinds of computer-mediated business models/productivity models/configurable electronic workspaces will be key productivity enhancers." However, he also added, "There will be an increasing problem with people 'disconnecting' during their so-called leisure time and immersing themselves in purely virtual realities for entertainment purposes. We've already seen how these can be addictive, and by 2020, the technological capability for them might be near ubiquitous—leading to perhaps an entire generation 'opting out' of the real world and a paradoxical decrease in productivity as the people who provide the motive economic power no longer are in touch with the realities of the real world."

ONLINE OVERUSE IS CLASSED WITH GAMBLING, ALCOHOL, ETC.

The use of the word "addiction" influenced most respondents to address this angle of the scenario exclusively in their responses. As author and sociologist **Howard Rheingold** noted, "The way the question is worded embeds some assumptions." The scenarios were written to set people off and spur deeply felt reactions; they did. Rheingold continued, "I have a serious addiction to reading; is that a social problem? Has the world 'lost' me?" Writer **Fred Hapgood** responded, "Of course it is totally arbitrary as to who gets to call whom an addict." And **Toby Miller** of the University of California–Riverside wrote, "Addiction is a bizarre metaphor to apply to forms of labor and leisure other than drugs. It buys into the medical model's attacks into popular culture."

Respondents predicting addiction will be evident in 2020 were pretty much divided into two camps: those who imply that an addiction to VR can simply be classed with other addictions such as alcohol, drugs, and gambling; and those who see VR in a different light as a new concern.

"There are lots of ways to get addicted, and the list changes with time," wrote **Roger Cutler** of the World Wide Web Consortium and Chevron's Information Technology Division. "It is very unlikely that this source of addiction will have any magic power that others don't." **Robin Gross**, executive director of IP Justice, responded, "VR is no different than offline temptations." **Joe Bishop**, a vice president with Marratech, wrote, "We lose some folks to gambling and drugs now. And if drug addiction isn't an alternative reality I doubt I know what is. I doubt that this will be a serious problem."

> "People will always triumph over the Internet. The Internet is a robot. No matter how much sexuality there is online, nothing can replace a hug of the closeness and touch of a fellow human."
>
> —Stan Felder,
> president and CEO,
> Vibrance Associates, LLC

Scott Moore has been working with virtual worlds for 10 years as the online community manager for the Helen and Charles Schwab Foundation. He wrote, "I disagree with any large-scale doom prediction surrounding virtual-reality addiction. However, such addiction will progress very much as addictive drugs do. Right now, we see this with the large corporate-based virtual worlds, which are like cocaine for some—expensive to produce and to consume. As the tools for creating such places become cheaper and easier to access, we will see lower quality virtual worlds that will have a wider reach to people with less disposable income (starting with the middle-middle classes and working down). We can see the very beginnings of this progression with the many free social-networking services. Some people will be completely sucked in and their lives ruined, much as what happens for drugs now. However, the toll will still be far less than the damage to lives and communities that chemical drugs can do."

Torill Mortensen of Volda University College in Norway wrote, "First, there is nothing virtual about digitalised space. It has real-life effects, rewards, and problems. Second, what do we lose people to today? Is it better to go jump off a mountainside for your kicks or do drugs than to spend it in some digital version of reality that feels better and more rewarding? The main problem isn't that 'virtual worlds' are addictive; it is that the physical world is not sufficiently challenging and rewarding. Blaming the media should not be a way out of fixing the very real social problems the world faces."

Bryan Trogdon, president of First Semantic—a company working on a realization of the Semantic Web—responded, "Wall-sized monitors in conjunction with speech recognition, artificial intelligence, wireless broadband, and computer power will take us from television to teleliving, a term defined by Professor William E. Halal as 'a conversational human-machine dialogue that allows a more comfortable and convenient way to shop, work, educate, and conduct most other social relationships.' I agree with his assessment that people will still crave real social relationships."

SOME DEFINE THE ISSUES
DIFFERENTLY—ENVISIONING A THREAT

Among those expressing concern over the future use of alternate realities is **Robert Shaw**, an Internet strategy and policy advisor for the International Telecommunication Union, who wrote, "This is already the case in immersive gaming environments, and virtual reality will be even more addictive. Policy and regulation will move increasingly from physical space into virtual space with analagous rules." **Fredric Litto**, a professor at the University of Sao Paulo, wrote, "Good legislation will make it obligatory to identify virtual objects and environments to users so that there can be no confusion between the real and the apparently real."

Sean Mead, a technology consultant, wrote, "Simulations will develop to where some players' experiences so closely mimic reality that the players will be stimulated with the same neurotransmitters that drive feelings of love and pleasure in the real world. There will be simulations as addictive as nicotine and cocaine, but without same degree of societal antipathy." Consultant **Thomas Lenzo** agreed, writing, "As the quality of virtual reality increases, it will attract more users and the numbers of cyber addicts will increase."

Rajnesh Singh, of PATARA Communications and the Pacific Islands chapter of the Internet Society, responded, "There needs to be significant research into VR and its likely effects on the human psyche. From current observations, a VR world could be a dangerous place indeed." **Mike Gill**, an electronics engineer with the National Library of Medicine, wrote, "Until addiction is better understood, VR will be a serious problem." **Cary Curphy**, an operations research analyst for the U.S. Army, responded, "This is already a limited problem with video gaming; just wait until the first really good online sexual-encounter application."

> "There is a strong likelihood that virtual reality will become less virtual and more reality for many. However, I see this as an addiction phenomenon that will likely inspire us to understand unexplored dimensions of being human."
>
> —Barry Chudakov,
> principal, The Chudakov Company

Steffan Heuer, U.S. correspondent for *brand eins Wirtschafts-magazin*, responded, "The social costs of too much information vs. not enough knowledge will only continue to rise." **Tiffany Shlain**, founder of the Webby Awards, wrote, "I already see many Internet junkies who need a fix more than they can be present in the moment."

Denzil Meyers, founder and president of Widgetwonder, expressed concern over a self-selected social stratification, writing, "These technologies allow us to find cohorts which eventually will serve to decrease mass shared values and experiences. More than cultural fragmentation, it will aid a fragmentation of deeper levels of shared reality."

Mirko Petric of the University of Zadar in Croatia wrote, "An interplay of the 'virtual' and 'real' reality will become more intense, but people will probably become more literate in dealing with it. 'Addiction' to alternate realities is already a reality, we will have to wait and see which form it will take. Other forms of 'addiction' to alternate realities (utopian, political) were easy to observe in the 20th century, and had a mass effect. The particular form of addiction that we are discussing here can be seen as one of these, only based on a different platform and happening in a different sociopolitical context."

Technology consultant **Robert Eller** responded, "A human's desire to reinvent himself, live out his fantasies, overindulge—addiction will definitely increase. Whole communities/subcultures, which even today are a growing faction, will materialise. We may see a vast blurring of virtual/real reality with many participants living an in-effect secluded lifestyle. Only in the online world will they participate in any form of human interaction. The gin holes of 19th-century London or the opium dens of Shanghai are very likely outcomes."

> "Real human interaction is an inherently difficult process...The ability to communicate with the anonymity afforded by something even as comparatively ordinary as e-mail makes it easy for anyone to avoid direct communication and contact. The possibility of virtual worlds will probably open up a whole new category of psychoses for discussion."
>
> —Al Amersdorfer,
> president and CEO,
> Automotive Internet Technologies

Nick Carr, an independent writer and consultant, wrote, "I'm not sure if addiction is the right word, but the shift of people's attention to online information, media, entertainment, and communities will erode culture and bring into being a colder if more efficient world." And **Hal Varian**, a professor at the University of California–Berkeley and consultant for Google, responded, "I think we can see this happening now. The question is whether this is really a bad thing. Personally, I think it is, but I'm not sure I could defend that view philosophically."

Addiction expert **Walter J. Broadbent** of The Broadbent Group offered a solution to VR addiction in his response. "I have studied addiction for 36 years. We already have tons of addicts in the world who STERB. That is, they use short-term energy-releasing behaviors to feel better. We already have millions who are addicts. The issue is not to regulate them but to offer a life in which such behavior is not needed, and that, too, can be accomplished on the Internet. We need to create valuable and helpful communities on the Web that will allow millions to connect."

SOME SPECIFICALLY ADDRESSED CONCERNS TOWARD YOUTH CULTURE

Ed Lyell, a pioneer in education and the Internet who now works at Adams State College, proposes that we take a close look at finding ways to provide guidance to young people as they create their alternate, online personalities. "This is already the new reality for many youth," he wrote. "Instead of dealing with the challenges and fears of teen identity definition, more and more youth are creating multiple 'virtual' personalities and losing themselves to each of those game scenarios. Who the 'actual' individual becomes or emerges as from such vivid role playing is unclear to me. Do we end up with much more mature, experientially compassionate people, or even more anxious, fearful, and disassociative personalities? It seems that even minimal intervention at appropriate stages of virtual personality creations could dramatically improve positive over negative long-term outcomes."

Michael Cann, Jr., CEO of Affinio Corporation, responded, "It will be possible for computer users to build 'alternate realities' around themselves, and some will find this environment to be so much more appealing and comfortable than the 'real world' that they will prefer it. I see a future epidemic, especially among children and teens." **Paul Craven** of

> "VR, like e-mail, IM, blogging, gaming, is a new and interesting technology that competes for time and, like the others, may become addictive. It will still be up to the individual."
>
> —Gordon Bell,
> senior researcher, Microsoft

the U.S. Department of Labor wrote, "Anyone with a teenager can tell you this is already a problem."

Heath Gibson, competitive intelligence analyst for BigPond in Australia, wrote, "Addiction to chat rooms and online gaming worlds is already emerging as an issue. Recent research has highlighted, for example, how teenagers' ability to learn during school hours is being impacted by a lack of sleep—caused by late-night SMS/chat sessions. There is a real risk that some people will become 'lost' to virtual worlds."

William Kearns of the University of South Florida shares concerns about the youth culture. "If the recent suicides of Japanese boys heartbroken over not being able to possess Lara Croft are any indication, we have much to be concerned about," he wrote. "I also personally am more concerned about the erosion of basic skills in children—boys especially—who play video games incessantly yet cannot figure out how to repair the most basic devices. Parents have left machines to raise the children, and they are being molded (or worse crippled) by their experiences or lack of parenting."

SOME CLASS VR WITH BOOKS, TV, AND OTHER COMMUNICATIONS ADVANCES

Some respondents drew comparisons with earlier communications innovations, including books, television, and films. "We will survive to discover new horrors beyond VR," wrote **Paul Saffo**. "The history of media is a history of addiction for some and moral hazard for others. Remember that half a century ago, Cervantes' Don Quixote was driven to windmill-tilting madness because he read too many books. Flaubert's Emma in *Madam Bovary* got into a jam for the same reason. A century ago, parents lamented that kids were spending too much time inside reading. In mid-century, the same fears were transferred to paperbacks, movies, and then TV. Now it is videogames and the Web. VR is clearly next, and its seductive hyper-realism will be seductive indeed.

But one generation's outrage is the next generation's mainstream tool. I will bet that in 2020 parents will be lecturing their children that they can't go out and play until they finish their VR-based simulation games."

John Quarterman, president of InternetPerils, Inc., wrote, "We've already seen this happen, so it's not really a prediction. Of course, we've also seen it happen with every previous technology. Teenagers spend huge amounts of time on the telephone; TV is everybody's whipping boy; radio led to that jungle music, rock and roll; even books led to porno addictions

> "As virtual reality gets better, people's ability to see through it gets better. Novels were the dangerous VR of their own day, just as TV was for us kids, and computer-simulated realities will be for our own kids."
>
> —Douglas Rushkoff,
> author of many books about Net culture; teacher, New York University

and modern propaganda. Some of these things have since become generally accepted; others we try to deal with and forge ahead."

Thomas Narten of IBM, a liaison for ICANN to the Internet Engineering Task Force, responded, "Like all technologies, there are good and bad consequences. For some, the bad will dominate. But on the whole I believe society will benefit."

WORLDS CONVERGE; HOW DO YOU DEFINE "REALITY"?

With many people getting "lost" daily in an online world of IM chat, e-mails, video conferencing, gaming, shopping, surfing, and work, some respondents said it's already difficult to draw a line between what we once called "reality" and the virtual world.

"The real and virtual are converging, and anyway, addiction is a disease for which we will soon find the cure; just a matter of suppressing the expression of a few genes here and there," wrote **Bob Metcalfe**, Ethernet inventor, founder of 3Com Corporation, and former CEO of InfoWorld.

Daniel Wang, principal partner with Roadmap Associates, wrote, "While area codes might still define geographic locations in 2020, reality codes may define virtual locations. Multiple personalities will become commonplace, and cyber-psychiatry will proliferate."

Martin Kwapinski, senior content manager for FirstGov, the U.S. Government's official Web portal, responded, "The distinction between 'real' and 'virtual' realities will continue to blur...Our definitions of what is 'real' will be tested and changed." **Raul Trejo-Delarbre** of Universidad Nacional Autonoma de México wrote, " 'Virtual reality' doesn't constitute a different reality. It is part of the reality that surrounds us."

Ted Coopman of the University of Washington wrote, " 'Virtual reality' is a pointless and dated term that has no meaning other than the technical (computer-science) definition. We live in a pervasive communication environment and this will only increase. The demarcation of virtual and real and mediated and nonmediated will have no meaning for most people and is an artifact of older generations. Reality will be one seamless world that spans face-to-face and digital areas of action. If anything, the ability to physically take a class or travel to meet with someone will be considered an elite privilege."

> "I wonder whether we live with the pleasant illusion that we share the same 'real world.' In the year 2020, the prevalent mode of thinking will be that we all live in virtual realities and have done so all the time. The trick is to bring those realities together in productive and pleasurable ways."
>
> —Charlie Breindahl,
> IT University of Copenhagen

Charles Hendricksen, a research collaboration architect for Cedar Collaboration, wrote, "For professional communities, 'virtual reality' is a meaningless term. Transactions made on the Internet are completely and totally real."

Clement Chau, of Tufts University's Developmental Technologies Research Group, responded, "Virtual reality will merge with 'real reality' in that some activities will be predominantly virtual, while others will be real. A new term will probably be coined to describe real reality. When this merging of the two realities happens, addiction problems will not be a concern because (a) the novelty wears off, (b) virtual reality REQUIRES participation in real reality, and (c) virtual reality will become part of the daily lives, as much as the telephone or e-mails has become part of our everyday routines."

Patrick O'Sullivan of Illinois State University wrote, "What people refer to as 'virtual reality' is still an aspect of all of our reality— it's not a separate reality any more than books, movies, video games, or our imagination is a separate reality. Saying someone is addicted to virtual reality will one day sound as ridiculous as saying some people today are addicted to books." **Bruce Edmonds** of the Centre for Policy Modelling in Manchester, U.K., wrote, " 'Game' environments are already becoming serious media for economic and political interaction." And **Alex Halavais**, of Quinnipiac University, responded, "Alternate to what realities? Phone realities? The most recent Pew study seems to belie this: Those with stronger virtual social ties have stronger ties generally."

Robin Berjon, affiliated with the World Wide Web Consortium and Expway, responded, "There is no such thing as virtual reality. To say that a discussion one has with another human being using a chat program is virtual is like saying that the music one listens to from a CD doesn't exist. Addiction to worlds that involve stronger imaginary components has always been, and will always be, a potential social issue. At least the Internet, apart from repetitive-stress injuries, poses a lesser health risk than many alternatives."

> "We will not be able to separate 'virtual' worlds from 'real' worlds; both will be the same reality."
>
> —Carlos Fernandez,
> CCRTV, Barcelona

THOSE WHO STICK TO THE "OLD-SCHOOL" VR DEFINITION MOSTLY DISAGREE

Most of the respondents who appear to define VR as a body immersion in a 3D experience were pessimistic that it would be fully developed and in wide use by 2020. "VR is cute, and fun, and great for computer games and various ISOLATED applications," wrote **Jim Warren**, founder of *Dr. Dobb's Journal* and a technology policy advocate and activist. "But I do not envision it as becoming widely deployed, other than in very limited areas, such as games and entertainment."

Ross Rader, director of research and innovation for Tucows, Inc., wrote, "Thirteen years ago we said the same thing about VR—today, we're still saying the same thing, but with no directional evidence to support it. It's an interesting contention, but way too far down the field to act as any sort of a compass." **Cliff Figallo**, an online communities architect, wrote, "Only a relative fringe of users will spend enough time in VR environments to be adversely affected." **Jason Nolan** of Ryerson University in Canada responded, "The term 'VR' is pretty meaningless. What 99% of folks do is work and interact digitally. There are not any major installs of anything close to VR itself, so there's no way to predict what it would be like. Of course, for those of use who have worked in collaborative VR, we know that as with digital interactions, there is always a pull to the real, as Howard Rheingold noted more than a decade ago."

Defining VR Has to Do With Defining "Presence"

Thousands of years ago, Roman naturalist Pliny expressed one of the earliest interests in perceptual illusion when he wrote about an artist who had "produced a picture of grapes so dexterously represented that birds began to fly down to eat from the painted vine" (Biocca, Kim, & Levy, 1995). Computer graphics and VR scientist Ivan Sutherland wrote in 1965, "The ultimate display would, of course, be a room within which the computer can control the existence of matter" (p. 507).

Most researchers say VR can be defined as a particular type of experience. It goes beyond the "goggles and gloves" systems first emerging in a useable form in the 1990s. Hardware, they say, should not be the focus in defining VR in terms of human experience. The ultimate goals of VR have been defined over time as the amplification of human cognition, perception, and intelligence. They say it has to do with one's "presence."

When perception/presence/cognition is not mediated by a communication technology, it reflects only immediate physical surroundings. A mediated environment can be considered an alternate reality or a virtual reality. VR is an experience in an alternate perception. VR researcher Jonathan Steuer of Stanford University has found that different individuals reach this state at different levels in differing ways. He said VR is distinguished from dreams and hallucinations because it requires perceptual input introduced through a communications medium. He also said participation in RPGs, MUDs, and online discussion groups can be the construction of a virtual reality in a virtual space (1995).

> **Predictions from respondents who chose to remain anonymous:**
>
> **"Greater productivity may be illusory."**
>
> **"They will claim they are not lost but have found their true world, and there will be serious debate about that."**
>
> **"Sign me up."**
>
> **"Augmented reality will become more common than virtual reality."**

As the levels of vividness and interactivity intensify the VR experience in the future, more users are likely to be spending more hours in VR. Steuer warned in a 1995 research article that as VR is perfected, it may present dangers: "Rapid advances in both multimedia computer technologies and high-speed data networks hasten the development of a truly global village, in which our ability to interact with friends, family and others who share interests similar to our own will no longer be limited...These new developments are also certain to enhance the possibility of using the media to manipulate and control beliefs and opinions...As an increasing proportion of most individual's experiences come via mediated rather than direct sources, the potentially detrimental effects of such manipulation increases exponentially" (p. 53).

"MIGRATING" TO SYNTHETIC ONLINE WORLDS

VR pioneer Jaron Lanier (the man who coined the term "virtual reality" in 1987) and researcher Frank Biocca predicted in 1992 that the market for VR entertainment would be fairly advanced by 2000, with VR "theaters" in malls, enabling people to watch VR "performances." There are no such elaborate theaters in 2006, although one might argue that productions shown in the best IMAX theaters might approximate a feeling of VR. While Mattel introduced the PowerGlove in 1989 (for $89) for use with Nintendo video games, and gamemaker Sega Genesis introduced a headset with VR goggles and earphones in the fall of 1993 for $150, the goggles-and-gloves VR idea has not been mainstreamed. Most "totally immersive" VR technologies have remained too expensive for use outside major industries such as medicine, the military, and flight-training services.

But millions of people have found in 2006 that they have become so immersed mentally in MMORPGs that they feel themselves to be physically living and moving about in these limited but effective synthetic worlds. They said they are already experiencing VR. This phenomenon is most overwhelmingly in evidence in Korea, where broadband is nearly universally available and where a majority of people spend at least some time most days populating online worlds of one type or another.

In his 2005 book *Synthetic Worlds*, Edward Castronova wrote that "a virtual reality brought about by games rather than devices" is gaining users at the rate of Moore's law (i.e., doubling every 2 years), and the current number of "hard-core" users numbers at between 10 million and 27 million people. He estimated the commerce conducted between people who spend time in synthetic worlds amounts to at least $30 million annually in the U.S. and $100 million globally, and the collective volume of annual trade within synthetic worlds is above $1 billion (pp. 2, 13, 55).

The currencies of online worlds have begun to be traded against the dollar, and many of them trade at a higher rate of exchange than real Earth currencies. Some of the most popular of these games in 2006 include *World of Warcraft, Second Life, Ultima Online, EverQuest, Lineage, Star Wars Galaxies, Legend of Mir, Eve, There, Mu,* and *Dark Age of Camelot.*

Second Life cofounder Philip Rosedale told *Wired* magazine that the monthly trade in his synthetic world is about $8 million and trending upward, and he added, "I'm not building a game; I'm building a new country" (2006). ICANN member Joi Ito testified in the same issue that he is a *World of Warcraft* "addict," adding, "It represents the future of real-time collaborative teams and leadership in an always-on, diversity-intensive, real-time environment—*World of Warcraft* is a glimpse into our future" (2006).

In his book, Castronova (2005) predicted what he calls the "migration" of more and more people to computer-rendered Internet communities and added, "Synthetic worlds are simply intermediate environments: the first settlements in the vast, uncharted territory that lies between humans and their machines...Add immense computing power to a game and...the place that I call 'game world' today may develop into much more than a game in the near future. It may become just another place for the mind to be, a new and different Earth...Ensuring that the technology serves such a marvelous end, rather than a less happy one, is the real challenge for the next few decades. We will be less likely to meet that challenge the longer we treat video games as mere child's play" (pp. 9, 18). Castronova added, "There is a huge throng of people just waiting at their terminals for a fantasy world to come along, one that is just immersive enough, under the technology they can afford, to induce them to take the plunge and head off into the frontier forever" (p. 71).

RESEARCHERS WARN ABOUT "TOXIC IMMERSION" AND OTHER THREATS

People are already using synthetic worlds like *Second Life* to host parties, offer schools, suffer wars, exhibit art, present theatrical stagings, exhibit political structuring and strife, and experience friendship, sex, and marriage. As humans begin to spend many hours there, they invest time and money, building personal assets. Security is a question, just as it is in the "real" online world, and researchers say there is a possibility of "toxic immersion."

Michael Shapiro and Daniel McDonald of Cornell University wrote in a 1995 research piece, "As the distinction blurs between the physical and computer environments, people will need to make increasingly sophisticated judgments about what is 'real' and what is not...we expect that aspect of communication research to become increasingly important as technologies like virtual reality make it possible to both mimic and to modify our perceptual bases of understanding in increasingly complex ways" (p. 323). They pointed out that whenever a new communications medium evolves and emerges, people have a tendency to apply their already-established judgment processes to the new mode of delivery. This often leads to errors and problems (e.g., the 1938 CBS radio-theater production of *War of the Worlds* led to a panic). It takes a period of adjustment for people to become sophisticated in their reception and perception of information delivered in a different way.

In his book, Castronova predicted three major threats presented by networked VR: (1) a sociopath might create an addictive world; (2) an unethical corporation might build a world that is a threat in some way; (3) an irresponsible government agency might seduce people into an addictive world or regulate other worlds in a way that endangers or causes injury or restrictions to users (2005, p. 253). He warned, "We are unprepared for the emergence of a peer-to-peer world that might expose us to risks that we would rather not face. We can see countless opportunities for research, education, and innovation, but only a small cadre of for-profit builders have mastered the craft of building worlds, and there are no training programs that teach it. In view of this general ignorance of synthetic world technology and all it might mean, perhaps the wisest policy of all at this point would be simply to support more research" (p. 283).

In 1991 VR pioneer Tom Furness predicted before the U.S. Senate Subcommittee on Science, Space, and Technology that "televirtuality promises to subsume the existing media of communications." He explained that both humans and computers are growing more intelligent and, as they do so, they are collapsing their differences and merging.

In responding to the 2006 Pew Internet survey scenario, **Marilyn Cade**, a technology consultant and policy expert, wrote, "We should acknowledge and embrace this as a challenge and look for solutions and remedies, and safeguards...We should not deny the value of the advances of technology because of the harm; we should embrace the technology and study and seek to provide any appropriate awareness and safeguards, harnessing technology/and managing it effectively. To benefit, and not to harm humankind is the next frontier, isn't it?"

ADDITIONAL RESPONSES

Many other survey respondents shared comments tied to the scenario about the pros and cons of living chunks of our lives in an alternate reality. Among them:

> "All human problems derive from problems the individual has with him-/herself. Virtual reality will allow people to avoid the need to face, acknowledge, and overcome these personal issues. It will keep them safe and therefore they will prefer it." —**Amos Davidowitz**, director of education, training, and special programs for Institute of World Affairs; Association for Progressive Education

> "Addiction to virtual worlds is already a big issue; some of these worlds even have their own currency. There will be more diversity in interfaces with computers and data, and VR will certainly be commonly used in business." —**Michael Steele**, Internet user since 1978

> "Such ambivalent effects are typical of all great historical changes." —**Mark Poster**, professor of film and media studies, University of California–Irvine

> "By 2020, the main industry will still be Distraction. The distractions will be richer, more expansive, and at least as engaging relatively as television or today's video games. The minimum production values of all distractions will increase proportionate to the technology available and production costs of the top-tier distraction experiences. Addiction to distraction will continue to become more acceptable.

The absolutely trivial will continue to undermine social, civic, and political sensibilities. Alternate realities of 2020 will likely make our 'Halo 2' console game look like a pair of dice." —**Sam Punnett**, president, FAD Research

"Process addictions like sex and gambling will be replaced by virtual-reality sex and gambling, gaming, and 'traveling.'" —**Michael Collins**, CEO, a respondent who chose not to share further identifying information

> "We won't 'lose' people, but people will likely find virtual reality more interesting than the offline world. There will be a few people who don't interact much with the outside world, but there is something in human nature that craves real, physical closeness."
>
> —Randy Kluver,
> director, Institute for Pacific Asia at Texas A&M University

"Hard to agree or disagree, since it's hard to tell what the point of this question is. I don't think that virtual reality will be so real that it will be addictive in the same sense that alcohol or heroin is addictive." —**Stewart Alsop**, investor and analyst; former editor of InfoWorld and Fortune columnist

"First, I am not convinced that virtual reality will be so advanced in 15 years. Second, a section of society is always addicted to something, whether it be drugs or the latest fashion craze. This group does not threaten the larger community." —**Adrian Schofield**, head of research for ForgeAhead, South Africa; leader in the World Information Technology and Services Alliance (WITSA)

> "The Internet is becoming increasingly transparent—just as the air is. We will use it all the time as part of our daily life, just as we constantly breathe air. Therefore, we cannot become addicts to Internet anymore than we can become addicts to air."
>
> —María Laura Ferreyra,
> strategic planner,
> Instituto Universitario Aeronautico;
> ISOC member in Argentina

"As some people are already now becoming predominantly thinking-addicted, losing conscious contact with their emotions and body, this is likely to happen." —**Pekka Nikander**, Ericcson Research, Helsinki Institute for Information Technology; past member of the Internet Architecture Board

"Virtual reality is overplayed. The Internet is creating a new reality for so many people that 'virtual' won't be necessarily in high demand." —**Michael Gorrell**, senior VP and CIO, EBSCO

"More people will become addicted, but the problem will be minor and self-correcting." —**Willis Marti**, associate director for networking, Texas A&M University

"In many respects today, the novelty of virtual reality and interactive technology has captured many people's imaginations, and certainly anyone who can be addicted could be addicted to something like virtual reality as well. However, by 2020, virtual reality will become an integrated part of our lives, not just for technos and gamers. It will be as commonplace as using e-mail, surfing the Web, and cell phones are today. When the handheld calculator and then the personal PC were introduced, they were a novelty, but they were also tools and as such have become intrinsically integrated into our lives. Virtual reality will be just another way that we interact and go about our daily lives." —**Tom Snook**, CTO, New World Symphony

"Huh? We lose some folks to gambling and drugs now. And if drug addiction isn't an alternative reality, I doubt I know what is. I doubt that this will be a serious problem." —**Joe Bishop**, VP, business development, Marratech AB

"I'd introduce a qualifier: Anything that relieves people from their awful, 'real' realities may become an addiction. But, some people will really be weathered and weary by 2020." —**Alejandro Pisanty**, CIO for UNAM (National University of Mexico); vice chairman of the board for ICANN; member of UN Working Group for Internet Governance; active in ISOC

"I don't think that excursions to alternative realities will be a serious social problem. People 'check out' in all sorts of ways, and this form of escape is at least social." —**David Clark**, Internet pioneer; senior research scientist at MIT

"Call this the 'Holodeck bogeyman.' There was a good *Star Trek: The Next Generation* episode with the above as the plot ('Hollow Pursuits'). It's just a TV screen. Reminds me of a joke told at MIT: 'DESAAD: Master, I have found it! "Doom" plus "Magic" plus "IRC" plus netnews plus MUDding! DARKSEID: You cringing fool! That is not the Anti-Life Formula, it is the

No-Life Formula.'" —**Seth Finkelstein**, anticensorship activist and programmer; author of the Infothought blog; EFF Pioneer Award winner

"I use the Internet to accomplish a lot. However, as powerful and important as the Internet is in accomplishing what I need done, I still travel to all continents except Antarctica on a regular basis for face-to-face meetings. For this to change, human dynamics have to be altered in a fairly fundamental way, and it's not obvious to me that this can be done in anything less than generations." —**Fred Baker**, CISCO Fellow, CISCO Systems; Internet Society (ISOC) chairman of the board; Internet Engineering Task Force

"This prediction is very hard for people in my generation (baby boomers) to judge. Younger generations are more in touch with the facts on the ground, and can sense how far role playing and virtual reality have penetrated." —**Andy Oram**, writer and editor for O'Reilly Media

"Addictive personalities needing escape will, I'm afraid, be lured into this as an alternate reality—same as they can be to other activities/behaviors." —**Cheryl Langdon-Orr**, independent Internet business operator; director, ISOC-Australia

"The signs are already there. Check out what the military is doing with simulations, VR collaborations, and game-based learning. Also check out the consumer sphere, with *Second Life* and others. Anyone who has read *Life on the Screen* knows that even in its pure textual days, the Internet was a place for exploring alternate realities." —**Joel Hartman**, CIO, University of Central Florida

"This has already happened, with MMORPGs being an obvious example. The people that 'inhabit' these worlds are able to become more powerful than anything they might hope to achieve in the 'real world.' They can amass vast virtual fortunes online that happen to have real dollar value as well, often generating enough to actually make a living from. However, while this activity will expand, there is little chance in it becoming pervasive, as virtual reality in the next 15 years, while becoming more immersive, will still remain the realm of online gaming." —**Philip Joung**, Spirent Communications

"Virtual reality is a drain in proportion to disaffection with the 'real world.' Although virtual reality can be culturally rich, we need people to be engaged in real-world issues like pollution, poverty, and peace." —**Karen Coyle**, information professional and librarian

"The possibility is real; but hopefully we (humans) will wake up and realize that the real world is much better than the virtual world." —**Sharon Lane**, president, WebPageDesign

"Virtual reality will not become a reality by 2020. That is, it will exist, but only as a tool, not as a primary 'anything.' The home will have ultra-high bandwidth providing for virtually any kind of communication, at a low subscription rate, but virtual reality is not going to be any kind of major factor." —**Don Heath**, board member, iPool, Brilliant Cities, Inc., Diversified Software, Alcatel, Foretec

"We lose people to online and other games today; we'll lose people to virtual reality games and communication tomorrow. Not a big deal." —**John Browning**, cofounder of First Tuesday, a global network dedicated to entrepreneurs; former writer for *The Economist* and other top publications

"We will not lose people to Internet VR more often or more intensely than we already do to other media—television being the classic example. Some escapism will always be necessary for most people, and to escape for good, one way or another, is an option that is already available. Media, including Internet VR, will remain to generate the type and means of escapism that will be socially accepted." —**Suely Fragoso**, professor, Unisinos, Brazil

"This has already happened in 2006. However, for some people these will be seen as realities rather than alternative realities." —**Mark Gaved**, The Open University, U.K.

"This scenario is only partially valid, even among geeks' communities. People will lose contact with real realities as a result of many other factors, including the transformation of the latter is pseudorealities, that is artificially constructed substitutes to the former and vanished real world (e.g., natural environment, true products 'as in the old times', etc.)." —**Michel Menou**, professor and information-science researcher

"'Virtual reality will turn us all into shut-ins!' What is this, 1996? *World of Warcraft* is the new golf. The reason it's so incredibly compelling is because it's FULL OF PEOPLE!"
—Cory Doctorow, blogger and cofounder of Boing Boing; EFF Fellow

"Virtual reality has existed since the beginning of human history. With storytellers, drugs, ecstatic experiences, etc. Yes, the information technology can create a more enveloping experience, but it is, by necessity of this very fact, a less personal one. The science-fiction image of the 'wire' junkie, of the kid that lives in VR, requires more than just a little more computing power to become feasible. It requires a complete revolution in our existing technology. The very best created worlds, those presented by the top end computer games, are far from convincing as reality. They depend entirely on two senses—vision and sound. Our experience of reality depends on at least three other senses—touch, smell, and taste—with smell being particularly powerful in our localisation of our selves. Until there is technology that can provide stimulation of these senses as well, VR will remain a tool or a toy, it will not become an alternative to reality." —**Robin Lane**, educator and philosopher, Universidade Federal do Rio Grande do Sul, Brazil

"'Serious addiction problems for many'—depends on the meaning of 'many.' This will be a social phenomenon, but probably limited to a small minority in the population." —**Gary Chapman**, director, The 21st Century Project, LBJ School of Public Affairs at the University of Texas–Austin

"Virtual reality will not be used seriously except for training simulations and games, until it can provide for all five senses and reproduce the world in exacting detail—and that won't happen until a much later date. Much more interesting is augmented reality and ubiquitous computing. These technologies will have a major effect on human interaction with each other and the physical world, enabled by wireless embedded systems and dramatic improvements in automated sensing equipment that are already well underway (such as RFID, GPS location, and automated barcode and context detecting using mobile phone cameras)." —**Simon Woodside**, CEO, Semacode Corporation

"Despite concerns in the past that the Internet would lead to a breakdown in human interaction, the opposite has proven to be true. Interaction with a virtual world may actually provide a safe environment for people with social challenges to build their confidence and skills for person-to-person communication." —**Rick Gentry**, acquisition coordinator, Greenpeace

"As the hi-def games increase in seductiveness, I do think more players will see the 'real world' as an alternate world where they eat, use the bathroom, sleep, and perhaps work and have sex. Of course there are many real-world obsessions where people may seem lost or disconnected from a well-rounded and varied set of life activities." —**Steve Cisler**, former senior library scientist for Apple; now working on public-access projects in Guatemala, Ecuador, and Uganda

"I think it could be a productivity boost in cases where the people are geographically distributed but interact frequently (e.g., 3D conferencing). It could also be a boost in prototyping physical objects (aircraft, cars, etc). I think the people that would get 'lost' in the virtual-reality world would be few and would probably be the same people who are currently lost in the gaming world." —**Rangi Keen**, software engineer, Centric Software

"There will be addiction, but it won't be considered a problem. Well, maybe in the way that watching television for over 4 hours a day is considered a problem. Losing people to alternate realities? I don't think these people would have stayed in our reality without the virtual world." —**Carlo Hagemann**, professor, Radboud Universiteit Nijmegen, The Netherlands

"The online world is only ever an extension of the offline world with a different set of constraints. Anything that can be a problem in the physical world can be a problem in the virtual world—positive and negative." —**Lisa Kamm**, has worked in information architecture since 1995 at organizations including IBM, Agency. com and the ACLU

"I don't believe there is a 'virtual reality' for many people, neither now nor then. The Internet will become increasingly important both economically, as the basis for media of communication as well as for learning and leisure; but online and offline will increasingly become integrated, and we'll learn how to manage the respective dangers and benefits.

There will be no more 'alternate realities' and addiction in respect to the Internet than what we can see in respect to TV today." —**Florian Schlichting**, PhD candidate and researcher, University College, London

"This is not new—fantasy production is old as fantasy, novels, films, plays, etc. Just another venue, and as in the old days, somebody gets addicted or flee into their own fantasy worlds." —**Arent Greve**, professor, Norwegian School of Economics and Business Administration

"I look forward to an updated version of DSM :-)" —**Andy Williamson**, managing director for Wairua Consulting Limited, New Zealand; member of the NZ government's Digital Strategy Advisory Group

"Disagree with the addiction premise. People have always had access to alternate realities. Some people choose to avail themselves; most don't." —**Sherida Ryan**, Internet analyst, Openflows Networks Ltd.

"Virtual realities will certainly be attractive to addictive personalities. However, it is a mistake to talk about this (especially in Washington) in terms of cause and effect. Virtual realities will not 'lead to' addiction problems. People with addiction problems may find an outlet for expression in virtual realities, but there will always be outlets for addictions, with or without virtual realities that are made possible by the Internet." —**Nan Dawkins**, cofounder, RedBoots Consulting

"The concern for Internet addiction is highly overrated—statistics show that in today's world (where the mantra of Internet addiction can be heard all the time) such addiction is actually only a minor problem affecting very small groups of people). I do not see why this should change in the future." —**B. van den Berg**, faculty of philosophy at Erasmus University, Rotterdam, The Netherlands

"Current research seems to suggest that those who spend much time interacting online also have many social ties in the face-to-face realm." —**Peter P. Nieckarz, Jr.**, assistant professor of sociology, Western Carolina University

"One needs to be careful how they operationalise 'addiction.' To date, the research has found that very few people are addicted to the Internet per se. There are others that use the Internet because of their addiction. For example, some gamblers use the Internet to gamble amongst many other avenues. In most cases, it is not an 'Internet gambling addiction' they have but a gambling addiction. —**Monica Whitty**, professor, Queen's University, Belfast

"Every age has suffered from analogous addictions. No great loss here." —**Edward Lee Lamoureux**, associate professor, Bradley University

"Virtual worlds, where the problems are not real and the pleasures can be heightened, will lead to addiction problems, just like gambling, alcohol, and drugs do now." —**Jim Jansen**, assistant professor, Penn State University

"Individuals who are predisposed to this type of 'addiction' will fall victim to virtual realities and escape from life. For others virtual technologies create powerful tools for design and for team collaboration." —**Kathleen Pierz**, managing partner, The Pierz Group

"I think the biological world still holds some attractions that are needed to survive and people will be able to moderate their virtual activities." —**Cleo Parker**, senior manager, BBDO

"In 2006 this is already the case. We are not discussing this enough." —**Deborah Jones**, freelance journalist; Canadian technology writer

"We have already lost a lot of young people to virtual worlds; god knows what will happen in 2020." —**Russell Steele**, owner, The Insightworks

"For some. This is already a problem with online gambling sites, video porn, and online interactive games. Especially in gaming, where preprogrammed action is increasingly being replaced by the spontaneous actions of real players, games are becoming even more compelling and addictive. The more compelling and realistic these experiences become, the more a certain profile of person will withdraw from the outside world. Clearly, new addiction problems will arise." —**Kerry Kelley**, VP, product marketing, SnapNames.com

"If one simply looks into the massively multiplayer gaming worlds of today, one quickly will see the impressive power and influence these type virtual worlds can and do have on the user communities. I anticipate that this Interactive Entertainment model will be duplicated in our private/social lives (SIMS) as well as the corporate and government worlds mainly for the betterment of mankind—but it can also be abused and become a replacement for drugs." —**Jim (Jacomo) Aimone**, director of network development, HTC

"I cannot comment here because I am too jealous of my own time to devote any of it to a virtual reality exercise. There is too much to do in the real world." —**Ralph Blanchard**, investor, information services entrepreneur

"Society loses people to alternate realities today through drugs, alcohol, gambling, reality shows, and sim games." —**Ted Summerfield**, president, Punzhu.com

"Addictive personalities will always find something to be addicted to; if virtual-reality worlds do not exist, they will find something else for their addiction. So, although I agree that it will lead to 'serious addiction problems for many,' it will be a displaced addiction, displaced from something else that would have borne the brunt of their addiction." —**Jeffrey Branzburg**, educational consultant for National Urban Alliance, Center for Applied Technologies in Education, and other groups

"While virtual reality may suck some into unbalanced lives, there is also the chance that face-to-face friends, family, and community will become more meaningful as complement to the online part of life." —**Janet Salmons**, president, Vision2Lead Inc.; consultant on organizational leadership and development and virtual learning

"Online life already supports offline life. People want to see each other face to face. Some people will get sucked into virtual reality—*EverQuest* players, for instance. This 'addiction' might be a problem for some but not widespread." —**Susan Wilhite**, design anthropologist, Habitat for Humanity

"Again, this will move faster than we realize if business moves to virtual reality. The place where it really makes sense is in medicine, earth sciences, science altogether—but most people won't be able to distinguish between the real world and their virtual world." —**Judi Laing**, Southern California Public Radio

"We are seeing signs of the escapist in children today, more and more spend time on the Internet (read: Pew Internet reports) living the virtual life! Would they know who they really are? Would we?" —**Alik Khanna**, Smart Analyst Inc., a business employing financial analysts in India

"For some, addiction to technology-based activities such as gaming or social networks is already a reality. As the technology improves and its reach widens, so will the number of people whose only means of establishing 'control' of their lives through a virtual existence to the cost of their real lives." —**J. Fox**, a respondent who chose not to share further identifying information

"The *Star Trek* holodeck is beyond 2020. Various forms of online addiction such as gaming are already reality. Is an online gamer more valuable than a passive couch potato watching TV?" —**Brian T. Nakamoto**, Everyone.net, a leading provider of outsourced e-mail solutions

"Most people will continue to associate in the 'real world' and use the virtual technology as a supplemental communication channel rather than an alternative experience." —**Ellen K. Sullivan**, former diplomat; policy fellow, George Mason University School of Public Policy

"I believe this statement is an adequate summary of the parallel contradictory trends. Many of the trends we will see will have contradictory countervailing trends as well. But the accumulation of power and control via the effective use of technology will have devastating effects in many unanticipated ways." —**Benjamin Ben-Baruch**, senior market intelligence consultant and applied sociologist, Aquent, General Motors, Eastern Michigan University

"I am quite confident that real is real, virtual is virtual. These two cannot be replaced with each other in our daily life." —**Yiu Chan**, Internet user since 1995

"Real-world addictive pursuits, such as gambling and using pornography, are easier to access online. This will pose problems for those with difficulties in this area." —**Mark Crowley**, researcher, The Customer Respect Group

"I also believe that virtual reality, once the technology begins to incorporate additional senses (especially tactile ones), will take virtual, commercial pornography to new—and dangerous—levels." —**Roger Scimé**, self-employed Web designer

"That covers it." —**Gordon MacDiarmid**, Lobo Internet Services

"Although some people prefer to be plugged in to *The Matrix*, most realise that the true benefit of online activity is how it can empower your 'real life'—not your 'second life.'" —**Peter Kim**, senior analyst, marketing strategy and technology team, Forrester Research

"Addiction is a feature included in a small percentage of the current release of human beings. Virtual-reality addiction will likely capture a portion of those who would otherwise have turned to more organic forms of addiction like alcohol, Sudoku, or chocolate." —**Jeff Hammond**, VP, Rhea + Kaiser

"People with addict personalities will have this problem, but not very different from the present." —**Mario Rios**, TDCLA (Tecnologías del Conocimiento, an e-learning group), Chile

"There's something else I'd like to add: Virtual reality will be a drain for the 'savvy communities,' too. To be within the 'savvy community,' it is a must to keep oneself updating. As time goes on, as age comes, the strength to keep oneself updated diminishes. When this strength is zeroed, is completely out of the savvy community. We won't lose people to alternate realities; we will lose people to mental problems." —**Ivair Bigaran**, Global Messenger Courier do Brasil, American Box Serviço Int'l S/C Ltda.

"Would we say that television has led to serious addiction problems for many and that we have lost people to alternate realities? Probably not, because TV has become so integrated into our culture. Maybe the same will apply to virtual reality." —**Henry Potts**, professor, University College, London

"We need to be aware of the way technology can isolate people from real relationships with others. Addictions are also a real concern. Technology often allows one to become more anonymous, thus leading to more destructive behaviors when not held accountable." —**Jeff Bohrer**, learning technology consultant, University of Wisconsin–Madison

"There are benefits and drawbacks to any technology use. It is possible to make the argument, I think, that we have 'lost' people to an agricultural society, which for the most part doesn't exist in the way that many wish that it would and that farm subsidies support a technology-based lifestyle at the expense of some other lifestyles. Separately, we may indeed lose people to alternate realities. The result of this choice of focus on the part of some may also benefit the human species." —**Mary Ann Allison**, chairman and chief cybernetics officer, The Allison Group, LLC; futurist

"Naa, my father will still be alive in 2020, and with life increase due to technology (ironic, *non*?) many of his generation so will be. Give it more time, as dinosaurs get extinct." —**Wainer Lusoli**, University of Chester, U.K.

"Yes, there will be a media-fueled awareness of 'VR addiction' and public-health campaigns will target it. However, the virtual communities formed via electronic networks will be far more powerful, transformative, and important." —**Daniel Conover**, new-media developer, Evening Post Publishing

"We have already seen examples of this in the recent past. Anyone that was an early user of AOL recognized its addictive nature. People were going broke because they paid for access by the hour. You could say the same thing about some computer games as well." —**Robert Lunn**, Focalpoint Analytics; senior research analyst on the 2004 Digital Future Report

"This has been the tired wail of every generation since Gutenberg threatened the world with the attractive alternate reality of literacy. Reality simply expands to take in the new 'alternate' and become richer." —**Walt Dickie**, VP and CTO, C&R Research

"It is not the type of technology that is addictive. Online community-type video games might have some people so addicted that they play for 8 or 10 hours per day. I can't see

where virtual reality can make the situation much worse."
—**Doug Olenick**, computer technology editor, *TWICE (This Week in Consumer Electronics)* magazine

"I don't believe that in a relatively short term of time, like it is 15 years, the virtual reality substitutes to the real world. The human being even has a lot of road that to travel in that sense."
—**Sabino M. Rodriguez**, MC&S Services

"I agree fully to the first part (I mean, I'm one of those ;-), but the second issue is more in the section of 'computer games addiction,' 'chat fever,' or something similarly harmless for ordinary people. Historically, numerous religious people have virtually lived 'in a world beyond' and I would argue that certain Eastern religions based on the unreality of the real world systematically promote a similar escapism via meditation, etc. Not a big issue." —**Mikkel Holm Sørensen**, software and intelligence manager, Actics Ltd.

"That already happens with drugs, gambling, church, and TV, but in a virtual world, one can now live 24/7, working, earning money, paying bills, and entertaining oneself." —**Alix L. Paultre**, executive editor, Hearst Business Media, Smartalix.com, Zep Tepi Publishing

"Already people are lost in virtual reality. Living in one's head is a basic human trait. As the telephone is an extension of the ear, the automobile is an extension of the leg, cameras are extensions of the eyes—computers can be said to be extensions of the brain. When it becomes easier to live inside your head, because you can bank online, order food online, entertain yourself online, and so forth, people are less motivated to move out of their brains and into their active, physical lives."
—**Elle Tracy**, president and e-strategies consultant, The Results Group

"Once propagated and adopted, the potential is very high for the emergence of a critical mass of alternate-realities applications that would dilute the gains in productivity yielded by the business adopters." —**Kevin McFall**, director, Online Products & Affiliate Programs, Tribune Media Services, NextCast Media

"This 'serious addiction' label is applied too loosely in many current scenarios and I'm sad to see it applied here. There are always individuals willing to give up their own autonomy, and if VR is an option, a few will fall that way. Overall, VR holds great promise for breaking down barriers both geographical and temporal." —**Suzanne Stefanac**, author and interactive media strategist, dispatchesfromblogistan.com

"The virtual reality provided by some electronic communication now I believe has social consequences—there are cases of new medical problems, for example, with individuals 'addicted' to SMS messaging. Although virtual reality may be a boon to productivity in some communities, it may be another diversion for many more. Ultimately, shouldn't technology serve reality?" —**Jean-Pierre Calabretto**, PhD student, University of South Australia

"There are many people in alternative realities now—drug addiction, gambling, shopping channel (ha ha). It would be surprising if VR does not claim a certain number of people as well." —**Jeff Corman**, government policy analyst, Industry Canada, Government of Canada

ANONYMOUS COMMENTS

A number of anonymous survey respondents shared comments tied to the scenario about the pros and cons of living chunks of our lives in an alternate reality. Among them:

"That is in the nature of it."

"Well, yes, but aren't some people addicted to 'real life' in equally unhealthy ways?"

"DUH."

"This is a very real danger."

"Not a big problem."

"The appeal of virtuality will lead to problems for some, as existence in virtual spaces becomes increasingly available and possible. Social resources will need to be shifted to address these concerns."

"How sad, but it's reality for the future."

"Greater productivity may be illusory."

"And they will claim they are not lost, but they have found their true world. And there will be serious debate about that."

"Augmented reality will be more common than virtual reality."

"There is a growing addiction in the making."

"The top addiction problem that will be addressed is our addiction to technology and computers."

"The alternate realities we create are part of our 'real world.'"

"Anecdotal evidence regarding suicide among those who play a lot of games seems to support this."

"This is already happening. I am trying to reclaim the time I used to spend reading but now spend tooling around on the Internet. Not only will we end up feeling drained, but more and more of the 'facts' we think we know we will be unable to identify where they came from. Without being able to recall where we read one thing or another, we will become more vulnerable to misinformation."

> *Some predictions from respondents who chose to remain anonymous:*
>
> **"Human beings began to alter the real a long time ago—whatever the word 'real' means."**
>
> **"Human interaction is essential. Only those already disconnected will drift off totally."**

"People will also be forced to use the Internet and technologies more, which will create a cycle of dependency and obsession over remaining connected for as much as possible."

"Virtual reality effects are exaggerated; however, non-face-to-face exchanges of all kinds, including sex, will grow."

"We already see evidence of this with MMOGs like *World of Warcraft* and *EverQuest* (referred to by many as EverCrack). However, AIrtual [editor's note—this refers to a mix of 'artificial intelligence' and 'virtual'] companies, development shops, etc., will put virtual reality to good use."

"We already are losing people not only to VR, but to interactive spaces, and the divide between passive media consumers and interactive media users is widening. The place to look is at teenagers and preteenagers, and the signs are ominous, not only of their weight problems, but of sharp divisions in cognition between young people who are awake and engaged and young people who seem consumed by an odd listlessness, a dullness that nothing, not even interactive media and VR, can penetrate. I'd argue that soon entirely separate school systems will be necessary, because there will be little crossover in that divide."

"Yes, just as people are so easily lured into the quicksand of drugs, people will also be lured into virtual worlds where they can experience the power that is denied them in the real world. So sad, but I see it coming."

"The people we are losing and will lose will be the youth of our country. Now, I realize that I sound like an aging individual… bummer. But the fact is that 'screen time'—and I mean TV, gaming consoles, PCs, etc.—appears to rob children of basic developmental processes. I witness limitations in the ability of younger individuals to think creatively, abstractly, and spontaneously. Does anyone tell their children to just 'go outside and play'? Virtual reality is created, conceived of, and presented by someone else…through the programs and AI it is delivered to another human…seems self-limiting."

"Too many people already have a serious problem discerning fantasy from reality, not to mention that they don't want to interact with other human beings. I see that this as a serious problem. I grew up when people were killing themselves because they believed that they were their characters in D&D—VR will just fuel the fire."

"There will certainly be VR addicts, mostly in gaming and porno worlds. But I doubt VR will replace the office."

"This is especially true in the area of men and pornography. It is wrecking lives today and careers, and as it becomes even more realistic, it will destroy families and committed relationships by making this stuff so easily accessible to so many that may have addictions to this stuff—the same as gambling."

"Until smell and tactile sensation is fully integrated into virtual reality, not a major problem—and I don't believe true five-sense virtual reality will be available in 2020. In addition, such a problem may only exist for the set of addictive personalities who are already abusing various escapes."

"People are addicted today to many different things. People were addicted to things in the past and will continue to be addicted to things in the present. Addictions will continue and change with the times."

"People do not get 'lost' in alternate realities. People choose to participate in alternate realities because they find it an efficient way to communicate with other people and build communities. This dystopian view of 'getting lost' was also prevalent when the Internet first became mainstream. However, people have not gotten 'lost' on the Internet, even when participating in alternate spaces such as MOOs (MUD—object-oriented) and MUDs (multiuser domains). If the VR structure is especially appealing to some, they will incorporate participation in it as part of their daily lives. The VR communities will supplement 'RL' (real life) with respects to entertainment, work, and social support."

"Those who are inclined to serious addiction will always find something to be seriously addicted to, whether it is watching sports, tending to a garden, or living in alternate realities. People who spend time in *EverQuest* were surveyed about whether they thought of themselves as citizens of the real world who sometimes play in *EverQuest*, or citizens of *EverQuest* who sometimes play in the real world. Something like 60% responded the latter."

> **Predictions from respondents who chose to remain anonymous:**
>
> "'Lead to'? Check out MMOR-PGs now—inhabiting a virtual world at the expense of the real one is already an issue."
>
> "It's this way today—ever played *World of Warcraft*?"

"There will always be a minority of people who are addicted to whatever there is to be addicted to. So, it will be alternate reality for some. This problem is overblown."

"We already lose people to alternate realities. I've known at least three people who fabricated enough of their life online that they just had to commit suicide in that life in order to retain their real one."

"Can you imagine an implanted chip that allows a person to enter an alternative reality anywhere or any time? Nightmarish image."

"This is already the case and it will increase with more immersive environments."

"Drug addiction will continue to be a bigger problem than 'Internet-related' addictions. Only if virtual reality mixes with 'meatspace' chemicals will the problem become more reality than sensationalist hype."

"People are designed for community. The pendulum will swing but ultimately we will find the need for others."

"Every new technology brings new problems and this is unavoidable. The measure of our societies is how we deal with the problems. Criminalise or socialise."

"I agree about the productivity. However, I think the addiction problem will happen for a very small minority."

"Virtual reality is dead. Everything is virtual. If by VR you mean persistent virtual worlds, or synthetic worlds, the question would be different, and so would the answers be."

"I don't think this will be too large a percentage of the population."

"A real problem will be the loss of some key social interaction skills for some."

"I don't know that computers are any more addictive than other obsessions that trap people in their grip—it's just that we tend to be more suspicious of computers than we are of alcohol and drugs and gambling."

Predictions from respondents who chose to remain anonymous:

"We will become vulnerable to misinformation."

"Non-face-to-face exchanges of all kinds, including sex, will grow."

"Real world and virtual world will have strong fights. In 2020, the heat of the battlefield will be over, and we will be licking our wounds."

"This seems to be already happening for some even with today's online games, and by 2020, today's most enthusiastic gamers will be well up the age scale."

"Human behavior sophistication/discrimination will help to maintain sanity."

"You can see it happening already in the antisocial behavior depicted by our children who consider a playdate to be each person taking their turn using the PSP or Game Boy."

"But so what? Some people have always chosen 'alternate realities' such as meditation, drugs, and even just eternal irresponsibility."

"There is in my opinion a single-digit percentage of the population that might be effected as described above."

"I definitely see this as an issue. Each new 'big thing' sees people who go overboard with it and leads to addiction. Virtual reality can certainly be abused, as can other ways to 'escape' reality such as drugs, alcohol, etc."

"The pervasiveness of virtual realities will allow people to create multiple identities; however, the human connection and the need to fit in with others will continue to be issues for most. Thus, those who do not have strong personal and human ties will be easily lured by the attractive nature of the virtual-reality worlds but at the cost of true lasting relationships."

"If it's virtual, it cannot be real. So this prediction is just a stupid formulation. What is sure is that the value will remain in the reaction to other users. The virtual world has no value if it does not bring a user benefit in the real one. But we can nevertheless be faced with misunderstanding from some customers."

"Yes, we're already seeing that by the 'EverCrack' and similar MMO games that take people away from the 'real world' in terms of entertainment and socializing. Teenagers rush home after school and IM with each other (although are they just IMing with ways to meet each other later?). Everything done beyond moderation can be addicting, whether it's Internet usage, going online in a virtual world, or drinking to excess.

Advances in virtual world technologies will only add one more thing that people can get addicted to. On the other hand, I do agree that virtual reality will allow more productivity for people in tech-savvy communities, as it will be easier for them to work without the distractions of the typical 'physical workplace.' As much as had been argued about the need for in-person meetings and the 'water cooler,' I don't think it's as important as people are arguing."

"Gaming is already being associated with mental illness. Cell phones and iPods are today's cigarettes. The overstimulation many young people face will cause them to burn out faster."

"I don't agree that this is bad. The line between this reality and virtual reality will increasingly become blurred. But it won't make a difference. Money will be the same in either reality, as will love and human contact. Ultimately, many people will juggle two lives, while some who are unable to cope, will settle on a single life—either in this reality or in virtual reality. That number will be a small percentage, and I suspect will be little different from the number of people who use drugs now as escapism."

"We're already having problems with people becoming addicted to online worlds—chat rooms, online gambling for teenagers, blogging for adults—yes, the problem will be worse."

> *Predictions from respondents who chose to remain anonymous:*
>
> **"We see evidence of this in MMOGs like *World of Warcraft* and *Ever-Quest* (referred to as EverCrack). However, AIrtual companies, development shops, etc., will put virtual reality to good use.**
>
> **"This problem is overblown."**

"Look at the insular world that is being created by iPods, noise-reducing headsets, and personalized video players."

"I am afraid this is a likely scenario with people being lost to virtual worlds."

"The sensations that can be delivered via electronics and mechanics will exceed the sensations created by drugs."

"Reality is relative anyway."

"How will those who live in poverty and diminishing opportunity today not be bitter and more activist in the future? Terrorism within our own population will be the cause of the biggest drain and those lost in virtual reality (whether computer or wealth simulated) will probably be the first victims. This is not a threat, but seems a sad possibility all around."

"The Internet is already a huge black hole for time."

"The workplace will not change that much in 14 years."

"Virtual reality will never surpass the fantasizing power of the human mind! It might as well be said that chronic daydreamers are 'imagination addicts.'"

"The question is irrelevant. Anything can be addicting and detrimental, and for many VR already is. So what?"

"I doubt that it will be worse than it is now. If, on the other hand, we dramatically improve our holographic, smell, and haptic (touch) capabilities, virtual reality could indeed become increasingly threatening to real-world relationships."

"Not only addiction, but time wasting on a level rivalled only by television. We've seen studies of work-unrelated 'puter use in the workplace; at home, by all ages, not just Runescape-addled teens, the computer sucks time from front porch neighborliness, home maintenance, physical activity, community involvement."

Predictions from respondents who chose to remain anonymous:

"Social resources will need to be shifted to address these concerns."

"I don't know that computers are any more addictive than other obsessions...it's just that we tend to be more suspicious of computers than we are of alcohol and drugs."

"'Real world' person-to-person jobs will always be important. There will be those who seem to prefer the alternate reality that technology brings them, but their numbers will not be significant."

"There are many people who can't handle technological progress, from a while back, like fire, wheels, cars, guns, etc."

"As this is happening with teleworking and IM/chatting already, the more impressive the presented reality the more this will happen."

"It's already happening with young people. They live online in ways they can't possibly stomach offline. If they can find a way to make money from these activities and they can keep most of them hidden from whomever they choose, they will continue to retreat into their cocoon."

"We see this trend in gaming already."

"This one is obvious. They don't call it 'EverCrack' for nothing. MMORPGs...are extremely addictive; we're already there."

"As we are learning from the gaming generation, online activities can encourage social behaviors. Addiction is a possibility, not a probability."

"Virtual reality by 2020 will likely be fully immersive—possibly to an extent made possible only by network connections to brain circuitry. But we will NOT see it in business except in narrow niches. As for addiction, we've heard that song before about video games."

"There will always be a portion of the population who will be 'addicted' to something—but I don't think this will become rampant."

"Moral panics have accompanied every new medium so far. Psychos as well as Lud-omaniacs will continue to abound, but will not be the product of virtual reality."

"For most people on the planet, living in the 'real world' is no bargain. That's why we have Disney World and Las Vegas. Virtual reality will be a much less expensive and safe way to escape the everyday burdens of life—a much needed improvement over drugs, alcohol, and what is otherwise truly self-destructive behavior."

"Whilst some will become addicted, the majority won't. Virtual reality will come in many different forms: holograms, virtual screens projected into specific areas of control (reality today), and any surface or nonsurface people want to communicate; VR will become a communications and life aid."

"Many people are already addicted to virtual realities (such as online games). Increases in immersive technology will only increase the problems. However, I believe the promises of VR at those levels are still further off than 2020, given the slow rate of global technological advances taken as a whole (e.g., disparity between industrialized and Global South nations with regard to technological infrastructure)."

"One could write an essay on this one. A short answer is that people will be no more or less in alternate realities than they ever have been."

"In my opinion, this is happening on many levels already."

"A doomsday, technologically deterministic view like many we have seen before."

"Participation in virtual-reality worlds has and will continue to have limits, similar to those of real worlds. The life cycles of community formation and dissolution will mark online worlds just as they do offline worlds. Moreover, as the novelty of virtual-reality worlds wears off, participation in them will hold steady or even decrease, thereby containing addiction to them."

"The greater problem will arise from the increasing knowledge and economic gap between those benefiting from the technological savvy and those 'left behind in the real world.'"

"People will increasingly not notice the technology; reality will include technology; the concept of VR will seem odd."

> **Predictions from respondents who chose to remain anonymous:**
>
> "I've known at least three people who fabricated enough of their life online that they just had to suicide that life in order to retain their real one."
>
> "People do not get 'lost' in alternate realities. People choose to participate in alternate realities because they find it an effective way to communicate with other people and build communities...VR communities will support RL (real life)."

"Look to current consumption of online games. While these participants are arguably different from the mainstream, in their early uptake of new technologies, for one example, other populations have demonstrated 'addictive' qualities with social software that is not online gaming."

"Virtual reality will disappear, as it ought to for a long time already—the Internet will be more and more part of everyday life, certainly not a disconnected and separated entity."

"This scenario will doubtless play out for at least 'some,' but I'm not sure it will for 'many.'"

"I think we have a good example already: a table of teenagers all sitting and talking on their cell phones rather than to each other."

"Humans control the technology. Sure, some of the virtual-reality applications will be good enough to imply reality, but it is still a virtual reality, the key word being 'virtual.'"

"We have to pay more attention to the impact of VR. Our world is going to be untrustable—e.g., we can't trust photos or video as the images there can be fake. This is going to be a serious social impact to our world."

"Even children make the difference between their tales and the reality. And they can switch at will."

"It is happening right now with many playing MMORPGs. If you have the best spaceship in a community it does matter, and you won't be so sad that you can't have the best car in the real-world neighborhood."

"Virtual reality would be in 'real-life' reality as much as telephone, radio, and TV. Fears and prejudice about it would be finally displaced. Everybody will know the difference between face-to-face and online communication and will use it as a tool to grow their support and work networks."

"Addiction may be the case with some, but only very limited occupations can shift online. This scenario concerns a limited, privileged number of people."

"I haven't seen much promise for this proposed 'virtual reality' idea. Either the technology hasn't evolved enough yet, or we haven't found any practical application for it. I do think that ubiquitousness of computing and connectivity will help productivity, but when the systems go down, there will be generations of people who don't know how to use a phone book."

"It's not clear that ICT has increased productivity in general, so why would VR on the Internet increase productivity?"

"Real world and virtual world will have strong fights. In 2020 the heat of the battlefield will be over and we will be licking our wounds."

"This seems inevitable. To not recognize this as truth is to hold that legal alcohol will result in zero hangovers. On the other hand, heroin and cocaine were once legally purchased from English pharmacies and the country didn't turn into gutter-dwelling addicts. Addiction will remain addiction—whether it's alcohol, gambling, drugs, or a fantasy life."

"The broader concern is that we are human-machine instead of human-human, losing the commons, losing the community."

"Serious addiction is most likely as virtual reality takes over gaming and recreation. It will work well for some people, but the majority will prefer the real world."

"Gamers already exhibit some of these problems."

"It's already happening today—I watch my 14-year-old son lose himself every day in a virtual-reality-based game. At the same time, he is incredibly productive in that world, building and creating."

"Not my cup of tea, but judging how my students behave regarding technology, this is a serious risk for some people."

"Technology doesn't always increase productivity."

"There will be a problem; indeed, there already is a problem—but the way this is phrased is over-stated. Plus, addictiveness will be very limited."

"We already have this problem with religion. The central issue is one of personality and behavioural defects."

"To be lured by such things is certainly a part of human nature and this can be damaging if it is not balanced."

> *Predictions from respondents who chose to remain anonymous:*
>
> "Money will be the same in either reality, as will love and human contact. Ultimately, many people will juggle two lives."
>
> "How will those who live in poverty not be bitter and more activist in the future? Terrorism within our own population will be the cause of the biggest drain, and those lost in virtual reality (computer or wealth simulated) will probably be the first victims."
>
> "If it's virtual, it cannot be real. So this prediction is a stupid formulation. What is sure is that the value will remain in the reaction to other users. The virtual world has no value if it does not bring a user benefit in the real one."

"People will still be interested in real life. For 50 years, large numbers of Americans sat in front of the TV every evening from 6 p.m. to at least 10 p.m. Is the Internet so different?"

"The terminology here is troubling: The tidy divide between 'virtual' and 'real' has never existed and/or long ago became very blurred. The hysteria about 'addiction' is a kind of moral panic around technology that we saw with TV and phones—telephony itself permits 'virtual reality' after all! It is nothing new. But the idea of teenagers, especially, descending into some unholy hell of virtuality where all is pleasure, where there is no responsibility, and they die because they forget to stop and eat, is just plain silly."

"This trend, whether it happens by 2020 or not, portends danger to individuals as well as to our societies. The 'addiction' to gaming that we see setting in among increasing numbers of adolescents and young adults reveals their vulnerability. Only yesterday, a local newspaper ran a story of a grandmotherly woman who spend 12+ hours a day online in *Second Life*; it appeared that her avatar was more dominant and more important to her life than her real persona."

"I don't disagree with the addiction prediction, but I do disagree with the productivity increase. Most people who use a computer still double-click on hyperlinks; they are a long way from being able to benefit from collaboration in a virtual world."

"Parts of this are true—but we have always had among us on earth those whose reality varied from the observable. I don't think that will increase much."

"Virtual work makes workers more effective but does not substitute for real world activities. Virtual-world trap is less dangerous than drugs and Disney movies."

"One only needs to look at the gamer community to understand that there can be too much of a good thing. Nevertheless, I think that only a small percentage of the population will face this problem."

"The medical-training virtual medical center currently set up in *Second Life* is an interesting example of virtual-world training supporting increased productivity and efficient use of resources in RL. It was not envisioned or directed by the games' owners, simply set up independently like the rest of the *Second Life* VR, and used for this private purpose. Addictive personalities may indeed have problems with this as such VRs continue to become more 'realistic,' and potentially more appealing than RL. On the other hand, by finding like-minded individuals unlimited by geography, these persons may also be afforded human connections and interactions rather than being isolated. Ultimately, I suspect it is a net/net situation, or nearly so, as individuals with this type of issue might well have become 'addicted' to video games in the '80s or '90s, or Home Shopping Network, or gambling, or something else some other time."

"The amount of people who are involved in online games and communities will swell as the technology gets cheaper and easier to use."

"We know that people do best with FTF (face-to-face) relationships. This fear has been around for a while, going back to at least MUDs (multiuser domains)."

"We already experiencing this type of issue with the dissemination of chatting and webloggers, exposing some Web surfers to the so-called e-addiction, but this type of addictive won't be in any manner a threat to society. Let people have fun with that virtual reality."

"We have yet to find evidence of any kind of real 'media addiction'—why do we expect that we will find one related to virtual media?"

"I fully agree on this issue, and the best example regarding addiction problem is in Bangladesh."

"It is already happening, South Korea being the unfortunate pioneer."

"Virtual reality is booming, but people can make the break from it so as not to be addicted. Some technologies can be exported, and this could cause workers to be affected and uncared for."

"I believe this will happen more and more in the homes, where people disconnect from their environments and immerse themselves in VR worlds."

"As with other 'new' fads like hula-hoops, hopscotch, television, video games, etc., the Internet and VR will lose much of their addictiveness, and will be commonly used for specific purposes in specific timeslots."

"The real community will always play a big role. Until we have virtual family/child raising, children will always be raised directly, and direct communication will be seen as a standard. Virtual communication will grow, and addiction will be a problem, but I don't believe to the extent you're stating...Virtual reality provides no more addiction than obedience, gambling, video games, television, caffeine, or sugar."

Predictions from respondents who chose to remain anonymous:

"So what? Some people have always chosen 'alternate realities' such as meditation, drugs, and even just eternal irresponsibility."

"If it's virtual, it cannot be real... What is sure is that the value will remain in the reaction to other users. The virtual world has no value if it does not bring a user benefit in the real one."

"Virtual reality was a wet dream in the '90s and is irrelevant these days. The whole notion of disembodiment has been proven wrong. This will be also the case in the two decades from now."

"Yes some people will have addiction problems, but I don't think it will be necessarily worse than any other addicting environments, e.g., casinos, that exist today. I think the virtual reality worlds will draw people together just as e-mail, the Internet, chat, and multiplayer online games do now."

"While I suspect that some will be affected negatively by additions to virtual-reality worlds, I don't believe the 'many' will be beyond the 'many' who suffer various addictions today (many addictions are to substances which also allow access to a world 'different' in some sense from the one to which people attempt to escape)."

"We are human beings. The tangible world is still the escape from technology."

"I believe the rate of 'loss' to this kind of phenomena is basically fixed. I'm also skeptical about how real these experiences will feel."

"No question on this. But I do wonder why we assume this is such a bad thing, or so much worse than many of the alternatives."

"The 'virtual reality' world indicated above will be that of computer games. The addiction to interactive computer games is likely to increase. Other than that, I do not think that virtual reality will have a big impact on society in 2020."

"More sci-fi! Yes, VR will be better than today and provide benefits—but people still have to eat and buy food, i.e., they live in the real world."

"This is already happening with many virtual-reality games, and that will likely attract the most attention. The more insidious virtual reality is the virtual reality that already engulfs many people, the virtual reality of news and media that surrounds us today. This is not called a 'game' but in fact it is the biggest game."

"If our experience with Trekkies, gaming addicts, and Internet junkies are predictive, people will completely lose a sense of reality or knowledge of how to interact with other people. By the same token, spoken and written communications will be reduced to blurbs and sound bites, and newspapers will more closely resemble texting-style English."

"E.g., gambling or prescription drugs online right now."

"There is no research to support the idea of large-scale addiction problems now, and there is no reason to believe VR would accelerate the problem. Further, it is unlikely that VR will take off."

"Work is not progressing well in this area—the only two Internet-based applications that most people use—e-mail and Web. This isn't anywhere close in R&D and hasn't advanced at all in the last few years. People don't want to pay more for communication and will be less likely to do so in the next 10 years—don't think 'virtual reality' is even the right concept."

"Again, the scenario is misleading by combining professional and private use. Addiction in private use will come from marketing, as we see now with videogames, not from the nature of technology nor the inclination of the users. This will not be measurable in any meaningful way."

"The prediction is that by 2020, world travel, as we know it today, will not be possible—there will simply not be the oil to freely move around the globe. Virtual reality will be the way we communicate globally and 'travel.' I am not sure that addiction to virtual reality is necessarily any more harmful than other addictions, and most people are not going to be lost to alternate realities."

The Internet Opens Access and Blurs Boundaries

Prediction: *In the bestseller* The World Is Flat, *Thomas Friedman wrote that the latest world revolution is found in the fact that the power of the Internet makes it possible for individuals to collaborate and compete globally. This scenario: By 2020, the free flow of information will completely blur current national boundaries as they are replaced by city-states, corporation-based cultural groupings, and/or other geographically diverse and reconfigured human organizations tied together by global networks.*

Respondents' Reactions to This Scenario	
Agree	52%
Disagree	44%
Did not respond	5%

Note. Because results are based on a nonrandom sample, a margin of error cannot be computed.

Consensus of Opinion: There will be increasing opportunity for global success, and people will form allegiances to geography-neutral

social and work groupings while maintaining a national and/or regional identity as well. Some inequities will continue to exist in regard to technology knowledge and access, and some nations and/or corporations will continue to try to restrict what people can accomplish online.

A great number of the people of China and India are using networked digital technology today to advance their economies to new heights and to change the landscapes of their lives. These countries are held up as the prime examples, but many groups and individuals across the world are less isolated than they were just a decade ago, thanks to their leveraging of a relatively new tool called the Internet. A commonly cited proof of this is India's IT offshoring revenue, which totaled $17.2 billion in 2005, with more than 1 million Indian IT workers serving overseas customers. While many people recognized the globalization brought about by networked communications before *New York Times* columnist Thomas Friedman published his bestseller *The Word is Flat,* Friedman's book brought many vital issues about the future to the attention of well-read people in the West. Where will accelerating social and technological progress take the world in the next 15 years?

Survey responses to this proposed future ranged from "this will never happen" to "it's happening now." Most respondents agreed to the primary thrust of this scenario: that national groupings are being displaced to some extent by reconfigured human organizations tied together by global networks—city-states, corporation-based cultural groupings, and/or other geography-neutral sets of people. As in most of the earlier scenarios, a significant number of people found fault in enough of this proposed future to disagree with it, and many wrote elaborations that both agreed and disagreed with aspects of this future.

> "I agree. The mechanism for doing this, however, is the Next Generation Network infrastructure, not 'the Internet.'"
>
> —Anthony Rutkowski,
> VP for regulatory
> and standards, Verisign

Hal Varian, an expert on economics and technology at the University of California–Berkeley and consultant for Google, wrote, "I certainly agree that the Internet allows small groups to compete globally; in fact, I've written about 'micro-multinationals' as becoming an important force. But I think that such forces only work well in some domains. People will still be plowing fields on their own." **Charles Hendricksen** of Cedar Collaboration wrote, "The nation-state will become an administration entity rather than a cultural organizer."

Luc Faubert of dDocs, president of Quebec's Internet Society chapter and an ambassador to the World Summit on the Information Society, wrote, "Both types of associations are needed and will coexist: (a) a cross-border, interest-driven virtual communities; and (b) local communities."

Daniel Wang, principal partner with Roadmap Associates, wrote, "Much like tectonic shifts moved land masses long ago to form world geography, the online shifts we're experiencing are reconfiguring the human experience to form a new world order—one without borders. Success, however, will depend on the accessibility to networks, and whether the flat world is going to be an equal-opportunity one."

Gordon Bell, a senior researcher with Microsoft, noted that an economic reconfiguration will result from this scenario. "In the intervening 15 years," he responded, "there is going to be a very large financial reconning, as power is rebalanced."

Marc Rotenberg, executive director for the Electronic Privacy Information Center, said politics are key. "Citizens may be less willing to allow the collapse of nation-states if they believe that international organizations lack accountability," he wrote. "The debate over the WTO is a precursor to the future." **Michel Menou**, an information-science researcher who has worked in nearly 80 nations, wrote, "The decline of the nation-state is much more the result of the subversion of those supposed to represent and defend the common interest by forces that represent particular ones."

SOME PROJECT THE POSSIBILITY
OF TURBULENCE AND EVEN VIOLENCE

Paul Saffo, forecaster and director of The Institute for the Future, responded, "I mostly agree, but strongly object to the panglossian overstatement. This trend will continue, but the old order will fight back. National governments will aggressively defend their power, and corporate incumbents will fight dirty against networked challengers. I thus believe that the 2020 networked world will be a turbulent place, full of opportunity and real innovation, but also real risks. Friedman's writings will take their place alongside earlier optimist tracts extolling the wonders of technologies-to-come that over the years touted the benefits of radio (1930s), television (1950s), and personal computers (1970s)."

Pekka Nikander of Ericcson Research and the Helsinki Institute for Information Technology, a past member of the Internet Architecture Board, also expressed concerns about aggression.

> "There will be increased conflict among states and social movements reacting against the homogenization of the world, the 'Westernization' of the world, etc."
>
> —Benjamin Ben-Baruch, senior market intelligence consultant and applied sociologist, Aquent, General Motors, Eastern Michigan University

"The hind side of this scenario," he wrote, "is that the collapse of nation-states and other existing power structures is unlikely to be peaceful, causing widespread low-intensity violence."

Robin Lane, teacher and philosopher at Universidade Federal do Rio Grande do Sul in Brazil, responded, "It may lead to less conflict between nations. However, it may also result in more conflict as it creates cultural interfaces that were not factors in people's experience prior to high-speed international communications."

Ted Coopman of the University of Washington wrote, "Friedman... missed the 'democratization' of mass violence. While there will certainly be mass cooperation and competition, there will also be the ability of heretofore ineffectual entities to project power in unexpected and disruptive ways. This will be especially true for those who hold totalizing worldviews. This will result in a constant, global, low- to medium-intensity insurgent warfare manifesting across all venues and using all manner of repertoires to further agendas or thwart others. This will not be an entirely bad thing, as cooperation and building affinities and alliances will be the keys to success, rather than coercion."

SOME SAY NATIONAL DIVISIONS
ARE TOO STRONG TO OVERCOME

Many respondents said the established political systems in current world governments will resist major erosion and remain dominant. "Nation-states can control access to the Internet if they choose to," wrote **Joe Bishop**, a vice president with Marratech AB. "I doubt that national boundaries will dissolve by 2020 unless we discover extra-terrestrial intelligent life."

John Quarterman, president of InternetPerils, Inc., responded, "Some countries, such as U.S., Japan, and China, will remain sufficiently nationalistic that even with blurring, they'll still be distinct. Even in Europe, the EU project has had recent setbacks, and while national boundaries are more porous than they used to be, national feeling still exists. Blurred, yes; completely, no."

> "China is not going away by 2020."
>
> —Charlie Breindahl,
> IT University of Copenhagen

Barry Wellman, director of NetLab at the University of Toronto, wrote, "First off, I said the first sentence before Friedman; he just has better P.R. I agree with the first sentence, but disagree with 'completely blur.' We still have bodies; we, states, and organizations still have territorially based interests (in the political sense of that word)." **Mark Gaved** of The Open University in Manchester, U.K., wrote, "There will be peaks and troughs in access geographically and economically. The Internet will create cultural crises (like the issue over the Prophet Muhammad cartoon) that will reshape how we deal with issues in a transitional manner."

Gary Chapman, director of The 21st Century Project at the LBJ School of Public Affairs at the University of Texas–Austin, wrote, "Nation-states are not going to go away, nor is nationalism." And **Fred Baker**, chairman of the board of trustees for the Internet Society, responded, "Gee, I'd love to see world peace, but I don't believe that the Internet alone will be able to accomplish it. Much of the thinking in *The World Is Flat* is valid. However, I doubt that the Western notion of a nation-state will significantly change during my lifetime."

Robert Shaw, Internet strategy and policy advisor for the International Telecommunication Union, wrote, "The contribution and creativity of individuals has always been important, way before the Internet, but what the Internet offers is a mechanism that connects and leverages individual creativity and behaviour into a collective mechanism that both rewards individual excellence and joint efforts. Therein lie the benefits. The individuals continue to live in nations, societies, and cities with their own value systems that are not going to be displaced by this behaviour."

Alan Levin, a network architect and chairman of the South Africa chapter of the Internet Society, responded, "I partially agree, as national boundaries will be even more emphasized in those countries where there has been political resistance (explicit or inadvertent) to the information age. These countries will effectively become outdated islands of information poverty."

> "It will take longer for this to be complete, if it ever is. It should be noted that even in a post-geographic world, geography isn't blurred; it just becomes a less important factor amongst many."
>
> —Robin Berjon,
> W3C and Expway

Peter Kim, senior analyst for Forrester Research, wrote, "I think this is feasible, but not in the time frame. Government regulation will slow the pace of this change as political constituencies fight to keep revenue sources local."

SOME TAKE ISSUE WITH THE PHRASE "COMPLETELY BLUR"

Most respondents see a great deal of the scenario as likely, but some took issue with the strong wording indicating that shifting social and economic groups will take the starch out of national boundaries. "Virtual connections *will* increase in scale, scope, and importance," wrote Internet policy analyst **Alan Inouye**. "I disagree about the magnitude of this change by 2020 (e.g., don't agree with 'completely blur'). Physical relationships and communities will continue to be important. Nations have a lot of history, ideology, and culture."

Esther Dyson of CNET Networks, former chairman of ICANN, responded, "I disagree with 'completely.' Moreover, if anyone can be successful, then those who are not successful (by whose definition?) must be responsible for their own failure." **Adrian Schofield** of South Africa's ForgeAhead, an ICT research and consulting firm, responded, "Although I agree in principle, there remains sufficient misguided nationalism to maintain borders between people—despots and dictators will still be in power."

Howard Rheingold, author and Internet sociologist, wrote, "I disagree with the word 'completely' here, but I agree that Friedman's 'flatteners' add up to a powerful force. I would also point out that the global economic flows enabled by communication infrastructure are highly dependent on cheap petroleum when it comes to moving matter around. That could change overnight."

Glenn Ricart, a member of the Internet Society Board of Trustees, responded, "The phrase 'completely blur' probably goes too far, but it's fair to say that new nongeographical allegiances will become as important and probably more

> "The world is flat, but it's also lumpy. We cluster together. Geography is one powerful attractor. So are interests. We're capable of maintaining many sets of relationships simultaneously."
>
> —David Weinberger,
> teacher, writer, speaker,
> consultant, and commentator
> on Internet and technology;
> Harvard Berkman Center

important than today's geographical communities. However, note that in addition to being connected with like-minded people, I also need to have economic intercourse with complementary groups. Hence, although I'm a PhD computer scientist and will want to connect with the same and equivalent worldwide, I also want to connect with farmers who grow and will ship me great produce. The real world counts because I still can't get fine dark chocolate to appear from my wireless PDA. In fact, I suspect I'll spend a minority of my time with like-minded people of all types (cultural groupings, etc.) and the majority of my time with complementary people and groups."

David Clark, a senior research scientist at MIT and one of the original architects of the Internet, responded, "I agree, except that I don't think national boundaries will be replaced. They will continue to play an important role. But it will be less unique. National identity will continue to be with us."

Technology writer and consultant **Fred Hapgood** took issue with the timing of the scenario. "It will all happen, but the right date is closer to 2120 than 2020; national cultures run deep," he wrote.

Does the Internet Weaken
or Strengthen Rural Areas?

Some respondents see networked communications technologies as a force that will draw people away from rural regions. "Most of the changes will be for individuals, not 'communities,' " wrote community-networking expert **Steve Cisler**, "because the individual is the one with the raised expectation and awareness, and while she may try and convey that to a surrounding neighborhood or town or tribe, she may decide it is best to move away and into places where she can grow and excel. For that reason, I see the Internet as an urbanization (globalization) engine that weakens many rural areas. [Traditional groupings] just can't change as fast as the individual—who becomes impatient with that stasis."

Some respondents see networked communications as a great resource that allows new advantages for those in nonurban areas.

"The Internet is, and will continue to, foster online livelihoods and collaborations not previously possible," wrote **Christopher Johnson**, CEO of ifPeople. "This is fostered by the increasing (business/ professional) service base of the economy. Increasing education and connectivity have grown the pool that contributes to professional services beyond typical boundaries. We have tapped this approach in our own business with a model that leverages a distributed workforce of micro-enterprises working in open-source technologies based on the model of fair trade. These cross-institutional collaboratives allow for agile learning organizations that can compete and adapt quickly."

Alex Halavais of Quinnipiac University wrote, "This also means the globalization of the hinterlands. While individuals in India, China, and ultimately Africa (though this will take much longer) will be part of these new global networks, there will inevitably be losers in this process: those who remain less connected. And here 'less connected' does not merely mean unable to access the Internet, but unable to call on a global network of financial and interpersonal resources. So yes, you will be able to find the First World more often in the Third, but also the Third World more often in the First."

Jeff Corman, government policy analyst for Industry Canada, wrote, "There will always be a flow of goods which are best served through local businesses, and I believe the Internet will also help local businesses better meet needs of local consumers of goods that are not necessarily suited to global enterprise. And in the developing world, this may be an even greater advantage of the Internet."

CORPORATE-BASED GLOBAL GROUPS DRAW FIRE

Concerns were expressed over the chance that business-based groupings with an emphasis on bottom-line financial goals will become too strong. "The Internet will open worldwide access to opportunities for success; it will also open ways for many dysfunctionalities," responded **Alejandro Pisanty**, an officer of ICANN. "Corporation-based cultural groupings may actually be one of the most destructive forces if not enough cultural, relational, and bottom-up social forces are built up. This does not detract from the prediction that a lot more people than today will have a good life through extensive networked collaboration."

Andy Williamson, managing director for Wairua

> "It will not be city-states so much as it will be corporations that become the sovereign entities transcendent of geographic space."
>
> —Peter Nieckarz,
> Jr., assistant professor of sociology,
> Western Carolina University

Consulting Limited and a member of the New Zealand government's Digital Strategy Advisory Group, wrote, "I suspect there is likely to be a huge backlash against the global corporatisation of the world and commodification of culture. I also do not see a free flow of information, given the current attempts by many to control it. However, localised and topical tribalism (and multitribal affiliations) seem likely to rise."

Scott Moore, online community manager for the Schwab Foundation, responded, "There was a time that one could literally connect a computer to the Internet and be on—now one must register the IP connection, which means such a connection can be denied. It is not freedom when a corporation or government holds the key to the cage."

Mirko Petric of the University of Zadar in Croatia wrote, "It can be hardly expected that current national boundaries will blur completely by 2020, but it can be predicted with a great deal of certainty that corporate-based power will continue to exert its influence, relying on the possibilities offered by the new technologies—not only the Internet but also beyond it. In any sort of prediction of this kind, some room should be left for cultural forms that will be a reaction to this state of affairs."

Sam Punnett, president of FAD Research, sarcastically replied, "The corporation-based cultural groupings will still be called countries in 2020."

WHERE DO NATIONS STAND IN THE NETWORKED FUTURE?

While many people replied that 2020 will find us in a mostly positive place where national boundaries are disappearing thanks to cross-cultural communications, a number of the survey respondents dismissed this scenario, using words and phrases such as "Pollyannaish," "Nice dream," "Piffle" and "Get real." Perhaps they are familiar with another recent book, *Who Controls the Internet?* by Jack Goldsmith and Tim Wu.

Predictions from respondents who chose to remain anonymous:

"The Internet is the greatest meritocracy in the history of mankind."

"For thousands of years, social order has been maintained by government and religion playing off of each other. Will new constructs for social responsibility develop and evolve quickly enough to beat back the chaotic nature of these kinds of alliances?"

"National boundaries will be replaced by knowledge clusters."

The authors, both American law professors, describe how political and economic interests have come into play over the past decade in making the Internet a much less "open" place than it was in the early 1990s. They dispel any notions that John Perry Barlow's free "civilization of the mind in cyberspace" (1996) might still exist, and even go so far as to say that a "geographically bordered internet has many underappreciated virtues." Their main points in support of this is as follows: "Citizens want their government to prevent them from harming one another on the Internet and to block Internet harms from abroad. Companies need a legal environment that guarantees stability in the network and permits Internet commerce to flourish. The bordered Internet accommodates real and important differences among peoples in different places, and makes the Internet a more effective and useful communication tool as a result" (Goldsmith & Wu, 2005, p. viii).

Goldsmith and Wu write that corporations and governments are working in concert to solidify their power, using the architectures of the Internet and the law in addition to leveraging the sort of economic coercion seen in China's Internet oversight and censorship.

Governments that wish to exercise control threaten a loss of access (this equates to a loss of corporate income) if Internet companies do not follow their wishes in regard to censorship, the sharing of the personal computing records of protesters, and/or the sending of "tracing" packets out on the network to identify the location of wanted users. Network-tracing technology and geo-identification was originally developed to help all nations fight online fraud and other crimes, to help certain nations retain their cultural identity (France is a leader in this regard), and to help corporations and other groups share information selectively on a regional level.

> *Predictions from respondents who chose to remain anonymous:*
>
> **"The world is not flat and never will be. The world is spikey. There is so much evidence of that: wealth, power, Internet access, resources, etc., are concentrated."**
>
> **"Nation-states will adapt to flat-world capitalism. The relationship between power and money is quite enduring."**
>
> **"We are pack-driven organisms, and while there may be some reordering of packs, the overall default of governments will continue."**

Goldsmith and Wu write that today's "bordered internet reflects top-down pressures from individuals in different places who demand an internet that corresponds to local preferences and from the Web page operators and other content providers who shape the internet experience to satisfy these demands" (2005, p. 89).

If the trend of the past decade continues, the Internet will continue to be more regulated at various levels (to fight crime, build trust in the system, etc.), and control of content will be easier to exercise, to positive and negative effects.

Those who prefer to see the glass half full might want to read *An Army of Davids: How Markets and Technology Empower Ordinary People to Beat Big Media, Big Government, and Other Goliaths,* by Glenn Reynolds, or *The Only Sustainable Edge: Why Business Strategy Depends on Productive Friction and Dynamic Specialization,* by John Hagel III and John Seely Brown. Reynolds said accelerating advances in technology will increase individuals' empowerment at an accelerating rate over the next few decades. Hagel and Brown (2006) said, "The acceleration of capability building will shift our individual and collective mind-sets from a worldview that focuses on static, zero-sum relationships to one that focuses on dynamic non-zero-sum relationships...This new worldview emphasizes the importance of the evolution of local ecosystems" (pp. 2–3).

COLLABORATION TOWARD OPTIMIZING USE OF THE INTERNET

All survey respondents agreed that those who have access to the Internet now and in the future, more highly regulated nor not, will have increased opportunities to learn and prosper.

The Massachusetts Institute of Technology, better known by its acronym, MIT, offers nearly all of its course material free online through its OpenCourseware program. The government of Egypt has signed an agreement with the University of California–Berkeley and Intel as part of the META (Middle East, Turkey, and Africa) Higher Education Initiative, focusing on technology education.

Corporations, which came under heavy criticism by some survey respondents, are working to help connect more people online—yes, they probably would not do it if there were no economic incentive, but more people are gaining tech knowledge and access through direct and indirect financing by major corporations. Google is one of a group of businesses noted earlier in this report for its financing of the $100 laptop project. Intel just announced it will spend $1 billion to bring technology to people in developing nations (Intel News Release, 2006). AMD is offering the "50 × 15" program (http://50x15.amd.com/), offering funding to any project that is targeted at getting at least 50% of the world's population online by 2015. Sun Microsystems launched the Global Education and Learning Community (GELC) that CEO Scott McNealy has described as a "free and open, self-paced, Web-based community for students to get access to the best curriculum on the planet" (Sun Microsystems, 2005, p. 2).

Nonprofit organizations and nongovernmental organizations[1] have been leading the way to closing the digital divide for many years. One such company is Inveneo (http://www.inveneo.org/), a San Francisco-based group working on making it possible to power and get Internet connections for computers in locations with no direct electrical or telecommunications access. The inhabitants of Nyarukamba, a village in western Uganda, have been surfing the Web with Wi-Fi computers and making voice-over-IP phone calls with solar-powered Inveneo equipment installed in the Ruwenzori Mountains. Inveneo also expects to provide such systems in outlying areas of Ghana, Swaziland, Senegal, and the Philippines (Bower, 2006).

And despite the dominance of big corporations, the Internet is still the best tool ever for people who want to start their own small business. One example is a start-up that is gathering people from all over to form a new cultural cluster based mostly on the Internet. This "global tribe" is being planned by two 26-year-old British entrepreneurs, Ben Keene and Mark James. They began in April 2006, seeking 5,000 people to sign up at http://www.tribewanted.com for the chance to live for 1, 2, or 3 weeks annually on a small Fijian island. Twelve "chiefs" will be elected, tribe members will pay annual fees of $220, $440, or $660 per year, and they will participate in the island's online community year-round. Members post their biographies, videos, and photos online and also lend their voices when island decisions are made.

> **Predictions from respondents who chose to remain anonymous:**
>
> "The EU is trying to do this and having some success. There is and will continue to be some tension from major power brokers."
>
> "People who succeed will become rich, while others remain poor."
>
> "The world will be more unified than ever, as is happening in Europe right now. The concepts of national borders will be deeply altered."

The Internet Society is encouraging worldwide participation in the first annual OneWebDay (http://onewebday.org) September 22, 2006. The event is billed as a way to "celebrate the human collaboration and connection the Internet makes possible." Internet Society chapters around the world will stage special events.

The first meeting of the Internet Governance Forum (http://www.intgovforum.org/)—a group that was inspired by the United Nations-led World Summit on the Information Society and its Working Group on Internet Governance—will take place in Athens, Greece, October 30–November 2. The IGF's international delegates will meet to identify common issues and make recommendations to the world. Technically, at this point it has no direct influence or power over the Internet. Themes identified for discussion at the first meeting include openness, security, diversity, and access.

While the U.S. has been a juggernaut of innovation and it has owned the world's biggest economy for a long stretch, analysts have seen the pendulum swing over the last decade. A great deal of this is tied to the ways in which people have been using networked communications to open new opportunities and markets; the enhanced connectedness brings it all together. A recent Goldman Sachs report projects that China will have the largest economy in the world by 2045. Clyde Prestowitz writes about this in detail in *Three Billion New Capitalists*, his book about the influence of increasing participation in the global economy of people from India, China, and the former Soviet Union.

In his response to this 2020 scenario, survey participant **Amos Davidowitz** of the Institute of World Affairs and Association for Progressive Education wrote, "The nation-state is an invention of the industrial world that allowed the most efficient management of resources both material and people. The information age needs the flow of ideas—the political form always follows the economic need. We will see a flattening of the nation-state in Western society. In Third World countries and networks of ethnic grouping such as the Arab world, we will see a desperate attempt to hold onto the framework as is. We cannot forget that Eastern Europe, Africa, and Asia lost many years, due to imperialism, to work through the various aspects of nationalism. It took Western Europe a thousand years and two very bloody world wars to work out the kinks of nation, culture, country, resource. The future is brighter since the source of wealth is no longer based on carbon, such as oil, minerals, land, which are limited—but based on information and creativity, which is limitless."

Additional Responses

Many other survey respondents shared comments tied to the scenario about global access to the success and the blurring of national boundaries. Among them:

> "Structurally, the issue for the world is much more about balance of power. Right now, there is no balance, and the United States is viewed as a threat because of its untrammeled ability to enforce its own rules and interests. If there is a balance of power, there will be a stability that allows the Internet to level the playing field for economic success and access." —**Stewart Alsop**, investor and analyst; former editor of InfoWorld and Fortune columnist

> "This is incoherent nonsense. The only meaningful element is that multinational corporations can rival national government as power blocs, and such corporations may gain even more power in the future. Information is a part of the economy— a big part. But it's still only a part." —**Seth Finkelstein**, anti-censorship activist and programmer; author of the Infothought blog; EFF Pioneer Award winner

> "I agree that virtual connections will increase in scale, scope, and importance. I disagree about the magnitude of this change by 2020 (e.g., don't agree with 'completely blur'). Physical relationships and communities will continue to be important. Nations have a lot of history, ideology, and culture." —**Alan Inouye**, Internet policy analyst previously with the Computer Science and Telecommunications Board of the National Research Council

> "Nice dream." —**Nicholas Carr**, independent technology writer and consultant

> "Although I agree in principle, there remains sufficient misguided nationalism to maintain borders between people— despots and dictators will still be in power." —**Adrian Schofield**, head of research for ForgeAhead, South Africa; leader in the World Information Technology and Services Alliance (WITSA)

> "I disagree with 'completely.' Moreover, if anyone can be successful, then those who are not successful (by whose definition?) must be responsible for their own failure. (Again, too

many thoughts mingled into a single prediction.)" —**Esther Dyson**, former chair of ICANN; now of CNET Networks

"Yes, in the sense that some of the institutions that relied on geographical particularity will be weakened (e.g., universities linked around physical libraries). BUT new distinctions/boundaries/groupings will arise to add 'texture' to this so-called 'global village.' In the medium term, there will be just as many barriers, in effect, to open global action/interaction." —**Bruce Edmonds**, Centre for Policy Modelling, Manchester Metropolitan University, U.K.

"The technology tends towards this openness, but our religious and political predilections now indicate otherwise." —**Douglas Rushkoff**, author of many books about Net culture; teacher, New York University

"I disagree with the word 'completely' here, but I agree that Friedman's 'flatteners' add up to a powerful force. I would also point out that the global economic flows enabled by communication infrastructure are highly dependent on cheap petroleum when it comes to moving matter around. That could change overnight." —**Howard Rheingold**, Internet sociologist and author

"In the intervening 15 years, there is going to be a very large financial reconning as power is rebalanced." —**Gordon Bell**, senior researcher, Microsoft

"My 'agreement' with this is more of a hope than a certainty. Most surely, there are massive forces—government, corporate, and 'religious'—who are doing everything they can to limit such egalitarian distribution of power. For, after all, timely access to adequate information, and the ability to timely communicate with the body politic, be it our neighbors, or a national or global audience—e.g., pollution recipients around the world—is the ULTIMATE power. If it were not, those in government and business who HAVE power would not be so all-fired zealous in trying to limit public access to information about themselves and their activities. However, it is not clear to me that we citizens will be successful in protecting our 'right' (ability) to communicate freely. That freedom may be choked by governments, by corporate managers, and by self-appointed censors who 'know what's best for us.'" —**Jim Warren**, Internet pioneer; founding editor of *Dr. Dobb's Journal*; technology policy advocate and activist; futurist

"Citizens may be less willing to allow the collapse of nation-states if they believe that international organizations lack accountability. The debate over the WTO is a precursor to the future." —**Marc Rotenberg**, executive director, Electronic Privacy Information Center

"It will be about adaptive dynamics and economics, with new comparative advantages and value propositions. Adaptiveness + Economics = 'Adaptnomics'—with credit to my friend Wale Adjadi." —**Tunji Lardner**, CEO for the West African NGO network: wangonet.org; agendaconsulting.biz; consultant to the UNDP African Internet Initiative

"I'd agree with the statement if the word 'completely' was deleted as a modifier for 'blur.' I don't think social transformation will be effected in the next decade and a half. But, barring additional polarizing events on the scale of 9/11, we should be well on our way toward a more global environment, both socially and economically." —**Reva Basch**, consultant for Aubergine Information Systems

"I think that this is already true, though it will take some time before it sinks sufficiently into the cultural background to be fully effective. Again, issues relating to assessing identity and trust will be key. For instance, it is often suggested that projects such as Wikipedia would be better if readers could more easily identify and trust the source(s), but conversely, the value of contributing would be greatly increased if contributers could be uniquely identified and if trust in them could be asserted. That being said, I believe that 'completely blur' is an overstatement and that it'll take longer for this to be complete, if it ever is. It should be noted that even in a post-geographic world, geography isn't blurred; it just becomes a less important factor amongst many." —**Robin Berjon**, W3C and Expway

"The Internet also makes it possible to preserve and nurture ethnic and cultural differences. People keep thinking that the latest change in technology is going to change human nature and society, and it just ain't gonna happen." —**Roger Cutler**, W3.org, senior staff research scientist at the Chevron Information Technology division of Chevron USA

"Completely agree. Like never before, the human race will be enabled to act as one entity." —**Michael Gorrell**, senior VP and CIO, EBSCO

"I think this contention is basically correct; however, a flat playing field also means you can lose big as well as win big. Where we'll lose out is that we have many computer users, but few of the people who have the great ideas are the same ones who can program software. For example, a man sending one e-mail, or even a batch of e-mails by using a 'cut and paste' feature from a list of addresses can never compete with a fully automated system that transmits e-mails 7 × 24 as fast as the processor will go. Most Americans have not transformed their work habits to use the computer to their best advantage unlike the Asians, the Indians and Pakistanis, and Chinese. Americans still think of it as a toaster and fail to see its potential. Consequently, we'll be eaten alive economically unless the quality of our educational institutions increases and people learn how to tap the power available in these systems." —**William Kearns**, assistant professor, University of South Florida

"Too much inertia in the current system to be replaced in 15 years, particularly as we won't be 100% connected." —**Willis Marti**, associate director for networking, Texas A&M University

"Since most war and exploitative pain in the world's history has arisen from nation-state 'ego' conflict, I am hopeful that emerging affinity networks and identification will lead to long-term, more peaceful networking toward mutual gain. As Elise Boulding taught me, the expansion of global NGOs is our best hope for a friendlier planet." —**Ed Lyell**, pioneer in issues regarding Internet and education; professor at Adams State College

"Most in the technology fields have seen this coming a long way off. *The World Is Flat* exposed to the rest of the world what many in technology have known for a long time, that the more communication that is available, the smaller the universe. When the first telephones were given out, no one wanted them, but they quickly made the world smaller and more mobile by creating access beyond the town hall or country store to the entire world. This will only continue as we realize that borders don't really exist and find even more ways to communicate with each other and that, in fact, it is a very small world." —**Tom Snook**, CTO, New World Symphony

"This is already starting to happen today. As corporations like Amazon and Google rush to compete with one another, they will act as an enabler to smaller organizations (even organizations of one) that will leverage the commodity services provided by the giants. The key lies not only with a free flow of information, but of service—service to which others will add their own value." —**Ross Rader**, director of research and innovation, Tucows, Inc.

"It is surprising that many people find this prediction original or novel. Since the advent of computer-to-computer messaging in the early 1980s (Videotext, BBSs [bulletin board services], Bitnet, and ultimately the Internet), it has become manifestly clear that space and time are together altered by the new asynchronous, highly capillarized data networks. You no longer have to be in a major city of the world to be able to develop a product, project, or service that makes the world beat a path to your door. And this is good, very good. So what else is new?" —**Fredric M. Litto**, professor, University of Sao Paulo, Brazil

"While this is theoretically possible, it ignores the fact that the Internet largely reflects the social, political, and economic hierarchies and networks outside of it." —**David Elesh**, associate professor of sociology, Temple University

"The nation-state will become an administration entity rather than a cultural organizer." —**Charles Hendricksen**, research collaboration architect, Cedar Collaboration

"This, like many of the other claims, starts with a reasonable premise (e.g., Internet makes it possible for individuals to collaborate and compete globally). But there is no reason that this ability to collaborate…[will] be associated with the withering of nation-states." —**Robert Kraut**, Human-Computer Interaction Institute, Carnegie Mellon University

"I agree, except that I don't think national boundaries will be replaced. They will continue to play an important role. But it will be less unique. National identity will continue to be with us." —**David Clark**, Internet pioneer; senior research scientist at MIT

"Yes, but this will happen within clearly defined cultures. Japanese will not mix with U.S.-Americans for the simple reason that U.S.-Americans will not learn foreign languages. Chinese cyberspace will be huge but by and large inaccessible because most non-Chinese will not have learned Mandarin. What Friedman writes might be the case for national boundaries but will not be the case for cultural limitations that cannot so easily be overcome." —**Geert Lovink**, media theorist, professor and Internet critic, Institute of Network Cultures, University of Amsterdam

"The power of the Internet in enabling collaboration is very important, and I would agree with Friedman's remarks on the ability of individuals to collaborate. The inference this question proposes (the complete blurring of national boundaries), however, requires, for example, that Syria and Israel decide that the border between them is no longer important. Gee, I'd love to see world peace, but I don't believe that the Internet alone will be able to accomplish it. Much of the thinking in *The World Is Flat* is valid. However, I doubt that the Western notion of a nation-state will significantly change during my lifetime." —**Fred Baker**, CISCO Fellow, CISCO Systems; Internet Society (ISOC) chairman of the board; Internet Engineering Task Force

"This has already happened—no need to wait for 2020." —**Robin Gross**, executive director, IP Justice

"This is again more of a utopian desire than any thing else, but is a major part of the benefits that an 'Internet for Everybody' can/will offer." —**Cheryl Langdon-Orr**, independent Internet business operator; director, ISOC-Australia

"Both types of associations are needed and will coexist: (a) cross-border, interest-driven virtual communities; and (b) local communities." —**Luc Faubert**, president of Quebec's Internet Society chapter; ambassador to World Summit on the Information Society

"Not likely. While there is much to be said about the enabling power of communications and the Internet, there is a deep-rooted nationalism that is part of the psyche of nearly all people worldwide. Many events only serve to strengthen that nationalism in both positive and negative ways, including wars and conflicts, financial systems, political messaging, and even the World Cup and the Olympics. This doesn't mean that groupings won't continue to happen as they have today, but they will continue to consist mostly of people with shared common interest that still end up living their own separate lives when offline." —**Philip Joung**, Spirent Communications

"This is one of the wonders that will evolve out of the Internet— free flow of information across physical and geographical boundaries. However, this must not come at the expense of a loss of identity of people involved." —**Rajnesh J. Singh**, PATARA Communications & Electronics Ltd., Avon Group, GNR Consulting, ISOC Pacific Islands

"I can see a trend toward regionalism and cross-border coop- eration, but it won't proceed as fast as this question suggests. National governments still have lots of financial, legal, and rhetorical tools at their command, and the change from one country to another can still be extreme. It will be a long time, if ever, before the force of last resort ceases to be the national government." —**Andy Oram**, writer and editor for O'Reilly Media

"We've been getting this prediction for a while, and it hasn't come true. Large corporations, with the support of strong nations, continue to have great control over economics and politics. There is no real basis for power in these dispersed city-states, and no one with power today is showing willing- ness to give it up. This could be a scenario for 200 years from now, but definitely not 2020, and getting there may not be through peaceful means." —**Karen Coyle**, information professional and librarian

"I partially agree, as national boundaries will be even more emphasized in those countries where there has been politi- cal resistance (explicit or inadvertent) to the information age. These countries will effectively become outdated islands of information poverty." —**Alan Levin**, programmer, designer, systems and network architect; chairman of the ISOC South Africa chapter

"We saw hints of this in the late '90s and the very first part of this century, only to see it 'interrupted' by the bursting of the 'bubble.' However, perhaps the bubble burst because we moved too fast too early and with insufficient thought to have sound business models. We will have learned in the next 15 years and we should see great collaboration by peo- ple to compete globally with any entity. Indeed, it's likely that that will, effectively, be the way of business—whether the 'individual' is essentially a 'corporation,' or virtually individuals, literally." —**Don Heath**, board member, iPool, Brilliant Cities, Inc., Diversified Software, Alcatel, Foretec

"Yes, to the extent that it is allowed by trading regimes. When the African farmer can see prices in European markets, he will be all the more outraged at foot dragging over liberalisations proposed in, e.g., the Doha round of trade talks." —**John Browning**, cofounder of First Tuesday, a global network dedicated to entrepreneurs; former writer for *The Economist* and other top publications

"The Internet's real power is that it allows individuals that share a common interest to interact and collaborate in ways simply not possible before. That ability will continue to erode traditional boundaries (e.g., national or geographic)." —**Thomas Narten**, IBM open-Internet standards development

"Reasons for collaboration have to exist. Finding them and making worthwhile for all involved will be a growth industry. I predict more jobs for matchmakers." —**Mike Gill**, electronics engineer, National Library of Medicine

"Although there is little doubt that we will see some pioneers in this area, politics and economics in general do not change that quickly, especially across borders. Too many incumbents have a vested interest in the status quo. When the 'old people' die, THEN we'll begin to see changes of this scope. Besides, people as a rule are not intelligent enough to mingle so deeply with other cultures." —**Michael Steele**, Internet user since 1978

"As Friedman correctly identifies, this will be a trend, but it will NOT 'completely blur' anything in the next 20 years, and may never do so." —**Peter Roll**, retired chief system administrator

"The Internet may be a great place for the flow of information, but I still have to buy food from my local supermarket, send my child to a local school, attend a local church, and so on. While online communities will have greater roles, the needs for real-world communities won't change." —**Jim Huggins**, associate professor of computer science, Kettering University

"Completely agree. I think Friedman nailed it. Also note the fact that we are emerging into an era of user-content creation and distribution. This is already becoming a disruptive force, affecting mass media of various types, the music and motion picture industry, and others." —**Joel Hartman**, CIO, University of Central Florida

"William Gibson foresaw this all in the 1980s and it appears he was right." —**Martin Kwapinski**, senior content manager for FirstGov, the U.S. government's official Web portal

"2020, as defined in the beginning of this question, is too early for current national boundaries to have become fully blurred. Also, the description above (not in bold) does not lead to what is stated in the main sentence (in bold—'The Internet opens worldwide access to success') as current national boundaries ceasing to exist do not imply everyone will live at the same conditions anywhere in the globe. Local differences will remain; we will just stop understanding them through the colours defined by current (artificial) national boundaries to read them according to how other, as artificial, lenses will have been tinted." —**Suely Fragoso**, professor, Unisinos, Brazil

"Countries will still want to retain their political power. As such, they need money to support their government, their infrastructure, and their military (unfortunately). Unless the system of collecting this money changes from the current business tax and import/export duties, it will be hard for a company to be completely agnostic to national boundaries. I do agree, however, that the Internet will make it easier to attain a global reach." —**Rangi Keen**, software engineer, Centric Software

"This question is hard to give an either/or answer to. I believe that the trend the question describes will be true, but only to a limited extent; national boundaries will persist, as will national identities, as strong or maybe even stronger than before. If you, on the other hand, talk about the years between 2050–2100, migrations may wipe out a lot of national identities, not so much the Internet, which can be used to maintain national identities." —**Arent Greve**, professor, the Norwegian School of Economics and Business Administration

"While the basic observation is valid and this will certainly become more important in the future, the prediction wildly overstates its effects. Among other things, it overlooks the existence of diverse languages and cultures, and all the other aspects of nations beyond the economic." —**Florian Schlichting**, PhD candidate and researcher, University College, London

"I see no decrease in nationalism." —**Leigh Estabrook**, professor, University of Illinois

"I didn't believe Friedman when he wrote that and don't believe that national boundaries will ever be so threatened by the Internet as to erase them. China is doing everything it can to allow all of its citizens to access the Internet even while it dictates to Google which sites will be blocked." —**Christine Ogan**, professor, University of Indiana School of Journalism

"It's already more difficult to travel than 20 years ago. National government power holders/structures will not go quietly." —**Michael Cannella**, IT manager, Volunteers of America-Michigan

"In spite of all our collaboration, the coffee machine (hopefully delivering real espresso by that time) remains a central meeting point for quasi-professional deliberation." —**Carlo Hagemann**, professor, Radboud Universiteit Nijmegen, The Netherlands

"This trend will be more developed, but by no means complete." —**Tama Leaver**, lecturer in digital communication, University of Western Australia

"Some individuals will be able to collaborate globally. Local operations will still have an advantage for anything that involves physical flow of objects." —**Grant Blank**, assistant professor of sociology, American University

"This is very likely to happen, but not 2020." —**Ben Detenber**, associate professor, Nanyang Technological University, Singapore

"The ability for individuals to collaborate and compete globally (which has been true since life appeared on this planet), on the one hand, and the reconfiguration of social groups around new foci at the expense of the nation-state, on the other hand. The latter phenomenon is not primarily dependent upon ICT. The decline of the nation-state is much more the result of the subversion of those supposed to represent and defend the common interest by forces that represent particular ones." —**Michel Menou**, professor and information-science researcher

"Yes, we will definitely see a weakening of the current nation-state barriers, but there will be other, very prominent barriers. Most importantly will be language, followed by digital access." —**Randy Kluver**, director, Institute for Pacific Asia at Texas A&M University

"All these statements are so absolute, I can't do anything but disagree. I agreed with the first part here, and was quite happy to have found a question where I could say, yes, that's how I imagine the future. Then it got around to a vision again of the totally smooth integration of nations, organisations, and individuals, and I have to say, sorry, not going to happen anytime soon. They burn Norwegian embassies in Syria over a cartoon drawn in Denmark. How is that kind of national and cultural conflict to be overcome in 14 years?" —**Torill Mortensen**, associate professor, Volda University College, Norway

"The Internet, in fact, connects to the world…but only if we have proper connections to the Net. The information flow is not plenty free: [It] is limited by the interests (money, politics, rivalries) of governments and corporations. That is not a surprise: [It] is part of the present and indeed the next realities in this world. [It] is difficult to think [this would occur] in a world of city-states in only 15 years. Our countries are much too complex to turn, suddenly or almost, in demarcations like Singapore." —**Raul Trejo-Delarbre**, Universidad Nacional Autonoma de México

"The death of distance doesn't flatten social hierarchies. In fact, the opposite is true: It promises MORE not less authoritarian control." —**Edward Lee Lamoureux**, associate professor, Bradley University

"This techno-centric view totally ignores the counter pressures of national-state loyalties, religious affiliations, and political alliances." —**Jim Jansen**, assistant professor, Penn State University

"Without clean drinking water and global basic education for women, there will always be a digital divide. Technology is just a detail in this regard." —**Jason Nolan**, associate professor, Ryerson University, Canada

"People talking erodes nationalism. The conversation is pervasive, and as people get to know each other, they will find how similar we all are." —**W. Reid Cornwell**, director, The Center for Internet Research

"This is a much broader process than can happen in the next 15 years." —**Rich Ling**, senior researcher and sociologist, Telenor Research Institute, Oslo, Norway

"I think this will probably happen, but perhaps not by 2020, and it won't be a pretty or peaceful transition either." —**Janine van der Kooy**, information management/librarian

"Nations aren't going away, but perhaps people will reach out more across them than now." —**Danny Sullivan**, editor-in-chief, SearchEngineWatch.com

"China (a nation-state) is very adept at controlling the free flow of information available to its individuals. China is not going away by the year 2020." —**Charlie Breindahl**, IT University of Copenhagen

"This is a question of degree. Will the Internet facilitate 'alternate mappings' for disparate communities of interest? Yes. Will communications barriers across national boundaries decrease in some ways? Probably. Will national boundaries completely disappear? No. National boundaries are sustained by economics, politics, cultural identity, religion, etc.—a whole host of complex systems that can't/won't be dissolved quickly or easily. It is important to keep in mind that opportunity is not the only necessary precondition for drastic change. The Internet is a tool that could just as easily be used to cloister and protect." —**Nan Dawkins**, cofounder, RedBoots Consulting

"While this collaboration and competition will increase, the prediction that these developments will completely blur national boundaries ignores the many forces that will maintain these social and political institutions. Instead of 'either/or,' it will be 'and'—ongoing national boundaries supplemented by geographically independent groupings. The dynamic between the two is where the most interesting questions lie." —**Patrick B. O'Sullivan**, director of the Center for Teaching and Learning, Illinois State University

"Although I do not completely agree with the complete blurring of current national boundaries, I fully agree that the

Internet opens up enormous opportunities for international collaboration. For the 'blurring' to be a reality, however, proven models of collaboration that have not yet seen the light of day must be developed, understood across cultural boundaries, and as easily accessed as the Internet itself." **—Paul Chenoweth**, Web developer, Belmont University

"Of course the Internet adds to other processes of globalization marking our times. However, locality will always remain an important factor in people's lives—the place (geographical, social, political, economic, etc.) in which people live forms the background against which they have their experiences. This phenomenon is part of the human condition and will not disappear through the rise of the Internet, despite its globalizing aspects and tendencies." **—B. van den Berg**, faculty of philosophy at Erasmus University, Rotterdam, The Netherlands

"You forgot language! This might be true for an elite of some industrial countries, but in many countries, we still have great problems with illiteracy, even in the U.S. And the Internet requires a high competence in literacy skills, and if it's global, you might be required to speak a foreign language as well." **—Oliver Krueger**, professor, Princeton University

"I'd like it to be that way, but I'm not sure that 15 years is realistic time for those changes." **—Lilia Efimova**, researcher, Telematica Instituut, The Netherlands

"We see this already with blogs, individual and joint, claiming space where mainstream media is losing ground." **—Deborah Jones**, freelance journalist; Canadian technology writer

"Not ALL individuals will partake in this free flow of information, but it will redefine our culture and our leadership." **—Kathleen Pierz**, managing partner, The Pierz Group

"I think the success part is right. I tend to think nationalism is more hardwired and unlikely to disappear." **—Cleo Parker**, senior manager, BBDO

"This seems like an unlikely outcome. Many people identify along ethnic, religious, and linguistic lines, and computers are unlikely to change that." **—Michael S. Cann, Jr.**, CEO, Affinio Corporation

"Many of us have been writing about such changes for at least a decade. That process is already well under way." —**Bud Levin**, program head/psychology and commander/policy and planning, Blue Ridge Community College; Waynesboro (VA) Police Department

"I agree that the Internet opens worldwide access to success, but I disagree that national boundaries will be replaced by city-states." —**Carter Headrick**, director, grassroots and field operations, Campaign for Tobacco-Free Kids

"National boundaries are too important to the most powerful interests on the planet. They will not lose their power to uncontrolled media. Global collaboration will happen to the extent it supports existing power structures." —**Michael Reilly**, GLOBALWRITERS, Baronet Media LLC, Hally Enterprises, Inc., State University of NY at Stony Brook, Global Public Affairs Institute

"It's happening now. It hurts my brain to think of what will happen in 15 years." —**Michael Collins**, CEO, a respondent who chose not to share further identifying information

"Unlike a few Yanqui fantasists like Friedman, most peoples around the world operate as collectives. Some wires won't change that!" —**Toby Miller**, professor, University of California–Riverside

"Why wait until 2020? This is happening NOW." —**Howard Finberg**, director of interactive media, The Poynter Institute

"Connectivity is essential to global peace." —**Russell Steele**, owner, The Insightworks

"This may happen, but not by 2020. Cultural identities take longer to blur than that. A flat world will certainly extinguish some cultural identities but will create new ones." —**Joel Bush**, a respondent who chose not to reveal more details about his identity

"I agree with Friedman's premise, but this will not be reality only 14 years from now. There are far more powerful forces working to strengthen and sharpen national and cultural boundaries, and these will override much of the individual convergence that is possible through the Web." —**Ralph Blanchard**, investor, information services entrepreneur

"Clearly, new business models and new types of social interaction will continue to evolve as the cost and friction in communicating globally falls. But this prediction is too sweeping. People are still a product of their local communities, customs, parental expectations, religious affiliation, etc., to be as plastic as this statement asserts. Over a generation or two, perhaps." —**Kerry Kelley**, VP, product marketing, SnapNames.com

"Internet will open worldwide access to success, but will not blur national boundaries." —**Sean Mead**, consultant for Interbrand Analytics, Design Forum, Mead, Mead & Clark and other companies

"Whereas I believe this will eventually come to pass, I don't think it will happen by 2020." —**Paul Craven**, director of enterprise communications, U.S. Department of Labor

"Commerce is only one domain of human experience. While commerce may create transaction-based groupings across political boundaries, the city-states may well evolve to fill the human need for tribal community that is based more on religious, ethnic, and cultural distinctions." —**Jeff Hammond**, VP, Rhea + Kaiser

"I've seen *Blade Runner* and read *Neuromancer*, too, but recognize the artifice as separate from the reality." —**Joseph Redington**, associate academic dean, Manhattanville College

"We can never forget the Internet 'unsuccess' to many during the '90s. Stating the Internet opens worldwide access to success is too risky." —**Ivair Bigaran**, Global Messenger Courier do Brasil, American Box Serviço Int'l S/C Ltda.

"With the Internet homogenizing the developed world, people will want to retain their identity rather than lose it. Not everyone who has access to the Internet will be able to do well. The 'www' also stands for World Wide Wastebasket. There will be a large amount of false information that will be detrimental to some." —**Richard Yee**, competitive intelligence analyst, AT&T

"While physical national borders will remain on the ground, the borderless universe available via the Internet will continue to flourish and bring together populations in ways never possible physically." —**Mitchell Kam**, Willamette University, OR

"Risk, security, trust, and personal identity issues will preclude this free one-to-all collaboration and social reconfiguration.

The test case for this is 'distance learning,' where 100% remote arrangements are less effective than combined remote-personal arrangements." —**Ellen K. Sullivan**, former diplomat; policy fellow, George Mason University School of Public Policy

"I especially agree with the part about the corporate city-states. Like stadiums named for corporations, corporate identity of governmental districts is a natural, especially if we secede responsibility for and acceptance of formal governance in general. Privatize everything, and the corporations will be able to slice up our lives in whatever way is good for their quarterly gains." —**Susan Wilhite**, design anthropologist, Habitat for Humanity

"Geopolitical boundaries exist in our minds only. The degree in which we choose to make them part of our lives depends on how much we value competing affiliations. Arguably, the trend is already there with multinational work forces, corporations, organizations, and confederations like the European Union." —**A. White**, a respondent who chose not to share further identifying information

"A qualified disagreement: Although I believe it will occur, I do not believe it will 'completely' replace current national boundaries. Our nationalistic tendencies, ethnic and religious groupings, will continue to exert a lot of influence for generations to come." —**Jeffrey Branzburg**, educational consultant for National Urban Alliance, Center for Applied Technologies in Education, and other groups

"Again, factor in the ever-present tension between government and business. A boon to business often produces anxiety in government, in this case due to loss of control. Therein lies repression or revolution." —**Ralph Mueller**, self-employed; Internet user since 1977

"People will have strong ties to reality beyond 2020. Online communities may be boundless, but they can be easily disrupted by offline actions." —**Brian T. Nakamoto**, Everyone.net, a leading provider of outsourced e-mail solutions

"Increasingly, we are being bound by a common bond and we are speaking a common language. The Internet has no boundaries; geographic boundaries shall become meaningless. It will not make a difference where you are till the time you are connected. Behavior is the function of learning, and the Networks shall be the common source of learning, a common platform where all netizens stand equal." —**Alik Khanna**, Smart Analyst Inc., a business employing financial analysts in India

"There will also be increased conflict among states and social movements reacting against the homogenization of the world, the 'Westernization' of the world, etc." —**Benjamin Ben-Baruch**, senior market intelligence consultant and applied sociologist, Aquent, General Motors, Eastern Michigan University

"I think that we have to be cautious regarding utopian predictions à la Friedman, who has his own liberal and globalization agenda. Utopian predictions regarding the Internet have been proven wrong for the most part. Power and hegemonic structures will not allow such 'access to success' to spread too widely and will adapt themselves to the new networked reality in an attempt to preserve their hegemony." —**Michael Dahan**, professor, Sapir Academic College, Israel; Digital Jerusalem

"I think national boundaries are too strong to be blurred by other groupings of humans, although I do agree that these alternative groups will become more numerous and more powerful." —**Mark Crowley**, researcher, The Customer Respect Group

"However, the participants in these 'cultural groupings' and 'human organizations' will still maintain ties to those outside 'the network,' and national boundaries will remain relevant in coexistence. Successful Indian entrepreneurs, for example, will not be indifferent between living in India and the U.S." —**Jonathan Sills**, SVP (strategy and corporate development), Provide Commerce, Liberty Media

"National boundaries will be increasingly blurred, but not 'completely.' So many processes and so much legitimacy is still tied up with the nation-state. On the other hand, I agree with Friedman in that individuals will work and compete globally." —**Olav Anders Øvrebø**, freelance journalist based in Oslo, Norway

"Generally, this seems to be the trend, but nation-states will continue to have an important role in this mix as recognized organizational units, if nothing else than for symbolic reasons of identity, even if their actual role is diminished. They may become more inclined to be police states or the security apparatus of some of the other main groupings, although this very power of physical violence will give them continued power within a global networked world." —**Shawn McIntosh**, lecturer in strategic communications, Columbia University

"The real question is how does anyone prepare for this? The cultural gaps remain wide and change much more slowly than the technology can bridge." —**Jill O'Neill**, director of planning and communication, National Federation of Abstracting and Information Services

"Research has been conducted that digital divide is deepening both between and within developed and developing states. In the long run, they will be more remote or even unconnected to each other." —**Yiu Chan**, Internet user since 1995

"I do believe that the Internet has opened up the globe for companies, but the blur of national boundaries isn't there. Companies still need to enter these countries delicately and learn to 'speak' the language and blend into that country's cultural world. If they don't, then they won't be successful, so this is why I think culture will still exist, thus creating 'boundaries.'" —**Jeff Gores**, Internet user since 1994

"Globalisation for the elite has almost been the case, from the 19th century onwards. Communication facilitated the connections between some groups, but this has not yet proven the case for most of the people. Local environment will most probably remain the key social reference. Very localised and very globalised might impact the levels between." —**Sylvain Grande**; Internet user since 1995

"Thankfully, the nation-state shows no sign of dying, even in an internetworked world. State governments didn't wither away when we shifted to a national economy after WWII powered in part by new technologies (air travel, telephony, air conditioning). National governments won't either. However, much better mechanisms to address cross-border issues will be needed." —**Rob Atkinson**, director, Technology and New Economy Project, Progressive Policy Institute

"As nations are essentially artificial and are resultants, at least in part, of a process of mutual identification between the member individuals of the nation, then if the Internet does not change how an individual creates their identity, it will not change the existence of nations. What the ease and speed of international communication may do, given time, is reduce the general level of xenophobia in the world. It may, and I hope that it does, lead to less conflict between nations. However, it may also result in more conflict as it creates cultural interfaces that were not factors in people's experience prior to high-speed international communications. There is a potential for peace and a potential for conflict present in the Internet, as there is in all forms of communication." —**Robin Lane**, educator and philosopher, Universidade Federal do Rio Grande do Sul, Brazil

"The next important step in the social-software revolution will be tools that enable the collaborative creation of capitalization for large projects. However, the significant factors in the development of global culture in the next two decades will have to do with the implementation of nanoscales and the conversion to new energy sources. Networked groups will multiply these effects." —**Daniel Conover**, new-media developer, Evening Post Publishing

"I don't know whether to agree or disagree. Of course, the power of the Internet makes it possible for individuals to collaborate and compete globally. But successful competition has been repeatedly proven to be very difficult: Marshalling resources in an effective and coordinated way takes organization well about the individual level. Geographically diverse organizations already compete with great success, but geographically and ethnically specific organizations show no signs of waning. This isn't a simple either/or issue." —**Walt Dickie**, VP and CTO, C&R Research

"Internet 2020 will help most developing countries catch up with advanced ones. Cheap access to the huge information capital available on the Internet will be used by these countries to move forwards very quickly." —**Louis Nauges**, president, Microcost

"I completely agree with this in the longer term, but not by 2020." —**Cary Curphy**, operations research analyst, U.S. Army

"While the Internet does blur national boundaries, it cannot eliminate the significance of geography, nor huge global economic disparities." —**Henry Potts**, professor, University College, London

"Human differences will be less based on geography." —**Dan McCarthy**, managing director, Neuberger Berman, Inc.

"National boundaries will be blurring somewhat, but the nation-state continues to be an important concept. Once humans thought the people in the next village were outsiders, now we have moved to considering a larger number of people somewhat like ourselves. But our old habits and our 'old' biology will not change this fast by 2020." —**Cheris Kramarae**, professor, Center for the Study of Women in Society, University of Oregon

"There is no way that in less than 15 years, nation-state boundaries will be literally blurred. Obviously, the global economy will become increasingly more complex, but traditional political systems and national identities cannot be blurred or lost in this short of time. However, keep an eye on Europe. I guess Europe will be the first place to experience potential 'blurring.'" —**Jeff Bohrer**, learning technology consultant, University of Wisconsin–Madison

"I agree, but I don't see it as a completely good thing. At least nations have some means of accountability. *Corporate states scare the bejesus out of me.*" —**Gordon MacDiarmid**, Lobo Internet Services

"Yes, and the phenomena will yield both boon and war." —**Denzil Meyers**, founder and president, Widgetwonder, Applied Improvisation Network

"I agree with the basic statement and premise. By 2020, nations will continue to exist; however, I'm not convinced that they won't try to control (and prevent) success of the masses." —**James Conser**, professor emeritus, Youngstown State University

"The issue is, will that result in harmony or will it become a variation of H. G. Wells' prediction in the novel *Time Machine*." —**Michael Castengera**, teacher and consultant, Grady College of Journalism, University of Georgia; Media Strategies and Tactics, Inc.

"The Internet opens worldwide access to success and skills, if you have the necessary skills and knowledge. For some under-privileged people, the Internet may make their situation even worse by increasing the competence they will have to face. Also, as the world's economy becomes more globalized, the entrance of large numbers of workers (from China, India, etc.) into this global employment market is reducing the workers' negotiation power and their wages." —**María Laura Ferreyra**, strategic planner, Instituto Universitario Aeronautico; ISOC member in Argentina

"I agree with the first part—'The Internet opens worldwide access to success'—but I disagree with the rest. The Internet is an enormous source of any type of information; it is a great road of communication, so much internal as external, public or private, but the individual will be always the one that takes the final decision." —**Sabino M. Rodriguez**, MC&S Services

"This is already the case. One can also live in both worlds. I have a 'day job' while also running my own Web site, pub-lishing my own book, and performing freelance work using the new tools provided by the Internet." —**Alix L. Paultre**, execu-tive editor, Hearst Business Media, Smartalix.com, Zep Tepi Publishing

"The Internet is not going to blur or eliminate national bound-aries. It will allow corporations spread around the globe to cooperate better with others and with their international divi-sions, but I doubt it will help individuals." —**Doug Olenick**, computer technology editor, TWICE (This Week in Consumer Electronics) magazine

"Thomas Friedman is absolutely correct in his globalization assumptions. For the world in general, this will be a positive thing. However, I don't believe Americans quite understand how this will vastly increase the amount of competition Amer-icans and American business will face. Such things as deple-tion of natural resources such as oil and global warming will have negative consequences as countries such as India and China gain an equal footing with the West." —**Mike Samson**, interactive media writer and producer, Creative Street Media Group

"Absolutely true. Every significant technology advancement has served to make the world smaller and smaller. Previ-ous developments in communication technology required substantial investments for creation and dissemination of material. The Internet affords this opportunity to virtually anyone who can afford a basic computer. Imagine the impact of television, × 1,000." —**Al Amersdorfer**, president and CEO, Automotive Internet Technologies

"Ever heard of the digital divide? What Internet are you talking about, then? 'Globally' seems to be First World global, in which case it is true that success is Net based. But in the big picture, Internet is—unless it solves its distribution and access problems—just another medium. Not to mention the irritating allusions to the golden era of the Greek polis (city-states). That dream was held on the shoulders of slaves, bear that in mind. Solve the digital divide, then we will have 'worldwide' success. In the meanwhile, it is mere rhetoric." —**Miguel Sicart Vila**, junior research associate, Information Ethics Group, Oxford University

"The Internet opens worldwide access to success—this is already true. However, the idea that this will fundamentally reconfigure human organizations is ridiculous. Physical proximity matters, it allows a much higher bandwidth communication to occur. We don't even understand all of that communication today, let alone reproduce it over a network." —**Simon Woodside**, CEO, Semacode Corporation

"Thomas Friedman connected all the dots leading to the future." —**Tiffany Shlain**, filmmaker; founder and ambassador of the Webby Awards

"Manufacturing will go to countries with cheapest labor sources…closest to raw materials. Ford and GM will become automotive 'marketing' companies…selling their designs manufactured by other countries and companies." —**Terry Ulaszewski**, publisher, Long Beach Live Community News

"Not by 2020. No way. There are too many geopolitical barriers. Folks will hunker down; want to be more in a place. Tech is not a warm blanket." —**Gwynne Kostin**, director of Web communications, U.S. Homeland Security

"I've followed Friedman—great read; made lots of money; interesting ideas: utopian rationalization of increasing global inequalities and free-market capitalism. Given his track record on predictions regarding Iraq, I'd not bet that he is right about the world, but rather, he is insightful about his corner of the world—even though he is well traveled." —**Joe Schmitz**, assistant professor, Western Illinois University

"This is substantially true, and I agree with parts (although many of Tom's points are shallow and simplistic). National boundaries may indeed be shifted, but the overarching politics will persist beyond technology policy. Corporate cultural groups will result for sure, but we may opt into several such clusters. I wonder if some cultural alliances will take shape based on ethnic or intellectual connections, and thus exacerbating the haves vs. have-nots of the globe." —**Gary Arlen**, president, Arlen Communications, Inc., The Alwyn Group LLC

"This is already happening. Geospatial boundaries are artificial boundaries, useful for some forms of governance but antithetical to real knowledge sharing." —**Meg Houston Maker**, director of external information services, Dartmouth College

"It also will continue to grow the digital divide. The global connected community will become more of a single entity vs. the city-state, etc., with very distinct lines drawn between those that know and use this tool to prosper." —**Jim (Jacomo) Aimone**, director of network development, HTC

"Absolutely. We're already seeing the effects of digital globalization and these trends can only accelerate. Individuals may well come to view themselves as citizens of philosophical and cultural milieus rather than nation-states. This is good and bad, of course, since individual responsibility becomes so dispersed in these scenarios." —**Suzanne Stefanac**, author and interactive media strategist, dispatchesfromblogistan.com

ANONYMOUS COMMENTS

A number of anonymous survey respondents shared comments tied to the scenario about global access to the success and the blurring of national boundaries. Among them:

"Blurring's already begun."

"People will begin to see all are one and one are all. It's a good thing."

"I would add international cultural groupings—'tribes,' religious, or other sociopolitical affinity groups."

"Agree completely. Geography will become meaningless."

"I agree provisionally; global communication could be seriously hindered by the intervention of private telecommunications companies and content cartels."

"This is not an individual-player economy—far from it—and too far to make it happen by 2020."

"Internet helps globalization and associated corporate interests, but human cultures are persistent and resilient—the idea they will all be wiped out is wrong thinking."

"This is probably an overly 'Pollyannaish' view of the power of technology."

"Absolutely. This will be taken for granted by 2020, and it'll be hard to remember a time when the world did not operate this way."

"This will continue to be one of the most dramatic effects of the Internet on our lives."

"Nation-states will continue to weaken as megacorporations become more and more powerful, but they won't disappear. Geography will still matter, but matter less."

"This is a growing concern because governments will have to collaborate to 'control' the interests of their corporations and allow fair competition."

Predictions from respondents who chose to remain anonymous:

"People who add no value or try to erect barriers will get voted off the island quickly. Groups will form and disburse as needed."

"People appear to be 'hardwired' through evolution to be attuned to geography and a geographic sense of home. I didn't understand this when I was younger, but I see and understand it more as I gain age and perspective."

"When someone selling crap on eBay can make a living from home, that just shows what's possible. Imagine all of the Internet entrepreneurs that will flow out of India and China. It's incredible."

"Nationalism is something that, no matter how evil, will never die."

"Worldwide competition will continue to grow but will be complicated by diplomatic barriers between nations. This will only be true if diplomacy, not war, takes center stage."

"National boundaries are getting stronger, not weaker."

"We have only scratched the surface with this technology; the future flow of information will only be restricted by the methods/hardware we use to receive it."

"Love Tom, but he is so idealistic in that book, it is absolutely painful! That's not to say he is wrong—he's just talking about the horizon as if it were here. He's looking at a distant oasis and acting like we can all start drinking the fresh water if we just believe and get down on our knees. In my opinion, his lake is out there—but the one he's describing may be only a mirage. There's going to be a lot of painful times in the near future—while blue collar workers and industrial-age trades-folk are simply put out to pasture. It's like the hackneyed example of the craftsmen of buggy whips in the town where they build a factory for horseless carriages...all the buggy-whip craftsmen can read Tom's book, and many will learn to craft steering wheels instead...but many will simply go out of business and starve to death."

"I totally agree. The Internet will allow thinkers and creative people to participate and compete in a way that people in remote areas of the globe couldn't do before. It's easier than many think—I work in a home office that's 200 miles away from my 'real office' and coworkers. I've done it for 5 years, and it works amazingly well. The Internet has allowed me to be productive at my job without physically being there."

"It's easier and cheaper to start a company today than it was 10 years ago by orders of magnitude. This trend will spread around the world as bandwidth and clock cycles become more affordable."

"I think this will happen, but not by 2020...maybe 2030."

"The nation-state as we know today will be eliminated. However, the free flow of information will not be able to overcome cultural/religious issues. Nations will be based on those factors. Successful 'nations' will embrace the new technology and thrive as part of an interconnected global network."

"Blurring of boundaries is occurring already for Internet-intensive users. If you look at this group only, your 2020 vision is here already."

"True, but the risk is that the gap between what Richard Florida calls the one-third of the population who are part of the creative class and the underskilled, undereducated rest will open even wider."

"That might work if we were all the same race, religion, socio-economic level."

"I agree with this prediction, but with the exception of individuals empowered to compete globally. Perhaps at first this will be the case, but power will be held by affiliation as described above."

"This is the best part of the Internet."

"Even on a small scale, we're already seeing a tremendous increase in collaboration on a smaller scale (individual and small-group level)."

"Much as I'd like it to be so, I think that nationalism will survive and even thrive. The Internet will be as powerful a tool locally as it is globally. A more powerful force will also emphasize separation: religion. The Internet is increasing, not blending, religious separatism, and I fear that, too, will only increase in the next 15 years."

"I do not believe that corporation-based cultural groupings will become more geographically diverse. They will be part of the controlling interests on this revolution."

"Culture will continue to rule…there may be global networks, but we can't get rid of the subjectivity in people, regardless of their time zone."

"Readily available Internet access isn't the only answer—fresh water, health care, food, and shelter are still going to be hindrances—the digital divide will be even greater."

"This comes at a cost—again, I am very concerned about who has access and who has the opportunity to participate."

"Ideally, I would hope that this would happen. However, religious and political strife will segment the Internet and further divide the human population. The traitorous actions by some companies in relation to kowtowing to Chinese limitations is point in fact."

"National cultures will continue to be quite dominant, even when the boundaries have apparently disappeared."

"Only starting to appear by 2020, though. We can all happily adopt multiple individual roles (which may sometimes appear to be in conflict)—this may result in multiple online identities for any one individual. Would then expect to see some confusion as to which of these emerge as the dominant grouping(s). So people will identify less with being 'American' or 'Chinese'—but whether they become predominantly a 'football fan' or a 'New Yorker' is open to doubt."

"I agree, but I also say, 'Good luck with that.' Most of us are not intelligent enough to fully take advantage of anything that the Internet has to offer."

"This is very dependent on whether English is the one globally chosen language. Boundaries are falling, but the danger is that new ones will arise—we have a knack for finding ways of walling out and walling in, no matter how we slice up the real and virtual geographies we inhabit."

"It's enough to say that the free flow will blur current national boundaries. What do you gain by adding 'completely blur'? Does that mean obliterate? If so, I don't agree. Blur is the right word."

"National boundaries will increasingly be seen as trivial compared to corporate allegiances that transcend borders, but am not so sure that individuals will be so empowered."

"No, the world is not flat. The world is shrinking some places or some leveraging functions. But this is not uniform. That is why some take advantage of it and some don't."

"Yes, on the condition that the Internet remains free. We've seen what happens in the television and radio industry, the telecommunications industry, and elsewhere when monopolies are allowed to form and block out competition."

"Nation-states and confederations (EU, ASEAN) will continue exercising power. Yes, there will probably be some blurring of national boundaries, just like corporations seem to expand across nations. But so far, corporations do not control weapons of mass destruction. If they do, then the end of nations is near."

"The current static boundaries that define states, companies, and organizations will become much more fluid and adaptable to whatever is needed and will be able to pull in whoever is needed."

"As long as there is real estate, our physical national boundaries will be powerful. It will take more than this to erase the cultural differences that fuel the fires of distrust and their related fire accelerants."

"We will see this occurring, but not in such stark terms."

"I just don't think we can/will move so quickly to change long-standing structures in which powerful people and cultures are invested. There is no doubt, though, that other cultural groupings and other organizations will be reconfigured by then, as more and more individuals work together (and play together) globally."

"There will be human organizations tied by global networks, à la al Qaeda, à la the eBay marketplace—and they will rise in number and impact—but national boundaries will still exist."

"Could happen, but again, one word: CHINA."

"In 2020, as today, there will continue to be cities and countries that are more attractive to live, due to their jobs, their culture, their attractions, their concentrations of people, their infrastructure, their sense of humour. Currently it's more expensive to live, and on average there's lower dispensable income from living in the most popular places. No network will be able to replicate being in the same room as another individual."

"Governments will balkanize the Internet and prevent this from happening."

"Globalization is a mixed blessing."

"Business is based on trust, which is founded on relationships, based on culture. The Internet is blind and mistrusted. Am I going to collaborate with a screen name?"

"Increased transparency eliminates boundaries."

"But this will not happen in the U.S., because the Internet in the U.S. will be a dumbed-down, slow-poke, walled garden that will only partially and unreliably connect to the rest of the world."

"Nation-states can still exist, and national groups can still identify as such, even as technology and various institutions allow greater transnational connection and identification."

"Hate to argue with [Tim] O'Brien, but I still think politics and culture will get in the way of the free flow of information and total collaboration."

"The economic reality of the 'global village' will not be leveled in 15 years to allow ALL inhabitants of Earth to interact in the manner stated."

"The notion that the power of nation-states as currently configured will dissipate radically in 14 years simply due to global information flows is naïve."

"The world in 2020 will be a very different place—one that we are unable to envision at this time, but very unlike what we know today."

"I agree except for the 'city-state' potential. Although I believe those knowledge collaborations will exist, certainly federal governments (and their tax interests) will preclude full realization of a boundary-less virtual environment."

"I agree that because of the Internet's ability to link disparate groups worldwide so that entities can pool resources, it seems likely that corporations will increasingly govern international politics."

"On the contrary, although on one level there will be globalization, on another, we are seeing clear acceleration of nationalism, ethnic centricity, and the collision of cultures. See Samuel Huntington."

"Thomas Friedman is a one-man cliché machine. I sure don't see complete blurring of national boundaries in 14 years, unless the Muslims get their international caliphate or the Communists try again and finally succeed in ruining everything. In either case, there won't be worldwide access to success…just worldwide misery."

"Very true. The first part, that is. Rest is piffle."

"It's not just the Internet that enables this success—government policy also dictates whether or not it succeeds."

"Ah. Disintermediation 2006. The old, new thing. I think we call this eBay today."

"This must be the position version of the prediction that the world will be undermined by loosely affiliated terrorist groups that communicate via the Internet. I think that what Friedman says may be true in the sense that individuals may create entities that thrive in the short term. But without being trained as an economist, my experience in watching high-tech companies is that there is intense value created in the short term and then, in most cases, the smaller entity is purchased or absorbed by a larger incumbent. Hmm. So maybe larger corporations will become larger, but I have no idea what Friedman means by 'corporation-based cultural groupings' and I expect he has a more benevolent view of corporations than I do. Maybe I should read his book."

"No, national boundaries will always carry great political and social history and stigma. I do believe that more global networks will collaborate on similar problems and issues."

"Looking at current global politics, this will hardly occur. National boundaries may be blurred, but ones based on religion and cultural differences are being erected at great speed. The case will look different to business people than the most of us. I suspect there will be increasing desire among some not to network with North America and Europe."

Predictions from respondents who chose to remain anonymous:

"Individuals will still have national boundaries and pay taxes where they live. The Internet will simply create a virtual geography extending the loyalty of those involved."

"The idea that people will stop fighting over land territorial space in exchange for pure territory of power networks is a fantasy."

"Agree with the concept—but disagree with the timeframe. I believe it will take longer—adoption cycles are not as fast as some would like."

"Maybe, but by 2050."

"There is a need to adapt in order to be effective and successful."

"It is in the interest of many industries reliant on the military that national borders and differences remain."

"We'll be on our way to that by 2020, but that's only 14 years away. The EU is still having problems, so certainly all government will not collapse in 14 years."

"I expect the Internet will afford the development of social networks (of individuals and/or other collectivities) that will not be isomorphic with current national boundaries, but I do not expect the latter to be displaced or replaced."

"This is already happening in the form of open-source, etc."

"I think people will be tied together, but I think states will become more reactionary and more insistent on national boundaries as they find their importance waning."

"Communication processes and resulting contacts have changed as a result of the Internet. But whether this will equal a totally 'free flow of information' remains a political, economic, and social issue. For instance, Google's sellout to Chinese authoritarianism, paid rankings on search-engine results, etc."

"The ends of WWI and WWII were supposed to lead to a new thinking with regards to nationalism. As we have seen, nationalism will not die. However, we are seeing increasing globalization. Communicating and associating with different people is not the same thing as identifying with them."

"This statement does not take into account that there is still a socioeconomic background to the processes taken place on and around the Internet."

"This is unrealistically utopian. The 'global village' assumes that economics and politics will cease to influence communications. I disagree."

"Religions, nationalism, criminal impulses, etc., are stronger than the Internet and will screw up the technological paradise envisioned by so many."

"Access only to some, not all. Digital inequality threatens to increase existing social inequalities."

"This scenario is less likely than interplanetary trade."

"I find this scenario plausible, and Friedman has been eloquent about its benefits, but I'm leary of the categorical modifier 'completely.' I'm not willing to go that far."

"Nationalism will be weakened, but it won't disappear."

"Not 'complete' blurring—I think there may be some blurring."

"The move to global networking will be (is being) paralleled by the rise, not of national boundaries, but of local identity. So there will at once be both a more complete global and local consciousness, which are not always working in the same direction."

"I do not think that national boundaries will be blurred. Otherwise, I agree."

"Internet opens worldwide access to success and increases global collaboration, yes. Completely blur current national boundaries, no. The nation-state still has staying power, at least within the timeframe of these predictions."

"The entrepreneur can make money currently on the Internet. With the growth of this medium, I can only predict that the possibility for enterprising individuals to succeed will also grow—exponentially."

"The nation-state is already losing importance. However, the Internet does not open access to success for everyone. Being

Predictions from respondents who chose to remain anonymous:

"Blurring is already happening in regard to taxation. The significant change would be extension of the blur to physical domains and ultimately to military power."

"Ha, ha. Probably a lot of this is true except for the 'success' part. I will be earning an Indian programmer's salary in Chicago, trying to pay my property tax and cursing the market crash that wiped out my 'Social Security' and realizing that I won't be able to retire until I am 85. The good news is I can spend my off hours in virtual reality! It will be too dangerous to go outside anyway without my Sunblock 1,000 and oxygen tank."

a part of the new city-states, corporation-based cultural groupings, etc., is a crucial factor in gaining access to technologically facilitated success."

"The elimination of national boundaries is a utopian fantasy long distant to our own times. While I agree technology allows people to create and be part of their own virtual communities, I do not see those groups supplanting the modern nation-state (and I could well see a backlash against such groups, depending on the nation involved)."

"We can already see this trend in the academic world, to say nothing of the various online communities that share common interests that transcend national and cultural boundaries. However, the power of the Internet is that it acts as a medium to draw together peoples of a diaspora. We can see that in the U.K., where immigrant communities, refugees, asylum seekers, and others use the Internet to maintain their cultural roots and identities."

"I agree with this scenario up to the point of 'completely blur' national boundaries. I don't think this will happen, but the trend is moving global."

"Not completely. Humans aren't that good nor that comfortable with absolutes."

"The result is complex and not really 'flat' but 'bent.'"

"This is the kind of provocatively sounding speculation that sells books, but is grossly oversimplified. So long as the government collects the taxes, commands the military, controls the borders (physical and virtual), upholds the law, incarcerates those who violate the law, protects the rich, and placates the poor...then the nation-states will be around a good many years beyond 2020 and China will still tell Google what it can or cannot do."

"This (like most of the predictions) will be true only in a weak form. Certainly there will be a globalisation effect breaking down barriers. But this exists within a preexisting world order that has nothing to do with technology."

"Agree, with the caveat that open connectivity will be challenged by governments (such as China) and by large business organizations with political clout. Until a paradigm shift occurs concerning the way that information flow is treated, these major entities will present major barriers to Internet openness."

"Fourteen years from now may seem like a long time, but this statement seems a bit far fetched to suggest that national boundaries will be blurred because of the power of the Internet. There's still way too much nationalism and national pride in much of the world to ever suggest that boundaries will disappear. The idea of corporation-based cultural groupings is also interesting, but the idea of individuals collaborating and competing globally would seem to erode at this idea. Doesn't the idea of using technology to make the world flatter suggest that you wouldn't need a corporation to achieve your goals? If anything, individual power will increase—more and more people will utilize technologies to create their own businesses and compete with these larger corporations who are slower to react. The future will be lots and lots of small businesses (who can all act global)—all that needs to happen is people who are unafraid to try it."

"Yes, but not to that extreme; the nation-state will still be alive and well for a long time to come."

"Partly agree—although I suspect the timescale will be longer."

"Agree about global access and interactions and blurring of certain national distinctions. Disagree that political entities would disappear."

"National boundaries will still be with us in 2020. It takes a lot more than simply allowing good communications across boundaries to eliminate borders!"

"On my optimistic days, I can imagine this. I worry, however, that power and politics will trump. I'll go with the optimistic— cautiously."

"This blurring of national boundaries may happen in Europe, but not in most of the rest of the world for quite some time."

"I agree it will happen, although I question if this will happen already by 2020. Maybe it's a bit later. But we will definitely see some very good examples of this."

"National boundaries will NOT be replaced—but they will be blurred much like we see in the European Union. Information does not trump common ethnicity, heritage, language, and history. Unfortunately, global corporations will be more powerful than ever (though not as depicted in the original 1970s film *Rollerball*) to the detriment of workers worldwide. Nations will find themselves increasingly unable to limit the power of corporations."

"Access will indeed be greater, but countries will still exist. A given individual will have many social and professional affinities, which will be constituted, dissolved, or maintained as circumstances require/facilitate."

"The 80–20 principle applies. Individuals can compete globally only if they are trained at the leading global institutions and then live in the leading global cities. I just returned from an Indian city of 500,000, and Internet access is difficult and there are few opportunities to get the people who can help run a globally competitive corporation. I need to go to a big city."

"Not disagreeing that the Internet will blur the lines and shrink the world, but cannot see virtual communities replacing existing real world communities."

"This success will only be for the already technology/ information rich. Digital inequality will grow."

"We should encourage diversity rather than homogeneity. We don't want a McDonald's world!"

"Just because it is possible does not mean it will happen. Just being able to access unknown people over the Internet does not mean that I want to do it."

"The year 2020 may be an early target, but I believe the Internet will continue to reshape the structure of social organizations and interaction."

"There will be a free flow of information, yes, but free information? The problem is not the flow but the content."

> *Predictions from respondents who chose to remain anonymous:*
>
> **"Traditional societies will co-opt the free flow of information to their own uses. We have seen it already. Technology is neutral. People make decisions about how to use it, and it often isn't pretty (e.g., cell phones setting off bombs.)"**
>
> **"Global collaboration is happening rapidly. Political ramifications and international laws will slow this, so it will not be completed by 2020."**

"I agree on this point, but people in developing countries have little scope of access to Internet. Their case must be considered first."

"This is so true and will happen so thoroughly that this is why it will be beyond 2015 that we can measure if the benefits will outweigh the costs."

"I agree that the effect will happen, but the national boundaries will remain as there are more factors that fall outside the global collaboration impact which will maintain the boundaries."

"I generally agree with this statement, but the identity of 'nations' will continue forward."

"By 2020, the sense of global community will be considerably stronger, but the concept of sovereignty will not have been completely transcended."

"The presence of taxation, armies, religious and cultural differences, and natural limitations on the movement of peoples will mean that we will continue to have countries and the imposition of their laws and restrictions will continue. The balance of the two trends will be an evolving dynamic."

"I suspect there is much truth to this thesis—as there is to much of what Friedman writes in this book. But I would argue there are just too many variables related to individuals' identification with today's institutions to suggest that we will replace national identification at some other level. I do think people will, to a large degree, be much more open to differences between individuals and cultures. I think this is enormously healthy for individuals, for the world as a whole, and for all the institutions in between (I don't see this is a threat to nation-states)."

"As a trend, this may turn out to be true, but I certainly don't think national boundaries will be 'completely blurred' in the next 14 years."

"Capitalism fosters the state form and vice versa. State-shaped power structures are needed to guarantee private property and to ensure the security of individuals. Rather the opposite— I expect a strengthening of the concept of the state, once the state has moved from being paper based to being code based. Code will become territory, users citizens, and transmissions transactions, with geolocally identifiable points of origin and termination and accountability of persons. However, there will be a trend of centralization of power structures around cities/places where data converges and is minded."

"A nice utopian view—sounds good across the developed countries where all can compete equally. Sounds less good for developing countries/individuals competing in developing countries. This question should have the danger flag on it!"

"So long as nationalism remains a strong, powerful, and vital social and cultural (and in many cases political) force, as I think it will for a long time to come, this is highly unlikely."

"Findability on the Internet is a greater issue; there might be 'regional' markets that allow vendors to offer their services."

"I partially agree with this statement. I do believe that the global networks will become more prevalent as more countries become high-stakes players in the world economy; however, I do not believe that national boundaries will be replaced. In my view, people will actually feel a bit threatened by globalization and so will react with a heightened patriotism."

"The lines started blurring when companies and people could talk across borders and time zones. The Internet may have accelerated this process, but the blurring of lines has been well underway for some time."

"One interesting way to look at this is to look at its other side. Friedman's story is essentially one of homogenizing results and the cost of that homogeny. So worldwide access to success, for me, reminds me of the axiom, which is better in a crisis—a friend or a neighbor? When we remove geography and proximity from our lives, we make it much easier to ignore and pass over the basics. So if a distant colleague fails—for whatever reason—how can we care? How can we help? Sure, we can judge and complain about unfinished tasks that make our jobs harder, but how can we physically express the caring and nurturing aspects of our relationship with our distant colleague? We can't. We can only leverage distant colleagues for our advantage and be forced to ignore the disadvantages. Something about this concept seems unbalanced to me."

"National boundaries are already skewed as we see from our competitiveness problem, including what is a U.S. company—they are now global."

"This one (just like Friedman's book) gushes too much. Yes, there already are and will be positive effects. But world hunger won't be solved, and world peace is not around the corner yet."

"Get real. All this by 2020? Multinational corporations, irrespective of the Internet, are doing more to obliterate national boundaries, and they are still a long way from having this kind of effect on the world."

"Internet business will increasingly become one to one as systems are developed to allow me to sell something to another, anywhere in the world."

"This statement is totally blind of the fact that there is such a thing as a relevant habitus in which one grows up. Cultural differences do not die away, and Internet will not be the melting pot. Imperialism of capital and instrumental mind will remain blind to some crucial questions of human existence.

Violent religious fundamentalism (in USA) thrives on this kind of blindness."

"Agree, for the most part; however, there will continue to be some small countries that will attempt to dictate what their population can watch, read, and access."

"I agree with the first part of the statement, but not on the second."

"Governments will find ways of keeping their people within their boundaries."

"The Internet allows faster information flow. Only the rich and developed countries would be benefited. For those undeveloped/developing countries, they can't get good benefits from the Internet, as their connectivity and availability is low."

"Friedman is right that the world is flat and will empower everyone and everything will change. But it will never blur current national boundaries."

"Yes, although the 'flat' is actually a landscape with potholes—some cultures and geographical areas (consumed by war or disease) will just not be able to catch up."

"No way will 'free flow of information blur current national boundaries'—but the many organizations and global networks will move in this direction. Agree with a lot of Friedman's thoughts—direction, except for end of nationalism, is largely correct. Corporations may hope that nations go away—they might get even stronger in response to the 'blurring'—believe what Michael Schrage says—unless people try to control us—UGH!—we will pretty much have cyberspace that mirrors reality with the good, bad, wonderful, and ugly...that's the way media has always worked—but then people have always tried to control it."

"Established interests still normalise the Internet; nation-states are polities of stability. When do these alleged revolutions ever happen? It is right that things will be different—and problematic in ways—but this is 1980s techno-futurism..."

"Contrary to the techno utopians, governmental boundaries have not faded away. There will be, to be sure, reconfigurations, but the nation-state will not disappear. There may, however, be EU-type regional groupings."

"With high-speed Internet access and some ideas, we'll be competing head to head with everyone."

"Forget 2020; it's happening now."

"This isn't the way people seem to have worked in the past...It is unlikely that they will do it in the short-term future."

"The world has seen sectarian fighting and battles for centuries. The Internet will not change this, especially since I don't believe that it will be as widespread and readily available to the masses as was predicted in an earlier survey. Attacks on U.S. soil, something that was fairly unthinkable to U.S. citizens, only began to occur with dramatic results in the last 10 years. If this prediction were true, these attacks would never have occurred."

"I wish you were right. Governments—'nation-states' are engaged in fighting back, and BACK, and BACK...Not all—and certainly not in a country near you/or me, but in some countries. Corporations have suffered from the ENRON/MCI megafraud situations, which while they may not resonate to you, resonate in capitols around the world...they wonder still at the corruption in corporate America (I note it was a very SHORT list), even as corruption in governments are the theme of some countries. To advance the benefits of end-to-end Internet, based on bringing all countries into electronic commerce, we still need to address underlying communications technologies in many countries. In the book, the idea that the Internet spontaneously combusts and just HAPPENS, thus everyone can benefit from the 'online world revolution,' doesn't address how to connect the rest of the 'world,' the rest of the users."

"Oh, Internet! How glorious you have been to we human beings. Without the surge of Internet, some anachronistic states, such as Russia and China, would not be able to realize political, economic, and industrial changes, as they are doing today. Even remote communities, such as those living along the Amazon River, are seeing some progress and waking up to the reality because of the Internet. This global network has revolutionized everything."

"This is no more different than a description one could apply to today's world…People will still compete for geographic space because at its foundation, land is a material resource that no one can live without. Specific land areas with unique material resources and strategic locations will always be at a premium. Certain values established by the power brokers who manage such real estate, as well as values brought by people attracted to such situations, will always to some degree influence the local culture."

"The pressure will be there from people, but the governments may not be responsive to that pressure."

"Yes, for those who embrace the technology. There will be a clear division between the haves and the have-nots."

"This is already happening—but note that there are powerful forces in opposition. It won't happen consistently or universally."

"While I agree with Tom's observations, I think it is going too far to conclude that national boundaries will be completely blurred."

"While I believe some aspects of this are true, it's also a very old phenomenon. Fox's *History in Geographic Perspective* describes how critical communication media (in the form of shipping) created communities by interconnection that competed with communities united by nation building."

"Agree in part, though this phenomenon is not exclusively based upon Internet technologies, but far more upon concentration of economic power and the destruction of the state as the protector of common good by policies driven by neoliberal ideology."

"The world is on a globalization trend, not a city-state trend; information is on a stifling trend (via copyrights and software patents), and national boundaries are shoring up against the information flow (e.g., to Muslim women). However, what little information is permitted in the public part of the Internet does indeed contribute towards success."

"2020 is too soon. This is primarily because of obstacles provided by certain governments and institutions, corporations, etc.

There are artificially imposed limitations on informational and technical transfer, on technologies perceived to be threatening to established entities, and on content. (Examples being file sharing, U.S. encryption-export restriction laws, religious or sexual content restrictions in various regions)."

ENDNOTE

1. For additional information about NGOs, see http://docs.lib.duke.edu/ igo/guides/ngo/ and http://en.wikipedia.org/wiki/Non-governmental_ organization.

Scenario 7

Some Luddites/Refuseniks
Will Commit Terror Acts

PREDICTION: *By 2020, the people left behind (many by their own choice) by accelerating information and communications technologies will form a new cultural group of technology refuseniks who self-segregate from "modern" society. Some will live mostly "off the grid" simply to seek peace and a cure for information overload, while others will commit acts of terror or violence in protest against technology.*

Respondents' Reactions to This Scenario	
Agree	58%
Disagree	35%
Did not respond	7%

Note. Because results are based on a nonrandom sample, a margin of error cannot be computed.

CONSENSUS OF OPINION: Resistance to effects of technological change may inspire some limited acts of violence, but most violent struggles will still be inspired by conflicts tied to religious ideologies, politics, and economics. Many people will remain "unconnected"

**due to their social circumstances; some will choose to be uncon-
nected for various reasons—all the time or sometimes.**

The word "Luddite" has come into general use as a term applied to
people who fear, distrust, and/or protest technological advances and
the changes they engender, and "refusenik" has become a term used
to refer to people who refuse to participate in the actions routinely
expected of a particular social group. These commonly accepted
terms were used to construct an approachable, shorthand generalization to describe particular types of nonadopters of the technologies of
networked communications for this 2020 scenario. Some respondents
argued over the terminology, which added some excellent insights to
the discussion. One also suggested an alternative term. "There will
be refuseniks, but not enough Unabombers to make it a trend," wrote
Barry Parr, an analyst from Jupiter Research, adding that " 'Luddite'
will be retaken by 'technoskeptics' as a positive term."

It is likely that most, if not all, people have some concerns about
the negative effects of new technologies. The level of concern differs
from individual to individual, and the reasons for such fears vary
as well. It is impossible to gauge the numbers, but Kirkpatrick Sale,
author of the book *Rebels Against the Future*, wrote the following in
his 1997 essay *America's New Luddites*:

> "A Russian scholar claimed five years ago that there were as
> many as 50 to 100 million people who 'rejected the scientific,
> technocratic Cartesian approach.' Surveys show that in the
> U.S. alone more than half of the public (around 150 million
> people) say they feel frightened and threatened by the techno-
> logical onslaught…in 1996 the trend was reported in maga-
> zines from Newsweek (*The Luddites are Back*) to Wired (*The
> Return of the Luddites*)." (n.p.)

Other recent "neo-Luddites" who have warned that technological
advances are a threat to our humanity include Stephen Talbott, author
of the 1995 book *The Future Does Not Compute*, and Theodore Roszak,
author of the 1994 book *The Cult of Information: A Neo-Luddite
Treatise on High Tech* and a New York Times essay headlined

Shakespeare Never Lost a Manuscript to a Computer Crash (1999). Neil Postman's *Technopoly: The Surrender of Culture to Technology* (1990) and his speech *Informing Ourselves to Death* (1990) are often quoted by those with concerns over the effects rendered by humans who wield new communications technologies. Clifford Stoll followed that with the 1995 book *Silicon Snake Oil*, and Bill Joy came along with an essay in *Wired* magazine titled *Why the Future Doesn't Need Us* (2000).

The most infamous neo-Luddite (and some who believe in the strictest definition of "Luddite" would say the *only* one) is Theodore Kaczynski, also known as the Unabomber and author of a famous *Manifesto* (see Kaczynski, 1995), who took violent action to draw the world's attention to his concerns, killing three and injuring 27 by sending 15 parcel bombs. While religious ideologies have been an underlying cause of violent acts throughout human history, concern over advancing technologies has rarely motivated destruction or death.

Most respondents agreed with this 2020 scenario—58% for one reason or another—while 35% disagreed. But once again, because the proposed future had so many levels, there was a great deal of variability in the reasons for these responses. The elaborations provide many interesting insights.

NATURALLY, PEOPLE WILL PROTEST—BUT TO WHAT EXTENT?

Many survey respondents said there are people who will not adopt the new technologies, adding that this is to be expected and it really will not make much of a difference in the great scheme of things.

"This is a pattern repeated through history and will not change," wrote **Adrian Schofield**, head of research for ForgeAhead, and a leader in the World Information Technology and Services Alliance from South Africa. "From 'flower power' to fundamental Islam, there will always be those who get their kicks from being outside of the mainstream of life."

> "Hype. Have you seen many radical Amish converts lately?"
>
> —Seth Finkelstein, Infothought

Douglas Rushkoff, author and teacher at New York University, responded, "They're called cults and survivalists. Y2K was a fantasy for many who feel too dependent on the grid."

Anthony Rutkowski of VeriSign wrote, "More likely they will simply remain disconnected (no violence)—which is fine if it's an informed choice."

Torill Mortensen of Volda University College in Norway wrote, "This I believe, but I don't think they will be Luddites. They may just be Chinese, poor, or really angry."

Jim Warren, founding editor of *Dr. Dobb's Journal* and a technology policy advocate and activist, wrote, "Yes, there will be some who live 'off the grid,' mostly disconnected from everyone except the few with whom they choose to have contact. There already are. There always have been! Yes, there will probably be *very* isolated incidents of a *very* few 'attacks' against information technology, just as there have always been attacks against all previous technologies—e.g., some people have been known to toss slugs into the coin-collection machines at tollbooths, or sugar in gas-tanks, and there were the occasional acts of the Luddites of a century ago."

Alex Halavais, a professor at Quinnipiac University and a member of the Association of Internet Researchers, wrote, "It seems natural that the social changes now under way will lead to those who act against them. What is less clear is whether they will do so without the help of technology. I suspect that effective challenges to these social and economic changes will only come about through the use of information technologies. The model here is not the Luddites, but the Zapatista movement."

VIOLENCE IS LIKELY, SOME SAY, BUT IT WILL BE LIMITED

A number of respondents said they expect outbursts of violence motivated by human reactions to and expectations of technological advancements. "We'll always have a few like Jim Jones and David

Koresh, and a few misguided folks will follow," wrote **Joe Bishop**, a vice president at Marratech AB.

Sean Mead of Interbrand Analytics responded, "Constant change will spook some into trying to slow everyone down through horrific and catastrophic terrorist attacks against the information infrastructure and all who rely upon it."

"Today's ecoterrorists are the harbingers of this likely trend," wrote **Ed Lyell**, an expert on the Internet and education. "Every age has a small percentage that clings to an overrated past of [a] low-technology, low-energy lifestyle. Led by people who only know the idealized past, not the reality of often painful past life styles, these Luddites will use violence to seek to stop even very positive progress. It is unclear to me how much of such aggression is the nature of the individual who seeks a 'rationale' for her/his more personalized or inherent rage versus the claimed positive goals of such actors."

Jim Aimone, director of network development for HTC, wrote, "Terrorists exist today in the form of hackers, and I anticipate as we relinquish more controls to computers and networks, they will be able to remotely commit any act they want."

SOME SAY PROTESTS WILL BE TIED TO ADVANCEMENTS, LIMITATIONS

There were respondents who expressed concern over the potential for damaging acts tied to effects of advancing technologies. "The real danger, in my opinion, is the Bill Joy scenario: techno-savvy terrorists," wrote **Hal Varian** of the University of California–Berkeley and Google.

Thomas Narten of IBM and the Internet Engineering Task Force responded, "It is not

> " 'Pro-life' never became a term until technology advanced to the point that abortions could be done routinely and safely—now some fringe groups have turned to violence...The increasing pervasiveness of technology could serve to anger certain individuals enough to resort to violence."
>
> —Philip Joung,
> Spirent Communications

Luddites who will do this, but others. By becoming a valuable infra-structure, the Internet itself will become a target. For some, the motivation will be the Internet's power (and impact), for others it will just be a target to disrupt because of potential impact of such a disruption."

Martin Kwapinski of FirstGov, the U.S. Government's official Web portal, wrote, "Information overload is already a big problem. I'm not sure that acts of terror or violence will take place simply to protest technology, though that is certainly a possibility. I do think that random acts of senseless violence and destruction will continue and expand due to a feeling of 21st-century anomie, and an increasing sense of lack of individual control."

Benjamin Ben-Baruch, a senior market intelligence consultant based in Michigan, responded that terror acts will be motivated by the same root causes that drive people today. "It will be those who are struggling against the losses of freedom, privacy, autonomy, etc., who lack the resources to struggle in conventional ways and who will resort to whatever methods are available to them in asymmetrical wars," he wrote. "Ironically, increasing reliance on vulnerable technologies will make cyber attacks increasingly attractive to the relatively powerless."

Howard Finberg, director of interactive media for the Poynter Institute, responded, "The new terrorism might be cyberterrorism. This will be a rebellion against the mass culture of technology." **Sharon Lane**, president of WebPageDesign, wrote, "I agree, but 15 years is too soon—it will take more time or a dramatic technology event/disaster before we realize what we have given up for technology."

Mirko Petric of the University of Zadar in Croatia wrote, "Terror acts, in my opinion, cannot be expected by neo-Luddites, but by the groups resisting modernization processes based on a more general rejection of values and cultural practices they bring about. People uneasy with technology in a 'modern,' 'Western' society will probably represent a small minority. However, cultural reaction to the all-pervasive technology is already happening. It is not of the Luddite/refusenik type, but evident in the predilection for drawing, handmade objects, and the like. Paradoxically enough, some of these practices then get 'recycled' in a computer-based context. Lots of interplay of these trends can be expected rather than an outright rejection of technology."

> "The 2020 version of the Luddite will be the open-sourcer— tech-savvy people who refuse not the technology but participation in the manipulative culture."
>
> —Daniel Conover, Evening Post Publishing

David Kluskiewicz of First Experience wrote, "Many people who are close to self-realization based on their connections or personality will be crushed by the rise of merit, intelligence, and civic engagement. They will be crushed by this new reality."

Suely Fragoso, a professor at Unisinos in Brazil, responded, "I do not think that people will commit acts of terror or violence in protest against technology directly, but against social, political, and economic conditions that bind the development of technologies, as well as other human endeavours."

And **Peter Kim** of Forrester Research sees a future where technology enables antitechnology complaints. "WTO-type protests grow in scale and scope," he wrote, "driven by the increasing economic stratification in society. Some fringe groups or even cults emerge that isolate themselves from society, using virtual private networks."

ACTS OF CIVIL DISOBEDIENCE HAVE VALUE

Marc Rotenberg of the Electronic Privacy Information Center asked that the motivations of protesters be considered before labels are applied. "This will happen," he wrote. "The interesting question is whether these acts will be considered terrorism or civil disobedience. John Brunner's [book] *Neuromancer* suggests that we should keep an open mind about this."

Some respondents welcomed a questioning of the advance of technology. "We need some strong dissenting voices about the impact of this technology in our lives," wrote **Denzil Meyers** of Widgetwonder.

"So far, it's been mostly the promise of a cure-all, just like the past 'Industrial Revolution,'" **Rob Atkinson**, director of the Technology and New Economy Project at the Progressive Policy Institute in the U.S., wrote. "Technology has been, is, and will be a force for liberation and progress."

Wladyslaw Majewski of OSI CompuTrain and the Poland chapter of the Internet Society pointed out the potential for acts of terror perpetrated by controlling groups. "There is no real data that would justify the connection of acts of terror with people refusing to use communication technologies,"

> "There will always be deviants. It is variety that helps ensure our survival, and even gives our survival meaning and hope. However, 'Luddite'-motivated violence will be limited compared to other motivations; we're going to have much more serious problems by 2020 (e.g., political/religious reform, energy crises, GMO [genetically modified organism] food scares, small entities developing WMDs [weapons of mass destruction], etc.)"
>
> —Michael Steele
> (workplace withheld)

he wrote. "In fact, [the] exact opposite is a real danger—governments, corporations, and privileged circles eager to use new technologies to facilitate terror and deprive people from their rights."

Andy Williamson of Wairua Consulting and a member of the New Zealand government's Digital Strategy Advisory Group responded, "Remember that the original Luddites did not want to destroy technology because they did not understand it. They did so because they saw that it simply made a small group rich and a large group poorer and even less able to control their lives. If ICTs continue to be used for personal gain and by powerful governments and corporations to control freedoms and limit opportunities for the majority, then the [proposed scenario] is not only likely, but highly necessary. Not quite storming the Winter Palace, but certainly information terrorism on Mountainview [the California location of Google's corporate headquarters] and Redmond [the Washington location of Microsoft's corporate headquarters]!"

A BATTLE BETWEEN "OLD" AND "NEW" VALUES

There were differences of opinion over whether current conflicts between traditionally conservative cultural groups and those with capitalistic, consumer-driven economies are actually a war over the advancement of technology. "The most important resistance to technology comes from those who oppose change for ideological, religious, economic, or political reasons," wrote **Gary Chapman**, director of the 21st Century Project at the LBJ School of Public Affairs at the University of Texas–Austin. "These are the forces that have used government power to stifle progress in many times and places and could do so again."

> "This is already happening. The Jihad with which we are now at war is being led by people who prefer the 7th century to the Internet."
>
> —Bob Metcalfe,
> founder of 3Com

Paul Saffo, forecaster and director of The Institute for the Future, responded, "The question is how many such attacks will happen and how large they will be. While antitechnology activists may capture our imagination, the risk will come from fundamentalists generally, and religiously motivated eschatological terrorists in particular. But the good news is that this trend will gradually burn itself. The caliphate will not return, the apocalypse will not happen, and eventually world populations will come to their senses. Even lone terrorists must swim in a social sea, and the sea will become less tolerant of their existence. Notions of 'super-empowered individuals' terrify us today in the same way that H-bombs terrified our parents and grandparents half a century ago. But if we are lucky, they will, like H-bombs, remain more looming threat than actual disaster."

But **Stewart Alsop**, former editor of InfoWorld, wrote, "Tech Luddites are like the survivalists of our current times. They have withdrawn and therefore don't matter in the grand scheme of things. Al-Qaeda are definitely NOT Luddites!"

Mike Kent, a professor of social policy at Murdoch University in Australia, responded, "It seems more likely to me that existing terror groups will attack the system from within, rather than without."

And **Robin Berjon** of the World Wide Web Consortium and Expway wrote, "Given the (re)rise of integrist religion worldwide (certainly pretty much for all monotheist ones) and their hankering for obscurity, I'm surprised that such acts of terror haven't happened yet. Instead, they seem to have embraced the Web as a means to broadcast their message, communicate amongst themselves, and recruit new members. It is certainly true that the fact that vast amounts of information are available does not mean that people access them, and it is very easy to remain insular on the Web. That being said, I'd be surprised if there wasn't at least one sect to attempt violent action against the Internet in the close future."

There have been reports in 2006 that terror organizations are implementing technology to their advantage. The United States has an intelligence team tracking nearly 1,500 extremist organizations through its "Dark Web" project, based at the University of Arizona–Tucson. The number of jihadist Web sites has grown from a dozen in 1998 to 4,800 today. Technology experts on the Dark Web team use algorithms to assess threats found on sites and in online forums ("The Future of Terrorism," 2006).

WHETHER THINGS GO QUICKLY OR SLOWLY, SOME SAY IT WILL NOT BE A PROBLEM

IT policy maker **Alan Inouye**, formerly with the Computer Science and Telecommunications Board of the U.S. National Research Council, said daily lives will not be impacted in ways that would inspire the radical differences that might lead to violence. "While I expect continuing advances in our ability to harness IT for societal good (and bad), I don't expect such dramatic changes in daily life," he wrote. "The past 15 years—1990 to 2005—represented the diffusion of the Internet and cell phones to the general population. The preceding 15 years—1975 to 1990—represented the diffusion of the PC to the general population. Although the advances in the past 30 years have been remarkable, much of daily life is not so different. Maybe we will finally see the long-threatened convergence of information technologies and, as a consequence, vastly improved capabilities. But I am not so convinced."

Glen Ricart, formerly of DARPA and currently with PricewaterhouseCoopers and the Internet Society Board of Trustees, predicts more breakthroughs, but says they will appear incrementally and not cause conflict. "I doubt there will be a new digital divide along the lines postulated here," he responded. "I think there will be a continuum of technology use that can be measured as 'face time' versus 'screen time.' I think there are good reasons that 'screen time' will never overtake 'face time.' Well, maybe one exception. There will probably be some pathological cases of being addicted to virtual realities. Interestingly enough, this may be caused by spending too much time in youth interacting with games (and perfecting that genre) instead of interacting with other kids (and perfecting the pleasures of interpersonal relationships in the real world). By the way, in 2020, it may no longer be 'screens' with which we interact. What I mean by 'screen time' in 2020 is time spent thinking about and interacting with artificially generated stimuli. Human-to-human nonmediated interaction counts as 'face time,' even if you do it with a telephone or video wall."

PEOPLE WILL RESIST TOO MUCH CONNECTION IN VARIOUS WAYS

"Off the grid" was originally a phrase constructed to refer to the idea of living in a space that is not tied to the nation's power grid. The definition has been sliding toward a more generalized concept of living an unnetworked life that excludes the use of items such as televisions and cell phones. Some people even aim to live a life that can't be tracked and databased by the government and corporations. Some survey respondents see resistance to connection as a possible trend.

"I'm already familiar with several colleagues who have chosen to only pay cash for items and to eschew cellular telephones because they can be tracked," wrote **William Kearns** of the University of South Florida. "Being 'always connected' is not healthy, any more than it's healthy to be always awake. It's also not particularly good for your survival to be out of touch with your surroundings (the wolf may be outside the door). Specialized intelligent filters will become popular to self-select information for people and filter out adware, pop-ups, nuisance mail, and everything we haven't thought of yet. The motivation will be to reduce the annoyance factor with dealing with the mountain of detritus that passes for information on the network. Humans do a remarkably good job of making decisions without having access to all the facts. We should revel in that ability."

> **"By 2020, every citizen of the world will be as closely monitored as the Palestinians are in the Gaza Strip today. No one will be able to get off the grid."**
>
> —Charlie Breindahl,
> IT University of Copenhagen

Martin Kwapinski of First-Gov wrote, "There will absolutely be those who attempt to live 'off the grid.' The changes these technologies are bringing are massive, difficult to conceive, and terrifying to many." **Mitchell Kam** of Willamette University responded, "Most will just choose to live in isolation and in separate societies." **Judy Laing** of Southern California Public Radio responded, "They'll probably pick up where the '60s left off; their communities will be the resorts of their time."

Brian Nakamoto of Everyone.net predicted, "Living off the grid (comfortably) will be extremely difficult in 2020." **Barry Chudakov**, principal partner of the Chudakov Company, agreed. "My sense is that technology will become like skin—so common that we forget we're in it," he wrote. "Devices will be infused with some manner of intelligence and fit into all manner of objects, from clothing to prescriptions. So it won't be a simple thing to live 'off the grid'—unless, of course, you're a Unabomber type. But those types are rare and live only at the antisocial fringe."

Walter Broadbent, vice president of The Broadbent Group, has a solution for that. "Allowing/encouraging others to create a place for themselves off the grid is a viable solution for them," he responded. "We can use the power and influence of the Web to support others and encourage them to participate."

"TRANSPARENT, HUMANE" TECHNOLOGY IS MOST LIKELY TO BE ACCEPTED

Some respondents said innovations in interface design will make technology more approachable and accessible for the mass population, thus making it less likely to inspire protests of any sort.

Frederic Litto of the University of Sao Paulo responded, "In 1994 an international conference in London on resistance to new technologies concluded that: (1) a certain amount of such resistance is useful to society because it serves as a 'rein' to con-

> "The greater the gap between the digital haves and have-nots, the greater the tension...We can imagine the UN (and Bono?) organizing 'upgrades' for countries with a disproportionate number of digitally disadvantaged people."
>
> —Ralph Blanchard,
> information services entrepreneur
> and investor

trol possible excesses in the use of the new technology; [and] (2) such resistance is frequently the product of bad design of the interface between the user and the system (like the first automobiles, which required every driver to know how to fix his own auto, because there were no mechanics on every street corner—today, the interface design has improved, and the whole auto is a 'black box' to every driver). Just as those who used to throw stones at 'horseless carriages' are no longer with us, so, too, the crazies who protest against very useful and environmentally friendly technologies will eventually be drawn to other pursuits."

Martin Murphy, an IT consultant for the City of New York, wrote, "In 2020 I will be 75 years old. Many of the 'baby boomers' will be over 70 years old. This large group of people may indeed be sick of the constant intrusion of technology and nostalgic for a more human-centered time. If they get together with young, philosophically inspired antitechnology activists, things could get interesting. The trick will be to make the technology transparent and humane."

Nan Dawkins, cofounder of RedBoots Consulting, responded, "It doesn't have to go this way; our choices in regard to access will impact this outcome substantially."

ADDITIONAL RESPONSES

Many other survey respondents shared elaborations to their responses to the scenario about the communications network enabling or inspiring terror acts and the need for people to sometimes get "off the grid" and unplug from the Internet and an "always on" life. Among them:

> "Never underestimate the hegemonic power of the postindustrial era. If there is social unrest, poverty (not information) will be at the heart of it." —**Peter P. Nieckarz, Jr.**, assistant professor of sociology, Western Carolina University

> "This is, I think, dangerous thinking—branding those who don't buy a vision of technology nirvana as terrorists is a type of blackmail." —**Paul Blacker**, head of broadband strategy, British Telecom

> "The association of acts of terrorism with lack of access to technologies has no basis in history or reality. There may be protests, but no 9/11s!" —**Ian Peter**, Internet pioneer; Internet Mark II Project

> "Of course there will be more Unabombers!"
>
> —Cory Doctorow, Boing Boing

> "That's a pretty safe prediction. What are the odds that there won't be anyone fitting that description in 2020?" —**Fred Hapgood**, author and consultant

> "In principal I agree, but the numbers will not be significant." —**Amos Davidowitz**, director of education, training, and special programs for Institute of World Affairs, Association for Progressive Education

> "There will be incidents, but I don't think they'll be widespread or particularly effective. After all, the nouveau-Luddites won't have the benefit of technology for planning and organizing, will they?" —**Reva Basch**, consultant for Aubergine Information Systems, an online research expert

> "With technology, the 'Luddites' won't be able to congeal enough to cause significant impact." —**Willis Marti**, associate director for networking, Texas A&M University

> "That is absurd." —**Tom Snook**, CTO, New World Symphony

> "And not just Luddites; also people of various political or religious stripes who want their own separate communities. Once again, why is this a prediction? This sort of thing has been

going on for a long time: Pilgrims, Amish, Branch Davidians, etc. If anything, it's becoming more difficult because everything is becoming more interdependent. However, better independent solar power generation could change that." —**John S. Quarterman**, president InternetPerils Inc.; publisher of the first "maps" of the Internet

"I agree to an extent. This is already happening today in a limited fashion (there is a measurable population that prefers 'not to adopt'). I don't believe that this group will adopt terror tactics to get their point across, though. Technological adoption is the sum of choices made by a market. Technical modernity can only progress so far as the mass market chooses to allow it. And those that don't choose in favor of technology will make other market choices. The equilibrium will, in all likelihood, be much more peaceful than the anti-techno-terrorist picture you've painted." —**Ross Rader**, director of research and innovation, Tucows Inc.

"Of course, there are the accidental acts that turn into harm; and there are potentially those who act against technology. I believe the latter are a very short list. I think that the former are a longer list and will not create harm, if informed of the risks, and if they indeed want to live without the technological benefits. There is a different group not mentioned, or perhaps I missed this: those who are left behind because of cost, handicap, etc., whose anger and displacement is targeted. What they want is access and the ability to fully participate. Their acts of anger or harm are those that we should prevent by addressing their needs." —**Marilyn Cade**, CEO and principal, ICT Strategies, MCADE, LLC; also with Information Technology Association of America, a business alliance

"Resistance has and always will be technical." —**Geert Lovink**, media theorist, professor and Internet critic, Institute of Network Cultures, University of Amsterdam

"There are those that will always find an excuse for antisocial and violent behavior, and no doubt a few of 'these' will grab at any excuse (though there are so many for them to choose from already). However, the value of accessing education/ information and trade/work opportunities though the Internet should allow those who choose to go 'on grid' to respect those who don't." —**Cheryl Langdon-Orr**, independent Internet business operator; director, ISOC-Australia

"Human diversity dictates that some humans will always disagree with the mainstream." —**Luc Faubert**, consultant, dDocs Information Inc.; president of Quebec's Internet Society chapter and an ambassador to the World Summit on Information Society; member of Computer Professionals for Social Responsibility (CPSR)

"I hung out with neo-Luddites in 1995–1996. This is not a new issue, and among them there was a big debate about proper responses. Of course, the antitech people in Earth First! felt violence against machines was okay. Most of the others, including Amish, antitech humanists felt this was quite wrong. I interviewed a green anarchist named John Zerzan. He is a 'primitivist,' yet in order to get speaking engagement to promote his philosophy he had to get an e-mail account. The colleges would not use the phone or U.S. mail to contact him!" —**Steve Cisler**, former senior library scientist for Apple, founder of the Association for Community Networking; now working on public-access projects in Guatemala, Ecuador, and Uganda

"This is an extremely alarming proposition akin to sci-fi movie story lines. However, it is indeed a possibility—the digital divide could indeed divide us into distinct cultural groups— no longer will it be the 'have' and the 'have-nots,' but more likely it will be the 'have-tech' and 'no-tech.'" —**Rajnesh J. Singh**, PATARA Communications & Electronics Ltd., Avon Group, GNR Consulting, ISOC Pacific Islands

"There are indeed Luddites and refuseniks, and there are terrorists in the world. They will continue to exist." —**Fred Baker**, CISCO Fellow, CISCO Systems; Internet Society (ISOC) chairman of the board; Internet Engineering Task Force

"Human nature being as it is, there will be acts of terror using the ubiquitous ultra-high bandwidth capabilities, but not to a paralyzing degree. Technology will always find a way to, if not 'stay' ahead of the 'bad guys,' at least to 'get' ahead of them and thus, keep these destroyers at bay." —**Don Heath**, board member, iPool, Brilliant Cities Inc., Diversified Software, Alcatel, Foretec

"I don't believe that the Luddites/refuseniks are to blame for this prediction, and whilst I suspect the prediction of the three kinds of people is correct, the people that are left behind will not mainly be by their own choice; it will be a choice made by their politicians or cultural leaders." —**Alan Levin**, programmer, designer, systems and network architect; chairman of the ISOC South Africa chapter; serves on the boards of Future Perfect Corporation, AfriNIC, and .za DNA

"Terrorists burn down laboratories in protest of animal testing today, and fell power lines in protest of fossil fuels. This will continue, sadly." —**John Browning**, cofounder of First Tuesday, a global network dedicated to entrepreneurs; former writer for *The Economist* and other top publications

"Sure, but this has happened for generations. I don't see it as anything more than what has always been—and going back to the desert has its attractions." —**Leigh Estabrook**, professor, University of Illinois

"I agree because it's such a big world that this scenario will surely play out somewhere. That doesn't mean that it will be important." —**Peter Levine**, director of CIRCLE (Center for Information and Research on Civic Learning and Engagement), University of Maryland

"I agree; however, these will be a very small number of people. History shows us that there will always be refuseniks living off the grid away from any current technology. There will always be those who choose not to access technologies even though they are able and capable (financially, socially, culturally), as well as those who would like to access but are unable." —**Mark Gaved**, The Open University, U.K.

"How could this not be true? There won't be many, but even one would make this prediction true. I don't anticipate this group will be very large." —**Randy Kluver**, executive director, Singapore Internet Research Centre

"I agree with this statement, though the acts of terror will likely be directed at those who are controlling the technology at the expense of others rather than the technology itself." —**Sam Punnett**, president, FAD research; consultant on strategy, marketing, and product-development issues related to e-business

"Every modern culture has a counterculture. Every culture has extremists willing to commit violence to express their views.

Nothing new here." —**Scott Moore**, online community manager, Helen and Charles Schwab Foundation

"This is possible, especially in light of the scenario just presented where individual lives lost their privacy. Technology changes so rapidly that keeping up with it can be both a burden and tiresome and often a distraction from just being able to get on with what you really want to do that I can well imagine some people forming communes without any of this modern communication technology." —**Barbara Craig**, Victoria University

"God bless them. Or was that us?" —**Edward Lee Lamoureux**, associate professor, Bradley University

"The advantage of the technical environment is choice. However, the long-term cost of these individual decisions may have to be borne by the folks who do engage the technology." —**Jim Jansen**, assistant professor, Penn State University

"It is highly probable that we will have terror acts in the networked information society, but not by technological discontents. To transform in active opposition, the Luddist disagreements would need to converge with another political or social ideologies." —**Raul Trejo-Delarbre**, Universidad Nacional Autonoma de México

"Technology is the key to small groups projecting power. While this may be the case in some instances, it will not be a major force, as the rest of the world will simply route around them. If anything, conflicts will be between those who use technology for different ends." —**Ted M. Coopman**, activist; social science researcher; instructor, University of Washington–Seattle; member of Association of Internet Researchers board of directors

"This will probably happen—people are already doing this in modern societies and committing acts of terror against modern societies, but I really wanted to disagree because it's too much like a synopsis for a Michael Crichton book/movie/TV series." —**Janine van der Kooy**, information management/librarian

"I'm sure it will happen, but I don't think it's going to happen a lot or with many people. We already have people, such as the Amish, who spurn modern technology." —**Danny Sullivan**, editor-in-chief, SearchEngineWatch.com

"This is pretty much impossible for people who want access to social resources. People who never had access may continue to not have access, but that is not Luddite. They may like not having access. However, those who have grown up with access to social resources have lost the skills to live without them, and they will be drawn back to the grid in times of need." —**Jason Nolan**, associate professor, Ryerson University, Canada

"We will suffer terrorist attacks, but not against technology. The terrorists will use the technology to accomplish their goals in economical terms or identity fundamentalism." —**Carlos Fernandez**, CCRTV, Barcelona

"There will be nonadopters, but that might not launch a terrorist cause. The true terrorists will continue to use the Internet for bad causes such as hacking and posting gruesome terrorists acts. The Internet provides more opportunities for terrorists to show their deeds. Thus, they would not kill the goose that lays the eggs." —**Richard Yee**, competitive intelligence analyst, AT&T

"For sure there is another Unabomber out there somewhere." —**Kevin Schlag**, director of Web development and IT for Western Governor's University, BYU-Hawaii

"Some people who do not or cannot adapt to these new technologies will feel threatened by them or by their power, and a small number will probably try to destroy them." —**Michael S. Cann, Jr.**, CEO of Affinio Corporation

"Maybe this will be true, but I believe it is much more likely that effective terrorists will be early adapters of technology and will use technological sophistication to organize and commit acts of terror." —**Carter Headrick**, director, grassroots and field operations, Campaign for Tobacco-Free Kids

"Yes, but nothing unusual nor something to get excited about. The sort of stuff you describe is what people do when their environment changes. This will be just another rendition of the same process." —**Bud Levin**, program head/psychology and commander/policy and planning, Blue Ridge Community College; Waynesboro (VA) Police Department

"Another niche. No big deal, though—mostly peaceful except when the wackos among every group strike randomly." —**Michael Collins**, CEO, a respondent who chose not to share further identifying information

"This is a dark reality, but call them any name, the have and have-nots are separated." —**Stan Felder**, president and CEO, Vibrance Associates, LLC

"Those attacking the system will be its critics from within, not without." —**Toby Miller**, professor, University of California–Riverside

"It is likely that this disruption will cause social frictions and acts of vandalism/violence." —**Steffan Heuer**, U.S. correspondent, *brand eins Wirtschaftsmagazin*

"We call them Luddites now; when they smash the nearby server farm, do we then call them servites?" —**A. White**, a respondent who chose not to share further identifying information

"A no-brainer—of course some will. And some may become violent. Hopefully, not too many, and not too often." —**Jeffrey Branzburg**, educational consultant for National Urban Alliance, Center for Applied Technologies in Education, and other groups

"It's difficult to imagine how someone would pose a terror act against something that is openly accessible to the masses. The Internet is not an 'institution' in the definition of social sciences. Anybody can use the Web if they like to, even if it's to publish anti-Web ideas!" —**Nicolas Ritoux**, freelance technology reporter for La Presse, Montréal, and other media outlets

"I am not sure that they will self-segregate; religious and nationalistic fundamentalism may restrict people's access." —**Janet Salmons**, president, Vision2Lead Inc.; consultant on organizational leadership and development and virtual learning

"There are other things to get riled up about—religion, national identity, and belonging—and other cultural elements will be far more irritating than any on-grid and off-grid dichotomy." —**Susan Wilhite**, design anthropologist, Habitat for Humanity

"My agreement with this prediction is based on violent actors' use of information as a pretext for their actions, rather than the spontaneous demonstration of an anti-ICT sect." —**Ellen K. Sullivan**, former diplomat; policy fellow, George Mason University School of Public Policy

"This is a premise for a sci-fi novel. To the extent that this occurs today, it will continue. But it will continue to be a fringe activity. If this were rephrased in terms of major political or religious spheres—e.g., North Korea, certain sects of Islam—opting out of global connectivity, there is a more interesting discussion." —**Kerry Kelley**, VP product marketing, SnapNames.com

"The nature of the technology is to facilitate communication between individuals, rapidly diminishing the likelihood that violent objection will accompany technological change. Did anyone violently object to cell phones? To instant messaging? To e-mail? The cat is out of the bag. People will be left behind—some by choice—but the majority will simply be unable to afford to participate in the pace of change, a technological change that is individual and consumer-driven, and consequently requires significant disposable income." —**Nicco Mele**, U.S. political Internet strategist

"Violent animal-rights activists already operate, demonstrating that groups in opposition to modern rationalism already exist." —**Henry Potts**, professor, University College, London

"There should have been another choice here: can't say. The psyche of Man is to grow as 'powerful' (interpret it for yourself) as thy neighbor, no one would want to be left behind. Violence and terror—may be the cause vanishes, may not be intraglobe but interplanetary (or intrauniverse!) Extremism may be passé!" —**Alik Khanna**, Smart Analyst Inc., a business employing financial analysts in India

"But it cuts both ways. Even today, a sign of one's importance or prestige in business circles can be seen by how little the person interacts with ICTs—CEOs having their assistants read all their e-mails and print out only relevant ones for them to read comes to mind—and this ability to filter out the informational noise will likely be as much a sign of one's power

and importance as the powerless person who drops out."
—**Shawn McIntosh**, lecturer in strategic communications, Columbia University

"Once again, this has happened and is happening. Why should we expect it to cease happening in the future? If there is a resolution out there, it will not have surfaced by 2020." —**Walt Dickie**, VP and CTO, C&R Research

"There are always extremists in our society, and I do not see how they could alter history in the long run." —**Yiu Chan**, a respondent who chose not to share further identifying information

"There have been contrarians to every domain of human existence. The Luddites may form loose confederations of cells, similar to current terror organizations. But in an adaptable, networked world, they will either be forced to use the tools they decry (which will make them accessible to law enforcement) or they will be ineffectual due to their isolation." —**Jeff Hammond**, VP, Rhea + Kaiser

"Some will make the choice not to participate online, and many of them will be happy. I also think we will have a third group that might be important. A great number of people will still need to do 'manual labor,' not having much benefit from the Web. Some will be poor, uneducated, etc. The socioeconomic gaps in society may become larger as a result." —**Sturle J. Monstad**, University of Bergen, Norway

"There's not much of a chance for this to happen, as the Luddites will—by definition—lack the communication tools that even the most primitive collaborations require today." —**Roger Scimé**, self-employed Web designer

"People who embrace technology will and do also commit terror acts. Depending on how one defines a 'terrorist act,' one can say that Enron traders acted like terrorists by shutting down power plants to drive up energy shares. New York City MTA strikers committed terrorist acts by disabling its customers and cohorts and their ability to move about New York City. Don't hackers and media pirates commit terrorist acts on technology and media businesses and the viability of the people who work in those industries? Simply taking advantage of technology does not make one immune from thinking about or committing terrorist acts." —**Elle Tracy**, president and e-strategies consultant, The Results Group

"Such groups will be too insignificant in size and importance if technology is not explicitly forced upon us by anyone (that's the only thing that truly causes violent and targeted reaction). —**Mikkel Holm Sørensen**, software and intelligence manager, Actics Ltd.

"And the other way round—nontechnophiles will be outcasts, social pariahs outside the 'compulsary' Net of information, data, and success—as long as we model this world without taking into account freedom of choice and ethics, that is." —**Miguel Sicart Vila**, junior research associate, Information Ethics Group, Oxford University

"Since the Internet will continue to be disruptive, it will garner the attention of Luddites and refuseniks. What will be interesting is to see how many of these develop from the Internet generation, those teenagers now who have grown up with Internet ever present. Will a portion of this generation be turned against the Internet?" —**Jeff Corman**, government policy analyst, Industry Canada, Government of Canada

"You betcha. I'm surprised that it is not already more prevalent." —**Cary Curphy**, operations research analyst, U.S. Army

"There will continue to be a continuum, from people who want the latest in information technology, whatever it may be, to those who seek pleasure and knowledge in other less-technical ways. Thank heavens." —**Cheris Kramarae**, professor, Center for the Study of Women in Society, University of Oregon

"I think the people left behind will fight to get the chance to get in. Internet is not a way of life; it is just an ordinary tool. For that reason, people who actually live in communities who chose to segregate from modern society are already using [the] Internet to fight for their right to stay apart and to connect with other communities like theirs." —**María Laura Ferreyra**, strategic planner, Instituto Universitario Aeronautico; ISOC member in Argentina

"Sadly, I agree with this. However, living mostly 'off the grid' will remove one of the best ways to stop terrorism— a citizenry that is informed and engaged, which tips the

balance to the ignorant who are far too prevalent today."
—**Mike Samson**, interactive media writer and producer, Creative
Street Media Group

"This could well be true if the Internet is totally commercial-
ized. In the same way that ecoterrorism has grown out of the
frustrations of environmentalists who feel that they have been
ignored and disenfranchised, so too could others if the Internet
becomes a capital-driven marketplace." —**Rick Gentry**, acquisition coordinator, Greenpeace

"It is possible that there is a division in the society between
people who favor and those who are against the new technologies, but I don't believe they will arrive in the end to commit acts of terror or violence in protest against technology."
—**Sabino M. Rodriguez**, MC&S Services

"NO. Dumb question." —**Doug Olenick**, computer technology editor, *TWICE (This Week in Consumer Electronics)* magazine

"As long as you recognize religious fundamentalists as Luddites as well." —**Alix L. Paultre**, executive editor, Hearst Business
Media, Smartalix.com, Zep Tepi Publishing

"Isn't this already the case? Technological advancement
always breeds a certain amount of displacement, and nothing
to date will compare to the eventual impact of the Internet as a
communication medium." —**Al Amersdorfer**, president and CEO,
Automotive Internet Technologies

"This question, itself, has a pro-technology, elitist bias. Probably some will do some of the outcomes suggested; it's presently worded in a too-contingent, inadequately nuanced way.
I suspect that some of the present Muslim antipathy results
from traditional economic inequalities and concerns with cor-
rupting effects of modern (read: Western) mass, information-
driven culture/economies." —**Joe Schmitz**, assistant professor,
Western Illinois University

"Sure. The Unabomber was only the first dissident to
actively attempt to subvert the overriding technology and
information mechanisms. But once again, this is just history
repeating itself. There will always be those seeking an idyl-
lic past and who view subversion of the present as the only

path." —**Suzanne Stefanac**, author and interactive media strategist, dispatchesfromblogistan.com

"The revolution of the have-nots will be based on failure to attain their expectations of the 'good life' and the sense of loss of control." —**Terry Ulaszewski**, publisher, Long Beach Live Community News

"The key word is 'some.' It seems likely to me that they will be a very small minority. I think the access to communications network technology will be so inexpensive that there will be few who are 'left out'; more may 'opt out,' but that may become harder to do as access becomes almost universal." —**David Irons**, VP, cofounder, AScribe Newswire

ANONYMOUS COMMENTS

A number of anonymous survey respondents shared thoughtful elaborations to the scenario about the communications network enabling or inspiring terror acts and the need for people to sometimes get "off the grid" and unplug from the Internet and an "always on" life. Among them:

> "We are just not all on the same level, and there is still a significant technology divide. People tend to lash out at what they don't understand."

> "However, just like the Amish, they will become hopelessly left behind and will become meaningless in an advancing technological world."

> "They exist today. There are many examples in history of people sabotaging advancing societies…"

> "The question is whether it will be just little sparks on the fringe or a full-fledged movement. For it to become a movement, they'll need to put to use the technology they abhor."

> "There will eventually be radical, and probably religious-based, terrorists groups that fight technology."

> "I think this statement misses part, however. There will also be positive influences of these groups who choose other methods

> **Predictions from respondents who chose to remain anonymous:**
>
> **"We need refuseniks; we need cultural diversity, and a technology monoculture is dangerous and stultifying."**
>
> **"I'm starting to feel a little Luddite myself."**
>
> **"Some will live off the grid because of 'always-on' burnout."**

than terrorism to add something to the world."

"That's what Idaho and Wyoming are for."

"I do not expect a significant amount of antitechnology terror. I would expect a greater degree of simple refusal to become assimilated."

"This phenomenon is already developing and taking shape; something to be prepared for, no doubt."

"The terrorism will be within the grid by rival groups."

"Luddite/refusenik/terrorist activities have declined since the ARPANET came online."

"I see this as an increasing threat over time."

" 'No-tracers' will become more prevalent (and noticeable) as technology becomes more pervasive. However, violence against technology will be indirect and cloaked in other agendas, such as religious, nationalistic, or ethical."

"They are evident in every society; history proves that we will have people who will attack what they perceive as the only thing that excludes them from being part of society."

"The Internet allows like-minded people to find each other, for good and bad."

"Terrorists commit their acts of violence for many reasons—it is reasonable to expect [that] some terrorist personalities will seize upon technology as a protest topic."

"Education, ideology, etc., will drive it more than those who refuse technology."

"At least in America there have always been 'refuseniks.' If technology makes personal lives more transparent and civil liberties and personal freedoms are lost, this group will grow in numbers and activity. Any group is capable of terror and violence to make its point, but I do not think this group has a higher propensity for violent behavior."

"It is up to us to ensure this change. If we start an open discussion with each other, people understand the way."

"What do you mean by 'some?'—a few hundred loners in Idaho, or entire populations?"

"I don't know that technology incites so much fervor as to make people violent. This is kind of like deaf people being their own culture. I can't imagine it will catch on in any meaningful way."

"Antitechnologists are not terrorists—plenty of religious fanatics, however, will occupy that ground."

"Luddites will just refuse technology. That is not to say they will attack it—largely as they may lack the knowledge to do so."

"Those unable or unwilling to accept wide-open communication and cooperation will always seek ways to destroy those tools which challenge their opinion."

"Usually an effective act of terror requires the use of technology, so if these folks are willing to be ironic, I suppose terror acts will occur. Otherwise, I think they will be like the Amish, content and left alone."

"Seeking peace with technology is just as valid as being a hermit, although it is not a way to be a productive member of society, even though some cultures value monastic and hermit life."

"Perhaps there will be isolated attempts at violently resisting an IT-enveloped world, but these groups will lack the resources and backing to resist for any length of time. They will be killed or jailed."

"Whilst I agree that many will choose an information-free lifestyle, unless a popular religion rises up opposing technology, I doubt we will ever see terror or violence in protest against it."

"The people 'left behind' (by technology) will just make up the poor class that hopefully will encourage their kids to get plugged in."

"They're already doing so."

"Already, the neo-Luddites make their rejections of technology apparent, whether it's Unabombers or smashing computers on stage at town hall. But most people will ignore this lunatic fringe."

"Should this 'brave new world' come to pass, I would imagine lucrative illegal enterprises that erase people from the grid. Dropping out is getting more difficult with each year that passes. Again, 'society' abhors those beyond its control. As cash transactions become more and more exceptional, even unacceptable in some circumstances, it will be increasingly difficult to be a 'mole.' Full autonomy will be impossible without physically leaving normal society and constructing enclaves. It would behoove society to quietly allow this."

"There will always be generational differences, but the benefits of technology will be practically universal and the reaches of technology-based systems unavoidable. I agree that this will probably happen, although it hadn't occurred to me until I read this prediction."

"While refuseniks will be part of the future, they will shy away from violence, since most modern forms of violence will be technology-intensive."

"Religious extremists who believe in the 'End Times' will increasingly view technology enhancements like biochips and national/universal IDs as signs. Some will help their ideology along by committing unrest."

"Where are the Luddites? The only person in recent memory who can rightfully claim the label of being a Luddite is the Unabomber. Will another one like him come along? Probably. But short of some catastrophe, a mass revolt or significant portion of the population retreating from technology is unlikely."

"Few people would be able to access info on enough systems to wreak havoc with them. I do think some people will live off the grid, because of a suspicion about what they don't know about happening with their information behind the scenes. It's a valid fear, but not everyone is willing to make the convenience trade-off for security or privacy, though."

"The same people who hate 'big government' will find the new intrusiveness too confining."

"There will always be antagonists. There will always be nuts out there who think violence is the best tool for getting the attention of society to hear their viewpoints. Sad, but true."

"In the future, the only way to bring the technology down will be to know it very well. It would be difficult for Luddite to know where the 'target' was."

"Who will be the Edward Abbey of the networked world village? I'm sure she or he is out there."

> *Predictions from respondents who chose to remain anonymous:*
>
> **"More people will move off the grid just to slow down their own lives."**
>
> **"The technology-oriented will commit terror acts, and these will affect more people faster."**
>
> **"The real danger is the increased lethality of new technology (especially bioweapons) accessible to such Luddites."**

"Yeah, but this won't be a huge problem. We've already got groups like this, from the benign Amish to the 'ecoterrorists.'"

"What seems unlikely is that the 'technology refuseniks' will be a cultural group in any sense. They will be members of many groups, but I do not see that their resistance to one technology or another is sufficient to identify them as a group."

"I don't think one big massive group of Luddites will form. I would not be surprised, however, if small groups dissatisfied with technology and modern culture decide to wreak havoc because they are disconnected from the rest of the world."

"I agree with statement that 'the people left behind (many by their own choice) by accelerating information and communications technologies will form a new cultural group of technology refuseniks who self-segregate from modern society.' The terrorist prediction may be exaggerated."

"I agree that some will opt to live off the grid, but these won't all be 'bad' people. There will also be many political dissidents and human rights activists who will be forced off the grid in order to survive."

"To some extent, but there will not be a major problem or a major acceleration."

"Even today, there are many individuals who refuse to have anything to do with 'that technology' and are either frightened or resentful of it. There will always be individuals who refuse to accept that changes that are taking place in their society, and while most will simply make the effort to 'drop out' of that society, others will attempt protests of varying degrees of violence."

"This question is not as interesting as the presupposed scenario it implies. It reeks of Cold War hysteria. Was it L. Ron Hubbard or J. Edgar Hoover who formulated this one? What is more likely to happen is that the pace of innovation will start to slow and then plateau at a certain level, instead of spiking off the chart into chaos as this question implies. Moreover, if history is any guide, the have-nots will be fooled into wanting to be like the haves, rather than trying to destroy what the haves possess."

"Don't know if acts of terror will be protests against technology. More so, the way that governments and businesses employ technology."

"The Unabomber was only the beginning."

"However, I think the threat of terror or violence motivated by this specifically is low. I do agree some will choose to live 'off the grid.'"

"Someone has been reading [William] Gibson's 'Bridge trilogy' here!"

"This is happening in many developing countries."

"These will be some of the same people also involved in ELF/ALF [the Earth Liberation Front and the Animal Liberation Front]."

"I think this will come, but not primarily from Luddites who self-segregate. The info technology will be an obvious target for anyone looking to disrupt the evolving status quo."

"Some will (and do) live off the grid—e.g., Mennonites—but I don't think that the refuseniks will act in large numbers to destroy information technologies. Repressive governments will simply block information using technology, as recently demonstrated by China's actions."

"I agree that some people will withdraw from or limit their participation in the world/society facilitated by information and communications technologies, but I don't expect them to commit acts of terror or violence in protest against these technologies."

"This is already happening and will no doubt continue. How big a problem it becomes is harder to predict."

"Some people will refuse to use new media. Violence is not in the cards."

"And they may be right! Or, at least, they may keep us honest. Most people agree that the industrial revolution was a good idea, but we sure do have ecoterrorists who fight against its ramifications."

"They will be regarded like the Amish…it is a lifestyle choice. Any terror or violence would be using technology rather than in protest of technology."

"This will be exacerbated by educational and financial differences that further separate the haves from the have-nots."

"There will always be individuals disconnected from mainstream society, and some will inevitably react violently."

"It's always been thus. The proportion will be small and the terror unsuccessful."

"I think this is also true—but not just in response to encroaching technology. A reasonable percentage of human populations have always had evil intentions—for all sorts of reasons (religious, political, social, etc.)—and new technologies will only give them new tools by which to execute their horrendous deeds."

"Yes, this happens already, but it would be a mistake to label such people purely as 'Luddites' or 'refuseniks,' or assume that they will commit acts of terror or violence. In all likelihood, those who don't self-segregate will have access to much more sophisticated and deadly forms of terror. It will be a mixed picture, not a divided class portrait as given here."

Predictions from respondents who chose to remain anonymous:

"Most people will seek refuge from time to time from their digitally dominated world. Can you say 'Digital-Free Club Med'?"

"This is an overblown issue that is used to legitimize out-of-control security agencies in need of threats."

"Off-the-gridders threaten no one: They're sustainable, in balance. Hackers, on a global scale, will bring the grid to its knees because it's in their nature to fiddle, not always in a Firefox/Unix/Mozilla benign mode."

"Absolutely, we see this taking place already with Middle Eastern fundamentalist religions that violently reject the modern world, while using technology invented there to seek its destruction."

"Not any more than normal with or without the Internet. There have been refuseniks for centuries and centuries…"

"As with John Connor, in 'T3' [*Terminator 3: Rise of the Machines*]. Yes, but acts of terror will be extremely limited in terms of impact. Terror on these networks will be more of an act of inconvenience, like a thunderstorm, than an act of terror that we see today."

"Terror acts are much more likely to be facilitated by technology than be the result of an objection to technology. This being said, there will always be malicious use of technology for its own sake—technological vandalism, such as spreading viruses."

"Please, they'll be watching cable in their free time."

"If 'terror acts' can be considered as taking down communications networks, then they will almost certainly happen.

As technology becomes more pervasive and the 'majority' of culture is aware and adept, the pendulum will swing in the other direction."

"I agree with the peaceniks, disagree with the violence. Those off ICT who act need to organize; to do that requires social involvement, social capital, etc. That requires skills associated with high SES [socioeconomic status], and thus most likely also with high ICT use. There may come an economic underclass that may commit violence, but it is not their ICT refusal that will create this."

"Not only terror or violence, but the human relations aspect of our world may not exist."

"I do think we are for a backlash against technology by some factions of the population who feel 'excluded'…that their income and/or education level prevents them from accessing technology and thus not succeeding in life."

"These individuals will be easier to identify by government agencies and laws—like the Patriot Act. Although they will be 'off the grid,' the collaborations by multiple agencies will make it easier to spot them while making it difficult for them to survive."

"I agree that some will choose to live off the grid, but I don't see people grouping into tech refuseniks and committing violence within that group."

"Even so, the current percentage of those choosing to be 'left behind' will decrease as technology is easier to use and the population ages."

"These terrorists will be splinter groups, something like White Supremacists. The overwhelming cultural presence will dovetail with technology and all its tempting offerings."

"I think they are already out there—just not violent—yet."

"There will likely be isolated cases. Consider the Unabomber, or the stereotypical 'gone postal' displaced worker. However, in these cases the issue is the unbalanced individual, not the technology. More commonly, I would expect to see individuals, or discrete groups such as Mennonites, Hutterites, Amish, etc., who have made a conscious decision to live 'simply' for religious or cultural reasons and self-segregate, but do not offer violent protest."

"This is quite possible—but not the intentional left-behinds, also the people that came under the wheels of the accelerating modernization quite possibly will turn to fundamentalism that embraces terror as an instrument of protest."

"I don't think they will be necessarily Luddites, but they will understand that the Internet has become (by 2020) the lifeblood of communication and commerce for the global economy. What better way to spread terror than to destroy what we all rely on so heavily? I think the refuseniks and Luddites will just exist happily 'off the grid' much the same way that some groups/religions now choose to avoid cars, television, or modern conveniences. They don't (so far anyway) commit acts of terror because of their choice."

"I don't believe the 'refuseniks' are active enough to get out of their chairs, let alone commit terrorist actions, or common graffiti. The information and communications divide is real, and cognitive (I'm not a fan of the 'great divide' theory of literacy, but this is a serious cognitive shift). I also link it to the use of psychochemistry in both young people and adults, but at best it is an active/passive split. Counterintuitively, this is in part fueled by Ritalin/Meth, two sides of the same coin. So long as the drug of choice is 'puppy-uppers,' any movement fueled by it is going to be more active and focused than consumerist somnambulism. The people being kept on the dull and passive side of the divide are educated in an authoritarian mindset, trained to do as they're told, buy what they're told. I don't expect rebellion or activism from them at all. Pot smoking, perhaps. I do predict that there will be off-the-grid activists, rebels, and a new cultural group somewhat akin to [William] Gibson's 'Lo Teks' in *Johnny Mnemonic*. They will be capable of advanced analysis of changes in the structure of the system, and they'll start building enclaves and havens and systems to protect themselves from oppression inside the grid, whether in China or the U.S. I see this sort of activism springing up from the free-thinking, free-wheeling, and pissed off attitude of the blogosphere. And it will also be better organized. Refuseniks, if they do try anything, will fizzle."

"Just as technologies cannot in themselves produce happiness for individuals, cultures, or societies, so 'terrorists' are likely to use technologies for whatever ends, not to destroy technologies as the root cause of inequality or evil."

"I agree, in the sense that the statement is vague—there will always be individuals or groups that will commit terroristic acts against 'the modern world,' but they will always be in the minority. See, for example, the broad range of modern environmentalists (or 'eco-friendly') versus the Earth First! 'monkey wrenchers.'"

"I doubt there will be many people who actually could live in the world without some sort of technology—whether they like it or not. Technology will become too enmeshed in the simple things we need for living—food, air, water, shelter, etc. I do agree that some will live off the grid because they already are at this point in time. I don't think that extreme 'refuseniks' will commit acts of terror, but maybe violence in protest against technology."

"I would hope this is not the case. Better that this stay in sci-fi stories."

"It will not be the Luddites that will be able to do this. It will be the power elite that fear the Internet most. They have the resources to be dangerous."

"There will always be some 'some' out there—some who will refuse to adopt new technologies, some who will hesitate to recognize technology. But violence will be a very small part of the resistance."

"It seems unlikely that terror or violence will be in protest against technology…I agree some will choose to be 'off the grid,' but [it is] unlikely they will want to protest in a violent manner."

"Instead of Luddites, we have the fundamentalists who stand strong against any sort of globalization and loss of identity for themselves. This is already happening, and I see that this extremism is going to get worse before it gets better. But they will use technology to their advantage, not fight against it."

"There have always been such and there always will be. I'm not aware of evidence suggesting there will be more of them."

"We already have this cultural group, manifested in several ways. I see no reason to think that it will become stronger. How could it? It's pretty strong right now."

"I completely agree that there will be generations and individual groups who are left in the dust of the technology race, but there are already significant examples in history of this happening that do NOT include a cause-effect relationship that includes violence. Using the Amish as an example, perhaps the opposite may be more realistic...individuals retreating 'off the grid' as an alternative to the unpredictable pace and unintended consequences that 'modern' society is sure to face."

"If the refuseniks shun technology, they will not be able to commit acts of terror. Acts of terror require a great deal of communication and coordination. So, terrorists will (and already do) exploit the information technologies to their full potential. Although it is possible that some people could live 'off the grid,' it will become increasingly difficult to survive in a society without encountering information technologies."

"We will have to use some of the technology described in previous statements to minimize the risk of being hit by these terrorists. I have a feeling more people will go off the grid than we might expect now."

"I'm not sure there are Luddites today. To commit the acts of violence, they will need the mobile phone to communicate."

"I agree that some will live off the grid, but I do not agree that some will choose to commit acts of terror of violence."

"Double-barreled question, not helpful. I agree that some people (probably many) will live off the grid for peace but don't necessarily agree that this will lead to others committing acts of terror, but acts of terror are committed for all sorts of reasons and there have been acts of violence against technology already. I disagree with the statement because I'm not sure about the formation of a new culture of refuseniks."

"We already have that, but not in the way you think. Al-Qaeda is a battle against modernity, although they use modern technology to do it (jet airplanes). The Republican Party, because it is controlled by fundamentalist Christians (as opposed to Al-Qaeda, fundamentalist Muslims), also wages a war against modernity, specifically science, and by denying evolution they deny scientific principles and thus all of science. Information overload has been a hollow concern for decades."

"These will be people left behind by/reacting against lots of modern things, not just against technology."

"Some may live off the grid, and there will probably be Unabomber-like acts of violence, but those will be relatively isolated."

"Those are not the only alternatives. There are many high-tech people who limit the technical interest of their children. There is a middle road."

"Though am not sure they will call themselves Luddites. Anti-globalists, pro-God, nationalists, etc., will be other labels used for similar sentiments."

"The irony of Luddite/refusenik terror is that certain technologies are used to protest others. The technologies that have so faded into the wallpaper as to be unnoticeable are used to protest those that have newly arrived on the scene and present unsettling challenges."

"Inclusive programs should minimize that risk, as happens today (it does mean that it is impossible to eliminate terrorism, but [it is possible] to control its impact)."

"This question, to me, treats people who do not fully embrace online life as part of their identity as subversive or inferior. This is way too broad of a characterization of those that do not want to be a part of the Internet-is-life movement. There will definitely be self-sufficiency movements that are seeking to minimize risk in the face of global resource crises, but please do not lump these people with terrorists! If you are trying to say, okay, not everyone will be on board…that is fine. But we don't have to associate those who are nonconformists with terrorism."

"It seems more likely that the 'terrorists' are making very effective use of the Internet and other computer-based technologies."

"These will be very few. On the whole, people do not avoid amenities/networks but do try to avoid political control/centres. Thus, new communities on the Internet, but separated from political control will (have) emerged and will continue to emerge. There will be a continual battle (as ever) between governments and anarchists."

"This will occur within the technology far more than without. There always are the opposites."

"I am sure one in a million (or billion) will do exactly this, which means 'some' will commit the acts you describe."

"I suppose there might be some extremely small and isolated examples. Past history has shown protests against technology (e.g., automobile), but I don't see this as anything to be concerned about. Why even bother to mention it in this survey?"

"However, these terrorist-type acts will not be limited to Luddites. It is equally possible that a cyber-hacker or bioterrorist not only has access to the necessary tools but [also] seeks to set back the forces of change."

"There are always people that wish to live outside the common society or are opposed to the society. However, this has nothing to do with the Internet. E.g., Amish people will not use the Internet, but that is not because of information overload."

"Put down that bong and switch off the reruns of *Star Trek*."

"Don't forget the religious fanatics of all stripes, which may or may not also be Luddites, and which are likely to be a much bigger and more dangerous problem. Yes, there are likely to be bad things happening."

"No different than we have seen in recent history—there will always be a fringe group of persons who will choose to be different."

"This is always true, but how many of these off-the-grid people are there, really? In any event, if the other predictions come true, it will be harder and harder to live off the grid, suggesting that only the most die-hard will attempt and achieve it."

"As global connectivity continues to improve, wage rates in the developed nations are likely to plummet. The result will be a large-scale migration of the retired to the developing world, and an influx of young, educated workers from the developing world to the developed world. As the U.S. exports its retired and imports new engineering blood, the young and uneducated will increasingly become marginalized, unable to afford housing or even food. They will band together in abandoned ghost towns in the Midwest and form extremist sects."

"Very few people leave technology on their own; it is the social and political structure that inhibits some from getting close to it under certain situations."

"It's hard to disagree with a 'some' sort of statement—after all, we had the Unabomber, so this is of course a possibility. However, I doubt we'll see violent acts of protest against technology—creative and important ones, perhaps, but probably not violent."

"I am not sure that the patronizing term 'refusenik' captures the possible magnitude of the problem, as the term suggests that nonuse of technology involves a choice. A protest against unequal (discriminatory) access to technology is different from a protest against technology itself. However, actions due to access inequity may be a bigger problem than those created by disenchantment."

"This is an utterly unhistorical understanding of the Luddite movement, which was about ownership textile frames, rather than about rejection of technology per se. I do expect there to be continued struggle over the ownership of technology and that some of that may result in refusal to use technology that cannot be owned or controlled by those who are impacted by it. If that technology is being used to exploit individuals (certainly true for textile frames in the era of the Luddites), then some violent reaction is likely."

"Getting off the Net is already there. This scenario is again a caricature, especially when pointing to acts of terror against ICT. Up to now, the acts of terror come more from agro-chemistry. It is also inappropriate to put a negative label upon those who refuse to embrace the technology/corporate push as it is. There is an obvious need for a critical examination of the most suitable ways to use technology in order to deal with real life issues as seen by the people, as well as the choices of needed technologies."

"Human beings can't live without technology. The only issue is how human beings cope with it. People may have different kind of reactions, but all these are natural and temporary as technology is ongoing developing."

"Mankind will always have a darker side to offer, it will always have some resented groups and organizations reluctant to any changes and progress. We had them in the past; we still have them in the present; we will have them in the future. But the world will always succeed over these demented minds."

RANKING PRIORITIES
FOR GLOBAL DEVELOPMENT

More than three-fourths of respondents—78%—identified building network capacity and the knowledge base to help people of all nations use it as the first or second priority for the world's policy makers and technology industry to pursue. It was selected as the first priority by 51% of the survey participants.

Following closely as a priority was "creating a legal and operating environment that allows people to use the Internet the way they want, using the software they want," which gained support from 64% of respondents as either the first or the second international priority. Falling far down the list were the other two choices in the setting of priorities—"developing and 'arming' an effective international security watchdog organization" and "establishing an easy-to-use, secure international monetary microcredit system"—which each gained only 8% of respondents' votes as a first priority. Many respondents wound up including support for two or more of the priorities in their written elaborations. They most often combined the ideals of total access/tech knowledge and an open legal and operating environment.

Setting Priorities for Development of Global Information and Communication Technologies

Respondents were asked the following: If you were in charge of setting priorities about where to spend the available funds for developing information and communications technologies (predominantly the Internet) to improve the world, how would you rank order the following international concerns? Please number these from 1 to 4, with 1 being the highest priority.

	First Priority	Second Priority	Third Priority	Fourth Priority	Did Not Respond	Mean Rank
Building the capacity of the network and passing along technological knowledge to those not currently online	51	27	11	4	7	1.67
Creating a legal and operating environment that allows people to use the Internet the way they want, using the software they want	32	32	21	8	7	2.05
Developing and "arming" an effective international security watchdog organization	8	12	23	50	7	3.25
Establishing an easy-to-use, secure international monetary microcredit system	8	21	36	28	7	2.90

Source. Pew Internet & American Life Project, Internet Issues 2020, November 30–April 4, 2006. Results are based on a nonrandom sample of 742 Internet users recruited via e-mail. Since the data are based on a nonrandom sample, a margin of error cannot be computed.

Accessibility and the Knowledge to Use ICTs Seen as Key

Respondents overwhelmingly agreed that bringing the tools of connection to as many people as possible and teaching them how to benefit from these tools will help improve the world.

"Capacity building should be the prime focus," wrote **Rajnesh Singh**, a leader in the Pacific Islands chapter of the Internet Society. "Not just machines, but people and getting them to do new and wonderful things with technology."

Fred Baker, president of the board of trustees of the Internet Society, responded, "Education is key to Internet deployment and use, and is something I am directly involved with."

"Providing access and literacy is paramount," wrote **Howard Rheingold**, Internet sociologist and author. "Without affordable access, knowledge of how to use the technology and the legal and operating environment that permits innovation, we won't see the creative explosion we see with personal computers and the Internet."

> **"The most important thing is for the Internet to remain an open, flat medium for high accessibility for everyone worldwide."**
>
> —B. Van den Berg,
> faculty of philosophy
> at Erasmus University, Rotterdam,
> The Netherlands

Robin Gross, executive director for IP Justice, wrote, "Building an open, inclusive, and interoperable infrastructure is the most important because all of issues will depend upon the infrastructure."

Ed Lyell, an expert on the Internet and education, wrote, "We enhance the positive potential of global communication commerce only by bringing as many into the network as possible. To continue to expand the current digital divide will bring on negatives of jealousy, income disparity, have/have-not battles, etc. This is a case when the economic common good must be nourished while minimizing the potential greed of individualized privatization. By this, I do not mean government run—but a structured system of individual incentives for excellence that lead to positive collective improvement."

Many respondents agreed with **Tunji Lardner**, CEO for the West African NGO network, wangonet.org, who wrote, "The challenge remains helping the majority of our brothers and sisters in vast underserved places in the world." **Lutfor Rahman**, executive director of the Association for Advancement of Information Technology at Pundra, Bangladesh, added, "Everybody should know the benefit and problems of using the Internet, and this should get first priority."

Nan Dawkins, cofounder of Red Books Consulting, wrote, "While ensuring access certainly impacts the Internet's potential as a change agent, it is important to remember that simple access is not enough. Giving a man (or woman) a laptop and a cheap connection is not sufficient to change his/her plight. The Internet is a tool with some potential, but it is probably not within the top 100 factors that can drive significant change in the world."

Seeking an Operating Environment That Is Open, Fair, and Full of Innovation

Respondents also put "creating a legal and operating environment that allows people to use the Internet the way they want, using the software they want" at the top of the priorities list. Their concerns in this realm include the positive and negative effects of a software monoculture; regulation's influence on security, trust, innovation, and access; and the outcomes caused by the imposition of various limitations by those in prevailing power structures.

"The social institutions of exchange and basic law (which requires some enforcement ability) are the most important for real development," wrote **Bruce Edmonds** of the Centre for Policy Modelling at Manchester, U.K. "This will allow new online institutions to emerge."

Wladyslaw Majewski, of OSI CompuTrain and the Poland chapter of the Internet Society, responded, "The only listed goal worth significant funding is to defend and promote human rights and activities."

John Quarterman, president of InternetPerils and an Internet pioneer, wrote, "Without software diversity, we're at the mercy of the monopoly software vendors, both directly and even more indirectly through ease of exploit

> "Giving people the ability to develop their own strategies and appropriate technologies as they see fit will always be a more powerful method of ensuring equitable uptake than by top-down measures or by allowing current power groups (e.g., corporate interests) to define the future environment."
>
> —Mark Gaved,
> The Open University, U.K.

of such software and especially ease of spread of such exploits, not to mention through the warping of political and social systems that happens as monopolists fight to maintain control…Distributed security is what we need, and the most effective first step is to deal with the software monopoly problem." **Baker** responded, "I would simply leave (this) to antitrust law."

Jeff Hammond, vice president for Rhea + Kaiser, wrote that innovation will trump any monoculture. "Creating a legal framework for the Internet should focus on intellectual property alone," he wrote. "I do not believe that the goals of 'using the Internet the way they want' means that a political solution should be sought for infrastructure or technology platforms. Political solutions are typically about *discouraging* human activities. Innovation is about encouraging human activities, many of which will be failures. If a software monoculture results, it will be because it is the solution that solves the greatest number of problems for the greatest number of people…it will also be temporary until the problems it creates are solved by the next wave of innovation."

Ross Rader of Tucows, Inc. wrote, "Various current legal environments are threatening to tear apart the fabric of the network (i.e., U.S. intellectual property law, communications regulation, etc.). This trend must be reversed. Without a fundamental right to choose platform, service, and application, there is very little merit left in the network. The edge must be left to its own devices, despite the economic pursuits of big business."

Robin Berjon of the World Wide Web Consortium and Expway wrote, "If there is no environment for open standards and multiple platforms, none of the two remaining points will be feasible, so I would place it at the top of the priority list because it is a prerequisite." And **Glenn Ricart**, a member of the Internet Society Board

> "Any effort to improve the world by means of development of information and communication technologies should be based on empowerment of the individual as user and various groups of users, and not be conducive to a business monoculture. In other words, the current trends of corporate domination in the area should be reversed. Public interest should be the top priority."
>
> —Mirko Petric,
> University of Zadar, Croatia

of Trustees, put it this way: "The highest priority is to make sure that the Internet can continue to foster economic and social growth and development for everyone (in all cultures) via innovation, competition, and free speech (e.g., uncensored and unmonitored packets)."

Simon Woodside, CEO of Semacode Corporation in Ontario, Canada, responded, "The legal environment today is excellent, and bodies such as ISOC, ICANN, and IETF, along with world governments, should continue to nurture and protect the open nature of the Internet."

Some respondents selected this priority as the first on their list and then made sure to emphasize the fact that the Internet should remain as *unregulated* as possible.

"Digital Rights Management, 'trusted computing' that bakes restrictions into hardware, and extensions of copyright law such as the Digital Millennium Copyright Act are roadblocks that could strangle a global creative renaissance before it can take root worldwide," **Rheingold** wrote.

Jim Warren, a pioneer technology policy advocate and activist, responded, "I do not imply that government and laws should do much. Quite the contrary—I want government and laws to mostly GET OUT OF THE WAY! First and foremost, government *mostly* serves itself first (and serves its most powerful supporters second)—and that is perhaps the foremost danger."

IF THE NETWORK IS NOT SECURE, WILL IT PROLIFERATE POSITIVELY?

At a June 2006 technical conference in Boston, Microsoft officials reported that a significant percentage of the world's computers have been infected by keystroke loggers, Internet Relay Chat bots, and rootkits. The company, which produces the Windows software that many people are referring to when they speak of the dangers of a software "monoculture," said that between January 2005 and June 2006, it removed at least 16 million instances of malicious software—one virus, Trojan, rootkit, or worm in every 311 times it scanned one of the 270 million computers running the Windows Malicious Software Removal Tool (Naraine, 2006).

A vocal minority of survey respondents pointed out the fact that the communications network will not be used or useful if it is not seen as a safe place to be, no matter how well connected everyone is. "Unless we find ways to curb spam, identity theft, cyber extortion, virus writing, and other such criminal activity, people will not WANT to use the enhanced IT environment that the other three choices present," explained **Eugene Spafford**, executive director of the Center for Education and Research in Information Assurance and Security. "Technology alone (or even primarily) cannot solve this problem—we will need international response to bad actors, with appropriate investigation and punishment."

Anthony Rutkowski of Veri-Sign, a company that includes a team of malware detectives based out of Dulles, VA, called the Rapid Response Team, responded, "Cybersecurity and infrastructure protection will remain the highest priority. Next Generation Network legal norms, regulations, and standards will likely have proliferated so as to

> "[We must] embed the openness with which the Internet began, the culture of creativity and connection and sharing and transparency. Standards will help that harmonization. Political and legal support will follow and should not lead...governments and commerce should have less valence than civil society and academia."
>
> —Sylvia Caras,
> disability rights advocate
> for People Who

allow for flexible use to the extent that is achievable given other priorities like security and infrastructure protection."

Amos Davidowitz of the Institute of World Affairs wrote, "People will not use it if they do not feel secure, so access and security are the primary goals."

> "Security has to come first. As long as we have...Trojan, spyware, malware, we will not be able to gain any true integrity of the Internet."
>
> —Terry Ulaszewski,
> publisher, Long Beach Live
> Community News

Marc Rotenberg, executive director of the Electronic Privacy Information Center, responded, "We need stronger safeguards for privacy and human rights before enabling greater security authority."

MANY EXPRESS CONCERNS OVER POLICING OF THE INTERNET

Interpol, the International Criminal Police Organization, is the group effort of 184 nations to facilitate cross-border police cooperation. It has been in existence since 1923 and has seen crime shift online in the past decade. It has limited influence, but is has concentrated some efforts on Internet crime and crime prevention. It hosted its First International Cybercrime Training Conference in September 2005.[1] In March 2006, an Interpol spokesman called on international politicians to make it easier for cybercrime to be fought across borders. He cited gangs that work online from Russia, China, the U.S., and other nations to target Internet users across the globe (Espiner, 2006).

In responding to the survey scenario of "developing and 'arming' an effective, international security watchdog organization," several participants wrote in support of the way that individual nations are working separately and together right now in preventing crime and leveraging punishments.

"Billions of dollars are already being used to build an effective international security watchdog organization," wrote **Charlie Breindahl** of the IT University of Copenhagen. "It goes under names such as NSA, CIA, and the Department of Homeland Security. Some of it is legal, some illegal. If there is a need to fulfill in this area, it is to put in place an international cyber-police controlled by the UN; that possibility is moot, of course."

Alejandro Pisanty, vice chairman of the board for ICANN and CIO for the National University of Mexico, responded, "A single 'watchdog organization' seems less preferable, and less viable, than an active network of national, functional, and cross-national and cross-functional bodies with solid agreements among them."

Fredric Litto of the University of Sao Paulo in Brazil said that "incentivated communication" is a better answer than employment of such a force, adding, "Leave policing to the last stage—you might not even need it."

And many people voiced strong dissent regarding the concept of a formalized international Internet-security group. **Ricart** wrote, "I will not willingly choose to give up my privacy so that some international security organization can decide to intervene when they think it appropriate." **Cory Doctorow**, blogger and cofounder of Boing Boing, wrote, "Why do we need Internet cops? How about Internet architecture that helps users protect themselves instead?"

Singh responded, "ICTs have become a new tool for criminals and terrorists, and it is important to think about and take the necessary protective measures; however, this must not be at the peril of freedom of expression and basic human rights." **Ted Coopman** of the University of Washington– Seattle wrote, "Any international ICT police force would not (based on my read of his-

> *"Qui custodiet ipsos custodies?* An effective international security watchdog organization will limit the possibilities of the other three."*
>
> —Alec MacLeod,
> associate professor, California
> Institute of Integral Studies

tory) be used to protect people or infrastructure in general, but protect those in power from those who are not."

Scott Moore, online community manager for the Helen and Charles Schwab Foundation, wrote, "A centralized 'enforcement unit' is utter bullshit. A watchdog group should do just that—use their resources to inform and spread the warnings so that people can be prepared. Arming a central organization against Internet criminals is like trying to destroy bad weather."

Lynn Schofield Clark, director of the Teens and the New Media @ Home Project at the University of Colorado, also emphasized the ideal that members of civil society can work together to help patrol the Internet. "We need a watchdog organization to oversee criminal and terrorist acts carried out through the use of ICTs, and we really need a series of well-supported, lower level watchdog organizations to ensure that ICTs are not utilized by those in power to serve the interests of profit at the expense of human rights. We need ICT specialists to augment the work of important organizations already in existence that are fulfilling this watchdog role. The need for the watchdogs will only increase as time goes on."

A treaty to help nations deal with cross-border crime has been in the works for many years. The Council of Europe Cybercrime Convention is open to signature by all nations, but conflicts over sovereignty and worries about speech and privacy rights have stalled it regularly since its beginnings in 1997.[2] Only a few nations have signed it, but the work continues.

The Organization of American States and the Council of Europe held a joint cybercrime conference in December 2005, and the Asia Pacific Economic Cooperation Forum also conducts annual conferences. Representatives of the Computer Crime and Intellectual Property Section of the Criminal Division of the U.S. Department of Justice conduct cybercrime workshops in cooperation with representatives of many other nations (2006).

> "A specialist tech-security watchdog sounds like a *really* bad idea: use a computer, go to jail."
>
> —John Browning, cofounder of First Tuesday, a global network dedicated to entrepreneurs; former writer for *The Economist* and other top publications

Individual countries have developed resources to educate Internet users and help them identify and report crimes. In the U.S., 5 federal agencies and 13 private organizations announced the January 2006 launch of OnGuard Online (http://www.onguardonline.gov), a site with information about monitoring credit history, the effective use of passwords and other security measures, and recovering from identity theft.[3]

SOME PEOPLE SEE ENHANCEMENT
OF ECONOMIC SYSTEMS AS A TOP PRIORITY

If economics is the root for the development of an equitable world, as many survey respondents pointed out throughout their answers to all of the scenarios proposed in this survey, then the fourth item on the list of priorities is of value. While a few respondents replied that it is not possible to make such a system secure and few selected it as a first priority, most said it is a worthy goal to work toward.

"The open-source development model must be applied to currency," wrote **Douglas Rushkoff**, author and teacher. "Interest-bearing, centralized currency is the final obstacle to a collaborative international network."

Ricart responded, "The ordinary industrial-finance system will get around to arranging an international monetary microcredit system as it is feasible to do so. Credit cards are getting close. I want trusted intermediaries to assure me that Ubu and Kwana's farm really exists and that the pictures are not from somewhere else."

Singh wrote, "A microcredit scheme would reach out to a new capital market that would benefit primarily those in the developing world who would otherwise find it hard to finance their small ventures. The funder would decide on the risk and partake in the necessary course of action (hopefully) without banking bureaucracy—a very practical outcome."

Dan McCarthy, managing director of equity funds company Neuberger Berman, Inc., responded, "Communities on eBay/PayPal/Skype, Google, or Western Union could facilitate microcredit well before 2020." **Baker** wrote, "I don't know that microfinancing as a vehicle for international philanthropy actually works, but finding ways to extend credit-/debit-card systems to developing countries can be a way of helping them close the digital divide in commerce."

There were those who disagreed. **David Weinberger** of Harvard's Berkman Center wrote, "Microcredit will just make it easier to charge per bit. I'd hate to lose the froth of sharing." And **Paul Craven**, director of enterprise communications at the U.S. Department of Labor, wrote, "I don't think it is possible to build a 'secure international monetary microcredit system.'"

> "Microcredit programmes have shown themselves to be some of the most useful and culture-enabling programmes yet developed. It's brilliant that people should be able to find them independent of the intermediaries currently involved in brokering the programmes."
>
> —Elle Tracy,
> president and e-strategies
> consultant, The Results Group

PUTTING ALL OF THE PRIORITIES TOGETHER

Most people could not resist including comments on the entire list of suggested priorities in their elaborations. Following are a few tightly woven responses.

Syamant Sandhir of Futurescape responded, "Basic safeguards need to be set up in a global legal framework that builds on current growth and increasingly takes in new communities. Keeping peace in these now-global communities would be paramount, and on the basis of this safe and secure framework, a microcredit system that helps communities would emerge."

"These are all critically important policy pursuits," wrote **Jim McConnaughey**, a senior economic advisor active in U.S. policy on access and the digital divide. "One result that I would expect to happen would be a natural flow towards greater democratic tendencies in many developing and even developed countries, including more participatory debates and a higher rate of participation in political elections (through secure electronic voting)."

Seth Finkelstein, author of the Infothought blog and an EFF Pioneer Award winner, wrote, "(1) The legal environment just might kill technological development. It's a palpable threat. (2) Diversity is helpful. (3) I have my doubts microcredit is solvable, but it's potentially useful. (4) Although scary, criminal and terrorist acts are relatively rare in the grand scheme of things."

Joe Bishop of Marratech AB wrote, "1 and 2 will bring commerce. Commerce will create some equalization of wealth in places where it does not now exist. That will prompt 3. Governments will take care of 4 out of paranoia."

Kerry Kelley, vice president for SnapNames.com, responded, "(1) Making the Internet friendlier to native languages, so that people can communicate more easily cross-culturally. (2) Being able to trust that who you are communicating with is who they say they are—as opposed to a security watchdog. (3) Reducing 'taxes' and 'tolls.' Cost of bandwidth, ISP subscriptions, PCs, and an 'affordable' micropayment system are key. (4) Doing what we can to head off the balkanization of the Internet into incompatible systems. These are more where I see priorities lying personally. Some are a rephrasing of the above."

Steve Cisler, a developer of worldwide community networks (including public-access projects in Guatemala, Ecuador, and Uganda), was among several respondents who said the meeting of basic human needs is the only real priority in many vast regions of the world today. "Non-Internet-related problems are a much higher priority than any of these," he wrote, "though I realize money will flow to these technological/policy challenges without taking care of more basic problems. This comes from the 8 months I spent offline talking to people not using the Internet. It's just not a high priority—except those of us/you in the ICT world."

DOMINANT U.S. INFLUENCE OVER THE INTERNET DOES NOT WARRANT MENTION

Interestingly enough, survey participants did not bring up U.S. influence as a major issue. In many venues over the past few years, there has been criticism of U.S. dominance in Internet policy decisions. Because most of the innovation of the network architecture took place in the U.S. and the U.S. was the first nation to overwhelmingly adopt the Internet in day-to-day communication, it had exercised the most control in network decisions. But the world has caught up and even surpassed the U.S. in Internet proliferation and usage over the past few years.

The United Nations and its affiliated communications organization, the International Telecommunication Union, called together representatives from all nations for two gatherings designated as the World Summit on the Information Society. These two gatherings of Internet stakeholders inspired the creation of the Working Group on Internet Governance (WGIG)—a body assigned to make recommendations about worldwide involvement in the positive development of the Internet as a tool for all.

There was some speculation that an international organization under the jurisdiction of the United Nations would be formally proposed as a replacement or competitor for ICANN and the Internet Society. This did not happen. Representatives of the U.S. and other nations opposed this idea and won their point over the course of negotiations over the course of 2005. ICANN remains a key authority, with the Internet Society's Internet Engineering Task Force and Internet Architecture Board also making vital decisions. The WGIG eventually recommended in the fall of 2005 that a new international consulting and recommending body—the Internet Governance Forum—should be formed. The UN announced that this group is "a new forum for multistakeholder dialogue on Internet governance" ("Working Group on Internet Governance Report," 2005, n.p.).

The IGF's power is expected to be limited to identifying issues to be addressed in order for all people to benefit from digital communications networks. For its first meeting in Athens in October 2006, the preidentified talking points are openness, security, diversity, and access, and the meeting announcement reports that "capacity will be a cross-cutting priority."

These themes generally match the policy priorities of most participants in this survey.

ADDITIONAL RESPONSES

Many other survey respondents shared comments tied to the question regarding the setting of world priorities for the successful diffusion of ICTs. Among them:

> "Unless we find ways to curb spam, identity theft, cyber extortion, virus writing, and other such criminal activity, people will not WANT to use the enhanced IT environment that the other three choices present. Technology alone (or even primarily) cannot solve this problem—we will need international response to bad actors, with appropriate investigation and punishment." —**Eugene Spafford**, director of CERIAS (Center for Education and Research in Information Assurance and Security)

> "Somewhere between 1 and 3..., invest in enabling lots of people (wisely chosen, perhaps) to create content, services, and communities on the Internet; and, regarding 2, attend to convergence with TV/radio/telephony/publishing/etc., in creating the legal environment. Regarding 3, a single 'watchdog organization' seems less preferable, and less viable, than an active network of national, functional, and cross-national and cross-functional bodies with solid agreements among them." —**Alejandro Pisanty**, CIO for UNAM (National University of Mexico); vice chairman of the board for ICANN; member of UN Working Group for Internet Governance; active in ISOC

> "The second and fourth items on the list...are, IMO [in my opinion], mostly irrelevant. The Internet is solving those problems on its own and doesn't need 'help' from governments (or whoever)." —**Thomas Narten**, IBM open-Internet standards development

> "The highest priority is to make sure that the Internet can continue to foster economic and social growth and development for everyone (in all cultures) via innovation, competition, and free speech (e.g., uncensored and unmonitored packets). My second priority among these is making the opportunities of the

> "My priority would be to build a 100-mg-per-second broadband pipe into every home."
>
> —Rob Atkinson, director, Technology and New Economy Project, Progressive Policy Institute

Internet and its commerce and social sharing of ideas available to all who wish to use it...I will not willingly choose to give up my privacy so that some international security organization can decide to intervene when they think it appropriate." —**Glenn Ricart**, executive director, PricewaterhouseCoopers Advanced Research; member of the board of trustees of the Internet Society

"Capacity and, next, enabling factors for effective 'global community' use should (in a perfect world) be a higher priority than the legal and monitoring issues, but I would personally prefer to see these four choices as two linked subsets of coordinated activity." —**Cheryl Langdon-Orr**, independent Internet business operator; director, ISOC-Australia

"Young Internet enthusiasts often forget that Internet rides on communication networks—yes, the old-fashioned telecommunication networks, a trillion-dollar industry. Therefore, we should emphasize both and not only Internet and its related software." —**D.K. Sachdev**, founder and president, SpaceTel Consultancy LLC

"Let's avoid paranoia!" —**Adrian Schofield**, head of research for ForgeAhead, South Africa; a leader in the World Information Technology and Services Alliance (WITSA)

"Where to spend the available funds? Available to whom? I am in charge of setting my priorities, and you, yours, so you must be asking about—what? The United Nations or something hellish like that?" —**Bob Metcalfe**, Ethernet inventor; founder of 3Com Corporation; former CEO of InfoWorld; now a venture capitalist and partner in Polaris Venture Partners

"I think the flow of information is more critical than the flow of money. There are alternatives for the flow of money. People will not use it if they do not feel secure, so access and security are the primary goals." —**Amos Davidowitz**, director of education, training, and special programs for Institute of World Affairs; Association for Progressive Education

"There are gigantic universes of human interactions that don't involve payment. MOST interactions don't involve payment. Why is payment on this list? —**Cory Doctorow**, blogger and cofounder of Boing Boing; EFF Fellow

"We need stronger safeguards for privacy and human rights before enabling greater security authority." —**Marc Rotenberg**, executive director, Electronic Privacy Information Center

"Providing the facilities to access and then to participate in the Internet-based economy are by far more important than policing and regulating our monoculture. The Internet is based on a collaborative and generosity-based culture. These by their very nature are self-policing and diverse." —**Michael Gorrell**, senior VP and CIO, EBSCO

"Personally, I don't have a lot of faith in international security watchdog organizations because they tend to get politicized. I also think the microcredit issue is open to widespread fraud and will be a non-starter, although it sounds like a wonderful idea. The legal and operating environment notion is also great, but national interests and protectionism typically favor big players (again, it's about the humans, not the network). So I'm left with capacity building as my first choice. The genie, technology, is out of the bottle, and we should simply accept the fact that unless the network is open to all, then it will be restricted for some and so potentially censored." —**William Kearns**, assistant professor, University of South Florida

"No one is in charge. A better question would be to ask what directions will get self-selected." —**Willis Marti**, associate director for networking, Texas A&M University

"It is all too easy to obscure the idea that unless a network is complete, it is not a network at all. Much the way railroads, then highways, pulled nations together and made them accessible across borders. For the Internet to be the tool that it is evolving into, there does need to be a method for keeping it from becoming a tool for criminals and terrorists. It needs to be a 'safe' place for people to communicate, so just as there is a need for police in cities and militias and armies in countries, there needs to be a way of deterring misuse. For the Internet to be a completely viable tool in the greatest of expectations that it can be, there needs to be interoperability between multiple platforms and the infrastructure to make them work together. Lastly, with the ability to do away with borders, there is great logic in allowing an international microcredit

system that allows a standardized method for commerce."
—**Tom Snook**, CTO, New World Symphony

"I do not believe that the level of harmony described can be achieved, despite investments in money and technology. World hunger will not be solved by 2020, so providing everyone with access to the Internet when some of the groups cannot afford the basics of life, seems somewhat far fetched. I do believe that (potentially) 85% of the world's countries will be able to share in this revolution." —**Mike McCarty**, chief network officer, Johns Hopkins

"You have to have the technology in place, up and working, in order for the population (whatever segments) can begin to use it. The physical network must be created first; then, investment (public or private) made to get content to ride on the network (do not forget Thoreau's quip when told in the 1870s that the first long-distance lines had been constructed and that now the people of Vermont could talk with the people of Georgia: 'Well, what if the people of Vermont have nothing to say to the people of Georgia?'). Incentivate communication. Leave policing to the last stage. You might not even need it." —**Fredric M. Litto**, professor, University of Sao Paulo, Brazil

"While these SOUND important, I don't think any of these are really issues to be concerned with. We do need increased capacity, but not with an emphasis on new areas: Many cultures are not economically prepared to 'waste time' on computers, since they can't eat computers. Software monopolies are being weakened by the inherent nature of the Internet, while open standards are being strengthened: If Bill Gates has hopes of monopolizing services or software, he should take a closer look at reality. Security is best implemented piecemeal, using creative ICE rather than OTC remedies whose weaknesses can be easily exploited. Forcing economic advances? Dream on! :) Funny you should pick Nigeria as an example. What we need most is protection from the government, which has shown itself to lack the intelligence to understand technology and the wisdom to refrain from hindering open communication. In an effort to control sex, for example, enforcement officials are distracted from terrorism and embezzlement. Diversity will grow the Internet more than any monoculture, especially diversity using open standards so that it is accessible to all." —**Michael Steele**, Internet user since 1978

"I believe we are giving control of our lives via the computer to corporate entities. And while I believe in a capitalistic society, I really hate being forced to 'compute' based on a corporate policy." —**Sharon Lane**, president, WebPageDesign

"While I think security is one of the top priorities, I could not rate the 'security watchdog organization' highly because I am afraid it would be ineffective and perhaps even oppressive. Good Internet security comes from hygiene at the individual level, along with voluntary cooperation among individuals and organizations." —**Andy Oram**, writer and editor for O'Reilly Media

"The only one of these four choices I would like to see implemented is the legal and operating environment. The others should happen naturally based on usage patterns and market forces." —**Peter Roll**, retired chief system administrator

"The more the have-nots can catch up to the haves, the more likely we will reduce the potential for conflict and misunderstanding. At the same time, we must have an environment that makes it easy to use the Net and not be burdened by paralyzing controls and, effectively, a police-state watchdog organization. The Internet has succeeded, wildly, by not having controls placed on it. The end-to-end philosophy permits efficiency; the end points can be employed, nicely, to allow sufficient controls without impacting the flexibility and efficiency of the Internet (or whatever the worldwide Net may be dubbed in 2020)." —**Don Heath**, board member, iPool, Brilliant Cities, Inc., Diversified Software, Alcatel, Foretec

"My priorities have been defined accordingly to my belief that less control will lead to better results in the long run. In the short run, there will be problems—because the new players have to learn how to play and control their eagerness, and because the old players have to come to terms with the new ways things will be done. The idea of the microcredit system appeals, but it has not been fully explained (the example given is clearly simplistic; the concept could be taken much further). It also seems too unlikely." —**Suely Fragoso**, professor, Unisinos, Brazil

"The Internet as a whole is already diverse (within the limits of standards), and good security is available to the knowledgeable. In terms of spending, these aims can best be furthered through widespread education. Extending the network is a good social policy, and the microcredit system sounds interesting, although I don't believe it will work for reasons that are beyond Internet technology." —**Florian Schlichting**, PhD candidate and researcher, University College, London

"We still need to build awareness and demonstrate value but also enable those who cannot access ICTs to gain access through empowerment. I think the legal environment is a second priority because getting this wrong could put us back years, and it's becoming more and more important. Yes, an international system for small transactions is useful, but it will likely emerge anyway and hopefully creating the legal system will include some effective controls, which, along with human intervention and a powerful watchdog community, will make 'arming' a last resort." —**Andy Williamson**, managing director for Wairua Consulting Limited, New Zealand; member of the NZ government's Digital Strategy Advisory Group

"All of these are commendable objectives; however, I feel that a micropayment system would solve many of our problems with current copyright regime. Couple a micropayment system with addressing current copyright and patent-law tyrannies and the world would be a better place for all manner of innovations." —**Sam Punnett**, president, FAD Research

"(1) Break the legal chains that governments and corporations use to control access and information flow. (2) Teach people to fish and they will teach you how to catch more fish. (3) With governments and corps out of the way and lots of people building new tech, several forms of secure micropayment (credit assumes banks which assumes we haven't actually succeeded at breaking the legal chains). (4) A centralized 'enforcement unit' is utter bullshit. A watchdog group should do just that—use their resources to inform and spread the warnings so that people can be prepared. Arming a central organization against Internet criminals is like trying to destroy bad weather." —**Scott Moore**, online community manager, Helen and Charles Schwab Foundation

"None of the above. The Internet should be free of any government's control. Market forces will level the playing field." —**W. Reid Cornwell**, director, The Center for Internet Research

"I think terrorism is the biggest threat to all of us in all parts of the globe at the moment, and the anonymity of the Internet has aided acts of terrorism in ways not envisaged in the early days of the Internet. The Internet has to be available to all if it is to be used for the economic and social benefits of all nations, and Third World countries need the tools to manage their own development at the grassroots level rather than relying on aid form outside." —**Barbara Craig**, Victoria University

"I don't think I have to put surveillance high on this list, as there are quite enough people already working hard to create systems for Internet control, censorship, and surveillance. Look to China, or to the U.S." —**Torill Mortensen**, associate professor, Volda University College, Norway

"I am taking a *Field of Dreams* approach. Build the infrastructure, and the other systems will follow." —**Jim Jansen**, assistant professor, Penn State University

"I assume that the development of the infrastructure puts equal emphasis on network and human resources. And that fair distribution of costs and revenues is also built in the scheme. Yet the goal should also be to make Internet relevant to the real needs of all groups of people." —**Michel Menou**, professor and information-science researcher

"These priorities (indeed most of the predictions in this survey) reflect a strong techno-determinist bias." —**Sherida Ryan**, Internet analyst, Openflows Networks Ltd.

"The same hardware that can liberate can also enslave—a bit overstated, but the legal and social policies that shape possible uses of technology are crucial to long-term potential. A monoculture is a concern, but more pressing is the fundamental design characteristics and policy implications of those designs that constrain or enable uses, and whether they empower the powerful at the cost of the less powerful or empower every person to take fullest advantage of enlightenment and social interaction that the Internet provides." —**Patrick B. O'Sullivan**, director of the Center for Teaching and Learning, Illinois State University

"By starting with a user-need basis rather than an engineer-design basis, international diffusion and acceptance has a higher potential for success. Building capacity to meet those needs and simultaneously protecting the users/infrastructure, including an electronic monetary system, should fall into a more natural progression." —**Paul Chenoweth**, Web developer, Belmont University

"The main impediment to the spread of technology that really serves people is the regime of control that makes supports systems based on influence and capital rather than utility. It is the choice between having a system that benefits incumbents or one that works the best. It is the classic engineers vs. accountant battle." —**Ted M. Coopman**, activist; social-science researcher; instructor, University of Washington–Seattle; member of Association of Internet Researchers board of directors

"Improving access and understanding will help create defenses against online evil based on understanding rather than the propaganda of an elite; I'm not seeing the finance system as a major impediment to progress right now." —**Cleo Parker**, senior manager, BBDO

"International security watchdog was my lowest priority because attempts so far to implement something like this has lacked authenticity and authority." —**Kevin Schlag**, director of Web development and IT for Western Governor's University, BYU-Hawaii

"The less structured the Net, the more neat stuff will happen. The more we constrain it, the less it will prove a tool that benefits mankind." —**Bud Levin**, program head/psychology and commander/policy and planning, Blue Ridge Community College; Waynesboro (VA) Police Department

"The growth and diversity of services and collaborative projects in the past decade leads me to believe that if we accomplish #1 and #2—i.e., if we provide capacity and capability—that those on the network will create everything else." —**Brent Crossland**, technology policy analyst

"The likely future of the Internet is presaged by your last two options—as a means of the spread of corporate capital."
—**Toby Miller**, professor, University of California–Riverside

"Usability is key to advancing technology. If watchdog organizations and legislation hinder activities that Internet users want to take part in, the online world will be held back."
—**Enid Burns**, editor, ClickZ.com

"In public libraries, we see people who have neither the knowledge nor the economic power to effectively use technology. Creating a more level playing field and providing a legal structure to limit predators would be my highest priorities. Systems to discourage identity theft and promote the ability to invest globally also seem important. I see no one I trust to create an international security watchdog without infringing on rights I think unwise to give up." —**Carolyn Wiker**, librarian, Pottstown Public Library

"Because of economies of scale, it is most important to get more and more people online. They must be able to communicate in an appropriate legal environment, in a secure manner. Monetary microcredit system—it will come, in due time."
—**Jeffrey Branzburg**, educational consultant for National Urban Alliance, Center for Applied Technologies in Education, and other groups

"I would prioritize building capacity for exchange of knowledge of all kinds, including access to online education, professional development, and lifelong learning." —**Janet Salmons**, president, Vision2Lead Inc.; consultant on organizational leadership and development and virtual learning

"I believe 'following the money' is more important for development, and that universal infrastructure is least important for development. The universal standards are likely to be spelled out in some highly cosmopolitan and elite technology center distant from local realities of the developing countries. The security activities rank right below the money activities because of the risk of misappropriating the technology benefits. The human infrastructure ranks third because it depends on strategic use of information, which remains a latent ability in many parts of the world." —**Ellen K. Sullivan**, former diplomat; policy fellow, George Mason University School of Public Policy

"1. This largely exists today, although monopolies such as Microsoft need to be kept in check. International standards organizations need more resources so they can move faster." —**Brian T. Nakamoto**, Everyone.net, a leading provider of outsourced e-mail solutions

"Number 4 is already on the radar with several sites up and functioning for just that purpose. Number 2 makes certain that everyone has the ability to get information and therefore be involved in decision making on every level. Number 1—security is a huge issue and must be dealt with." —**Judi Laing**, Southern California Public Radio

"I strongly feel that the key of any successful venture is systems. Once systems are in place, we can invite people from the other side over. Else, it may be unimaginably uncontrollable." —**Alik Khanna**, Smart Analyst Inc., a business employing financial analysts in India

"It is misleading to assume that just because people have Net access, they will be able to have the knowledge to use it for productive or good means—it may just lead to more commercialization and increases in media power. However, it is important that at least people have access—what they do with it can be dealt with later." —**Shawn McIntosh**, lecturer in strategic communications, Columbia University

"Crime and money are always bedfellows. Waiting before tackling Internet crime head on using a global taskforce would allow a prohibition-era-like foothold situation to occur." —**J. Fox**, a respondent who chose not to share further identifying information

"I don't believe technology should be expanded into cultures that are not prepared to adopt it. Security is my greatest concern and should be a major consideration. I don't think it is possible to build a 'secure international monetary microcredit system.'" —**Paul Craven**, director of enterprise communications, U.S. Department of Labor

"The discouragement of monopoly (as opposed to the enabling of it, as U.S. policy has for the past 25 years) should always be seen as the fundamental role of legal and political structures in a capitalist society, since only competition encourages innovation—*Wealth of Nations* still has some applicability to our current age." —**Joseph Redington**, associate academic dean, Manhattanville College

"I think we have to be careful that some societies don't go too far beyond others. I think if other societies want to be online, they should have that opportunity. It should be a social and intellectual barrier, not an economic one." —**Lori Keith**, Internet marketing consultant for Mannington Mills

"Building the infrastructures is the most efficient investment to get 'offline' people on. Every thing else will be easier and no country will be able to stop people, once infrastructures are available." —**Louis Nauges**, president, Microcost

"If the technology spreads, the regulatory framework will develop." —**Henry Potts**, professor, University College, London

"Priorities: freedom from corporate domination, (appropriate) safety measures, democratization, activism." —**Denzil Meyers**, founder and president, Widgetwonder, Applied Improvisation Network

"Basic safeguards need to be set up in a global legal framework that builds on current growth and increasingly takes in new communities. Keeping peace in these now global communities would be paramount, and on the basis of this safe and secure framework, a microcredit system that helps communities would emerge." —**Syamant Sandhir**, leader in experience design and implementation, Futurescape

"Security is largely an illusion anyway. The first steps must be about getting the economics and laws right so that content creators can be paid for their contributions." —**Daniel Conover**, new-media developer, Evening Post Publishing

"Imagine international voting online in real time. For all of it to work, there must be a legal cultural framework for it to rest on. Second, the infrastructure. 3 and 4 should be done together." —**Gordon MacDiarmid**, Lobo Internet Services

"First capacity and comfort must be established, then ease of use and freedom within reasonable guidelines/rules of the road. Third, a monetary system for business and personal commerce will make international transactions possible, and next a security system to protect users." —**Robert Kurdziel,** CEO, Beam Wireless

"First, give access and teach the potential. Next, create a level economic playing field. Then, create various safeguards, both legal and cultural, then use the Net to create a safe and sane world." —**Walter J. Broadbent**, VP, The Broadbent Group

"We need to avoid letting the digital divide become an impassable gulf." —**James Schultz**, principal, Pretty Good Consulting; Institute for Work and the Economy

"I'll answer these in low- to high-priority order. Lowest: building the capacity of the network and passing along technological knowledge to those not currently online. (This question was asked by someone who's never used technical support.) Next lowest: developing and 'arming' an effective international security watchdog organization. To watchdog for what? Who decides what's right and what's wrong in this organization? Who's a fundamentalist—a Muslim or a Mormon? Why fear (laud) the fundamentalist? The governments of more developed nations can behave in more magnanimous ways toward developing nations, by not only showing up in force when there's a disaster, but by showing up with the little things like drugs and inoculations, birth control, education for women, and so forth. These would be more worthwhile national and international pursuits than funding a 'security watchdog organization.' Second highest: creating a legal and operating environment that allows people to use the Internet the way they want, using the software they want. This will happen over time as usefulness evolves. Hardware and software monopolies are passé. The key point here, however, is the business case necessary to enable such a solution. The key architecture of the Internet's (as we know it) predecessor was survivability. The communications system had to survive war and the ravages of war. But consider this: There are still, more than 100 years after its invention, cultures where people do not know how to drive a car. But they do benefit from the 'public cars' made available to them. Perhaps the Internet will spawn similar public benefits over time. Highest: establishing an easy-to-use, secure international monetary microcredit system. Microcredit programmes have shown themselves to be some of the most useful and culture-enabling programmes yet developed. It's brilliant that people should be able to find them independent of the intermediaries currently involved in brokering the programmes. But you'll still need somebody motivated and involved to post and publish all the details necessary for the receiving beneficiary. And this, again, is a business case for a remaining intermediary." —**Elle Tracy**, president and e-strategies consultant, The Results Group

Anonymous Comments

A number of anonymous survey respondents shared comments tied to the question regarding the setting of world priorities for the successful diffusion of ICTs. Among them:

"Access is the most important thing—after you have access, anything else can be solved. Keeping the network open is also important. Financial operations are useful but not absolutely necessary. Cyberterrorism is overhyped and can be solved through the existing services. There is no need for yet another bureaucracy. Security must be the first tack. Without a secure network, the network can't exist."

"Universal literacy would be a good starting place to implement universal information literacy and to pass along technological knowledge."

"A framework—technical and legal—must come first."

"It's important to get more people on board, making it a number-one priority."

"Right now, I don't think a world network would work—can't rate."

"We desperately need to discourage hardware or software monoculture and promote and support open-source technologies."

"Fixing some of the problems that we have today will be necessary before we seek to expand the network. A 'watchdog' organization will hinder the growth of the Internet."

"Infrastructure and security first!"

"Standards and facilitation of economic activity within a secure framework are key to the ultimate future of the Internet."

"The infrastructure needs to be in place before anything else should be developed and worked on."

Predictions from respondents who chose to remain anonymous:

"The dark side of the Internet will continue to dog the heels of expansion and development."

"The toughest challenge will be balancing freedom with security."

"Cybercrime has enabled the rise of a techno-mafia that will... eventually unleash the cyber equivalent of Pearl Harbor—an attack that will empty the bank accounts of millions within hours, triggering mass panic and hysteria...major financial institutions will teeter on the brink of collapse."

"The monoculture will be the death of us, the death of the system, just as surely as Monsanto's propagating of sterile seeds will engineer planetary famine. Those with foresight will make it a top priority, because without it, nothing else can exist. The open environment is crucial and must be accessible, just as surely as FDR's Tennessee Valley Authority wired the rural South. Every city should be wireless, and it should be provided as a city utility like water and electricity. The growing power of the telcos to create choke points to regulate the system has to be broken, or else a parallel shadow system that is open must be developed, like the black market that sprang up in the Soviet Union's oppressive command-and-control economy. Just because this so-called 'capitalist' system is being run by corporations doesn't mean it is any less command and control with multinational corporations in the drivers' seats. We are living in an age of corporate neofascism, and the time has passed when we can sit by and let it happen. The last two items frighten me beyond words, and I'd rather not give them numbers at all. Getting us all connected seamlessly and allowing everyone, everywhere, to benefit from the Internet should be everyone's top priority."

"Making the capabilities of the Internet more readily available to a greater number of people would be the first priority.

Making it easy and safe to use would be the next important level."

"Making the Internet more an economic incentive rather than adding government restrictions would be more beneficial in the long run."

"The top priority should be to experiment with 21st-century improvements to democratic systems. Stock markets collect billions of votes daily on competing leaders, policies, and decisions. The same needs to be explored as soon as possible as para-political organizations."

"Technology is only widely adopted if it makes sense to the way of life of the people involved. The current legal and technical environment of ICTs is very strongly biased toward the Western culture. To make it truly global, the assumptions behind the models of users have to vary according to the culture of those users. Then there is a problem of infrastructure to be overcome in the majority of the world. This would be best addressed by providing training and incentives to local operatives. Allowing countries to develop networks that are adapted to the local needs, and not necessarily those that would be created by external developers. A microcredit system is nice, but not urgent, and security against terrorism is only a factor when there is some external motivation. Crime prevention is a problem, but one that depends more on the individual user being educated and properly equipped than it does on the spending of development funds."

"The legal environment is still in its infancy at the local, state, and country level, let alone international law...Microcredit or some sort of internationally accepted monetary system will help flatten the networked economy. I don't believe an international security watchdog is possible or useful until a system of law is accepted across the network."

"Freedom of expression is of paramount importance, securing monetary transactions will build trust in transactions, protecting it becomes the next priority. By implementing these tasks you can then afford to connect those who are currently not online."

"The legal environment is very important, and we also must get more people online. The monetary systems are being developed by firms, and quite soon we will have several, probably."

"We really need to educate people in a sensitive way first in order for any other advances to be embraced by the masses."

"Access to networks and information is just as critical as access to clean water, health care, and so on. If you don't have a connected world, the other priorities don't really matter."

"This seriously overestimates the place of the Internet and computers in the lives of the vast majority of the world's population."

"The absence of competition against giants like Google and Microsoft is a big threat to the network and to the people. It is the role of these companies to transform themselves into monopolies. It is the role of the states to protect competition and interworking."

"I'd err on the side of promoting open standards and expanding the network, rather than government regulation."

"It is a waste of time to play this game, as business and politics will drive the evolution of the Net."

"The free market will work it out."

"The world (and the U.S.) needs a better infrastructure available to support the wider acceptance and use of technology. Multiple platforms must work the same way when interacting with the Internet. There cannot be barriers created by particular software or hardware platforms."

"If this is a supposedly democratizing agent, then those who currently do not have access should be granted it."

"The Internet is at its best when it's all about the end user."

"Sharing technological know how with developing countries should be the top priority."

"I'm somewhat worried about an 'international security watchdog.' I would love to see the virtual world more secure, but I would not like to see a virtual 'Patriot Act.' Frankly, I think the politics of this will keep it from happening by 2020."

"There are other issues that need to be considered that impact the order of priority and importance."

"CTs? Global secure micropayments would be higher on my I'd like a simple micropayment system to buy an interesting movie download from Asia. Maybe such a system is already in development via Visa/MasterCard or PayPal. But the global 'flat world' economy you've mentioned earlier will need a payment system for routine business, not just occasional funding."

"The question seems to presume that all four alternatives are desirable. They are not. [But this respondent does not elaborate further.]"

"Let the system develop itself."

"It is essential to work to help those who are disenfranchised to become better integrated in any and all resource networks."

"Wealth is important for every person."

"Don't necessarily trust watchdog outfits. 'Who watches the watchers?'"

"Internet should be developed without adding to Microsoft monopoly, or other similar ones. Local applications and initiatives need space to thrive."

"I'd love to (explain and add to my answer), but I'm doing this at work, and the elaboration to this question would take an hour!"

> *Predictions from respondents who chose to remain anonymous:*
>
> **"The competitive advantage of those nations with the Internet will encourage us to separate ourselves from the have-nots of the globe. It will not bring us closer."**
>
> **"There are three development pillars: health, education, infrastructure. This is the role of governments. The rest is the role of society."**

"The last one (4) seems like the only one I'd want anything to do with."

"Numbers 2 and 3 are unnecessary. Number 4 would be a bad thing."

"No way on 3 and 4."

"Avoid #4 at all costs."

"Without 1 first there is no need for the rest; the rest supports 1."

"Equalizing the experiences of the most vulnerable would be my top priority. Then comes safety for the rest."

"The Internet is not a social-engineering tool. We can deal with the terrorists, but keep the government out. Don't trade human rights for security."

"The promise of the Internet to be a means of improved human communication needs to be encouraged at all levels of society. Unless and until people are allowed to have access to this incredible tool, the historical record of suspicion and conflict will continue forever."

"The network should be central to commercial and banking activity; whatever it takes to support that transformation should proceed.

"Openness, decentralization, and participation are not just trends—they are the reality of technological development."

"I would leave the microcredit thing off the list; we can do that now (except for the U.S., because our banking system is 'off the grid')."

"I like the idea of supporting other people in other nations."

"Private networks, such as banks and maybe even the World Bank, will establish and operate global microcredit functions."

"Since we are already shopping globally, an international monetary unit would really help. However, given the undervaluation of some currencies, this could be difficult to implement."

"My first is a no-brainer. It's important that those with little or poor access be encouraged and helped to get access (systems, training, support). It's also really key that technology be used to help offset the evils technology can be used for (child pornography, for instance)."

"All of these choices are only marginally positive. As for 'building the capacity of the network'—that's what is being done now. What will happen is that religious and political groups will take the knowledge and build their own segregated network, thus cutting off global knowledge from their population. As for 'creating a legal and operating environment'—legal for who? The whole world? Impossible. The world is too segmented. As for 'developing…international security watchdog'—again, it would only be recognized by a few countries, at best. Not possible in today's political climate. And as for 'establishing…monetary microcredit'—again, it won't be recognized by majority of countries. Religious and political strongarms will prevent this from happening, unless they get a cut of the action. What do we need? Well, an invasion from outer space might help…at least until we beat them (or are beaten). Then things would be back to what passes as 'normal'…continuous religious and political strife."

"Developing and arming an international security watchdog org seems a bit too Orwellian for my liking! I believe our biggest priority now should be access and knowledge."

"Better and more widespread access is the key to the future, but we also need to find a way to deal with the myriad of legal issues surrounding copyrights and intellectual property before we drown in lawsuits. I would say the monetary system is number 3, but I think there is already enough ability to conduct business in the appropriate currency to push that down a little in the priority list."

"(1) Given the current U.S. congressional discussions over potential 'ISP favoritism,' i.e., providing better data throughput or access to paid partner's content, as well as various issues of browser interoperability, and the EU issues with Microsoft monopolistic browser/media player technologies—without this, the rest is toast! (2) Ditto, with the

Predictions from respondents who chose to remain anonymous:

"The rise of terrorism will result in the developing and 'arming' of an international security watchdog organization."

"The hardest to undo are laws passed in haste to regulate the Internet."

"Encourage the development of a global public network instead of the privately held one we are currently forced to accept."

stipulation that it read 'enable' rather than 'force.' There would be no eBay without a PayPal equivalent. I can buy a book from Japan or U.K. as easily as my own country, and I do. As access and payments become easier, it might be just as easy to buy my recycled silk sari yarn directly from Nepalese weavers rather than through a retailer, doubtless increasing the producer's income. (3) With the additional goal of open information transfer and intellectual freedom. (4) Fraud is an increasing problem and will need increasing policing and enforcement. It is tempting to put it higher, but without the structure to support it, it's not going to be effective anyway."

"Access is important, but it is also important that we don't make a deal with the devil and cede control over the future of the Internet to large corporations in exchange for access. Access needs to happen under a paradigm of open, democratic control of the network. Security and economic growth are important priorities also, but if we allow the Internet to become a privately controlled network, the Internet as we've come to know it will no longer exist in any meaningful way."

"The order should be 4, 2, 1, 3. Number 3 is jurisdictionally unlikely as some sort of international body that would ever be universally accepted...it already exists anyway as a cooperative effort among various national governments."

"I listed 'Developing and "arming" an effective international security watchdog organization' last because I believe this is counterproductive. Anytime an individual or group takes it upon itself to decide how the others shall live/work, trouble surely follows. Even when the original goal is meant to be helpful, it can become self-serving and exclusive. The Christian church comes to mind."

"(1) Leaving the Internet open will help with greater dissemination of ideas, continued innovation, and economic competition that will help keep the costs down. Openness benefits everyone, especially people in developing countries. (2) Although access by itself will not ultimately alter a society, it is only first step to become a player in the global community. Education, training, and business skills will also be necessary. Access will be the first step in a society towards greater fundamental change, which might be resisted or in the least take at least a generation or two to occur. (3) Individual investments on a global scale can really change the dynamics of global economics. However, this type of change comes with a lot of political, economic, legislative, etc., baggage. The benefits of this change would be difficult and not immediately apparent. (4) The first question that comes to mind is who will monitor the watchdog organization? There is too much room there for corruption, using the organization to push political agendas, and traipsing over people's rights."

"I wish one of these options had been 'finding a way for individuals to reduce the commercialization of public space and the loss of privacy that is accompanying this.' This seems at war with option one, which I chose—but I was identifying with the last sentence of that choice."

"These choices would not be my top priority. I would (1) ensure continued innovation as the keystone to continued global benefits; (2) ensure Internet users have basic freedoms to connect any device, access any information, or use any software over the Internet; and (3) spur telecom competition as a way of driving down broadband prices and increasing consumer choices."

"Number 4 suggests that the Internet is only about commerce, and if that is the case, what would be offered online that people who earn $100 a year could afford? Although 3 is ideal, I doubt it would be effective. Number 2 is also something of a problem because 'technical ability' may not have anything to do with the reasons why people don't use the Internet. So the item I ranked first is the only one in the list that I think should be pursued."

"We may not know the answers, but people from other cultures may have ideas that could contribute to the other three elements. Furthermore, they would not be left behind."

"Undertaking any of these things will take vigorous work at the grassroots level. Therefore, building capacity is most critical. Enabling the flow of funds is also hugely important because of the impact of small money movements and the importance of...what's it called when people send money home to their home countries? This should be easy and inexpensive."

"Capacity building has to come first if we are to move from today's fragmented, divided access to universal access and use. Establishing monetary and legal operating environments are the next steps. Although I marked the development and 'arming' of an effective security watchdog organization 4th, that's not where I'd spend effort. We have no models of effective organizations of this sort, and because I don't think that our current nation-state organizations will be transformed by then, I cannot envision that within less than 15 years we can build an organization that everyone (or anyone) could trust."

> **Predictions from respondents who chose to remain anonymous:**
>
> **"We need to teach people not only how to operate $100 PCs, but also how information can be used to improve their lives."**
>
> **"Ensuring interoperability and adherence to open standards is critical for a truly global Internet."**

"The monetary microcredit system seems too idealistic in our current global economy. There would need to be major economic change before any such thing could hope to be implemented."

"The highest two priorities are guaranteeing anonymity and scanning the world's documents online, particularly the older documents being rotted away in people's private collections. The third-highest priority is backing up the Internet so that stuff does not disappear the next day."

"In the hierarchy of needs, I put security over connectivity, then follow with software utilization over unification of monetary systems."

"I actually believe that only number 1 is important. I would have put 4 in the other three choices."

"By establishing a 'monetary microcredit system' first, you enforce change and increase the population in developing countries. This is in my opinion an excellent starting point for new markets. That is why I put 'opacity of network...' on second place. 'Creating a legal and operating environment' would be my third choice, as I see that it takes the most time to succeed. By prioritizing the other tasks, we strive for a faster success. I put 'an international security watchdog organization' in fourth place, as I think everybody is responsible for their own behavior on the Internet. Though there should be checks on illegal behavior on the Internet, it is my opinion that you cannot secure everything. People should start learning that you cannot prevent bad things from happening."

"The 'microcredit' thing sure is out of left field. Did you mean to say 'micropayment'? Enabling easy commerce between anyone and anyone will produce FAR, FAR more benefit than enabling easy tiny loans to developing countries."

"Number one is far more important than the other three. Computers are not the only solution to the world's economic problems."

"Hmmm. 1, 2, 3, 4 is the obvious order—some bias here."

" 'Build it and they will come' (*Field of Dreams*)."

"I believe, in general, technology is good and everyone should have access to it. The rest—not so sure about any of them. Regarding security, if the Internet becomes too dangerous, then having everyone with the opportunity to be online is irrelevant because no one will use it except the bad guys."

"If I could, I'd drop my 4th-ranked priority to, oh, about 10th. I'm concerned about the free-speech/expression implications of an 'international security watchdog organization.'"

"I question if the last two of these priorities should really be priorities at all."

"I am not sure that these are even the right four statements—in fact, I'm sure they aren't—wouldn't even put 3 and 4 on the list."

"An effective international security watchdog? Who are you kidding?"

"I gave 'arming an effective international security watchdog organization' a zero/0 because it is a 0. Start with improving how national entities cooperate, and then cross-network with each other. Creating an international 'watchdog organization' is a threat to privacy and, unfortunately, doesn't address the concerns you started with. So, no. Nada…give me a break."

"Getting people online and having them do what they want is more important now then safeguarding everything. That will happen more if there are too many 'accidents.' Information wants to be free, other services will be paid for, but a new international monetary microcredit system will not help (and I don't believe we will ever see one that most people will agree on)."

"I believe my #1 is the *sine qua non* for all the others."

"Paying attention to security is underrated in many people's minds. For me, it is a serious issue as it is the one issue most likely to undermine the continued globalization of infrastructure and its use."

" 'Cultivation of universal infrastructure standards' is another word for monoculture. So second item is politically correct but paradoxical."

"There are only three pillars for development: health, education, infrastructure. This is the role of governments; the rest is the role of the civil society."

"Without popularity, it is meaningless to do other things. When the network is secure, monetary activities can be implemented easily."

"Now is the time to start developing the security measures. If we pack the functionality before thinking through the security, it will take longer than 14 years to work through all of the bugs to make it secure enough to be effective. The others flow in a natural order."

"The global network needs to be available to as many people as possible before we can even think about the other three options. What good is a system that possibly might need to be restructured after others are brought online. Seems like putting the cart before the horse—you don't develop systems and regulations for something that is not close to being finished."

"The free market will determine what gets developed where. If people want to protect personal info, use the software they want, or share knowledge with the less fortunate, they should do so themselves; it may not be government or business appropriate to develop. The more people blog, contact companies and governments with opinions, and make decisions in their life in line with their ideals, they will affect things in the way they feel is progressive and right. People's privacy may be at risk, but public opinion will monitor and respond in a way that meets the needs of the majority of people. I am also excited about the Internet technology working in two directions to deliver real-time info on everything you need in your daily life and allow you to have two-way communication with all of it, making us less couch potatoes, and more participants in the world."

ENDNOTES

1. The First International Cybercrime Investigation Training Conference Web site is available online at http://www.interpol.int/Public/TechnologyCrime/Conferences/1stCybConf/Conference.asp.
2. The following U.S. Department of Justice site has a number of links to details regarding the treaty: http://www.usdoj.gov/criminal/cybercrime/intl.html.
3. To see an online summary of recently prosecuted computer crime cases in the United States, see http://www.cybercrime.gov/cccases.html.

REFLECTIONS

**THE ISSUES ARE THE SAME, BUT THE STAKES
ARE HIGHER THAN EVER BEFORE;
LOOKING AHEAD IS VITAL**

Hope and fear can be found threaded throughout the wisdom shared by respondents to this survey. This is a predictable outcome, since all human progress has had its negative and positive influences; as social communications theorist **Mark Poster** pointed out in one of his survey elaborations, "ambivalent effects are typical of all great historical changes."

The hope found here appears in common future visions of people helping people through connections on a massive, collaborative, open, worldwide communications network. The Internet is already an overwhelming tool for social networking, for *connection*. Innovations such as Wikipedia, MySpace, Flickr, and *Second Life* are showing the power of individual participation and creativity and the wisdom of crowds. In addition, the number of Internet initiatives for the public good is on the increase as the economics of connectedness are beginning to flatten. One of these positive projects is the Center for Information Technology Research in the Interest of Society (CITRIS), based out of the University of California system units at Berkeley, David, Merced, and Santa Cruz. The efforts of CITRIS, supported with corporate dollars from tech companies are responsible, for instance, for a Wi-Fi wireless network that allows eye specialists in the Tamil Nadu region of India to examine patients in remote clinics via high-quality video conference. The program is now expanding to include 50 clinics that will serve up to 500,000 patients each year. CITRIS also hosted a June 2006 international conference in Helsinki on the convergence of future communications technologies; the environment, energy, and sustainability; and services, security, and society.[1]

A lot of the fear about the future of the worldwide communications network is expressed in concerns about the outcomes of political and economic power struggles in the new age of human networking.

Throughout the history of communications innovations, every new-media mechanism has been perceived by political and business powerbrokers in the old-media paradigm. For instance, decision makers applied their experiences with the telegraph when evaluating how best to deploy radio, and they looked at the diffusion of television with radio-tinted glasses. The old-media rules, regulations, pecking order, and associated social, political, and economic power structures are always superimposed upon the latest breakthrough technology. As Carolyn Marvin observed in her book *When Old Technologies Were New*, "New practices do not so much flow directly from technologies that inspire them as they are improvised out of old practices that no longer work in new settings" (Marvin, 1988, p. 5).

As we are now witnessing corporations' and governments' attempts to extend their power by defining the Internet in the old-technology paradigm, there is a mournful tone—sometimes tinged with frustration—underlying a significant percentage of the written responses to several of the proposed scenarios in this survey. Many respondents reflect disappointment in seeing the Internet's open, neutral potential being muted by the influences of competing old-media companies, brash new-media companies, and nations with less than optimal human-rights records. They would like to see the Internet defined in a new way, not in the telephone/television paradigm, and they would like to see hope restored for an Internet that can help topple oppressive regimes and allow individuals everywhere to self-actualize.

Survey participant **David Clark**, an original Internet architect who is working to help inspire a new, improved Internet, said in a 2006 interview with *Red Herring* magazine that it is vital to stop struggling with the past (the old paradigm) and dream of how good the future can be. "We don't presently have a roadmap of where we are trying to go with the Internet, where we would like to be in 10 to 15 years," he said in the interview. "If the story is compelling enough, people will figure out how to get there" (n.p.).

ENDNOTE

1. The Center for Information Technology Research in the Interest of Society site is available online at http://www.citris-uc.org/.

METHODOLOGY

This Web-based survey, sponsored by the Pew Internet & American Life Project and conducted by Princeton Survey Research Associates International, elicited a nonrandom sample of 742 Internet stakeholders. The interviews were conducted online, via WebSurveyor, between Nov. 30, 2005, and April 4, 2006. Details on the design, execution, and analysis of the survey are discussed next.

SAMPLE DESIGN AND CONTACT PROCEDURES

E-mail invitations to participate in the survey were initially sent to 550 select Internet leaders, both stakeholders and skeptics. The initial list included as many members as possible from the "200 Internet Figures" identified in the research project that began Imagining the Internet, the Elon University/Pew Internet & American Life Predictions Database project (http://www.elon.edu/predictions/200briefbios.aspx), and the board of directors lists for major Internet organizations such as the Internet Society, the Working Group on Internet Governance, the World Wide Web Consortium, ICANN, and Internet2.

In addition, leaders of top Internet organizations were asked to send an open invitation to participate in the survey to members of their groups. These e-mail invitations provided a direct link to the survey, and contained the following language:

> *Internet leader,*
>
> *The 2005 Pew Internet Predictions Survey is now online. It is aimed at helping illuminate important issues and concerns. It is only effective if the best and brightest people take part. We would appreciate it if you would share the address for the survey with people who are on the membership list of the major world Internet organization in which you are a leader. We are inviting ISOC, W3C, WGIG, IEEE, and Internet2 members to participate, in addition to other top technology leaders who have been previous survey participants.*
>
> *Please look at the following list and share the appropriate PIN for your organization with your membership in the e-mail in which you inform your group about the survey address:*
>
> *- Internet Society (ISOC): 1111*
> *- Association for Computing Machinery (ACM): 2222*
> *- World Wide Web Consortium (W3C): 3333*
> *- Working Group on Internet Governance (WGIG): 4444*
> *- Institute of Electrical and Electronics Engineers (IEEE): 5555*
> *- Association of Internet Researchers (AoIR): 6666*
> *- Internet2: 7777*
>
> *The address of the survey is:*
> *http://www.psra.com/experts*
>
> *Here is a sample introduction paragraph you might want to send to your group's membership along with the site address and PIN number:*
>
> *ISOC, W3C, WGIG, IEEE, and Internet2 members and a select group of additional top technology leaders are being asked to participate in the 2005 Pew Internet Predictions Survey. The Web-based survey asks respondents to assess the future impact of the Internet in order to illuminate important issues and concerns.*
>
> *You can participate by going to the survey site:*
> *http://www.psra.com/experts*

At the start of the survey, please use the PIN number:
****(((INSERT YOUR GROUP'S PIN FROM ABOVE IN THIS
SPACE)))***

If you receive more than one invitation, please only respond to the survey once. The Pew Internet Project will issue a report on this survey in the winter of 2006.

If you have any questions, please feel free to contact Pew Internet Project Director Lee Rainie at lrainie@pewInternet. org or 202-419-4500.

Thank you!
Your participation will help us illuminate important issues and create a useful document that will be of importance for years to come.

Thanks very much for your assistance. We hope you will take advantage of this opportunity to inform members of your organization about the survey.

Pew Internet encouraged the initial sample of experts to forward the e-mail invitation to any colleagues whose thoughts on the future of the Internet they would consider useful and important. In addition, respondents were encouraged to share with Pew Internet the e-mail addresses of people who would be excellent participants in the survey. These addresses were collected, and an e-mail invitation was also issued to these people to participate. This created an additional snowball sample of Internet experts, whose ideas are also included in the final data.

The survey title page gave the following brief description of the survey and its sponsors, along with instructions for how to complete the survey:

Predictions Survey

Welcome to the Pew Internet Project's 2005 Predictions Survey!

If you received an e-mail invitation from the Pew Internet Project with a personalized identification number (PIN) for taking this survey, please enter it below.

Those who were invited to participate by a friend or colleague should use guest PIN 900.

If you did not receive either an individual or guest PIN, please enter 999 and proceed.

ENTER PIN.
General Survey Instructions

Thank you for agreeing to assess the following predictions about the Internet. Most are provocative extensions of recent statements by leaders in science, technology, business and politics.

Immediately below each question/prediction is a space for you to elaborate on your answers; we hope you will take the opportunity to expand the body of knowledge about Internet issues by contributing your personal thoughts. Likewise, if you disagree with the premise or wording of a question/ prediction, please tell us why in your elaboration. You are free to skip any questions you do not wish to answer.

This survey is confidential, but we encourage you to take credit for your responses. To do so, please type your name AT THE START of the elaboration section immediately below each question/prediction. We will only credit to you the individual elaborations that have your name AT THE BEGINNING. Please remember that accredited statements have more validity and add a great deal more to the body of knowledge than those for which people do not take credit. The predictions made here are offered in the spirit of testing ideas about how the future might unfold. They are not meant to represent our "best guess" or our preferences about the future. Neither the Pew Internet Project nor Elon University advocates any policy outcomes related to the Internet.

By the year 2020...

The first section of the survey asks you to assess predictions about what the Internet will be like in 15 years. Here's a preview of the kinds of predictions and questions you will encounter as you move through the survey:

Where will things stand in 2020?

A global, low-cost network thrives.

English is displacing other languages online.

Technology advances to the point where humans have lost control of many aspects of it.

People's activities, preferences, transactions, and whereabouts are logged and profiled, making life more efficient but also more transparent; there is an ensuing lack of privacy.

Virtual reality is a boon and a drain.

Success is more attainable for people living outside of nations that dominated the 20th century, allowing them to become important contributors.

Luddites will commit acts of violence and terror.

Please proceed to share your views about these proposed scenarios...

Following this section, participants were given fuller descriptions of seven different scenarios for the year 2020. In each section, they had three options: skip the question, agree with the scenario, or disagree with the scenario. They were asked to provide written elaborations with their answers, and each participant began each elaboration by typing his or her name if willing to be identified with any direct quotations taken and used in this report or the online version of the survey data.

Respondents were also presented with four different proposed priorities for using the Internet to better the world and they were asked to rank them in order from first to last. They were asked to also suggest issues for Pew Internet to give further study.

QUESTIONNAIRE DEVELOPMENT

The questionnaire was developed by PSRAI in collaboration with staff of the Pew Internet & American Life Project and their partners at Elon University.

APPENDIX

SELECT BIOGRAPHIES

This collection of more than 250 brief biographies describing some of the 2006 Future of the Internet Survey respondents includes data for many of the participants who were willing to be quoted on the record for one or more of their statements in answer to the survey. Dozens of additional well-connected Internet leaders/stakeholders preferred to remain anonymous, keeping their comments off the record; you will not see their names here although they did participate in the survey. The list includes leaders from ITU (International Telecommunication Union), ISOC (Internet Society), ICANN (Internet Corporation for Assigned Names and Numbers), IETF (Internet Engineering Task Force), IEEE (Institute of Electrical and Electronics Engineers), ACM (Association for Computing Machinery), AoIR (Association of Internet Researchers), and CPSR (Computer Professionals for Social Responsibility).

Among the *Future of the Internet II* survey respondents who were willing to forgo total anonymity were the following people:

Matthew Allen, associate professor of Internet studies at Curtin University of Technology, Australia, and founder of its Internet studies program, which offers one of the few BA degrees in Internet studies in the world; president of the Association of Internet Researchers; Internet user since 1992.

Mary Ann Allison, chairman and chief cybernetics officer, The Allison Group, LLC; she has worked with Microsoft, the Alliance for Public Technology, Glasgow's Urban Learning Space, and other major businesses, governments, and NGOs to improve their capacity to change; Internet user since 1981.

Stewart Alsop, investor and analyst with Alsop Louie Partners, a venture capital firm; former editor-in-chief and executive vice president of InfoWorld; columnist for *Fortune* magazine; Internet user since 1994.

Al Amersdorfer, president and CEO, Automotive Internet Technologies, a provider of Internet marketing solutions for the retail automobile industry; Internet user since 1985.

Jim Archuleta, senior manager, government solutions, Ciena Corporation; manages partnerships with research and government entities to deliver advanced networks; Internet user since 1989.

Gary Arlen, president, Arlen Communications, Inc., The Alwyn Group LLC; founder and former long-time director of the Internet Alliance; expert in new applications and policy implications of broadband and interactive services; Internet user since 1982.

Nick Arnett, director of business intelligence, Liveworld, Inc. (online communities for businesses); formerly of Senti-Mentrics Partners, MCC Media, Opion, Inc., Invisible Worlds; MCC Media; Verity; a cofounder of Multimedia Computing Corp. with Tim Bajarin of Creative Strategies; former InfoWorld writer; Internet user since 1988.

Rob Atkinson, director of Progressive Policy Institute (a think tank); author of "New Economy Index" series and the book *The Past and Future of America's Economy: Long Waves of Innovation that Power Growth*; previously project director at the Congressional Office of Technology Assessment; Internet user since 1993.

Fred Baker, CISCO Fellow, CISCO Systems; Internet Society (ISOC) chairman of the board; Internet Engineering Task Force (IETF) leader; he has worked in the telecommunications industry since 1978, building servers, bridges, and routers; an architect of the Internet and Internet user since 1987.

Reva Basch, consultant for Aubergine Information Systems (online research expert); active longtime member of The WELL, one of the earliest cyberspace communities; author of many books, including *Researching Online for Dummies*; Internet user since 1973.

Rashid Bashshur, director of telemedicine, University of Michigan; a catalyst for the development of telemedicine systems since the 1970s who has worked at the National Academy of Sciences and has been awarded National Science Foundation funding for telemedicine research; Internet user since 1980.

Gordon Bell, senior researcher, Microsoft; an Internet pioneer, he proposed a plan for a U.S. research and education network in a 1987 report to the Office of Science and Technology in response to a congressional request by Al Gore; earlier in his career, he was a technology leader at Digital Equipment Corporation; Internet user since 1986.

Benjamin Ben-Baruch, senior market intelligence consultant and applied sociologist, Aquent, General Motors, Eastern Michigan University; Internet user since 1980.

Robin Berjon, World Wide Web Consortium and Expway (Paris, France), where he is a research scientist working with XML in constrained and high-performance environments; member of the SVG Working Group and active in the Perl XML community; Internet user since 1996.

Ivair Bigaran, Global Messenger Courier do Brasil, American Box Serviço Int'l S/C Ltda.; Internet user since 1994.

Joe Bishop, VP, business development, Marratech AB, a Swedish company that develops and markets software solutions that allow remote groups to collaborate; representative to Internet2; Internet user since 1994.

Paul Blacker, head of broadband strategy, British Telecom, with more than 20 years of telecommunications work in the U.K., Portugal, Spain, Malaysia, and Saudi Arabia; Internet user since 1993.

Ralph Blanchard, investor; has a PhD in economic history; formerly worked as CEO for a franchised information-services business, now managing a private real-estate firm; Internet user since 1994.

Grant Blank, assistant professor of sociology, American University; author of *New Technology in Sociology* and coauthor of *Desktop Data Analysis with SYSTAT*; Internet user since 1987.

Jeffrey Boase, Internet researcher and coauthor of the 2006 Pew Internet report *The Strength of Internet Ties*, PhD student, University of Toronto, where he works with NetLab; a former fellow at the National Center for Digital Government; Internet user since 1992.

Michael Botein, professor and founding director, Media Center, New York Law School; consultant to the FCC in international telecommunications law and the regulation of cable TV; he wrote *International Telecommunications in the United States* and *Cases and Materials on Regulation of the Electronic Mass Media*; Internet user since 1985.

Jeffrey Branzburg, educational consultant for National Urban Alliance, Center for Applied Technologies in Education and other groups; former supervisor of instructional technology for New York; columnist for *Technology & Learning* magazine; Internet user since 1997.

Charlie Breindahl, external lecturer, University of Copenhagen, IT University of Copenhagen; research areas include the aesthetics of new media and Internet dating; Internet user since 1996.

Greg Brewster, associate dean, School of Computer Science Telecommunications and Information Systems, DePaul University; formerly worked at Bell Laboratories for AT&T; recipient of National Science Foundation networking grants; Internet user since 1979.

Walter J. Broadbent, vice president, The Broadbent Group; expert in addiction and recovery; Internet user since 1994.

John Browning, cofounder of First Tuesday, a global network dedicated to entrepreneurs; former writer for *The Economist* and other top publications; Internet user since 1989.

Enid Burns, managing editor for statistics at ClickZ.com, a major resource of interactive marketing news, research, and reference; Internet user since 1994.

Lillian Buus, E-learning Lab: Center for User-Driven Innovation, Learning and Design, Aalborg University, Denmark; research interests include change processes and virtual-learning environments.

Marilyn Cade, CEO and principal, ICT Strategies, MCADE, LLC; also with Information Technology Association of America (business alliance); represents the technology industry in international forums, including the OECD, ITU, CITEL, ICANN, WIPO, and the World Summit on the Information Society; former director of Internet policy for AT&T; Internet user since 1986.

Jean-Pierre Calabretto, staff member and PhD student, Division of Information Technology, Engineering, and the Environment at University of South Australia; Internet user since 1989.

Michael Cannella, IT manager for Volunteers of America-Michigan, member Computer Professionals for Social Responsibility.

Sylvia Caras, disability-rights advocate for People Who; Internet user since 1993.

Nicholas Carr, independent writer and consultant whose work centers on information technology; Internet user since 1987.

Michael Castengera, teacher and consultant, Grady College of Journalism, University of Georgia, Media Strategies and Tactics, Inc., a media consulting firm; Internet user since 1992.

Gary Chapman, director of The 21st Century Project at the graduate school for public policy at the University of Texas–Austin; executive director of Computer Professionals for Social Responsibility from 1984 to 1991; served on selection committee for the Turing Award—the computer-science field's equivalent of the Nobel Prize; Internet user since 1982.

Clement Chau, research assistant and program coordinator, Tufts University, Developmental Technologies Research Group; Internet user since 1995.

Barry K. Chudakov, principal, The Chudakov Company, specializing in strategies for complex adaptive systems; Internet user since 1989.

Steve Cisler, former senior library scientist for Apple, founder of the Association for Community Networking, now working on public-access projects in Guatemala, Ecuador, and Uganda; Internet user since 1989.

David Clark, from 1981 to 1989 the chief protocol architect of the Internet; senior research scientist at MIT; past chair of Computer Sciences and Telecommunications Board of the National Research Council; now working under a major National Science Foundation grant to rethink the architecture of the Internet; Internet user since 1975.

Lynn Schofield Clark, director of Teens and the New Media @ Home Project, University of Colorado; member of the international study commission on Media, Religion, and Culture; Internet user since 1991.

James Conser, professor emeritus, Youngstown State University; expert on criminal justice and coauthor of *Law Enforcement in the United States*; a leader of Police Futurists International and member of the World Futures Society; Internet user since 1985.

Ted M. Coopman, activist; social-science researcher; instructor, University of Washington–Seattle; member of Association of Internet Researchers board of directors.

Jeff Corman, government policy analyst, Industry Canada, Government of Canada; Internet user since 1995.

W. Reid Cornwell, director of The Center for Internet Research; former CEO of Intratech, a high-tech executive search firm; author of *A Primer of Internet Marketing, Metrics, and Management*; Internet user since 1974.

Todd Costigan, National Association of Realtors, Center for Realtor Technology; Internet user since, 1985.

Karen Coyle, information professional and librarian, active leader of Computer Professionals for Social Responsibility; expert on Internet privacy; Internet user since 1983.

Paul Craven, director of enterprise communications, U.S. Department of Labor; Internet user since 1993.

Brent Crossland, government technology policy analyst based in Illinois; specializes in securing digital identities and information; Internet user since 1992.

Mark Crowley, researcher, The Customer Respect Group; Internet user since 1995.

Claudia Cruz, online editor of elPeriodico, based in Guatemala.

Roger Cutler, W3.org (the World Wide Web Consortium, Tim Berners-Lee's Web development group), senior-staff research scientist at the Chevron Information Technology division of Chevron USA.; Internet user since 1994.

Cary Curphy, operations research analyst, U.S. Army; Internet user since 1989.

Michael Dahan, professor, Sapir Academic College, Israel; Digital Jerusalem; his works include the paper "National Security and Democracy on the Internet in Israel"; led projects to foster peace in the Middle East through new technology; Internet user since 1989.

Amos Davidowitz, director of education, training, and special programs for Institute of World Affairs; Association for Progressive Education; founder of Global Peace Experiences; Internet user since 1994.

Nan Dawkins, cofounder of RedBoots Consulting; has more than 20 years of experience in marketing communications with J. Walter

Thompson and other agencies; a frequent speaker on search engines, blogs, and online advocacy; Internet user since 1997.

Jascha de Nooijer, Universiteit Maastricht, The Netherlands; research studies teens and use of the Internet for health information; Internet user since 1995.

Ben Detenber, associate professor, Nanyang Technological University, Singapore; research interests include media effects and information and communications technologies.

Cory Doctorow, self-employed journalist, blogger, coeditor of Boing Boing, a leading blog; born in Canada, he now lives in London; he worked as the European Affairs Coordinator for the Electronic Frontier Foundation before quitting to work on writing and speaking full time; Internet user since 1987.

Georg Dutschke, Universida Sevilla, Forum Criança, Cortefino; research interests include the impact of new technologies, organization development, and marketing; Internet user since 1996.

Esther Dyson, editor Release 1.0 (now part of CNET Networks), investor and advisor to start ups, and member of many boards, including Electronic Frontier Foundation and the Global Business Network; former chair of ICANN (Internet Corporation for Assigned Names and Numbers) board; Internet user since 1985.

Bruce Edmonds, Centre for Policy Modelling, Manchester Metropolitan University, U.K.; his research has included work on social intelligence and the construction of AI and social agents; Internet user since 1992.

Lilia Efimova, researcher, Telematica Instituut, The Netherlands; research interests include personal knowledge management and weblogs; Internet user since 1993.

David Elesh, associate professor of sociology at Temple University; an expert on political fragmentation in metropolitan areas and consequences of industrial change; Internet user since 1983.

Leigh Estabrook, professor, University of Illinois; research includes a study of the impact of the USA Patriot Act; recipient of the 2003 Association for Library and Information Science Award for professional contributions to education; Internet user since 1978.

Luc Faubert, consultant, dDocs Information, Inc.; president of Quebec's Internet Society chapter and an ambassador to the World Summit on Information Society; working on the creation of the North American Regional At-Large Organization (NARALO) within ICANN; member of Computer Professionals for Social Responsibility (CPSR); Internet user since 1985.

Bret Fausett, an intellectual property and Internet attorney and a partner with Hancock, Rothert & Bunshoft, LLP in the Los Angeles area; he has done work tied to ICANN, urges its reform, and produces a blog and podcasts about it.

Stan Felder, president and CEO, Vibrance Associates, LLC; publisher of the health/medical Web sites hisandherhealth.com, newshe. com, and ourgyn.com; Internet user since 1985.

María Laura Ferreyra, strategic planner, Instituto Universitario Aeronautico; active leader in the Internet Society chapter in Argentina; Internet user since 1996.

Cliff Figallo, online communities architect, SociAlchemy; was managing director of the WELL (Whole Earth 'Lectronic Link, one of the best-known conferencing systems and virtual communities in the U.S. in the 1990s) and a director of the Electronic Frontier Foundation's Cambridge office in the early 1990s; Internet user since 1985.

Howard Finberg, director of interactive media, The Poynter Institute; was named the Newspaper Association of America "New Media Pioneer" in 2000; a journalist for 30 years, he previously worked at *The Chicago Tribune, New York Times, San Francisco Chronicle,* and *Arizona Republic*; Internet user since 1991.

Seth Finkelstein, activist and programmer, author of the Infothought blog and an EFF Pioneer Award winner; he devoted hundreds of hours of time over the span of several years to decrypt and expose to public scrutiny the contents of censorware blacklists, raising the level of public awareness about the freedom of speech issues on the Internet.

Richard Forno, principal consultant, KRvW Associates (information security), Infowarrior.org; CMU Software Engineering Institute; formerly the chief information security officer for Network Solutions; author of *The Art of Information Warfare*; publishes a Web site with information on computer security; Internet user since 1992.

Gary Foster, Gary D. Foster Consulting, a consulting company that concentrates on Christian marketing and management; Internet user since 1990.

Suely Fragoso, professor and researcher at the Center of Communications Science, Unisinos, Brazil; active in Association of Internet Researchers, research interests include the digital divide; Internet user since 1994.

Mark Gaved, The Open University, U.K.; research interest is community activism; Internet user since 1987.

Rick Gentry, acquisition coordinator, Greenpeace USA; Internet user since 1995.

Heath Gibson, competitive intelligence manager, BigPond, a provider of broadband customer Web sites in Australia; Internet user since 1994.

Mike Gill, electronics engineer, National Library of Medicine; Internet user since 1988.

Michael Gorrell, senior VP and chief information officer for EBSCO publishing, responsible for all technology and product development for this online research platform; member of Internet2; Internet user since 1994.

Stine Gotved, cultural sociologist, University of Copenhagen; her research looks into cyber-sociology issues, including online communities, time/space relations, mediated interaction, and the sense of belonging.

Arent Greve, professor of organization theory, the Norwegian School of Economics and Business Administration; research topics include organization theory and the development and diffusion of technology; Internet user since 1983.

Robin Gross, executive director, IP Justice, civil liberties organization that promotes balanced intellectual property law and defends consumer rights to use digital media worldwide; Internet user since 1988.

Carlo Hagemann, professor, Radboud Universiteit Nijmegen, The Netherlands; member of the Association of Internet Researchers; Internet user since 1989.

Alex Halavais, assistant professor, Quinnipiac University; graduate director for the informatics school at Buffalo; he studies how social networks are formed on the Internet and promotes the practice of "self-Googling"—establishing your own identity on the Internet; Internet user since 1984.

Jeff Hammond, VP, Rhea + Kaiser; expert on strategic planning, design, and implementation of interactive communications; Internet user since 1992.

Fred Hapgood, technology author and consultant; an accomplished freelance writer in technology and science; in the 1990s, he took on the role of moderator of the Nanosystems Interest Group at MIT, and has written a number of articles for *Wired* and other tech publications since then; Internet user since 1981.

Joel Hartman, CIO, University of Central Florida; chair of the EDUCAUSE Learning Initiative Planning Committee; member of the Microsoft Higher Education Advisory Council; representative to Internet2; and on the board of Florida LambdaRail; Internet user since 1970.

Caroline Haythornthwaite, associate professor, University of Illinois at Urbana-Champaign; active leader with the Association of Internet Researchers; research areas include social networks and the Internet in everyday life; Internet user since 1996.

Carter Headrick, director of grassroots and field operations for Campaign for Tobacco-Free Kids; engaged in creating online activism; Internet user since 1993.

Don Heath, Internet pioneer and president and CEO of the Internet Society from 1996 through 2001; board member, iPool, Brilliant Cities, Inc., Diversified Software, Alcatel, Foretec; member of U.S. State Department Advisory Committee on International Communication and Information Policy; Internet user since 1988.

Charles Hendricksen, research collaboration architect for Cedar Collaboration in Redmond, WA; research interests include development and evaluation of geospatial information technologies for decision support; Internet user since 1968.

Steffan Heuer, a German journalist who covers the technology industry, U.S. correspondent, *brand eins Wirtschaftsmagazin*; Internet user since 1994.

Buff Hirko, virtual reference coordinator, Washington State Library; an expert on virtual reference, she is a frequent speaker at regional and national conferences; Internet user since 1988.

Donna Hoffman, professor of management and codirector, Sloan Center for Internet Retailing, Vanderbilt University; founder of eLab, and an internationally known expert on Internet marketing strategy and consumer behavior online; Internet user since 1975.

Scott Hollenbeck, director of technology, VeriSign (provider of global infrastructure services for telecommunication, content, Internet, and Ecommerce services); active director in the Internet Engineering Task Force; expert at developing applications and systems; Internet user since 1988.

Jim Huggins, associate professor of computer science, Kettering University; research interests include theory of computation, computing history, programming language design, computing ethics, cryptography; Internet user since 1989.

Christian Huitema, general manager of wireless and mobility at Microsoft in the Windows Networking and Devices group; pioneering Internet engineer (on the Internet Architecture Board from 1991 to 1996; Internet Society leader from 1995 to 2001; still active in building the Internet).

Alan Inouye, U.S. Internet policy analyst previously with the Computer Science and Telecommunications Board of the National Research Council, where he completed several key studies, including "Trust in Cyberspace" and "A Digital Strategy for the Library of Congress"; formerly worked at Atari and Verbatim; Internet user since 1990.

David Irons, VP, cofounder, Ascribe: The Public-Interest Newswire; consultant on strategic communication; formerly public affairs director at Harvard's Kennedy School of Government and UC Berkeley's business school; Internet user since 1993.

Jim Jansen, assistant professor, Penn State University School of Information Sciences and Technology; has published more than 90 articles on information technology and systems; recipient of an ACM Research Award; Internet user since 1993.

Jakob Linaa Jensen, assistant professor in media studies, University of Aarhus, Denmark; participant in Modinet, a study of mediated democracy.

Christopher Johnson, cofounder and CEO for ifPeople, Inspiring Futures; a life member and chair of the Working Group for Computer Professionals for Social Responsibility (CPSR); Internet user since 1995.

Philip Joung, works for Spirent Communications (wireless positioning products); representative to Internet2; Internet user since 1989.

Lisa Kamm, has worked in information architecture since 1995 at organizations including IBM, Agency.com, and the ACLU; started the first ibm.com Information Architecture department; leader in the Association for Computing Machinery; presenter at Computers, Freedom & Privacy conference; Internet user since 1987.

William Kearns, assistant professor at the University of South Florida; representative to Internet2; Internet user since 1992.

Susan Keith, assistant professor in the school of communication, information, and library sciences at Rutgers University; research interests include the issues arising from the junction of "new" and "old" media; Internet user since 1996.

Thomas Keller, domain services, Schlund + Partner AG (a Germany-based Web-hosting company—one of the largest ICANN registrars in Europe); he represents Schlund in the Registrar Constituency and is a member of the GNSO (Generic Names Supporting Organization) Council; Internet user since 1995.

Kerry Kelley, vice president for product marketing, SnapNames. com, a Portland-based company that helps customers "back-order" a currently registered domain name to secure it when it becomes available; Internet user since 1986.

Mike Kent, professor of social policy, Murdoch University, Australia; research interests include the Internet, literacy, and access to technology; Internet user since 1994.

Alik Khanna, Smart Analyst, Inc., a business employing financial analysts in India; Internet user since 1996.

Peter Kim, senior analyst, marketing strategy and technology team, Forrester Research, Boston; specializes in e-strategy and management, social marketing, blogs; Internet user since 1993.

David Kluskiewicz, a senior account executive at First Experience, a marketing communications company.

Randy Kluver, director of the Institute for Pacific Asia at Texas A&M University; former executive director, Singapore Internet Research Centre, Nanyang Technological University; Internet user since 1989.

Gwynne Kostin, director of Web communications, U.S. Homeland Security; responsible for content strategy and integration, program development, Web evangelizing; coordinates public Web communications during incidents of national significance; Internet user since 1993.

Cheris Kramarae, professor, Center for the Study of Women in Society, University of Oregon; Internet user since 1976.

Robert Kraut, Human-Computer Interaction Institute, Carnegie Mellon University; an expert on the design and social impact of information technologies in small groups, in the home, and in organizations; author of *Computers, Phones, and The Internet: Domesticating Information Technology.*

Oliver Krueger, visiting professor, Princeton University Center for the Study of Religion; a native of Germany who previously worked at Heidelberg University; research areas include media and religion; Internet user since 1995.

Martin Kwapinski, senior content manager, FirstGov.gov, the U.S. Government's Official Web Portal; Internet user since 1997.

Jeannette LaFrance, The Shpigler Group (providing data, analyses, and strategic recommendations on subjects such as BPL, metropolitan networks, fiber-route feasibility, and "utelco" business models); Internet user since 1990.

Mark O. Lambert, former utilities commissioner, State of Iowa; consultant; futurist; Internet user since 1989.

Edward Lee Lamoureux, associate professor, director of the multimedia program, and codirector of the New Media Center, Bradley

University; research interests include new media and intellectual-property law.

Robin Lane, educator and philosopher, Universidade Federal do Rio Grande do Sul, Brazil; Internet user since 1990.

Cheryl Langdon-Orr, independent Internet business operator and director for ISOC-Australia; she is a board member of AUDA, the group in charge of Australian Domain Name registration, and she is a member of ICANN At Large; Internet user since 1977.

Tíscar Lara, assistant professor at the School of Journalism, University Carlos III Madrid, Spain; Internet user since 1995.

Tunji Lardner, CEO for the West African NGO network: wangonet. org; agendaconsulting.biz; has held various consultancies for the World Bank and UN as well as being a resource person and consultant to the UNDP African Internet Initiative; Internet user since 1988.

Pierre Le Fèvre, president, Yomux Media, Inc., based in Montreal, Canada; Internet user since 1990.

Russell Lefevre, vice president for Technology Services Corporation in Los Angeles; former Institute of Electrical and Electronics Engineers-USA Congressional Fellow.

Thomas J. Lenzo, technology consultant with 30 years of experience, clients include Kaiser Permanente, Parsons Engineering, and others; Internet user since 1979.

Alan Levin, programmer, designer, systems and network architect; chairman of the South Africa Chapter of the Internet Society; active in ICANN; serves on the boards of Future Perfect Corporation, AfriNIC, and .za DNA; Internet user since 1994.

Bud Levin, program head/psychology and commander/policy and planning, Blue Ridge Community College; Waynesboro (VA) Police Department; Internet user since 1988.

Peter Levine, director of CIRCLE (Center for Information and Research on Civic Learning and Engagement), University of

Maryland; works with the Prince George's County Information Commons (a nonprofit Web site for community, produced by youth), National Alliance for Civic Education, Deliberative Democracy Consortium; Internet user since 1993.

Rich Ling, senior researcher and sociologist, Telenor Research Institute, Oslo, Norway; author of the book *The Mobile Connection: The Cell Phone's Impact on Society*; associate editor for The Information Society and for Norsk Mediatidskrift; Internet user since 1984.

Fredric M. Litto, professor and director for the School of the Future at the University of Sao Paulo, Brazil, an interdisciplinary lab investigating the question of how new communications technologies can improve learning; president, ABED-Brazilian Association for Distance Education; representative to Internet2; Internet user since 1993.

Geert Lovink, media theorist, professor and Internet critic, Institute of Network Cultures, University of Amsterdam; in 2005–2006 he is a fellow at the Wissenschaftskolleg, the Centre for Advanced Study in Berlin; Internet user since 1993.

Robert Lunn, Focalpoint Analytics; worked as a senior research analyst on the 2004 Digital Future Report: Surveying the Digital Future, produced by the USC Annenberg School Center for the Digital Future.

Wainer Lusoli, University of Chester, U.K.; originally from Italy; former research fellow, European Studies Research Institute (2003–2005); member of Association of Internet Researchers; research initiatives include the Internet & Elections Project and a look at the impact of the Internet on the 2005 U.K. general election; Internet user since 1994.

Ed Lyell, pioneer in issues regarding Internet and education; professor of business and economics at Adams State College, Alamosa, CO; designer and consultant for using telecommunications and high-touch/high-tech methods to improve school effectiveness; Internet user since 1965.

Mike McCarty, chief network officer, Johns Hopkins; Internet user since 1992.

Jim McConnaughey, senior economic advisor active in U.S. policy on access and the digital divide, including work at the Federal Communications Commission, Harvard, and the National Telecommunications & Information Administration.

Kevin McFall, director, Online Products & Affiliate Programs, Tribune Media Services, NextCast Media; Internet user since 1984.

Alec MacLeod, associate professor, California Institute of Integral Studies; his research interests include the visual culture of the Internet; Internet user since 1989.

Shawn McIntosh, lecturer in strategic communications, Columbia University; a coauthor of *Converging Media* who formerly worked as an editor and freelance writer for newspapers and magazines in the U.K., U.S., and Japan; cofounded Netgraf, which examines issues and trends related to online journalism; Internet user since 1992.

Ursula Maier-Rabler, assistant professor, University of Salzburg, Austria; research interests include ePolicy, eDemocracy, and eGovernment; Internet user since 1982.

Wladyslaw Majewski, OSI CompuTrain SA, a leader of ISOC Polska—the Internet Society chapter in Poland; Internet user since 1989.

Meg Houston Maker, director of external information services, Dartmouth College; active in Association for Computing Machinery; Internet user since 1993.

Willis Marti, associate director for networking, Texas A&M University; former builder of large networks for TRW, Martin-Marietta, and SYtek; research interests include security, fault tolerance, distributed platforms, distributed operating systems; leader with Internet2; Internet user since 1983.

Andrea Matwyshyn, executive director, Center for Information Research; assistant professor of law, University of Florida; an affiliate of the Centre for Economics and Policy at the University of Cambridge; research focuses on information security and information technology and privacy regulation; Internet user since 1992.

Sean Mead, networking consultant, for Interbrand Analytics, Design Forum, Cannon Retail Technologies, Mead, Mead & Clark P.C., and other companies; Internet user since 1989.

Nicco Mele, Internet strategist, political Web architecture expert, CEO for EchoDitto, an online communications firm serving nonprofits and political organizations; born in West Africa, but now extremely active in politics in the U.S., he's known for heading the breakthrough Internet strategy for Howard Dean's 2004 presidential campaign.

Michel Menou, professor, consultant, and information-science researcher; born in France, he has worked in nearly 80 nations since 1966; research is concentrated on information policy, including significant studies of information technology and its impact in Africa; on the editorial board of seven scholarly journals; Internet user since 1992.

Bob Metcalfe, Internet pioneer, invented Ethernet when working at Xerox PARC in 1973, founder of 3Com Corporation, former CEO of InfoWorld, now a venture capitalist and partner in Polaris Venture Partners; director of the Pop Tech executive technology conference; winner of IEEE Medal of Honor and the U.S. National Medal of Technology; Internet user since 1970.

Denzil Meyers, founder and president, Widgetwonder (internal branding consultants and facilitators of corporate storytelling), Applied Improvisation Network; Internet user since 1993.

Vincent Michon, strategic marketing manager, France Télécom; Internet user since 1979.

Toby Miller, professor, University of California–Riverside; an Australian with research interests in cultural policy and political economy; Internet user since 1990.

Sturle J. Monstad, Research Centre for Health Promotion, University of Bergen, Norway; Internet user since 1989.

Scott Moore, online community manager, Helen and Charles Schwab Foundation; an expert on online communities; Internet user since 1991.

Torill Mortensen, associate professor, Volda University College, Norway; her research interests include media theory and reader-response theory; Internet user since 1991.

Martin F. Murphy, IT consultant, City of New York; Internet user since 1993.

Brian T. Nakamoto, Everyone.net (a leading provider of outsourced e-mail solutions for individuals and companies around the world); author of the blog Information Overload; Internet user since 1990.

Thomas Narten, IBM open-Internet standards development, based out of North Carolina; involved in networking for more than 20 years, he is the Internet Engineering Task Force (IETF) liaison to the ICANN Board of Directors; he has been the IBM technical lead for Internet Protocol v.6; cochaired the IETF multi6 Working Group; Internet user since 1983.

Louis Nauges, president, Microcost (an IT services and hardware company based in France); Internet user since 1990.

Peter P. Nieckarz, Jr., assistant professor of sociology, Western Carolina University; research interests include the emergence of community and social structure on the Internet; Internet user since 1993.

Pekka Nikander, engineer at Ericcson Research, Helsinki Institute for Information Technology, Finland; past member of the Internet Architecture Board; Internet user since 1987.

Christine Ogan, professor, University of Indiana School of Journalism; working with two other professors under a NSF grant to study recruitment and retention of women in information technology disciplines in U.S. universities; Internet user since 1986.

Doug Olenick, computer technology editor, *TWICE (This Week in Consumer Electronics)* magazine; Internet user since 1996.

Jill O'Neill, director of planning and communication, National Federation of Abstracting and Information Services; Internet user since 1986.

Andy Oram, writer and editor specializing in free software and open-source technologies for O'Reilly Media, based in Boston; member of Computer Professionals for Social Responsibility; Internet user since 1983.

Olav Anders Øvrebø, freelance journalist based in Oslo, Norway; Internet user since 1995.

Cleo Parker, senior manager, BBDO (international agency for networked, multichannel communications solutions); Internet user since 1993.

Barry Parr, analyst for the media group, Jupiter Research; formerly e-commerce research director for International Data Corporation; former vice president of news at CNET; and former managing producer of the San Jose Mercury News's Mercury Center; Internet user since 1990.

Craig Partridge, Internet pioneer and early leader in the IETF; active member of the Association for Computing Machinery's SIG-COMM and the IEEE Communications Society; he chaired a National Research Council study of how the Internet functioned during the 9/11 attacks; now chief scientist, BBN Technologies; Internet user since 1983.

Alix L. Paultre, executive editor, Hearst Business Media, Smartalix.com, Zep Tepi Publishing; author of *Cyberchild*; Internet user since 1996.

Pascal Perrin, futurologist, France Telecom; Internet user since 1998.

David Perry, president, Consensus Point (formerly Foresight Technologies), a prediction market organization based in Nashville; Internet user since 1990.

Ian Peter, Internet pioneer, helped develop the Internet in Australia and the Asia-Pacific region in the 1980s; maintains a project on the future of the Internet—the Internet Mark II Project; Internet user since 1986.

Mirko Petric, lecturer in media theory and semiotics, University of Zadar, Croatia; Internet user since 1996.

Kathleen Pierz, managing partner, The Pierz Group (consultants in directory assistance/enquiry); Internet user since 1985.

Alejandro Pisanty, CIO for UNAM (National University of Mexico); vice chairman of the board for ICANN; member of UN Working Group for Internet Governance; active in ISOC; Internet user since 1977.

Nathaniel Poor, lecturer in the Department of Communication Studies at the University of Michigan; research areas include the convergence of Internet use and international engagement.

Mark Poster, professor of film and media studies, University of California–Irvine; studies the ways social communications have changed through the introduction of new technologies; author of the book *Second Media Age*; Internet user since 1983.

Henry Potts, professor, Centre for Health Informatics, University College, London; Internet user since 1990.

Sam Punnett, president, FAD Research; has worked in the field of interactive digital media since the 1980s in the music business, social research, broadcast production, equities analysis, electronic game design, and for the last 9 years, on strategy, marketing, and product development related to e-business; Internet user since 1988.

Polly Purvis, executive director ScotlandIS, a trade association; formerly of the Royal Bank of Scotland, Matrix Management, and the Scottish Software Federation; board member for Technology Ventures Scotland and Scottish Technology Forum.

Teddy Purwadi, secretary-general of the Indonesian Internet Service Providers Association; active in work with ICANN; leader of the Indonesian Chapter of the Internet Society.

John S. Quarterman, president InternetPerils, Inc.; a founder of Matrix.Net, Inc., which began publishing the first maps of the Internet in 1993; conducted the first demographic survey of the Internet; Matrix News, which he started in 1991, was the earliest continuing commercial newsletter published over the Internet; Internet user since 1974.

Ross Rader, director of research and innovation, Tucows, Inc.; works with ICANN in the Registrars Constituency, part of the GNSO (Generic Names Supporting Organization); Internet user since 1991.

Sheizaf Rafaeli, professor in the graduate school of business administration, Haifa University, Israel; director of INFOSOC, the Center for the Study of the Information Society; contributor to Globes (a business journal); founder and coeditor of the Journal of Computer-Mediated Communication; Internet user since 1982.

Lutfor Rahman, executive director of Association for Advancement of Information Technology and vice-chancellor of Pundra University of Science and Technology, Bangladesh; Internet user since 1996.

Gisela Redeker, professor, University of Groningen, The Netherlands; member of the editorial boards of the journals Linguistik Online, Poetics, and Tijdschrift voor Communicatiewetenschap; Internet user since 1981.

Michael Reilly, GLOBALWRITERS, Baronet Media LLC, Hally Enterprises, Inc., State University of New York at Stony Brook, Global Public Affairs Institute; Internet user since 1972.

Howard Rheingold, Internet sociologist and author; one of the first to illuminate virtual communities; in the '90s he published the webzine

Electric Mind; he wrote the books *Virtual Reality, Smart Mobs,* and *Virtual Community*; he also was the editor of *Whole Earth Review* and the *Millennium Whole Earth Catalog*; Internet user since 1990.

Glenn Ricart, executive director, PricewaterhouseCoopers Advanced Research; member of the board of trustees of the Internet Society; formerly CTO at Novell and a founder or cofounder of three successful start ups; former program manager at DARPA (Defense Advanced Research Projects Agency); won the first NSF grand for networking and created the first operational regional TCP/IP network; Internet user since 1968.

Mario Rios, TDCLA (Tecnologías del Conocimiento, an e-learning group), Chile; Internet user since 1997.

Nicolas Ritoux, freelance technology reporter for La Presse, Montréal, and other media outlets; Internet user since 1995.

Nuno Rodrigues, 4EMESmultimédia (a multimedia development company based in Portugal); Internet user since 1992.

Sabino M. Rodriguez, MC&S Services; Internet user since 1994.

Hernando Rojas, a native of Colombia and a professor in the department of life sciences communication at the University of Wisconsin–Madison; consultant for the UN Development Program.

Peter Roll, retired chief system administrator; Internet user since 1981.

Marc Rotenberg, founder and executive director Electronic Privacy Information Center; he won an Electronic Frontier Foundation Pioneer Award in 1997 for his work as a "champion of privacy, human rights and civil liberties on the electronic frontier"; Internet user since 1978.

Douglas Rushkoff, social theorist, journalist, and teacher, New York University; wrote *Cyberia: Life in the Trenches of Hyperspace, Media Virus! Hidden Agendas in Popular Culture, Exit Strategy,* and *Coercion*; he is a recipient of the Neil Postman Award for Career Achievement in Public Intellectual Activity; Internet user since 1985.

Anthony Rutkowski, an Internet pioneer who helped establish Internet protocols, he works as vice president for regulatory and standards, VeriSign; he is a cofounder and former executive director of the Internet Society and he is an active leader in International Telecommunication Union (ITU); Internet user since 1979.

Sherida Ryan, Internet analyst, Openflows Networks Ltd. (provider of news, analysis, network facilities and tools for open-source); Internet user since 1995.

D.K. Sachdev, founder and president, SpaceTel Consultancy LLC (management and engineering support to organizations engaged in operating and/or developing total systems for broadband, multimedia, Internet, telecommunications, and digital satellite broadcasting); early developer of XM Radio; Internet user since 1987.

Paul Saffo, forecaster and strategist with more than two decades of experience exploring long-term technological change; director, Institute for the Future; serves on many boards, including the Long Now Foundation; Fellow in the Royal Swedish Academy of Engineering Sciences; chairman of Samsung Science Board; Internet user since 1978.

Janet Salmons, president, Vision2Lead, Inc.; consultant on organizational leadership and development and virtual learning; Internet user since 1985.

Mike Samson, interactive media writer and producer, Creative Street Media Group; Internet user since 1989.

Syamant Sandhir, leader in experience design and implementation, Futurescape; Internet user since 1995.

Kevin Schlag, director of Web development and IT for Western Governor's University, BYU-Hawaii; Internet user since 1993.

Jan Schmidt, professor, Bamberg University's Forschungsstelle Neue Kommunikationsmedien, Germany; research includes the principles and practices of networking with a focus on Weblogs and social software; Internet user since 1993.

Adrian Schofield, head of research for ForgeAhead (focused on ICT research and consulting in Africa), South Africa; a leader in the World Information Technology and Services Alliance (WITSA); Internet user since 1994.

James Schultz, principal, Pretty Good Consulting; Institute for Work and the Economy (a consortium studying challenges posed by new immigrants in the labor market); former executive at Walgreen's; Internet user since 1995.

Robert Shaw, senior Internet strategy and policy advisor for the International Telecommunication Union (ITU); ITU is an organization with 189 member states based in Geneva, Switzerland, responsible for the global development of telecommunications networks and services; Internet user since 1987.

Tiffany Shlain, filmmaker; founder and ambassador of the Webby Awards; named one of *Newsweek*'s "Women Shaping the 21st Century"; Shlain has also directed 10 films, including *Life, Liberty and the Pursuit of Happiness*, a selection at the 2003 Sundance Film Festival, and a profile of Intel founder Gordon Moore; Internet user since 1987.

Rajnesh J. Singh, PATARA Communications & Electronics Ltd., Avon Group, GNR Consulting, chairman of the Pacific Islands chapter of the Internet Society; member of IEEE; Internet user since 1993.

Tom Snook, chief technology officer, New World Symphony; representative to Internet2; Internet user since 1967.

Jonathan Sills, SVP (strategy and corporate development), Provide Commerce, Liberty Media; Internet user since 1993.

Kerri Smith, Elexio (Web design, content management and enterprise solutions for nonprofit organizations); Internet user since 1997.

Chris Sorek, senior vice president of public communications, SAP (provider of client/server enterprise application software); formerly with the International Federation of the Red Cross and Red Crescent Societies in Geneva, where he directed global communications activities; Internet user since 1980.

Mikkel Holm Sørensen, software and intelligence manager, Actics Ltd. (ethical management systems); Internet user since 1997.

Eugene Spafford, Internet and executive director for Purdue University's CERIAS (the Center for Education and Research in Information Assurance and Security—a Web-based incident-response database); Internet user since 1980. Member of U.S. President's Technology Advisory Committee and advisor to National Science Foundation and other agencies; leader in ACM (Association of Computing Machinery).

Suzanne Stefanac, author/interactive media strategist, dispatches-fromblogistan.com; freelance technology writer with 15 years of work in publications such as *Wired*, *Macworld*, *Salon*, *PC World*, *Publish*, *Rolling Stone*; formerly of MSNBC; founding editor of Macworld Online and cofounder of RespondTV; Internet user since 1989.

Russell Steele, president, The Insightworks (provider of tools for research and teaching in economics and public policy); Internet user since 1995.

Danny Sullivan, editor-in-chief, SearchEngineWatch.com (a guide to how search engines operate); producer of search-engine strategies conferences in the U.S. and U.K.; Internet user since 1994.

Ellen K. Sullivan, former diplomat; policy fellow, George Mason University School of Public Policy; spent several years in Romania and Singapore, looking at how government employees use technology to filter information; Internet user since 1988.

Elle Tracy, president and e-strategies consultant, The Results Group, based in Seattle; formerly senior Web strategist at Circle.com; Internet user since 1993.

Raul Trejo-Delarbre, political science professor, Universidad Nacional Autonoma de México; author of the book *The New Magic Carpet: Uses and Myths of the Internet, the Network of Networks*; Internet user since 1993.

Bryan Trogdon, president, First Semantic (working on a realization of the Semantic Web); Internet user since 1995.

Terry Ulaszewski, publisher, Long Beach Live Community News; Internet user since 1989.

B. van den Berg, faculty of philosophy at Erasmus University, Rotterdam, The Netherlands; Internet user since 1993.

Miguel Sicart Vila, junior research associate, Information Ethics Group, Oxford University; Internet user since 1997.

Hal Varian, a professor at University of California–Berkeley and a world-renowned expert on the economics of information technology, he has also taught at Oxford, MIT, Stanford, Michigan, and other universities around the world; he is a paid consultant for Google and writes a monthly column for *The New York Times*; Internet user since 1986.

Daniel D. Wang, principal, Roadmap Associates (coaching and advisory company); Internet user since 1995.

Jim Warren, Internet pioneer, founding editor of *Dr. Dobb's Journal*, technology policy advocate and activist, futurist; in 1992 he organized the first Computers, Freedom, and Privacy Conference. When he won an EFF Pioneer Award in 1992, he was noted as being "instrumental in assuring that rights common to older mediums and technologies are extended to computer networking"; Internet user since 1970.

David Weinberger, teacher, writer, speaker, consultant, and commentator on Internet and technology; fellow at Harvard's Berkman Center for Internet & Society; author of the "Cluetrain Manifesto"; Internet user since 1986.

Barry Wellman, researcher on virtual communities and workplaces; professor and director of NetLab at University of Toronto; expert on human-computer interaction and social networks in communities and organizations; winner of achievement award from the International Network for Social Network Analysis; Internet user since 1976.

Nancy White, principal, Full Circle Associates (communications consultants); active in Computer Professionals for Social Responsibility; Internet user since 1998.

Monica Whitty, psychology professor at Queen's University, Belfast; research focuses on Internet relationships, including trust online, cyber-stalking, and Internet privacy and surveillance; Internet user since 1994.

Susan Wilhite, design anthropologist, Habitat for Humanity; interests include authority and reputation in an open-source world, online social networks, domestic space uses, and identity; Internet user since 1993.

Andy Williamson, managing director for Wairua Consulting Limited, New Zealand; a member of the NZ government's Digital Strategy Advisory Group; an authority on community informatics; active in e-Democracy efforts and helps establish community-based groups; Internet user since 1990.

V. K. Wong, PhD in physics, director of IT campus initiatives and CARAT (Collaboratory for Advanced Research and Academic Technologies), University of Michigan; Internet user since 1981.

Simon Woodside, founder and CEO, Semacode Corporation, based in Ontario, Canada; Internet user since 1992.

Richard Yee, competitive intelligence analyst, AT&T; Internet user since 1995.

Norito H. Yoshida, new business development manager, Yahoo Japan; Internet user since 1993.

Jonathan Zittrain, cofounder of the Berkman Center for the Internet and Society, Harvard University, and a top forum administrator for CompuServe; holds the chair in Internet Governance and Regulation at Oxford University and is a principal of the Oxford Internet Institute; active in work with ICANN.

REFERENCES

Barlow, J. P. (1996, February 8). *Declaration of independence for cyberspace.* Retrieved October 23, 2008, from http://homes.eff.org/~barlow/Declaration-Final.html

Biocca, F., Kim, T., & Levy, M. (1995). The vision of virtual reality. In F. Biocca & M. Levy (Eds.), *Communication in the age of virtual reality* (pp. 3–14). Hillsdale, NJ: Lawrence Erlbaum Associates.

Bower, A. (2006, May 22). Villagewide Wi-Fi. *Time.* Retrieved October 23, 2008, from http://www.time.com/time/magazine/article/0,9171,1196418,00.html

Bridis, T. (2006). Google compromised principles. *Associated Press.* Retrieved June 7, 2006, via *Yahoo! News,* from http://news.yahoo.com/s/ap/20060606/ap_on_hi_te/google_censorship_3

Castronova, E. (2005). *Synthetic worlds: The business and culture of online games.* Chicago: University of Chicago Press.

comScore. (2006, May 4). *694 million people currently use the Internet worldwide according to comScore networks* [Press release]. Retrieved October 20, 2008, from http://www.comscore.com/press/release.asp?press=849

Crystal, D. (2003). *English as a global language* (2nd ed.). Cambridge, U.K.: Cambridge University Press.

Dutton, W. H., di Gennaro, C., & Millwood Hargrave, A. (2005, May). *The Internet in Britain.* Oxford Internet Surveys (OxIS). Retrieved October 21, 2008, from http://www.oii.ox.ac.uk/research/oxis/oxis2005_report.pdf

Espiner, T. (2006, March 21). Interpol: Give us the tools to fight cybercrime. *ZDNet.co.uk.* Retrieved October 23, 2008, from http://news.zdnet.co.uk/Internet/security/0,39020375,39258540,00.htm

French, H. (2006, May 9). As Chinese students go online, little sister is watching. *New York Times.* Retrieved October 23, 2008, from http://www.nytimes.com/2006/05/09/world/asia/09Internet.html?_r=1&oref=slogin

Frey, T. (2004, September 16). *Top 10 trends in innovation: Key factors most affecting innovation in the US. DaVinci Institute.* Retrieved October 21, 2008, from http://www.davinciinstitute. com/page.php?ID=60

Furness, T. (1991, May 8). *New developments in computer technology.* Committee on Commerce, Science, and Transportation, U.S. Senate. Washington, DC: U.S. Government Printing Office.

The future of terrorism: Is technology making us safer or more vulnerable? (2006, July). *Discover* magazine. Retrieved October 24, 2008, from http://discovermagazine.com/2006/jul/cover

Glenn, J. C., & Gordon, T. J. (2005). *2005 state of the future.* Washington, DC: American Council for the United Nations University.

Goldsmith, J., & Wu, T. (2005). *Who controls the Internet? Illusions of a borderless world.* New York: Oxford University Press.

Hoare, T., & Milner, R. (Eds.). (2004). *Grand challenges in computing research.* British Computer Society. Retrieved October 21, 2008, from www.ukcrc.org.uk/gcresearch.pdf

Institute for the Future. (2005). *2005 Ten-year forecast perspectives [SR-891].* Retrieved October 21, 2008, from http://www.iftf.org/system/files/deliverables/SR-891_2005_TYF_Perspectives.pdf

Intel News Release. (2006, May 2). *Intel commits $1 billion to further emerging markets strategy.* Retrieved October 23, 2008, from http://www.intel.com/pressroom/archive/releases/20060502 corp.htm

Internet Society. (2005). *2004 annual report.* Retrieved October 21, 2008, from www.isoc.org/isoc/reports/ar2004/ISOCar2004.pdf

Ito, J. (2006, June). The World of Warcrack: Rob Pardo and the Blizzard team. *Wired.* Retrieved October 23, 2008, from http://www.wired.com/wired/archive/14.06/warcraft.html

Joy, B. (2000, April). Why the future doesn't need us. *Wired, 8*(4). Retrieved October 24, 2008, from http://www.wired.com/wired/archive/8.04/joy_pr.html

Kaczynski, T. (1995, September 19). *Industrial society and its future.* Retrieved October 24, 2008, from http://www.time.com/time/reports/unabomber/wholemanifesto.html

Kaplan, N. (1995, March). What Neil Postman has to say. *Computer-Mediated Communication, 2*(3). Retrieved October 24, 2008, from http://www.ibiblio.org/cmc/mag/1995/mar/hyper/npcontexts_119.html

Kapur, A. (2005). *Internet governance: A primer.* UN Asia-Pacific Development Information Programme e-Primers for the Information Economy, Society and Polity. Retrieved October 21, 2008, from http://www.apdip.net/publications/iespprimers/igovprimer.pdf

Kay, A. C. (1989, Autumn). Predicting the future [Speech delivered to the 20th annual meeting of the the Stanford Computer Forum]. *Stanford Engineering, 1*(1), 1–6. Retrieved October 24, 2008, from http://www.ecotopia.com/webpress/futures.htm

Krauss, M. (1992). The world's languages in crisis. *Language, 68,* 6–10.

Lanier, J., & Biocca, F. (1992). An inside view of the future of virtual reality. *Journal of Communication, 42*(2), 150–172.

Last, M., Liebowitz, B., Pister, K., & Warneke, B. (2001). Smart dust: Communicating with a cubic-millimeter. *Computer, 34,* 44–51.

Mallon, J. (2006, May 18). *Industry and market overview.* Abstract for presentation at 4th Annual Microelectric Engineering Packaging and Test Engineering Council Conference, San Jose, CA. Retrieved October 23, 2008, from http://www.memsinfo.jp/whitepaper/WP75MPT.pdf

Marvin, C. (1988). *When old technologies were new: Thinking about electric communication in the late nineteenth century.* New York: Oxford University Press.

McDonald, D., & Shapiro, M. (1995). I'm not a real doctor, but I play one in virtual reality: Implications of virtual reality for judgments about reality. In F. Biocca & M. Levy (Eds.), *Communication in the age of virtual reality* (p. 323). Hillsdale, NJ: Lawrence Erlbaum Associates.

Naraine, R. (2006, June 12). Microsoft: Trojans, bots are significant and tangible threat. *eWeek.com*. Retrieved October 23, 2008, from http://www.eweek.com/article2/0,1895,1974620,00.asp?kc=ewnw s061206dtx1k0000599

Neild, I., & Pearson, I. (Eds.). (2005, August). *2005 BT technology timeline*. Retrieved October 21, 2008, from http://www.btplc.com/ Innovation/News/timeline/TechnologyTimeline.pdf

Newitz, A. (2006, May). The RFID hacking underground: They can steal your smartcard, lift your passport, jack your car, even clone the chip in your arm. *Wired*. Retrieved October 23, 2008, from http://www.wired.com/wired/archive/14.05/rfid.html?pg=1&topic =rfid&topic_set

Pool, I. d. S. (1983). *Technologies of freedom*. Cambridge, MA: Harvard University Press.

Postman, N. (1990, October 11). *Informing ourselves to death* [Speech for the German Informatics Society]. Retrieved October 24, 2008, from http://www.frostbytes.com/~jimf/informing.html

Red Herring staff. (2006, April 10). The future of the Internet: In a decade, the Net will dig deeper into our lives [interview with D. Clark]. *Red Herring*. Retrieved October 23, 2008, from http:// www.redherring.com/Home/16391

Rose, R. (2005, April). *Language, soft power and asymmetrical Internet communication*. Research Report 7. Oxford, U.K.: Oxford Internet Institute. Retrieved October 23, 2008, from http://www.oii.ox.ac.uk/ resources/publications/RR7.pdf

Rosedale, P. (2006, June). The other fed chief. *Wired*. Retrieved October 23, 2008, from http://www.wired.com/wired/archive/14.06/ rosedale.html

Roszak, T. (1994). *The cult of information: A neo-luddite treatise on high-tech, artificial intelligence, and the true art of thinking*. Los Angeles: University of California Press.

Roszak, T. (1999, March 11). Shakespeare never lost a manuscript in a computer crash. *The New York Times*. Retrieved October 24,

2008, from http://www.nytimes.com/library/tech/99/03/circuits/articles/11quil.html

Sale, K. (1997, February). America's new Luddites. *Le Monde Diplomatique*. Retrieved October 24, 2008, from http://mondediplo.com/1997/02/20luddites

Schneier, B. (2006, May 4). Everyone wants to "own" your PC. *Wired*. Retrieved October 23, 2008, from http://www.wired.com/news/columns/1,70802-0.html

Smith, D. (2005, May 22). 2050 and immortality is within our grasp. *The Observer (London)*. Retrieved October 23, 2008, from http://observer.guardian.co.uk/uk_news/story/0,,1489635,00.html

Spooner, J. G. (2006, April 4). The lessons of the $100 laptop. Interview with Nicholas Negroponte. *eWeek.com*, April 4. Retrieved October 23, 2008, from http://www.eweek.com/article2/0,1895,1945967,00.asp?kc=ewnws040506dtx1k0000599

Steuer, J. (1995). Defining virtual reality: Dimensions determining telepresence. *Journal of Communication, 42*(4), 73–79.

Stoll, C. (1995). *Silicon snake oil*. New York: Doubleday.

Sun Microsystems. (2005). *Global Education and Learning Community (GELC)*. Retrieved October 23, 2008, from http://se.sun.com/edu/pdf/gelc-datasheet-051101.pdf

Sutherland, I. (1965). The ultimate display. *Proceedings of IFIP Congress, 2*, 506–508. Retrieved October 23, 2008, from http://www.cs.uiowa.edu/~sbabu/The%20Ultimate%20Display.htm

Tabott, S. (1995). *The future does not compute: Transcending machines in our midst*. Sebastopol, CA: O'Reilly. Retrieved October 24, 2008, from http://netfuture.org/fdnc/index.html

United Nations Educational, Scientific and Cultural Organization (UNESCO). (2005). Measuring linguistic diversity on the Internet. Retrieved October 23, 2008, from http://portal.unesco.org/ci/en/ev.php-URL_ID=20804&URL_DO=DO_TOPIC&URL_SECTION=201.html

U.S. Department of Justice. (2006, March). *United States activities to improve cybercrime legislation and investigate capacities.* Retrieved October 23, 2008, from http://www.coe.int/t/dg1/legal cooperation/economiccrime/cybercrime/T-CY/(T-CY%20_2006_ %2006%20-%20e%20-%20US%20Activities%20to%20ipmrove %20cybercrime%20l_205)_en.pdf

U.S. National Intelligence Council. (2004, December). *Mapping the global future: Report of the National Intelligence Council's 2020 project.* Retrieved October 21, 2008, from, www.foia.cia. gov/2020/2020.pdf

U.S. National Science Foundation. (2005, December 28). *National Science Board 2020 vision for the National Science Foundation.* Retrieved October 21, 2008, from, www.nsf.gov/pubs/2006/ nsb05142/nsb05142.pdf

Williams, D. (2006, May 31). New vehicle for dissent is fast track to prison: Bloggers held under Egypt's emergency laws. *Washington Post Foreign Service*, p. A10. Retrieved October 23, 2008, from http://www.washingtonpost.com/wp-dyn/content/ article/2006/05/30/AR2006053001178.html

Working Group on Internet Governance report. (2005, June). Retrieved October 22, 2008, from http://www.wgig.org/docs/WGIGREPORT. pdf

World Summit on the Information Society (WSIS). (2005). *Tunis agenda.* Retrieved October 23, 2008, from http://www.itu.int/wsis/ docs2/tunis/off/6rev1.html

CONTRIBUTOR INDEX

AUTHOR INDEX

Subject Index

CPSIA information can be obtained at www.ICGtesting.com
Printed in the USA
BVOW03*2003060314

346913BV00001B/4/P